'Antonia Fraser has written an excellent book which unravels the whole story of the plot, exploring the background, keeping close to the evidence, and, above all, bringing the characters to life … a judicious and very readable account'

Hugh Trevor-Roper, *Literary Review*

'Every few years a work of history appears that succeeds in connecting its subject to the deeper questions troubling modern society. This is one such book'

Amanda Foreman, *Independent*

'It has a fine narrative flow, for Antonia Fraser recognises that history is essentially a story, and a gripping one at that. She writes with verve and imagination'

Kenneth Baker, *Daily Telegraph*

'Fraser's meticulously researched book is an excellent read … Antonia Fraser has shed much light on one of the most controversial episodes in English history'

Martin Jacques, *Observer*

Since 1969, Antonia Fraser has written many acclaimed historical works which have been international bestsellers, as well as a mystery series featuring Jemima Shore. Her efforts in Non-Fiction have been awarded the James Tait Black Memorial Prize, the St Louis Literary Award, the CWA Non-Fiction Gold Dagger and the Wolfson Award for History. In 2000, she was awarded the Norton Medlicott Medal by the Historical Association and was made DBE in 2011 for her services to literature. She was married to Harold Pinter, who died on Christmas Eve 2008: her bestselling memoir of their life together *Must You Go?* was published in 2010. Her autobiography *My History: A Memoir of Growing Up* was published in 2015. Visit her website at www.antoniafraser.com.

By Antonia Fraser

Non-Fiction

The Gunpowder Plot
Terror & Faith in 1605

ANTONIA FRASER

History to the defeated
May say Alas but cannot help nor pardon –

W. H. AUDEN, Spain, 1937

WEIDENFELD & NICOLSON

A W&N PAPERBACK

First published in Great Britain in 1996
by Weidenfeld & Nicolson
First published in paperback in 1997
by Mandarin Paperbacks
Reprinted in 1999
by Arrow Books

This paperback edition published in 2002
by Weidenfeld & Nicolson,
an imprint of Orion Books Ltd,
Orion House, 5 Upper St Martin's Lane,
London WC2H 9EA

An Hachette UK company

9 10 8

A CIP catalogue record for this book
is available from the British Library.

ISBN 978-0-7538-1401-7

Typeset by Input Data Services Ltd, Bridgwater, Somerset

Printed in Great Britain by
Clays Ltd, St Ives plc

The Orion Publishing Group's policy is to use papers that
are natural, renewable and recyclable products and
made from wood grown in sustainable forests. The logging
and manufacturing processes are expected to conform to
the environmental regulations of the country of origin.

www.orionbooks.co.uk

Elizabeth Queen of Bohemia daughter of James the First

there was an obvious flaw in this argument, at least from the Catholic point of view. The King indicated that Catholics might be tolerated, just so long as their numbers did not increase. But Catholic toleration almost certainly *would* bring about an increase in numbers. The religious climate would be balmier and the Church Papists would venture forth again under their true colours.

These were ideas being floated rather than plans being made. But some time in 1602 Henry Percy 9th Earl of Northumberland initiated a more down-to-earth correspondence on the subject with the King. He came of a family (like the Howards) that had suffered much for the King's unfortunate mother. Cecil's father might have been responsible for Mary Queen of Scots' head being cut off (as James was rumoured to believe) but Northumberland's uncle had lost *his* head in 1572 for his part in the Northern Rising on behalf of Queen Mary. Born in 1564, the 9th Earl was two years older than James VI and a magnificent peer with massive estates in northern England, as well as in the south, where he had an establishment at Petworth in Sussex. Highly gifted, his scientific experiments and his remarkable scientific library would later earn him the sobriquet of the 'Wizard Earl'. But Northumberland also had something remote about him (to which his deafness contributed) and his speech was inclined to be slow. At times shy – 'a kind of inward, reserved man' – and at other times a manic gambler with a temper that flared up, he constituted a puzzle to his contemporaries.[4] His lofty position aroused in others not only respect but jealousy.

Northumberland's status at the court of Elizabeth was further complicated by a troubled marriage. His wife Dorothy was the sister of the Queen's favourite Essex, and for this, and her own sweetness of character, Elizabeth bore her great personal fondness. The Queen took Dorothy's side when the couple separated. A brief reconciliation resulted in the birth of a longed-for heir in 1602, but then the marriage again broke up. In general Northumberland does not seem to have exercised good judgement in his various relationships. Nowhere

was this more apparent than in his employment of a certain Thomas Percy as his go-between with King James.

Thomas Percy was a poor relation, one of those hangers-on that flocked around great men, petitioning for preferment. The connection was actually quite remote: Thomas Percy was a second cousin once removed, being the great-grandson of the 4th Earl (not an illegitimate half-brother of Northumberland as is sometimes suggested).[5] But a kind of clan system existed by which a comparatively distant relation such as Percy would look to the proverbially generous Northumberland as his patron. In 1596 Percy was made Constable of Alnwick Castle, the great Percy fortress on the borders of Scotland, and thus the agent for the family's northern estates. Northumberland declined a post as ambassador from Queen Elizabeth (his deafness made him draw back) but he did hold a command in the Low Countries from 1600 to 1601, where Thomas Percy joined him before the death of Queen Elizabeth. At some point Percy's particular energies convinced Northumberland that he was the man to handle the somewhat delicate Scottish mission.

Presumably Percy's religion was the clinching factor. Northumberland himself was summed up by a French ambassador as one who was 'a Catholic in his soul'. Northumberland put it rather differently when he wrote to James to say that, although he was not a Catholic himself, there were sundry people in his entourage who had 'oars in that boat'.[6] He was referring by this to a few old recusant servants lingering in his house: the sort who would threaten no one. But Percy was different. He was a much more political animal, and his Catholicism more determinedly active.

Percy was a controversial figure in his own time – 'a subtle, flattering, dangerous knave' according to one verdict. He was in his forties at the death of Elizabeth (although his white hair made him look older) and a striking figure with his exceptional height and formidable build. He had a certain charm, despite the general seriousness of his manner, and a great deal of energy. This energy was physical as well as mental and as a

result Percy had a tendency to sweat and used to change his shirt twice a day, giving 'much labour to his laundresses'.[7]

The personality of Thomas Percy still exercises a baleful influence on the events surrounding the Gunpowder Plot in the minds of historians, as, it might be argued, it did over the unwisely generous Northumberland. According to a Catholic source, Percy had had a wild youth in which he 'relied much on his sword and personal courage' and relished being among 'foul-mouthed, ribald people'. His conversion to Catholicism – or at any rate his moving from some form of Church Papistry to more ardent belief – was supposed to have calmed him down.[8] Nevertheless, some wildness seems to have remained, since he left his wife for another woman. In an age before the official registration of marriage or for that matter any possibility of legal divorce, men dealt with the situation by simply marrying again in another part of the country, which is what Percy appears to have done. His first wife, born Martha Wright, whom he married in 1591, was abandoned in London, in Holborn, 'mean and poor', to support herself as best she could by teaching the daughters of recusants. The other wife was in Warwickshire.[9]

The first marriage, even if a failure in personal terms, had important consequences for Percy. Martha Wright came from one of those stubbornly recusant families in Yorkshire, whose womenfolk were celebrated for their constancy. Her mother Ursula Wright – 'a great prayer' – served many years in prison for refusing to attend Protestant services. Another of Ursula's daughters, who married into the Yorkshire recusant family of Ward, became the mother of the remarkable proponent of female education and founder of the Institute of the Blessed Virgin Mary, Mary Ward, born in 1585. At Ploughland Hall, in east Yorkshire, the young Mary Ward spent five years in grandmother Ursula's care.[10]

Martha was, in the family tradition, 'an honourable good lady' and her teaching was still remembered with gratitude over forty years later by 'those that were her scholars'. Apart from her work, Martha lived 'very private', due to the fact that she frequently harboured priests.[11]

Thomas Percy himself was clearly a clever man. If he were not, Northumberland's continued reliance on his administrative abilities in the north would not make sense. At the same time, Percy was in some ways unscrupulous. He was not the only unjust steward to seek to benefit from the profits of a master immeasurably more wealthy than himself. Nevertheless, it was hardly to his credit that charges of dishonesty relating to the handling of the Percy estates were at one point brought against him, and proved. Yet Percy unquestionably had Northumberland's trust. It was Percy who was sent on a confidential mission to Scotland, before the death of Queen Elizabeth, on behalf of the English Catholics. Northumberland intended to 'deliver' the English Catholics to King James, and the King seemed to be ready to 'receive' them – on his terms.

Northumberland's plan was to build up a power base in the new reign and with the new sovereign, to make up for the Elizabethan family disgrace. There was also the need to counteract the rising influence of Cecil, in that perpetual dance to the music of jealousy which occupied sixteenth-century courtiers. As for the English Catholic faction, its floating quality, stressed in the previous chapter, made it easy for outsiders to overestimate its importance. Afterwards, when everyone was busy rewriting history to assert their own innocence (or the guilt of others) Northumberland would assert that the mission had been Percy's idea.[12] For all Percy's power to manipulate his patron, this does not ring true. Northumberland had a clear agenda in which he intended to make use of the Catholics to his own advantage.

Percy seems to have made three visits altogether to Scotland before 1603, carrying Northumberland's secret correspondence. He was genially received by King James. Father Oswald Tesimond, often known under his alias of Greenway, wrote an account of it later in his *Narrative*, which is one of the important Catholic sources for the events surrounding the Powder Treason. Tesimond, a Jesuit priest from the north, knew many of the participants well and was a first-hand witness to a

number of the happenings. Thus we have King James in Tesimond's version making 'very generous promises to favour Catholics actively and not merely to free them from the bondage and persecution in which they were then living'. It got better: 'Indeed, he would admit them to every kind of honour and office in the state without making any difference between them and the Protestants.' And even better: 'At last he would take them under his complete protection.' As the King pledged his word as a prince, he took Percy by the hand and 'swore to carry out all that he had promised'. That was the thrilling story of his royal encounter which Thomas Percy now spread everywhere among the Catholics.[13]

If all this was true, it is easy to imagine the elation with which Percy returned to England, hastening to pass the good news to his co-religionists. Similarly, one can understand only too easily their own rising excitement. As Father Tesimond explained, the report as it spread in secret did an enormous amount of good for the King, 'winning over as it did the allegiance of the Catholics and filling them with the highest hopes'. But was it true?

The consensus of opinions among historians is that King James did give certain assurances, but that they were verbal. In cultivating the Catholics his clear intention was to foster exactly those 'highest hopes' to which Tesimond alluded. This was how King James operated. (One should point out that he was making similarly encouraging noises, at precisely the same period, to the English Puritans, who would have been mortally offended at the merest hint of toleration for the Catholics.) The sort of thing he probably had in mind was to allow what Northumberland called 'a Mass in a corner' – that is, in a private house, giving no public offence. In his correspondence with Northumberland, King James continually stressed his unaggressive feelings towards those Catholics who were not 'restive'.[14]

But all this was a very long way from the wild message of future royal 'protection' spread by Percy. Also, Percy, eager to establish his own importance, had been given a perfect

opportunity by these unwritten promises to impress his patron Northumberland, and his fellow Catholics. There is no question that the account of Tesimond shows a degree of exaggeration on Percy's part. At the same time, equally fatally, the King promised much more than he would admit to later.

King James' surviving correspondence with Northumberland is of a very different tone. At the start Northumberland knew exactly the right note to strike: 'My conscience told me of your succession right.' This was Northumberland's message: 'It were a pity to lose so good a kingdom' by not tolerating private Masses so long as the Catholics 'shall not be too busy disturbers of the government of the state, nor seek to make us contributors to a Peter [i.e. Catholic] priest'. King James' written reply to Northumberland was along the same lines. As for the Catholics, he would neither persecute 'any that will be quiet' and give outward obedience to the law, nor fail to advance any of them who genuinely deserved it through their 'good service'.[15]

Between this kind of sober, not unreasonable talk and Percy's exaggerated account of a glorious future, there was an enormous, potentially lethal gap.

Not all the English Catholics, however, were prepared to conduct themselves quite so quietly. The cause of the old religion in England had not been helped – how could it be? – by an angry split which developed in the late 1590s between the Jesuits and another group of priests, the so-called Appellants.[16] The dispute emerged into the open in the prison of Wisbech Castle in Lincolnshire where a great many priests were held. It was immensely disruptive within the narrow confine of the prison, and outside in the wider world even more so. Most importantly, from the point of view of the future, the dispute encouraged the Appellants to paint the Jesuits to the government as treacherous emissaries of the Pope who owed to him their first loyalty. This of course was almost exactly the government's own declared position on those 'hellhounds' the Jesuits.

All the priests concerned were English-born, and most had

had spells of education and training abroad since such training was of course impossible in England. But between the Jesuits and the Appellants there was a basic difference of approach over the restoration of Catholicism to their country. Was the right course to hold to the sacred tenets of Catholicism, spread them where possible, die in the attempt if not? This, simply put, was the Jesuit mission as they saw it. The Appellants for their part believed in establishing some kind of compromise with the state and in pledging their fervent loyalty to the government (even to the extent of denouncing the Jesuits as foreign-based trouble-makers). In this way they could set up a form of Catholicism as an unthreatening minority religion which would be officially tolerated. It is a dispute which has often been mirrored since, under totalitarian regimes where Christianity (and other doctrines) have been proscribed.

It is possible to sympathise with both points of view; unfortunately, the situation was complicated by personalities and personal rivalries. The brilliant, intellectual Jesuits – Fathers Garnet and Gerard – were envied by the Appellants for the civilised lives they led in the great houses that nurtured them. This was petty and, given the disgusting deaths of the Jesuit priests when they were captured, it was also unfair. The Appellants had more of a case when they dwelt on the turmoil stirred up by the Jesuits. Their case – if one was necessary between co-religionists – was stronger still when they accused the Jesuits of supporting the power of the Pope to depose a given sovereign.

This was the most damaging charge which could be made in the eyes of the English government and it had been given substance, as has been noted, by the disastrous Papal Bull of 1570 excommunicating Elizabeth. Jesuits like Father Garnet and Father Gerard, busy trying to stay alive and out of sight, busy trying to restore Catholics to their Faith equally out of sight, were not in business to depose any lawful sovereign. But some Jesuits of an older generation had taken a different view. Living in exile abroad, they had seen no reason not to support, from time to time, the invasion schemes of the Spanish King Philip II.

Father Robert Persons was one of these. He had been born at Nether Stowey in Somerset, one of eleven children, in 1544, three years before the death of Henry VIII. (He was thus eleven years older than Father Garnet and twenty-two years older than Father Gerard.) He was outstandingly clever and supposedly had the best mind of all the English Catholics. He was also unswervingly loyal to the cause and on certain issues uncompromising to a degree that those who came after him were not. For example, Persons supported plainly the power of the Pope to depose sovereigns.[17] Leaving England in the 1580s he had spent some time in Spain – hence his spirited advocacy of the Archduchess Isabella – before arriving in Rome in 1597.

A notorious challenge was put to priests in England when they were captured by the authorities: the so-called 'Bloody Question'. It ran as follows: 'Whose side would you take if the Bishop of Rome [the Pope] or other prince by his authority should invade the realm with an army...?' Most English priests, thus challenged, tried to evade the issue, taking refuge in silence or prevarication: the most sensible course.[18] But Father Persons, had the Bloody Question been put to him, and had he answered truthfully, would have backed the 'Bishop of Rome'.

Apart from being a hate figure to the English government, Persons was a particular target of Appellant dislike. He was accused of trying to run the entire (subterranean) English Catholic organisation as a kind of Jesuit fiefdom. The very question of that organisation aroused Appellant indignation. The Appellants proposed a form of episcopacy where English Catholic bishops would have the traditional powers of conse- cration and confirmation. (This would of course have distanced them in practice from Roman control and helped forward their concept of a minority religion with tacit government approval.) Instead, in 1598, they got an overlord known as the Archpriest in the shape of Father George Blackwell. Father Blackwell, although a decent, likeable man, was not the vigorous character needed in these difficult circumstances to weld (or hammer) the English Catholics together. Although not a Jesuit, to the

Appellants Blackwell gave the impression of being completely under the Jesuits' thumb.

Father William Watson was an Appellant with all their worst qualities of bitterness and self-pity, plus a few bad qualities of his own. He was coarse-mannered and very vain. (It is a sad truth that those who are able to compromise – or, as their enemies would put it, collaborate – are not always the most inspiring of characters personally.) The Jesuit Father Persons, alluding symbolically to Watson's prominent squint, called him 'so wrong shapen and of so bad and blinking aspect that he looketh nine ways at once'. The worst of Watson was his manic self-confidence on the subject of his own abilities which would lead him, as we shall see, into intrigues which were half crazy and wholly dangerous. Watson excoriated Jesuit control, wanting to make an addition to the Latin Litany which in English read: 'From the machinations of Persons, free us, O Lord.'[19]

Father John Mush was another Appellant who detested Persons with a vigour which would have made Robert Cecil proud of him. Mush, who hailed from Yorkshire, was a pious man (he had been the confessor of Margaret Clitheroe) but he was also notably irascible. He described Persons as 'stationed at his ease' in Rome, while the Appellants in England, 'innocent of any crime and ignorant of his dangerous machinations', underwent the punishment which his imprudence and audacity alone merited.[20]

Ironically, the efforts of the Appellants to reach an official accommodation with the Elizabethan government were not successful, despite some heavy attempts to do so in the last months of the old Queen's life. The French Ambassador tried to play a helpful role, given the kind of toleration which the Huguenots had in France, but was told that in England at least there was to be only one religion within one country.[21]

A proclamation of November 1602 was more encouraging since a distinction was officially drawn between the 'traitorous Jesuits' and the Appellants. The latter were given three months to declare their allegiance to Queen Elizabeth and throw

themselves on the government's mercy. However, the Appellant position was not as secure as its priests hoped. An Appellant 'Protestation' of January 1603 went a long way towards shrugging off Papal temporal claims. Yet it was dismissed by the English Council because it did not go far enough. The Council took a hard line: priests would be safe only so long as they did not actually celebrate the Mass. To abandon the Mass was certainly not what the Appellants, dedicated priests like Father Mush, had in mind, for all their faults.

The dispute between Jesuits and Appellants, between integrity and compromise, each policy with the aim of preserving English Catholicism, was like a canker eating away at the heart of the recusant world. However, if the new monarch did indeed tolerate 'diversity of opinions' in religion, it was possible that this painful dispute would begin to fade away.

Not all unquiet Papists in England were priests. Thomas Percy had two brothers-in-law, John (always known as Jack) and Christopher (Kit) Wright, who, unlike their female relations, did not believe in heroic but passive resistance. They were an impressive couple physically, burly and well above average height. They would never be described as handsome but Jack had 'pleasing features' and Kit had a healthy, ruddy face. In general they conducted themselves as a couple of strong, silent Yorkshiremen. This natural taciturnity, coupled with a reputation for loyalty, made the brothers prized associates for any kind of venture needing action (with the sword) rather than argument. And they were both devout Catholics.[22]

Jack Wright was one of the young men who, with his great friend Catesby, had formed part of the entourage of the Earl of Essex. He had been in the thick of the fierce if short-lived fighting of the Essex Rising in 1601; thereafter he did a spell in solitary confinement. Jack moved his family from Yorkshire into Twigmoor Hall in north Lincolnshire which, even before the Essex Rising, was noted as 'resort of priests for his [Wright's] spiritual and their corporal comfort'. A government report put it in less flattering terms: 'This place is one of the

worst in her Majesty's dominions and is used like a Popish college for traitors' in the northern parts.*²³

The Wrights were representative of what was, in effect, a younger generation of English Catholics. Jack and Kit Wright were born in 1568 and 1570 respectively. Guy Fawkes, whose name would eventually become synonymous with the Gunpowder Plot, was like the Wrights a pupil at St Peter's, York; he was also born in 1570. Robert Catesby, born in 1573, was slightly younger: his first cousin Francis Tresham was born in 1568. Another pair of Catholic brothers to whom Catesby and Tresham were related were Robert and Thomas Wintour of Huddington Court, Worcestershire. The Wintours, who had both Throckmorton and Vaux blood, were born in 1568 and 1571 respectively. The Wintours' sister Dorothy was married to a neighbouring recusant John Grant, who was roughly the same age.

These scions of recusant families, or sympathisers, grew to manhood in the 1590s. A comparison might be made to the young people, born after the Second World War, who came to adulthood in the 1960s, with revolutionary results. In the 1960s, however, the young, standing on the shoulders of a previous generation wearied by war, were able to help themselves to a new kind of personal liberty. In the 1590s, the aims of the restless young men were on the surface much more idealistic: religious freedom. At the same time there was a special capacity for violence within them, due to the suppression in which they had been nurtured, which the children of the 1960s, busy making love not war, in general did not feel.

It cannot be a complete coincidence that so many of the young males associated with the Gunpowder Plot were admired by their contemporaries for being expert fighters and in particular swordsmen – the gallant art that signified the gentleman. It was as though they were able to work out their

---

* Twigmoor Hall still bears traces of numerous subterranean passages; on one occasion in 1940 a tenant farmer Percy Chappel discovered a complete room with stabling for a horse underground when the leg of his wife's grand piano went through the floor.

disappointments in the manly sphere of combat: with the additional lurking possibility of one day wielding their swords in
the cause of the Catholic Faith. Jack Wright for example was
especially renowned for his valour, and was popularly considered to be the best swordsman of the day. His brother Kit was
also admired for his skill. Robert Catesby was much respected
'in all companies of such as are counted a man of action' for
his elegant way with both a horse and a sword. 'Great courage'
and 'intrepid courage' were qualities associated with the
Wintour brothers. Guy Fawkes the military man had
'considerable fame and name among soldiers'.[24]

There was no possibility of a university degree for such men
in England unless by compromising their Faith and passing as
Protestants, and no possibility of advancement in the endless
purlieus of governmental service (both involved taking the
Oath of Supremacy). Any kind of Catholic education or career
had to be sought abroad, most conveniently in the Spanish
Netherlands for geographical reasons, or in Spain itself. These
young men suffered as a result frustrations unknown to the
previous generation.

It is true that in many cases their parents had been imprisoned and fined – Sir Thomas Tresham and Ursula Wright
come to mind – but these same parents, having lived through
the five Catholic years of Queen Mary Tudor's reign, would
have had different expectations. What had happened once –
the restoration of Catholic England by a Catholic sovereign –
might happen again. They practised endurance and submission
to the will of God. The young men, resentful where their
parents and their family finances had suffered, were much
more disposed to seek remedy in positive action.

The Essex Rebellion was a case in point. While the main
thrust of the rebellion was to further the ambitions of Essex
himself, young Catholics such as Catesby, Tresham and Jack
Wright had a different agenda. Father Henry Garnet (who
greatly disapproved of an involvement reflecting so badly on
recusant loyalties) described these young men as having joined
in the vain hope that, if Essex won the day, 'there would be an

end of the penal statutes against Catholics'. The abrupt failure of the rising meant that this avenue was blocked. However, it was possible that Spain might help to build up their faction again to a position of strength. With this in mind, Thomas (Tom) Wintour made an expedition to Spain from Flanders in 1601, travelling under the alias of Timothy Browne.[25]

The Wintour name originally came from the Welsh Gwyn Tour, meaning White Tower – and was always spelt by the family with a 'u', thus commemorating its origins. 'Wyntour' was a variant in signatures but not 'Winter' (a fact which will turn out to be of some importance in this narrative). The Wintours' mother was Jane Ingleby, daughter of Sir William Ingleby of Ripley Castle, near Knaresborough. Her brother Francis Ingleby was a priest: he had been hung, drawn and quartered in 1586. This tragedy, with its gruesome details, could hardly have failed to leave a stark impression upon the Wintour family.[26]

Robert Wintour, as the elder of the two, inherited Huddington Court near Worcester and a considerable fortune. Huddington was one of those mellow, beautiful, moated Tudor houses which, like Baddesley Clinton, lay in an essentially private situation concealed by woods. Robert Wintour used his large fortune to good effect and had an attractive reputation for generosity. In general, he was held to be a reliable and decent fellow, if somewhat more low-key as a character than his lively brother Tom. As a result, it was commonly believed that the younger, cleverer brother influenced the tractable older one, rather than the other way round.

Robert was known to be a devout Catholic. He had also made a grand marriage to Gertrude Talbot, kin to the Earl of Shrewsbury, which brought him yet deeper into the Catholic world. His wife's family had suffered much for recusancy: her father, John Talbot of Grafton Manor near Bromsgrove, had spent nearly twenty years in prison, and her mother, a Petre, was the daughter of Queen Mary Tudor's Secretary of State and sister to that hospitable Sir John Petre who was the patron of William Byrd.[27] Maybe it was Gertrude Wintour's influence

which made Robert so strong for the Faith, or maybe he had deliberately sought out a devout Catholic bride. At all events, Huddington Court, under the sway of Robert Wintour, was a known refuge for priests, where secret Masses could and would be celebrated.*

Tom Wintour, intelligent, possessed of a strong personality, with neither the burden nor the advantage of an estate, grew up to be an operator rather than a benefactor. Here was a reverse of Jack Wright: not a strong silent man with a sword but an argumentative one, with the reputation of being skilful in debate, inclined to win the day over his opponents. He was a short, stocky man and like Robert was physically very fit. Lack of stature did not prevent Tom being considered good-looking, with his sparkling eyes and a face that was 'round but handsome'. Having received an education as a lawyer – a natural profession perhaps for one of his disposition – he took to a life of 'dissipation', in Father Tesimond's words, at least for a while.[28]

Tom, like so many others of his class and background, crossed the sea to Flanders in the Spanish Netherlands. At first, however, he enrolled in the English army fighting Spain in the Low Countries on behalf of the Protestant rebels: dissipation did not match with religious enthusiasm. Tom had always been interested in history and he now acquired a special interest in military history, as well as experience as a soldier. Naturally he became familiar with the Flanders scene: expatriates, intriguers as well as fighters, and many who were all these things. He also fought in France and maybe in Central Europe against the Turks. He certainly learnt Spanish – which would be important – as well as French and Latin.

Then something changed Tom Wintour. About 1600 he became as passionate a Catholic as his soberer brother, who

---

* Huddington Court, still privately owned and still in Catholic hands, is another house which remains as an eloquent memorial to the events of 1605; two hiding-places can still be seen, probably constructed by Nicholas Owen. One is off a top room which would have been used, for reasons of security, as a chapel; it also has an inner hole, barred by an extremely heavy door: this might remain undiscovered if the searchers were satisfied with their first find. There is another hiding-place in the attic room opposite.

went often to the Sacraments. Tom Wintour gave as his reason that he had come to see the injustice of the English war in Flanders, supporting the cause of the Protestant rebels against the *imperium* of Catholic Spain. But he must also have been convinced of the paramount truth of Catholicism. It therefore seems more likely that Tom, in his late twenties, first reverted to the traditions in which he had been raised, a spiritual journey which is not particularly unusual, and then threw in his lot with Spain.

One might add in parenthesis that a conversion of this sort, a rejection of youthful misdemeanours, a ricochet towards ardent piety, has been the sign of many fanatics in history, not all evil but some sanctified (such as St Augustine). It is another common factor among the so-called Plotters which is surely not altogether coincidental: at least four of them – as it happens, the leading figures – had undergone this very same process.

At all events, Tom Wintour changed sides. Late in 1601 he arrived in Spain, with the aim of contacting the Council on behalf of various Catholic dissidents left behind, rudderless, after the execution of their patron Essex. His primary aim seems to have been to secure Spanish money to provide modest English Catholic help as and when a Spanish invasion took place. Meanwhile not only would the Catholic faction in England be strengthened but the Spanish King would 'have them at his devotion'. Wintour's hope was for a faction vigorous enough to press for toleration.[29]

Nearly five years later, this mission, together with a second mission of 1603, was christened the 'Spanish Treason'. It would be the subject of fearful denunciation on the part of the English government. Details were altered (including the personnel involved) to suit the government's purpose. Sir Edward Coke, for the government, would furiously declare that Wintour had promised 'two thousand horses' from the English Catholics to help the Spanish on their arrival in England: horses, fit for military service, to be kept in permanent readiness for this happy event.[30]

If Wintour did make such promises, believing them himself, he was certainly living in the realm of fantasy since there was no question of these famous 'Catholic' horses existing. Furthermore, the point about horses suitable for military service is an important one: in an age dedicated to the horse as a means of transport, one horse was by no means like another. The English Catholics may well have possessed, among them, two thousand horses of different varieties all over the country. But the horses which the Spaniards had in mind were exceptionally strong, heavy animals with great powers of endurance – war-horses, in other words, which, if truly kept in readiness, would be obvious targets for government inspection. They would also be extremely expensive, both to buy and to maintain.

Wintour was not a fantasist. At the same time he was a natural advocate – and a trained one – who knew exactly the picture he wanted to paint to the Spanish court. He intended to portray the kind of English Catholic readiness which would duly inspire Spanish financial subsidy. So while Wintour certainly did not promise exactly what Coke said he had, he may well have touched up the picture in rather more vivid colours than the situation actually warranted. He would have seen it as being in the best interests of his co-religionists to exaggerate their numbers and strength in order to lure the Spanish forward.

Further red herrings arose in later accounts of the affair. The visit by Father Oswald Tesimond to Spain in the spring of 1602 on some kind of mission to do with the Appellant controversy was one of them. Wintour's introduction from Father Henry Garnet to the English Jesuits in Spain, and their Superior Father Joseph Cresswell, was another. This introduction was by no means a unique event: Garnet often provided such links to Cresswell. In this case, it seems likely that he believed Wintour's mission was to secure Spanish pension money for destitute Catholics (another objective which was comparatively common) rather than anything more militaristic.[31] But these connections could, much later, all be drawn into a damaging web.

Wintour, with the probable aid of another Englishman in Spain called Thomas James, found himself grappling with the Spanish Council at an unpropitious moment. Invasions were no longer popular projects. The Spanish attack on Kinsale of 1601, when Spanish troops landed in the south of Ireland in support of native Irish rebels, had been a disastrous failure. It was however true that Wintour had an ally in Father Cresswell, whose position gave him access to the Spanish Council and Philip III. It was a connection which Father Cresswell had long utilised to lobby energetically for an armed assault on England.

Perhaps it was Cresswell's assiduity, perhaps it was Wintour's eloquence. For the evidence does point to some kind of promise of Spanish money being given in the summer of 1602, as a prelude to unspecified Spanish armed help. Certainly no practical details were included, the name of the commander, for example, or the number of troops involved.[32]

Such vague assurances on the part of Spain, which could if necessary be denied later, were the stuff of diplomacy (as King James was demonstrating about the same time in Scotland). By the autumn of 1602, in any case, Spanish attention was turning ponderously in the direction of peace with England. In the event, the money would never be paid. Yet Wintour and others in his circle were convinced still that Spain would provide them with a solution.

King James in Scotland had declared that he would not shed blood for the sake of 'diversity of opinions' in religion, so long as the Catholics remained quiet. Tom Wintour and his associates could hardly be said to fit into such a peaceful scenario. It was unfortunate that on the eve of the King's arrival in England the Catholics themselves were exhibiting a diversity of opinions as to how they should proceed. At certain levels they suffered from unhappy internal divisions, and at other levels were ominously restless. And yet the mood was one of optimism on both sides.

Ten years earlier at a time of great persecution in the north of England, Father Henry Garnet had convinced himself that

the Faith was still flourishing in spite of these privations: indeed it shone more brightly every day 'like gold in the furnace'. Despite the testing of his confidence in some dark years, he felt that in time all would observe 'the religious conduct of Catholics'. By the summer of 1603, Father William Wright, a priest recently returned from abroad, prophesied that: 'It will come to pass that we in England shall have a toleration as the Huguenots have in France.'[33]

As for King James, a man in his mid-thirties, coming to the promised land, he was almost childish in his joy, and in his expectations of the English. He was quite confident that they would prove a great deal easier to manage than the Scots: 'Alas, it is a far more barbarous and stiff-necked people that I rule over.' Scotland was 'a wild unruly colt', wrote the King, with a passion for equestrian sports, whereas in England 'St George surely rides upon a towardly [docile] riding horse.'[34]

It remained to be seen which of these contrasting expectations – if any – were well founded. For the Catholics at least there were some cheerful portents. An early recipient of the royal favour was the crypto-Catholic Henry Howard, whose much disgraced family the King now embraced: 'I love the whole house of them.' Howard was given the precedence due to a duke's son and made a Privy Councillor by a King 'not ignorant of how many crosses he has sustained'; the following March he was created Earl of Northampton.*[35] In early July the recusant Sir John Petre of Ingatestone Hall, uncle of Gertrude Wintour, was created Baron Petre of Writtle: William Byrd's Mass for the Feast of St Peter and St Paul (29 June) may have been written as a play on his patron's name, in tribute to the event.[36]

But the most significant royal appointment, at least from the Catholic point of view, was that of Northumberland. He had continued to play his unofficial role of Catholic emissary at his first meeting with King James in early May, before the King reached London. Northumberland presented a petition on the

---

* But for simplicity's sake he will now be described as Northampton in the text, anticipating the creation.

Catholic behalf, although he took care not to sign it himself (he was after all not actually a Papist, even if many of his best friends were). Now he was installed as Captain of the Gentleman Pensioners, the royal bodyguards. This was an important as well as a prestigious post. Not only did it keep Northumberland in close contact with the King, but it gave him opportunities for personal patronage in appointing further royal bodyguards such as the ambitious and unscrupulous Thomas Percy. It was an appointment which would, in the next few years, alter the whole direction of Northumberland's life.

PART TWO

The Horse of St George

Saint George surely rides upon a docile riding horse...

KING JAMES VI
to Robert Cecil

A King and his Cubs

This fair inheritance from the loins of our ancient
Kings ... your Princely offspring.

WELCOME SPEECH OF THE SHERIFFS OF LONDON
AND MIDDLESEX
to James I

'**D**o you not think my Annie looks passing well?' King
James asked a courtier at Windsor on 30 June 1603.
After this informal invitation to comment on the looks
of his Queen, the King took his daughter Elizabeth in his arms
and gave her a kiss. 'My Bessie too is not an ill-favoured
wench,' added the fond parent. 'And may outshine her mother
one of these days.'[1]

It was not the unceremonious style of James I which made
such a scene startling to the English. Although they would
come to miss their gracious and dignified old Queen, this was
still the honeymoon period for James, the robust male
monarch who had come to do the work for which his sex was
best fitted, after years of 'unnatural' female rule. This was a
mood expressed with fervour (if not talent) by Cecil's brother
Burghley in an ode of acclamation:

> And all the way of James he loudly sang,
> And all the way the plain
> Answered 'James' again.[2]

For England, 'the horse of St George', it was this phenomenon

of a Royal Family – as opposed to a solitary individual on the throne – which was so striking because it was so novel.

Queen Anne had brought Prince Henry and Princess Elizabeth south with her in a triumphal progress of perpetual entertainment which occupied most of June. Great houses were almost as eager to welcome the distaff side of the new dynasty as they had been to bow before their sovereign. As for the great ladies, eagerly anticipating rich pickings at the new parallel court of the Queen Consort, they vied with each other in rushing north, as earlier their husbands had done. The race was won by the enterprising Lucy Countess of Bedford, who became one of the Queen's closest friends.

There had not been a Queen Consort's household – an elaborate structure second only to that of the King – since the days of Queen Catherine Parr, last wife of Henry VIII. But Catherine Parr had been by birth a commoner whereas Anne of Denmark was a king's daughter. Thus the true comparison was felt to be with the much more magnificent household of Henry's first wife, the Spanish Princess Catherine of Aragon. This was also true of Queen Anne's financial arrangements: Robert Cecil's notes on her jointure refer back specifically to that period, almost a century before, of domestic royal innocence when Henry VIII made his first marriage.[3]

In the south King James grew cross with some of the appointments made by his 'Annie', threatening to 'break his staff of Chamberlainship' over one man's head. He also occupied himself, in his pedantic way, with giving orders about the old Queen's jewels and her heavily encrusted dresses (considered with reason treasures of state in their own right). By custom these went to the new incumbent, but James thought it necessary to have sent north only those things judged suitable for 'the ordinary apparelling and ornament' of his wife.[4] None of this could mitigate Queen Anne's sheer enjoyment of her new life. She bade fair to love riding the horse of St George quite as much as her husband, if for different reasons.

Queen Anne loved pleasure and quickly found that in England there was more pleasure to be had than in Calvinist

Scotland. But she was no fool and certainly not a Philistine. Her family had had a tradition of literary patronage, particularly her mother Sophia of Mecklenburg, who had supported the philosopher Tycho Brahe. The Queen's new best friend the Countess of Bedford – 'Lucy the bright' as Ben Jonson called her – was one of the most cultured women of her age. When Emilia Lanier, Shakespeare's Dark Lady, envisioned Queen Anne as a patroness of female talent in a petition at the beginning of her reign, her words did not, like so many other petitions to royalty, have an utterly ludicrous ring:

> Vouchsafe to view that which is seldom seen,
> A woman's writing of divinest things ...[5]

Queen Anne's own idea of pleasure was dancing in a masque written by Ben Jonson, with scenery and costumes designed by Inigo Jones (or having a palace built for her at Greenwich, also by Inigo Jones). These were royal tastes for which the English should be suitably grateful in view of the rich heritage which they handed down to posterity. All of this, of course, was extremely expensive, as pleasures usually are. The King's grumbling (and Cecil's more discreet moans) would become fearful. On the Queen's journey south, however, as in so many royal beginnings, the mood was halcyon.

The most luminous of all the entertainments was a production of Ben Jonson's masque *The Satyr* at Althorp in Northamptonshire on 25 June. The host was Sir Robert Spencer (created Lord Spencer, as a reward, in July).[6] It was the Queen's first encounter with Jonson's work but she could hardly fail to be touched by verses which were both flowery and friendly. As fairies skipped about, and an eponymous satyr emerged from the undergrowth to apostrophise the visitors, the general tone of the proceedings was that which Disraeli would recommend when dealing with Queen Victoria two centuries later: 'Everyone likes flattery; and when you come to Royalty, you should lay it on with a trowel.' Two days later the King was reunited with his family, not seen since April, at Easton Neston, near Towcester.

On 2 July Prince Henry was invested as a Knight of the Garter at Windsor. At nine years old he was a tall, handsome boy, full of self-confidence. The wish expressed in *The Satyr* – 'O shoot up fast in spirit as in years' – seemed likely to be fulfilled. Prince Henry made an excellent impression during the ceremony, just as he had on his way south with his dancing skills. Not only was his 'princely carriage' admired but also the intelligent, lively manner in which he answered the ritual questions. At the altar he performed his obeisance with grace. Like his mother, but unlike his father James, Prince Henry already possessed the kind of easy royal manners which courted popularity. The following spring at the procession before the Opening of Parliament, Prince Henry showed himself 'smiling and overjoyed' as he acknowledged the loyal cheers by bowing this way and that. All this was described as being to the 'eternal comfort' of the people.[7]

And there was more comfort to come, apart from the engaging Prince and the pretty Princess. For James did not delude himself about his daughter Bessie, who at just on seven years old was indeed an exceptionally attractive child, a natural enchanter like her grandmother Mary Queen of Scots. There was known to be another little princeling still in Scotland, Prince Charles, who would be four in November. True, Queen Anne had miscarried, in May, of the child she was bearing at the death of Queen Elizabeth, and another son, Prince Robert, had recently died at four months old. But there was every hope that she would continue to justify her reputation as 'a most fruitful and blessed vine'.[8] She was after all only twenty-eight.

It was notable how the congratulatory addresses to King James on his arrival stressed the importance of his family. A speech, given in the name of the Sheriffs of London and Middlesex by one Master Richard Martin of the Middle Temple, referring to 'this fair inheritance from the loins of our ancient Kings...your Princely offspring', hailed the return of 'the sacred royal blood' which had been lent for a hundred years to adorn the north.[9] And that was the point. It was

indeed a hundred years since England had enjoyed the spectacle of a king and queen living in public amity, with a quiverful of young children: for Master Martin was referring to King James' great-great-grandparents, Henry VII and Elizabeth of York.

The rhetoric of royal addresses and the ceremonial investiture of the young Prince Henry were both intended to focus the nation's mind on the amazing fact that after roughly a century of uncertainty on this vital question of the royal succession, there were now two heirs and one heiress in direct line to the throne, with the possibility of more. This was a radical change, and a politically important one, quite apart from the sentimental delights of a young Royal Family as a public spectacle. It was a change which meant that further changes could not be expected, or, if so, they would not be brought about by a change of dynasty.

This was an aspect of the new reign fully appreciated, for better or worse, by the Catholics. Gone were the days of eager speculation on the subject of the Archduchess Isabella or even that reputed Papist sympathiser, Lady Arbella Stuart. As Father Tesimond succinctly put it, the succession was now assured by the King's 'numerous progeny'. And it was to be a Protestant succession: for these were children 'raised and thoroughly instructed in the opinions and doctrines of the father'. In Father Garnet's words, not only the King 'but the son that follows him' had to be reckoned with, in regard to Catholic grievances. Father John Gerard also pinpointed a new feeling among the Catholics that things were now set in an unalterable pattern, given 'the likelihood of continuance of that flourishing issue' with which God had blessed the King.[10]

This power of instant 'continuance' was (and is) one of the theoretical strengths of hereditary monarchy as a system of government. It was a system which Gibbon would describe memorably two hundred years later as presenting at first sight 'the fairest scope for ridicule' yet establishing none the less an admirable rule of succession 'independent of the passions of

mankind'.*[11] Certainly, the presence of a young prince, a direct heir, concentrated everybody's attention.

The late sixteenth century, like our own, was an age when the assassination of leaders featured as a much dreaded phenomenon (these deaths included that of Henri III, King of France, who died at the hands of a fanatic in 1589; Elizabeth I had been considered by the government to be the target of a series of assassination attempts). For many years England had not enjoyed the particular strength of a hereditary monarchy, the possibility of instant 'continuance'. But from 1603 onwards, if James departed, it would be once more a case of: 'The King is dead, long live the King.'

This vision of an endless line of Protestant Stuart monarchs might induce enthusiasm among loyal subjects. (*Macbeth*, with its ghostly procession of Banquo's descendants, ending with King James, was written in the first years of the new reign.) But in some Catholics it might induce melancholy.

In a further striking aspect to the subject, any effort to change the government of England by force would have to reckon with this materialisation of 'Princely offspring'. For one thing, it would not be feasible (even if desirable) to destroy the entire family. Quite soon, according to custom, Prince Henry and Princess Elizabeth would be given their own vast households, providing new employment for many beaming courtiers. Princess Elizabeth was given Lord Harington (Lucy Bedford's brother) and his wife as governors, and set up in state at Coombe Abbey in the midlands near Rugby.

Prince Charles was brought down from Scotland late in 1604, and the Queen gave birth to another princess, Mary, in April 1605.† By then, you might say that the Royal Family to its enemies had become that mythical beast, the Hydra with

---

* Gibbon commented: 'we shall cheerfully acquiesce in any expedient which deprives the multitude of the dangerous ... power of giving themselves a master.'
† Princess Mary, born on 9 April 1605, was the first royal child actually born in England since the future Edward VI, child of Henry VIII and Jane Seymour, in October 1537. Theoretically at least this English birth set her apart – favourably – from her siblings, born in Scotland.

whom Hercules struggled, growing a new head for each one cut off. There was an alternative way of thinking. A multiplicity of heirs could also mean that one or other was adopted to front a new regime. But of course, in the high summer of 1603, a time of rising Catholic expectations, the royal children were not so much hydra heads as 'young and hopeful olive plants'.[12] (The allusion, as with the description of Queen Anne as a vine, was to Psalm 128: 'Thy wife shall be as a fruitful vine by the sides of thine house: thy children like olive plants round about thy table.')

At this early period there was still much Catholic confidence in the active piety of the Queen. This confidence, like so many other Catholic dreams, did however gradually fade. Perhaps more should have been deduced from Queen Anne's treatment of some Catholic ladies of Lancashire who came to York to 'put up supplications' in order to have 'by her means' toleration of their religion. The Queen's answer was, from the Protestant point of view, 'wise enough': that is, gracious but non-committal.[13] Cecil's notoriously anti-Catholic brother Lord Burghley heaved a sigh of relief.

In Spain, however, Queen Anne was referred to openly as the 'Catholic wife', a description she herself seems to have done nothing to discourage, at least where the Catholic powers abroad were concerned. The emissary of the Grand Duke of Tuscany was assured by the Queen that she wished to live and die a Catholic. The French Ambassador, Comte de Beaumont, believed that Queen Anne was speaking to the King 'very frequently' on the subject of the Catholics. The Papal Nuncio in Brussels, Ottavio Frangipani, became over-excited. He even suggested that the ancient English-born Duchess of Feria, who as young Jane Dormer had been the play-fellow of Edward VI, should be brought back from Spain to her native country to act as an unimpeachably Catholic lady-in-waiting to the new Queen. It was an unrealistic plan not only because of the good lady's advancing years and failing health, but because Rome, ever ambivalent towards Spanish political influence, gave the notion a chilly welcome.[14]

The coronation of King James and Queen Anne took place on 25 July, one of those days which give English summers a bad name. It bucketed down with rain throughout. It was additionally depressing that fear of the plague had led to any unessential pomp being omitted. Common spectators, seen as carriers of the plague to mighty persons, were judged to come into this category of unessential pomp, and so the stands to house them at Westminster were abandoned. The deluge fell upon a mass of half-finished scaffolding.

But the Catholics were gleeful when it became known that the Queen had declined to take the Protestant Communion during the ceremony. Here was one who, as the Venetian Ambassador reported, might attend Protestant services in public as part of her queenly duties, but went thankfully to Mass in private.[15]

The optimistic quiescence of the English Catholics in general was thrown into sharp contrast by the emergence in this first summer of the reign of a conspiracy among certain 'discontented priests and laymen' which was both desperate and foolish. Father Watson, the manic Appellant priest, was involved, as was another priest, Father William Clarke. The laymen included George Brooke, brother of Lord Cobham, and Sir Griffin Markham. Father Watson was one of those who had been received by James in Scotland before his accession and given that kind of 'gracious and comfortable answer' on the subject of Catholic toleration in which the King specialised. However, the answer he brought back to England was even more gracious and comfortable, as he admitted later to the English Council. To boost his own standing among the English Catholics, he spoke of instant toleration, exaggerating much as Thomas Percy had done.[16] In 1603 Watson felt personally humiliated by the failure of this instant toleration to appear and turned to conspiracy.

The plan, apparently, was to hold the King prisoner in the Tower of London until he granted a wide series of demands to the Catholics, including, of course, full toleration. The King's

advisers particularly associated with the persecution of Catholics – notably Cecil – were to be removed. This plot became known as 'the treason of the Bye' to distinguish it from another conspiracy of the same period, also involving George Brooke, dignified as 'the treason of the Main'.

The Main Plot, which involved Lord Cobham, the Puritan Lord Grey de Wilton and in some manner Sir Walter Ralegh as well, had as its aim the far more drastic elimination of 'the King and his cubs'. In place of the Royal Family, Lady Arbella Stuart was to be elevated to the throne, since now that the succession had been settled in favour of the Stuart line, Arbella, as King James' first cousin, was fourth in line for the crown, after his three existing 'cubs'. However, Lady Arbella was much enjoying her new glorious precedence as the first (adult) lady in the land after Queen Anne and had become, according to an ill-wisher, 'a regular termagant' on the subject.[17] She found it all so much more gratifying than the spiteful treatment she had received from the old Queen Elizabeth, and was wise enough to refuse any overtures from Lord Cobham.

All those concerned in both Bye and Main Plots were arrested in July, held prisoner and tried in the autumn. Lord Cobham and Sir Walter Ralegh were both sentenced to death but subsequently reprieved (the former when he was actually on the scaffold). In the event, Cobham was held in the Tower of London. Sir Walter Ralegh was also kept in prison. Sir Griffin Markham, like Cobham, was given a last-minute reprieve on the scaffold, but George Brooke was executed. Naturally both priests, Fathers Watson and Clarke, were put to death in the usual grim way.

The English Catholic community as a whole, including priests, reacted with absolute horror to all this. Could anything be more criminally reckless – and more ill-timed? It was, wrote Father Garnet to Rome of the Bye Plot, 'a piece of impudent folly, for we know that it is by peaceful means that his Holiness [the Pope] and other princes are prepared to help us'. This verdict of 'impudent folly' was certainly likely to be well received in Rome. Here, Claudio Aquaviva, General of the

Jesuits, was himself advocating prudence: there was to be no meddling by priests in anything 'that did not concern their apostolate'. As for the Papacy, there were still happy dreams of King James' conversion: a Mass had just been celebrated to mark his 'happy entrance' into England.[18]

Further communications on the same subject came from Garnet in July and August. The message was the same. The Pope should instruct the English Catholics to behave peacefully: 'quiete et pacifice'. (Such letters were always in Latin, the international language of the Catholic Church.) Meanwhile the Archpriest, Father George Blackwell, was equally forthright to his flock. As the chief Catholic pastor in England, he forbade the priests under his authority to participate in any such enterprise in the future.

Pleas and prohibitions after the event were all very well. Even so, the Catholic reputation for loyalty would have inevitably suffered in England had it not been for the bold action of two priests, one of whom was the Jesuit Father John Gerard. It was these priests who, on hearing something of the projected Bye Plot, along the Catholic network, hastened to tip off the Privy Council. This action to dissociate the Catholics from the conspirators was approved by the Archpriest and Father Garnet. One may conjecture that the Jesuit dislike of the Appellant played its part here: but then the Bye Plot showed, did it not, how dangerous Appellants could be ... In any case, there was absolutely no question that this tip-off was the correct, indeed the vital, move to make, from the point of view of the Catholic future. Gerard had acted 'with care and fidelity' to save the King, as a fellow Catholic wrote.[19] At a stroke – or so it seemed – the situation had been saved.

King James was grateful. Furthermore, he gave his gratitude practical expression. As part of his coronation festivities, he allowed pardons to those recusants who would sue for them. In a gesture which can hardly have pleased the Exchequer, but relieved and delighted the burdened recusants, he remitted their fines for a year. The consequences of this generosity are borne out by the figures concerned. The receipts from these

fines for the previous year had totalled something over seven thousand pounds, whereas for 1604 they were just under fifteen hundred pounds: a prodigious drop.[20]

A protestation of loyalty on behalf of leading Catholics headed by Sir Thomas Tresham was received by King James at Hampton Court. In 1602 Sir Thomas had been hailed for his leadership as 'another Moses' by a Catholic priest on the eve of execution: 'if thou hadst not stood in the breach of the violators of the Catholic faith, many...would not have battled so stoutly in the Lord'.[21] Now the Catholic Moses, who had suffered long imprisonment and vast fines in the previous reign, was leading his people, as he hoped, towards a more tranquil, less financially straitened future – if not yet towards the promised land.

The financial point was especially important to Sir Thomas Tresham, since his fortune – that fortune which Francis Tresham would inherit on his death – had been depleted by more than fines. For Sir Thomas was that fatally expensive component of any family history: a lavish host, as we have seen, but also an energetic builder. Rushton Hall in Northamptonshire was a vast monument to this energy, and there were other projects, including Triangular Lodge, constructed on architectural principles to commemorate the Holy Trinity.* He was also immensely litigious (another expensive taste). More attractively but equally extravagantly, Sir Thomas gave generous portions to his daughters on marriage, way beyond the norm of his generation.

Sir Thomas Tresham's predominant instinct was to get benign control, as he saw it, of his fellow men and women, whether as a host, builder, litigator or leader of the English

---

* Triangular Lodge is still standing, as is Lyveden 'New Bield' near Oundle, an unfinished shell begun in the 1590s, in the shape of a Greek cross. Rushton Hall (now an R.N.I.B. School for the Blind) preserves much of the stately atmosphere created by Sir Thomas. An aperture in the cellar leads to a hiding-place, using the drainage system of the house which lies in a direct line below what would have been the chapel on the top floor. It was discovered in 1979 by a local archaeologist: a small *Sanctus* bell dated 1580 and other objects consonant with recusant practice were found inside the hole.

Catholics. This was particularly true of his wide family circle: he had eight children (three more died in infancy) and then there was the Vaux connection, among the numerous links to other recusant families. Not everyone accepted the leadership of the patriarch with quite the submissiveness which Sir Thomas considered to be his due. That formidable pair, Anne Vaux and her sister-in-law Eliza Vaux, the Dowager of Harrowden, stood up to him, as we have seen, and Francis Tresham, his eldest son, was not easy to handle.

A modern psychologist would have no difficulty in explaining why Francis Tresham grew up both resentful of his father's authority and profligate with his father's money. While he was quite young, Francis Tresham had committed a brutal assault on a man and his pregnant daughter, on the ground that the family owed his father money. For this he did time in prison. Later he became involved in the Essex imbroglio, for which his father had to buy his freedom. Sir Thomas, however, lacking these psychological insights, simply expected that his son, like the other Catholics, would follow his peaceful example in the new reign. It would – for the Tresham family as a whole – be yet another expensive error of judgement.

A psychologist might also have made something of a solemn new public thanksgiving to which the English were introduced by King James on 5 August 1603. It celebrated the King's deliverance three years earlier – while in Scotland – from a situation of acute physical danger. The sacred royal person had been held captive in a locked room in a hostile castle by Earl Gowrie and his brother, only to be rescued in the nick of time. Whatever the final truth of the Gowrie Conspiracy, as this murky plot was known, the sense of a miraculous deliverance from physical peril was so important to King James that he insisted on its annual remembrance.

Since both Gowrie brothers were troublesome and both were killed during the King's rescue, there were Scottish critics who suggested that the Gowrie Conspiracy was a set-up, a means of getting rid of the family. King James himself rebutted this charge. He told a Scottish minister who tackled him on the

subject that he was not a bloodthirsty man, and in any case he had plenty of reasons to have the Gowrie brothers put to death by others without risking his personal safety: 'I needed not [to] hazard myself so.'[22] Both parts of his answer were true: King James was not in love with violence and he was in one crucial respect, his obsession with assassination, a physical coward.

We should not perhaps judge King James too harshly for his cowardice when we bear in mind his early history. Even the ante-natal influences were violent: when Mary Queen of Scots was six months' pregnant with James, daggers were pointed at her womb by her leading nobles who, having threatened her unborn child, proceeded to murder her secretary Riccio. As a five-year-old boy James saw the bloodstained body of his dying grandfather the Regent being carried past him at Stirling Castle. The new Regent Morton, an old ruffian, terrified the little King. At the age of eleven, James was kidnapped as a result of a feud between rival gangs of nobles and was – not surprisingly – said by the English Ambassador to be 'in great fear'.[23] There were plots and counter-plots throughout the King's adolescence to seize him or rescue him, since in a lawless country possession of the royal person was considered to be at least nine points of the law, if not the whole of it. Worst of all was the campaign of physical threat carried on against the King by Francis Earl of Bothwell (nephew of the noble who had been his mother's nemesis). At one point Bothwell set fire to the King's door, having pursued him through the castle to a remote room, leaving James, who could not afford armed guards, cowering inside.

King James of course expected the horse of St George to be infinitely more tractable than the wild unruly colt which was Scotland.* Yet these Scottish experiences had left an indelible impression upon him. The Spanish envoy took note that the

---

* One only has to remember that Essex committed a major crime in interrupting Queen Elizabeth at her *toilette* (on his unauthorised return from Ireland, before he rebelled) to understand the vast differences in attitude towards *lèse-majesté* between the two countries.

King was a 'timorous character'. Plague – 'God's devouring Angel' as James termed it – was a further morbid fear: another silent assassin which might come at him out of a crowd.[24] It was ironic that the King on the hunting field was fearless in pursuit, reckless of his own safety. His courtiers might have preferred him to lose himself less on the hunting field and cut more of a martial figure in public.

One should not underestimate the depth of the trauma which the Bye conspiracy caused the King, for all the unrealistic nature of the plot itself. Despite the fair words King James spoke to the recusants led by Sir Thomas Tresham at Hampton Court, despite the efforts of the Jesuits and others to tamp down their explosive co-religionists, the fact remained that the first evil threats to the royal safety – and that of 'the cubs' – had come from the Catholics. It was an association of Catholicism with menace which a King haunted by fears for his own safety was not likely to forget.

CHAPTER FIVE

Spanish Charity

The present case of the Catholics of England is one
of charity and not of justice.

CARDINAL DE ROJAS Y SANDOVAL
Primate of Spain, 1603

In mid-July 1603, Guy Fawkes set out from Flanders for
Spain. It was around the time that Sir Thomas Tresham
and other English Catholics presented their loyal petition
to King James at Hampton Court. But Fawkes' objective was
neither loyal to King James nor was it peaceable. He intended
to proceed further with the plan which had long obsessed
certain Catholic activists, to prod Spain into a genuine commitment to the invasion of England. In spite of King James' calm
accession, Fawkes still managed to believe that the time was
ripe.

Guy Fawkes was now a man of thirty-three. His life is
sometimes described as an enigma: but while certain details
have been obscured by the thunderclouds of mythology surrounding his name, the essential facts are known. There may
be ambiguous or at least puzzling characters in the large cast of
the drama later called the Gunpowder Plot, for example Lord
Monteagle. But Guy Fawkes is not one of them. Far from
being enigmatic, he was a straightforward soldier – or you
could say mercenary, since he had been enlisted in the Spanish
army in the Low Countries rather than in the army of his
native land.

Fawkes' appearance was impressive. He was a tall, power-fully built man, with thick reddish-brown hair, a flowing mous-tache in the tradition of the time, and a bushy reddish-brown beard. His physical courage was an important element in his make-up, and he was also steadfast. At the crisis of his life, he showed himself capable of extraordinary fortitude. He was neither weak, nor was he stupid. Although Fawkes was a man of action (hence Tesimond's reference to his 'considerable fame among soldiers'), he was capable of intelligent argument as well as physical endurance, somewhat to the surprise of his enemies.[1]

Guy Fawkes was born in 1570, in York in a house in Stonegate which belonged to his parents, Edward Fawkes and the former Edith Jackson.[2] Although the exact date of his birth is not known, it is likely to have been 13 April since he was unquestionably baptised in the nearby church of St Michael-le-Belfry three days later, and that was the customary gap.* Guy Fawkes' family was not outwardly Catholic. Edward Fawkes was a conventional Protestant, having followed his own father's profession of notary public, and succeeded him even-tually as Registrar of the Exchequer Court. This of course meant that Edward Fawkes had sworn the Oath of Supremacy to hold office. Guy's paternal grandmother, with whom he spent some time in early boyhood, born Ellen Harrington, came of a line of Protestant public servants: lord mayors and sheriffs. Guy Fawkes' descent on his mother's side was, however, different. The Jacksons were listed among the recu-sants of West Yorkshire, while Edith's sister's son (Guy's first cousin), Richard Cowling, became a Jesuit priest.

When Guy was eight, his father died. Two or three years

---

* His place of baptism is also the key to Guy Fawkes' birthplace in his parents' house. The site is now occupied by numbers 32–34 Stonegate next to the Star Inn (then as now a York landmark). York Civic Trust have placed a plaque on the eastern end of Blackwell's bookshop frontage (number 32): 'Hereabouts lived the parents of Guy Fawkes of Gunpowder Plot fame who was baptized in St Michael le Belfrey Church in 1570.' A house in Petergate has also been suggested but it does not lie in the parish of St Michael; the entry of Fawkes' baptism can still be seen in the York Minster Archives (S/2).

later his mother remarried a recusant, Denis Bainbridge. Their
life at Scotton near Knaresborough brought Guy formally into
the Yorkshire Catholic orbit. Nevertheless Edith Jackson
Fawkes' second marriage suggests that she had never lost the
recusant sympathies in which she had been brought up.

The earliest strong Catholic influence upon Guy Fawkes was
however exerted by St Peter's School, York.* His schoolfellows
included those taciturn swordsmen Jack and Kit Wright (the
latter was Guy's exact contemporary), as well as at least three
men who became priests, Oswald Tesimond, Edward Oldcorne
and Robert Middleton, put to death at Lancaster in 1601. It is
evident that this outwardly conformist school was in fact
something very different underneath. The previous headmaster
had spent twenty years in prison for being a recusant. The
current headmaster John Pulleine called himself a Protestant
because otherwise he would have lost his job, but the Pulleines
as a whole were notable Yorkshire recusants.

Pulleine himself played along with the authorities, and on
one occasion denounced a priest to them: further proof of his
loyalty, necessary for one of recusant stock. But there were
surely many other masters, less visible than the head, who contributed to the atmosphere of this 'Little Rome' (to adapt the
term used of Magdalen Viscountess Montague's Sussex home).
At any rate, Guy Fawkes in the prime of life was known to be
a devout Catholic, like Tom Wintour after his conversion,
assiduous in attending the Sacraments and taking Communion.
Father Tesimond made the further comment that Fawkes' kind
of 'exemplary life' was rare among soldiers.[3]

Guy Fawkes took himself abroad in the early 1590s to serve
in an army where he could exercise his talents and practise his
Faith freely. Before that, he had acted for some months as a
footman to the 1st Viscount Montague, Magdalen's husband,

---

* St Peter's School, York, still survives. Although it has moved its site since the
days of Guy Fawkes, the school retains a strong tradition of interest and even
fondness for its best-known old boy. Guy Fawkes was however tactfully
described by a recent head boy as 'not exactly a role model' (*The Times*, 5
November 1992).

at Cowdray in Sussex. (This was a good position for a young man in the household of a great lord, not a servile one.) Fawkes seems to have been dismissed by the venerable old peer 'upon some dislike he had of him'. But he was subsequently reemployed by Montague's grandson, Anthony, who succeeded as the 2nd Viscount Montague when he was eighteen. According to the young lord, this was at the suggestion of his steward, Spencer, who was kinsman to Fawkes. Spencer pleaded for Fawkes to be allowed to wait at table and Montague gave in, although by his own subsequent account he 'scarcely thought' about the matter.[4] It may well be, however, that Montague, by inheritance one of the leaders of the Catholic community, went further. He may have actually helped Fawkes on in his army career by providing an introduction along the Catholic network, as would have been common practice. But Montague, who found his mere employment of Guy Fawkes embarrassing enough in 1605, was hardly likely to admit anything which was not already of record.

There is another question mark over the early life of Guy Fawkes. According to one account, he married Maria Pulleine while he was still in Yorkshire and she bore him a son, Thomas Fawkes, in 1591.[5] A Pulleine bride would have been plausible for Guy Fawkes, since he was already connected to the family because of his mother's second marriage. However, not one contemporary account at the time of Guy Fawkes' greatest fame – or infamy – refers to him as a married man, nor is there any reference to his wife or child either in England or in the Low Countries.* If the marriage did indeed take place, perhaps it was very brief, with both wife and son dying almost at once, while Guy was still in Yorkshire. Such tragedies were all too common and maybe the loss precipitated Guy's journey, first south, then abroad. But this is to speculate. What is known is that Guy Fawkes, the successful and admired soldier, was also leading a clean life unusual for his profession.

* No entry concerning the marriage or baptism has been found in the register of Farnham Church, near Scotton, although the marriages of Fawkes' sisters Elizabeth and Anne are recorded in 1594 and 1599 respectively.

Whatever the background to his 'exemplary' conduct, the picture is created of a kind of soldier–monk, a man with a mission which did not include family and children.

Guy Fawkes' army career in the Spanish Netherlands prospered. Flanders was at that point 'the mother of military invention', as Tesimond described it. Fawkes was given a position and became an *alferez* or ensign and by the summer of 1603 was being recommended for a captaincy.[6] His commander there in the service of Spain was Sir William Stanley, a veteran soldier in his mid-fifties.

Stanley had probably always been a Catholic at heart, yet his interesting military career under Elizabeth illustrated just how difficult it was for the government to decide who was and who was not a Papist, providing the person concerned did not obtrude it. Stanley had been knighted for his services in the English cause in Ireland in 1569, and in the Low Countries served under Elizabeth's favourite Leicester, who praised his courage at the siege of Zutphen in 1586, calling him 'a rare captain' and 'worth his weight in pearl'.[7] Unfortunately the very next year Leicester's rare captain, now Governor of Deventer, surrendered his fortress to the Spanish and formally announced his change of sides (and religion). It was, in a sense, a good career move for one finding himself in the Netherlands, especially if Stanley had always held Catholic sympathies. But the English were understandably outraged. Stanley, the traitor, was high on the government's hate list.

Hugh Owen, another veteran, but a veteran spy rather than a soldier, also featured on this list. The 'Welsh Intelligencer' as he was sometimes known (he had been born in Caernarvonshire) was sixty-five at the death of Queen Elizabeth. For the last thirty years, since he fled from England, Owen had managed to have a finger in most of the conspiratorial pies in the Netherlands, his natural capacity for intrigue being greatly enhanced by his ability to communicate in Latin, French, Spanish and Italian, as well as English and, perhaps less usefully, Welsh. Owen, like Stanley, had supported the claims of the Archduchess Isabella. Whether it was Welsh

antipathy or not, he had a passionate dislike of King James, whom he designated 'this stinking King of ours' and 'a miserable Scot'.[8] The two men, Owen and Stanley, had visited Spain together, and for a long time shared a belief in the future of Spanish military intervention as a means of solving the Catholic problem. Stanley himself had in the past been responsible for various forays against the English and Irish coasts.

Yet vast tectonic plates were moving slowly beneath the surface of the diplomatic world. Sure enough, this invisible movement would one day produce its visible earthquake. The age-long hostilities between Protestant England and Catholic Spain would be brought to an end, and a treaty between the two countries negotiated. Already by the time of Guy Fawkes' unofficial mission on behalf of English Catholics, sensible men, close to the councils of the great, were beginning to appreciate that the time for violent solution had passed.

Guy Fawkes, a soldier rather than a diplomat, and certainly not close to the councils of the great, was not aware of this potential upheaval when he set out for Spain. The tectonic plates were moving, but the earthquake was still far off. It is only recent researches into the secret Spanish correspondence of the time which have revealed how doomed the Fawkes scheme was from the start. At the time the Spanish Council and Philip III continued to give amazingly friendly answers to Fawkes and his colleague Anthony Dutton, who had come from England and travelled to Spain via Flanders.[9] They experienced much civility, just as Tom Wintour had a year earlier. It was not in the Spanish interest to give a yea or a nay, when elaborate courtesies would serve their purpose better and mask the changes which were occurring. However, a man in international politics who has not spotted a subtle change in direction tends to suffer an ignominious fate, or worse, as the story of Guy Fawkes shows.

As for Dutton, from his arrival in Valladolid in May, he had already displayed himself as an incorrigible optimist (or another ardent advocate like Tom Wintour). Dutton asserted flatly that the English Catholics were ready and waiting to rebel, and that

it would not even take very long to secure success. 'With work, speed, secrecy and good weather,' declared Dutton, 'we will have the game in six days.'[10] How far from reality all this was! This was the same period when the Catholic Moses, Sir Thomas Tresham, was in the throes of declaring his loyalty to the crown, Catholic priests were denouncing the fanatical Bye Plot and being rewarded for their loyalty, and Catholics in general were eagerly awaiting that toleration which they believed had been promised to them in Scotland by their new King.

Fawkes' memorandum (in his handwriting, preserved in the Spanish archives) has an even more bizarre flavour, given that in July 1603 King James had been over two months happily resident in England and had recently remitted recusant fines. Fawkes wrote that the King's claims to inherit were scorned all over England as illegitimate. Then James was repeatedly described as 'a heretic', one who intended 'in a short time to have all of the Papist sect driven out of England'. His table-talk was said to be equally crude: 'Many have heard him say at table that the Pope is Anti-Christ which he wished to prove to anyone who believed the opposite.' Any overtures to Spain for peace, Fawkes declared, were to be treated as royal subterfuges of the basest sort. The King's true intention was to enrich himself with the property of Catholics and, once grown powerful as a result, join with other Protestants 'to wage war on the rest of the Christian princes' who were not heretics.[11]

So far, so passionate and, given King James' genuine desire for international peace, so wrong-headed. But there is another aspect to the memorandum and this is its fierce anti-Scottish bias. Fawkes concluded the memorandum with this prophecy: 'There is a natural hostility between the English and the Scots. There has always been one, and at present it keeps increasing [due to grievances felt by the English against the King's advancement of his Scottish favourites]. Even were there but one religion in England,' went on Guy Fawkes, 'nevertheless it will not be possible to reconcile these two nations, as they are, for very long.'

It has to be said, however, that Guy Fawkes' raging against the all-pervasive Scots was the one aspect of his memorandum which would have commended itself to the majority of his fellow Englishmen. It certainly gave notice of a new, potentially rebellious feeling among the English: deep resentment at being passed over in favour of the greedy new men from the north.

Although the Spanish Council did solemnly debate the propositions of Dutton and Guy Fawkes, a percipient point was made in the course of the discussion by the Duke of Olivares, the King's chief minister. 'Any increase in men to a Catholic faction is composed of the malcontents,' he remarked.[12] And the debate was not ultimately favourable to the Englishmen's cause.

In the meantime Father Cresswell, Superior of the English College, who a year previously had been encouraging action, along with Tom Wintour, had now changed his tack. He begged the Council to send Dutton and Guy Fawkes away, on the ground that they were endangering the negotiation of a diplomatic peace. In Rome, the Pope was equally resolute in asserting that 'the way of arms', in the phrase of Philip III, would simply result in the destruction of those English Catholics that remained.[13]

The only real memento that Guy Fawkes took away from this unpromising mission was a change of name: henceforth he would be known universally as Guido, the name he also used for his official signature. It was a name which might be said by his enemies to make his foreign allegiances clear. But that was not how Guido Fawkes saw the matter. In his eyes, he was both a sincere Catholic and a patriotic Englishman, an Englishman abroad but with the true interests of his country at heart.

From the point of view of English Catholic liberty of conscience, one crucial journey did take place in the summer of 1603: not the expedition of that amateur diplomat and adventurer Guy – now Guido – Fawkes, but the important mission

of Don Juan de Tassis, from Spain to England. (The fact that Tassis could set out, travelling via Brussels, while the Spanish Council had still not officially ruled out providing armed support is characteristic of the ambiguity with which they operated.) Tassis' brief was to pave the way for an Anglo-Spanish treaty and in so doing explore the whole matter of liberty of conscience for English Catholics.[14]

For example, should toleration be a precondition of any treaty? Should the Spanish King hold out for it at all costs? In any case, what was the nature of the English Catholic community? Strong, armed, rebellious? Or crushed, weak and disorganised? There had been many wild reports recently from visitors, including Wintour and Fawkes, and Tassis was going to test the truth of these claims.

A peaceful tide was flowing across Europe and King James was by temperament the right man to go with it. Guido's denunciation of him as a militant was extremely wide of the mark. It was the personal motto in which King James would take pride, *Beati Pacifici* (Blessed are the Peacemakers), which expressed the truth. Although Spain and England were still technically at war, the immediate Anglo-Spanish ceasefire which James had ordered on his accession provided the diplomatic excuse for Tassis' journey. It was now a matter of protocol that Spanish royal congratulations should be conveyed to James on his accession. Meanwhile the Archduke Albert and the Archduchess Isabella were so enamoured of the possibilities of the new reign that they despatched their own welcoming envoy without consulting Spain, the mother country. The new King's friendship was precious, Isabella had written in April, 'as a chance of peace'.[15]

The presence of an embassy from a foreign Catholic power had an important side effect for the Catholics of England. Traditionally the government did not interfere with the private celebration of the Mass in an embassy chapel, nor seek to question too closely the status of the embassy officials, some of whom might be priests: embassies were in theory foreign soil. Englishmen could therefore slip into the great warrens of

houses where such embassies were based and not only attend
Mass but also enjoy Catholic contact. They could do so, if they
were prepared to endure the ordeal of Cecil's spies, eager to
report who paid this kind of suspicious visit, as a method of
discovering secret Papists. It was all part of the deadly game
which Papists and their priests played, balancing the Mass
against imprisonment.

The arrival of an envoy from the greatest Catholic power of
all, Spain, produced incredible excitement. One of Don Juan
de Tassis' official escorts, Sir Lewis Lewkenor, thought it his
duty to advise Cecil that 'some gentlemen known to be recusants' had rushed to greet him, and some of them in their
eagerness even awaited his landing at Dover on 31 August.[16]

Tassis came from a family which (under the other version of
the name, Taxis) had given nearly a century of service to the
Habsburgs. He himself had acted as Court Chamberlain to
Philip III since 1599. While Tassis clearly enjoyed the trust of
his King, he was not a trained diplomat but a court official.
Moreover his instructions betrayed a startling naivety concerning the English scene. He bore with him letters of greetings to
many members of the English nobility, including ten dukes –
but there were no dukes at all in England at the present time.*
Tassis was also supposed to greet ten marquesses which was
slightly easier to achieve since there was actually one
marquessate in England, that of Winchester.

Tassis' stay in Brussels *en route* had been no more helpful in
preparing him realistically for what he would find in England.
Secret conferences were held 'at a late hour to protect us from
[English] spies', with men like Sir William Stanley and Hugh
Owen and a Jesuit, Father William Baldwin, who was part of
their counsels. There was more talk of Catholic troops in
waiting – the figure of twelve thousand men was mentioned.
And Tassis' card was marked concerning the English nobles he

---

* The Dukedom of Norfolk was still under attainder [prohibited from use], following the execution of the 4th Duke in 1572, and was not restored until 1660;
Prince Charles, the King's younger son, was not created Duke of York till January
1605.

would encounter, and how friendly they were to the Spanish (Catholic) cause. Even here the familiar anti-Scottish note struck. The new Scottish favourites at the English court, such as Sir George Home, were said to be unenthusiastic about Spain – but it was thought that they would change their opinions if bribed.[17]

Tassis, if not a trained diplomat, was shrewd and practical. It is to his credit that once in England he realised very quickly how false the picture was that he had been given. His letters back to Spain reflect a complete change of approach from the lofty militarism of the high summer. Lewkenor complained that the recusants continued to accost Tassis in the course of his 'slow journey' to Oxford, which was destined to be his first official resting-place. Some Spaniards in his train took the opportunity to slip into the prisons and visit 'the seminary priests...detained prisoners'.[18] Lewkenor, however – and Cecil – would have been gratified rather than angered if they had had the opportunity to read the reports despatched by Tassis back to Spain. For Tassis was not impressed by what he found.[19]

The recusants 'go about in such a timid fear of one another', he wrote, 'that I would seriously doubt that they would risk taking to arms' unless there was a clear and definite opportunity. A month after his arrival, he was expressing serious disappointment. The numbers of active Catholics had been grossly inflated. In short, he had no expectation of any Catholic 'stir' (a commonly used word for a rising).

One of the activists that Tassis did meet was Tom Wintour. He was privately of the opinion that Wintour was a Jesuit, although Wintour introduced himself merely as one that had kissed the hands of the King of Spain 'less than two years ago' in the course of negotiations with members of the Spanish Council. Wintour's fluent Spanish was useful once more on this occasion since Tassis spoke no English. Even so, he failed to convince Tassis that '3,000 Catholics' were ready, only needing the promised money from Spain to spur them forward.

Tassis was finally received by King James on 8 October in a series of ceremonies which lasted for three days. (Not only had the King been away hunting since his arrival, but there remained the persistent fear of plague which led him to avoid official duties.) Tassis presented the King with some fine Spanish horses – under the circumstances, a suitable gift – and for Queen Anne there were magnificent jewels. There was however one hitch. The King was disconcerted to find that Tassis did not have plenipotentiary powers to negotiate the coming treaty. These had been granted to a member of the Spanish Council known as the Constable of Castile, who was still in Spain.

Tassis also had to make an adjustment. Writing back to Spain he poured cold water on those rumours of King James' conversion to Catholicism. James was a Protestant and likely to remain so, despite the hints so casually dropped by his emissaries in the 1590s. Even more to the point, James' current attitude to Catholic ceremonies was not at all what Tassis had been led to expect. Great care was being taken to ensure that the King had no official knowledge of any Mass being said: it was a case of a discreet 'Mass in a corner' here and there in private (Northumberland's term to James in Scotland), nothing more public. There was general doubt whether King James would ever 'permit' the Catholic religion to be practised, but it was also viewed as fatal if the Spanish King was seen to be trying to set up his own religion 'in this country'. On 12 October, the day after he parted from King James, Tassis wrote quite frankly to Philip III to say that the question of the free exercise of the Catholic religion 'should be left aside until the peace has been negotiated'.[20]

Disappointed by the quality of local Catholic support, Tassis now believed that the English Catholics should continue to play that passive role for which they seemed best fitted. They were not after all Spanish subjects. If they had been, King Philip would be obliged to help them as a matter of justice, but as Cardinal de Rojas y Sandoval, the Primate of Spain, succinctly expressed it, the present case of the Catholics of

England was 'one of charity' from the Spanish King 'and not of justice'.²¹

This was a message appreciated by Philip III, who at long last gave up playing with the notion of a 'stir'. In a letter the following February, he summed up the new official line: it was essential that 'these Catholics' (the English) should avoid arousing the suspicions of their sovereign at this crucial moment when there was a real prospect of a treaty.²² In short, the diplomatic solution was to prevail.

There was, however, some question of *buying* liberty of conscience for the Catholics. To some, including the Pope, this was an abhorrent idea: Clement VIII denounced it as 'unworthy and scandalous' since it would mean using unclean money to interfere with the divinely ordained timescale for these things. The Spanish Council was also worried by the proposition, not on moral grounds, but more pragmatically, because other religious minorities might request the same lavish treatment.²³

In England, however, Tassis found himself entering the sweetly corrupt world of the Jacobean court, where bribery was not so much unworthy as a thoroughly worthy way of life. The promise of pensions – paid secretly by Spain – became a weapon in maintaining a pro-Spanish party at court. Of course the Spanish records of the money promised do not necessarily confirm that the money was actually received (Tom Wintour was after all still waiting for that promised Spanish subsidy). Whether all the promised money was paid over or not, it has to be said that very few names of prominent courtiers are missing from the Spanish pension records during the first decade of James' reign. In general, the desire to amass money was like a fierce universal lust in the Jacobean period. (Both Cecil and Henry Howard Earl of Northampton had acquired large fortunes and great properties by their deaths, despite having begun, for different reasons, as poor men.) Most of James' courtiers, as Tassis found, would have agreed with the aphorism of Francis Bacon, the lawyer and politician recently

knighted for his loyalty to the crown: 'Money is like muck, not good except it be spread.'

Outstanding for her avarice was the beautiful, wilful Catherine Countess of Suffolk. Her husband, formerly known as Lord Thomas Howard, a son of the executed Duke of Norfolk, had been given his Suffolk title in July as part of King James' rehabilitation of the Howard family that he loved. The new Earl of Suffolk was thus a nephew of Northampton and, like Northampton, he had tasted the bitterness of family disgrace in youth. As Lord Thomas Howard, however, he had won the Queen's favour by his distinguished service as a naval commander both at the time of the Armada and after. To Queen Elizabeth, in consequence, he had been her 'good Thomas'.

Now in his early forties, the Queen's good Thomas was resolved to be the King's good Suffolk, but the glory days of naval warfare were over for him and it was as a leading courtier that he intended to shine – a courtier and hopefully a rich man. He was given the post of Lord Chamberlain of the Household while Catherine Suffolk was made Keeper of the Jewels to Queen Anne.

The kindest thing that can be said about the Suffolks, as a couple, is that they had a huge family to maintain: Catherine Suffolk bore at least ten children, seven of whom were sons. But, even as parents, they cannot be said to have shone. A Suffolk daughter, Lady Frances Howard, would one day, with her second husband, the Earl of Somerset, be accused of conspiracy to murder Sir Thomas Overbury; she spent some years in the Tower. It is a story that lies outside the timescale of this narrative, as does the final fall of the Suffolks from grace, thanks to their amazing peculations. Even Catherine Suffolk's famous beauty did not escape scot-free. As in a morality play, 'that good face of hers' which had brought much misery to others 'and to herself greatness' was ruined by smallpox in 1619.[24]

At the beginning of James' reign, however, the Countess of Suffolk was in her prime, and Tassis was mesmerised by her.

She had already indicated Catholic sympathies and pro-Spanish feelings to an emissary from the Archdukes in Flanders before Tassis arrived in England; she had emphasised the prime importance of pensions and gifts in the delicate matter of establishing liberty of conscience. He allowed himself to be convinced that the key to 'all the affairs of the bribes' lay within her pretty grasp and that she was an essential ally in the preliminaries of the Anglo-Spanish negotiations.

Here, in Tassis' opinion, was 'a person of great judgement'. Catherine Suffolk was also a Catholic, although not publicly so, and planned to die 'within the Catholic Faith'. Furthermore, she was an advocate of a Spanish marriage between King James' son Henry and a daughter of Philip III, who would of course be a Catholic. It may be that Tassis' lack of diplomatic training blinded him to the faults in this charming harpy. Charm she certainly had: gossip linked her name to that of Robert Cecil, who would leave her a jewel worth one thousand pounds at his death, although Cecil scarcely shared her Spanish sympathies. However, when the Constable of Castile finally arrived in England to negotiate the treaty with Spain, he had no difficulty in seeing through 'her excessively grand pretensions'. Far too much weight, thought the Constable, had been placed on 'the word of a fickle woman'. But by that time Catherine Suffolk had thoroughly infiltrated herself into the process by which Spanish money was to be paid over in return for English influence at court. She received at the least twenty thousand pounds, possibly more, as well as certain wonderful jewels.[25]

It was ironic that while Tassis bemoaned the weakness of the English Catholics, the Protestant English were equally indignant at the evident increase in Catholic strength since March 1603. King James' generous relaxation of penalties, his friendly reception of Sir Thomas Tresham and his associates, was having exactly the effect which James himself had dreaded while in Scotland: the Catholics were beginning to 'multiply'. That is, they were *visibly* multiplying.

There must always remain some considerable doubt about the figures of increase which were bandied about in late 1603 and afterwards, given the ambiguous nature of Church Papistry. Father Persons, in Rome, believed that by 1605 the Catholics in England had almost doubled since the death of Elizabeth. Were there really all of a sudden far more Catholics in England – or were they just finding the courage (with due respect to Tassis) to declare themselves? What Tassis did not know was exactly how bad things had been before. There was a sensible point to be made that the Catholics appeared to be more numerous only because Mass could be said more openly.[26]

Later Parliament declared that the number of priests in England had swollen from one hundred to one thousand within three years of the accession of King James. But this was inaccurate on two levels. There were probably already about two hundred and fifty priests present in 1603, while there were certainly not as many as a thousand, even in the deepest hiding, by 1606. Similarly, when King James arrived in England, he was told by the bishops that there were only 8,500 recusants in the country, whereas the true figure was more like 35,000. Yet by the end of 1603 it was believed that a hundred thousand people were attending Mass. The important point to the Protestant interest was not so much statistical as psychological. In the words of Sir Henry Spiller, in a subsequent speech in Parliament, 'the strength of the Catholic body, with the suspension of persecution, at once became evident'.[27]

Claudio Aquaviva, General of the Jesuits, had delivered a stern warning to Father Garnet in July 1603 on the continued need for circumspection. 'By the unfathomable mercy of Christ, our Lord,' wrote Aquaviva, 'I implore you to be prudent.' He reiterated the need for prudence at the end of his letter, passing on a similar message from the Pope.[28] But for many of the English Catholics, buoyed up by the King's favourable reception of Percy and others – surely in Scotland James had given 'his promise of toleration' – it was not so easy to be prudent. Then there was the spectacle of a court riddled

with chic crypto-Catholics, high in the royal favour, which was hardly likely to encourage the rest to remain discreet. The difficulty of maintaining the 'nil gain' situation has been mentioned.* Most English Catholics were not even prepared to try.

'It is hardly credible in what jollity they [the Catholics] now live,' wrote Ralph Featherstonehalgh from Brancepeth in County Durham in mid-November. Among known Papists close to the King he instanced the eighteen-year-old Earl of Arundel, Suffolk's nephew. From Lord Sheffield, the Lord Lieutenant of Yorkshire, came a similarly outraged message: the Catholics were beginning 'to grow very insolent and show their true intentions' now that they were receiving 'graces and favours' from the King.[29]

Already the Catholics were 'labouring tooth and nail for places in Parliament', wrote Lord Sheffield with disgust. And it was true. The fear of the plague which haunted everyone at this time because it made all crowds potentially lethal carriers had at last diminished. The first Parliament of the new reign was to be held in the spring of 1604. Many Catholics hoped for great things from it. After all, in private talks, King James had frequently mentioned the need to refer the question of liberty of conscience to Parliament. They were expecting justice from their sovereign. But like their adventurous co-religionists Guido Fawkes and Tom Wintour in Spain, the Catholics in England were to be cruelly disappointed.

---

* There is a comparison to be made with racist outcries in the 1960s against Asian immigrants from the former British Empire into Great Britain by those who professed themselves in favour of immigration but ended by saying: 'If only they wouldn't have such big families.'

Catesby as Phaeton

~

Gallop apace, you fiery-footed steeds
Towards Phoebus' lodging; such a waggoner
As Phaeton would whip you to the west,
And bring in cloudy night immediately.

Romeo and Juliet

The New English Parliament was summoned on 31 January 1604. Six weeks later, the King and Queen journeyed in splendour from the Tower of London for the official Opening ceremony. This was the first public procession of the reign. The fear of plague which had marred the coronation and restricted its pomp had now at last receded: so 'the city and suburbs' became 'one great pageant'. Among those who walked from Tower Bridge to Westminster was Shakespeare's company of players, wearing the King's livery.

A good time was had within the Tower by the Royal Family in the days leading up to the solemn procession. There was a striking contrast between the dignified royal apartments and the dungeons for state prisoners – not far away – that the ancient edifice also housed. As John Taylor, the Water-Poet, put it:

For though the Tower be a castle royal,
Yet there's a prison in it for men disloyal.[1]

During this time the ten-year-old Prince Henry was more interested in the spectacle of the zoo, also within the Tower's

confines. He watched a lion being baited by three dogs: two of them died, but, when one looked likely to recover, Prince Henry ordered the dog to be cosseted and spared further ordeals: 'He that hath fought with the King of Beasts shall never fight inferior.'[2]

It was all part of the Prince's high profile as the King's heir. His appearance in the royal procession on its way to Whitehall was the first opportunity that the public – as opposed to the court – had had of inspecting the boy they took to be their future sovereign. King James rode a white jennet (possibly one of the Spanish horses presented by Tassis the previous October) under a canopy carried by Gentlemen of the Privy Chamber. His duties included listening to two speeches by Ben Jonson and several by the playwright Thomas Dekker, delivered under seven wooden arches specially erected for the occasion and intricately carved. King James was said to have borne 'the day's brunt with patience', although crowds, even when not plague-ridden, always made him uncomfortable and aroused his latent fears about his own security. Anne of Denmark on the other hand charmed everyone with that wave-from-the-elbow so characteristic of royalty down the ages. In return she was greeted outside St Paul's Cathedral by musicians from her native country to make her feel at home. But it was the tall, good-looking boy, Prince Henry, bowing this way and that to acknowledge the cheers, who provided the novel focus of attention.[3]

Spectators could not fail to be impressed that an Opening of Parliament was now a family occasion and an opportunity to express loyalty to the composite image in public. 'Men disloyal', in Taylor's phrase, might of course see such a state occasion as a perfect opportunity to wipe out the major royal players at one fell swoop.

Prince Henry had also accompanied his father to an ecclesiastical conference held earlier in January at Hampton Court. King James, wrapped in furs against the cold, presided over a series of theological discussions which were intended to sort out the Puritan element in the Protestant Church, with its

tiresomely obstreperous attitude to royal authority. Afterwards some Catholics – notably Father Tesimond – believed that 'all our miseries' had begun at that point, with the King pronouncing 'emphatically and virulently' against the Catholic Church, in order to balance his hostility to the Puritans. Yet not all the King's pronouncements at that time were anti-Catholic. Once again he invoked the hallowed name of Mary Queen of Scots when he complained how the equivalent of the Puritans in Scotland had misused 'that poor lady my mother', and had then ill-treated him during his minority. Now the Puritans were once more making trouble about the episcopacy: what institution would be next – the monarchy? 'It is my aphorism "No bishop, no King",' he commented drily.[4]

On 19 February, however, King James did publicly announce 'his utter detestation' of the Papist religion which he condemned as 'superstitious'. Three days later a proclamation ordered all Jesuits and priests out of the realm, while the fines for recusancy were once more imposed. On 19 March the King's speech in Parliament effectively crushed those Catholic hopes for liberty of conscience which had sprung up in the warm climate of his Scottish promises.[5] The pro-Papist and pro-Spanish courtiers were still in place, indicating that the King's amiable personal tolerance had not changed. The pro-Spanish Queen still wrote lovingly to the Pope and heard Mass in private. But the negotiations for the Anglo-Spanish Treaty were winding on without reference to the subject of Catholic toleration, since Philip III had officially abandoned his interest in the subject.

Instead, the Constable of Castile, with his powers to clinch the deal, was in Flanders *en route* for England. He would shortly be negotiating with the jewellers of Antwerp for suitable presents for King James. A careful man (or a pessimist), he hoped to acquire them sale or return, in case the treaty fell through at the last moment. But that did not now seem a likely prospect. The King would get his jewels. In any case, secure on his throne, James wanted nothing more from his Papists. The days of bargaining were over.

There was a further blow for the Catholics. The King devoted his real energies in this session of Parliament to establishing an Anglo-Scottish Union rather than Catholic toleration. Anglo-Scottish Union was an unpopular cause with most Members of Parliament, as the debates showed. But it was where the King's heart lay.

The King's speech in Parliament placed heavy emphasis on the blessings of peace which, as he firmly if not modestly expressed it, 'God hath in my Person bestowed upon you all.' First, there was peace abroad with all foreign neighbours; thanks to James, 'and only by mine arrival here', the country was now 'free of a great and tedious war'. The second, internal peace was to be achieved by a proper Anglo-Scottish Union, not simply the joining of the two countries under one crown.

Here James waxed eloquent, as he propounded the utter rightness of this union in a series of fanciful images, in which the King was the 'Husband' and the whole island was his wife, the King was the 'Head' and the island his body, the King was the 'Shepherd' and the island his flock. Was a Christian king to find himself a polygamist with two wives? Was the head to preside over 'a divided and monstrous body'? Was 'so fair a Flock (whose fold hath no wall to hedge it but the four Seas)' to remain parted in two?

Unfortunately the subsequent debate would show that none of these elaborately intellectual concepts had proved especially convincing to the King's English subjects. There was, instead, a remarkable display of gut feelings of dislike for the Scots: that is, the Scots in England, 'an Effluxion of People from the Northern parts'. The flock was indeed a fair one, but it was an English one, and the English sheep had no intention of sharing their richer pastures with their northern neighbours – not if they could help it. So the Members of Parliament contributed their own hostile comparisons. There was talk of plants which are transplanted from barren ground (Scotland) into a more fertile one (England) and how they always 'grow and overgrow'. Analogies were made to the cunning widow of a

London merchant who sells all her own goods at a profit in order to 'live upon the Husband's stock'.[6]

A suggestion that the entire island should be known by the name of Britain – 'which is most honourable' – met with a disgusted response. This was a particular hobby-horse of King James: years later, a hostile pamphlet would refer to Britain as 'your word'. King James was the first English monarch to have himself depicted in Roman Imperial style on an accession medal which showed him as Emperor of the Whole Island of Britain, and he loved the legendary family tree which had him descended from one Brute, 'the most noble founder of the Britains'. The ancient (if bogus) pedigree seemed to him to supply a historical basis for the union he craved.* In 1604, however, Parliament was distinctly unimpressed by the claims of Brute's descendant to change the name of their country, much preferring the glorious and famous name of 'our mother England'.[7]

On 21 April Sir Francis Bacon read a statement on the King's behalf in which he complained of all this 'carping'. Some of the hares started were indeed thoroughly captious. For example there was a notion that if the King died without issue the English crown would be alienated by passing to his heir on his father's side, a Scot without any English Tudor blood.[8] In reality, James' next heir after his three children was clearly his father's brother's daughter, Lady Arbella Stuart, who lived in England and enjoyed exactly the same share of Tudor blood as the King himself. Nevertheless there was an unmistakeable message here for the King, whether he cared to accept it or not: the Scots who had come to England in his train and been promoted lavishly by him were extremely unpopular.

This kind of ugly resentment of the outsiders given advancement was expressed not only in Parliament but outside it – travelling as far as Flanders where both Hugh Owen and Guido Fawkes gave vent to anti-Scottish outbursts. Of the

* When, in 1610, the antiquarian Thomas Lyte presented the King with 'a most royally ennobled genealogy', which tactfully started with Brute, he got the famous Lyte Jewel, containing a miniature of James by Nicholas Hilliard, as a reward.

Jacobean Scots at court, the 'new elite', the unpopular royal favourite Sir George Home, who came south with his master, was made Keeper of the Wardrobe for life on 1 June 1603.[9] He certainly did not help his cause in English eyes by selling off the richly embellished garments of the old Queen which were in his custody and thus making a killing for himself. But Sir George prospered: he was made a Privy Councillor, as were other Scots, and created Lord Home of Berwick. When it came to the more intimate role of Gentleman of the Bedchamber (which was a coveted court appointment) the King also promoted the Scots. It was not unnatural, perhaps, but it scarcely pointed to the impartiality of a true 'Briton'.

The next year, Ben Jonson aroused the royal anger in his satire *Eastward Ho!*, which mocked the King's Scottish courtiers. Parodying the popular play *Westward Ho!* by Webster and Dekker, Jonson included in his *dramatis personae* Sir Petronel Flash, 'a new-made knight', referring to those numerous Scottish adventurers who had taken the road south with the King and been rewarded. The gibe which stung concerned the Scots' population of the new colony of Virginia: 'I would a hundred thousand of them were there,' ran the offending lines, 'for we are all one countrymen now, ye know; and we should find ten times more comfort of them there than we do here.' Jonson did a spell in prison which incidentally seemed to bother him less than the embarrassing nature of his offence. 'The cause (would I could name some worthier) is, a (the word irks me) ... a play, my lord,' he confessed to Cecil, pleading for release.[10] Jonson was duly let go and the gibe was removed from subsequent performances.

The Scots were also derided for their accent, which was considered uncouth, despite its being the accent of both King James and Queen Anne. The Scots were generally considered to be lacking in hygiene: the crude word 'stinking' so rudely applied by Hugh Owen to the sovereign was also regularly directed at his northern subjects. Young Lady Anne Clifford, the privileged English heiress, shuddered at finding herself 'all lousy' through sitting in the chamber of Sir Thomas Erskine,

another Scottish favourite, recently created Captain of the Yeomen of the Guard.[11]

If the newly rich Scots were said to be greedy (as well as unwashed), then the attitude to the Scottish lower classes was scarcely likely to be more enlightened. The poor Scots established a colony in Holborn known as 'little Scotland', but the prospect of immigrants huddling together did not please either, in spite of the 'Scots Kist' (Scottish Box) placed at a house in Lamb's Conduit, a large brass-bound chest to which more prosperous Scottish nationals contributed. The beggars with their hateful accent were the most resented of all (as Irish beggars would come to be resented later in the seventeenth century). There were gangs called Swaggerers whose speciality was to prey upon the vulnerable homeless Scots in London.[12] King James had them arrested, but unfortunately he could not have all the Swaggerers in Parliament similarly treated.

The King's precious scheme of a Union languished, and it would not be effected for over a hundred years. In 1604 the spectacle of Scottish advancement was another aggravation to those already discontented with their lot. The recusants in particular would come to have an honest grievance. The money to reward this covetous crew had to come from somewhere. One simple method of acquisition was to allow the religious fines – the 'benefits of recusancy' – to be collected by the King's Scottish protégés at court.

In his speech of 19 March, King James was on much surer ground – at least where his Protestant audience was concerned – when he came to the topic of the third treasured peace which he intended to secure for the realm. This was the peace of God which could be secured only 'by profession of the true religion'. In one sense the Venetian Ambassador was right to report that the King's remarks which followed were quite conciliatory.[13] His language was not the language of detestation and persecution. He even spoke wistfully about a general Christian Union (like many would-be negotiators, the King was a great believer in unions as inevitably working towards peace). As so often before, he underlined his instinctive revulsion

Elizabeth I with Time and Death: towards the end of her life, Queen Elizabeth fell into a profound melancholy, underlined by the deaths of her old friends.

James I by an unknown artist: King James was thirty-six when he ascended to the English throne. The English found him at first encounter to be affable and 'of noble presence'.

Accession medal of James I, as emperor of the whole island of Britain: the King (unlike the English courtiers) was enthusiastic about the concept of 'Britons'.

Henry Prince of Wales and Sir John Harington by Robert Peake, 1603: the handsome young heir to the throne won golden opinions, a Royal Family being a new phenomenon in England.

Anne of Denmark by Marcus Gheerhaerts the Younger, c. 1605–10: there had not been a Queen Consort in England since the days of Henry VIII. The King's gracious wife was welcomed by the crowds.

Charles Duke of York (the future Charles I) as a child by Robert Peake: unlike his athletic elder brother, Charles was physically frail and only learned to walk at the age of four.

The monuments in Westminster Abbey to two daughters of James I, Mary and Sophia, who died young: Princess Mary, who was born in England in 1605, was considered by some to have a better claim to the throne than her elder siblings born in Scotland.

Arbella Stuart by an unknown artist, 1589: the first cousin of King James, with both Tudor and Stuart blood, but brought up in England, Arbella was a possible contender for the throne.

Archduchess Isabella Clara Eugenia by Franz Pourbus the Younger, c. 1599: some Catholics hoped that this Habsburg descendant of John of Gaunt – co-Regent, with her husband, in the Spanish Netherlands – would be backed by military force to succeed to the English throne.

(right)
Princess Elizabeth (the future Elizabeth of Bohemia) by Robert Peake: the charm and dignity of this nine-year-old girl, who held a little court in the midlands, encouraged the conspirators to think she might make a suitable puppet Queen.

FOR

Edward who would have defended them
Lucy who would have hidden them
Paloma who would have succoured them in exile

Contents

Contents

Illustrations

Elizabeth I with Time and Death *(Weidenfeld and Nicolson Archive, London)*

James I *(National Galleries of Scotland)*

Accession medal of James I *(British Museum, London)*

Anne of Denmark, Marcus Gheerhaerts, *c.* 1605–10 *(Weidenfeld and Nicolson Archive, London)*

Henry Prince of Wales and Sir John Harington, Robert Peake, 1603 *(Metropolitan Museum of Art, New York)*

Charles Duke of York (the future Charles I), Robert Peake *(City of Bristol Museum and Art Gallery)*

The monuments in Westminster Abbey to Princesses Mary and Sophia *(Dean and Chapter of Westminster, London)*

Arbella Stuart, anon., 1589 *(National Trust Photographic Library, London/ John Bethell)*

Archduchess Isabella Clara Eugenia, Franz Pourbus the Younger, *c.* 1599 *(Royal Collection, Windsor © Her Majesty the Queen)*

Princess Elizabeth, Robert Peake *(National Maritime Museum, London)*

Engraving of the conspirators *(Bodleian Library, Oxford)*

Ben Jonson *(Weidenfeld and Nicolson Archive, London)*

William Shakespeare *(Weidenfeld and Nicolson Archive, London)*

Henry Percy, 9th Earl of Northumberland, Van Dyck *(National Trust Photographic Library, London / Roy Fox)*

Robert Cecil, 1st Earl of Salisbury, (attrib.) John de Critz
(National Portrait Gallery, London)

Sir Everard Digby *(Ashmolean Museum, Oxford)*

Thomas Wintour's two signatures *(Weidenfeld and Nicolson Archive, London)*

Thomas Habington of Hindlip and his wife *(British Library, London)*

Vestment embroidered by Helena Wintour *(Stonyhurst College, Lancashire)*

The Browne Brothers, Isaac Oliver *(Burghley House, Stamford)*

Life in a recusant household, illustrated by a scene from the childhood of Mary Ward

Rushton Hall, Northamptonshire *(Hulton Getty Collection Ltd, London)*

Hindlip House, Worcestershire *(British Library, London)*

Baddesley Clinton *(Hulton Getty Collection Ltd, London)*

Coughton Court *(Coughton Court, Warwickshire)*

Huddington Court *(Huddington Court, Worcestershire)*

Map of Westminster *(Weidenfeld and Nicolson Archive)*

Tower of London, *c.* 1615, Van Meer *(Edinburgh University Library)*

Ashby St Ledgers *(Ashby St Ledgers, Northamptonshire)*

The Cellars of the House of Lords *(Hulton Getty Collection Ltd, London)*

Guy Fawkes entering Parliament *(Ashmolean Museum, Oxford)*

A contemporary Dutch print of the Gunpowder Plot *(Hulton Getty Collection Ltd, London)*

The anonymous letter delivered to Lord Monteagle *(Public Record Office, London)*

The delivery of the Monteagle letter to the Earl of Salisbury *(Weidenfeld and Nicolson Archive, London)*

Garnet's straw *(Hulton Getty Collection Ltd, London)*

Father Henry Garnet, SJ, by Jan Wiericx *(Hulton Getty Collection Ltd, London)*

St Winifred's Well, Holywell, Clwyd *(Hulton Getty Collection Ltd, London)*

Father Garnet's last letter to Anne Vaux *(Weidenfeld and Nicolson Archive, London)*

Sir Edward Coke *(Hulton Getty Collection Ltd, London)*

The entry in the Commons' Journal for 5 November 1605 *(House of Lords Record Office, London)*

Letter of King James authorising the torture of Guy Fawkes *(Public Record Office, London)*

Instruments of torture at the time of the Gunpowder Plot *(Royal Armouries, HM Tower of London)*

Guido Fawkes' signatures before and after torture *(British Library, London)*

A late eighteenth-century print of the execution of the conspirators *(Hulton Getty Collection Ltd, London)*

Embroidered cushion depicting the defeat of the Armada and the Gunpowder Plot, *c.* 1621 *(Bridgeman Art Library, London)*

Engraving of Father Garnet on the scaffold, C. Screta *(Hulton Getty Collection Ltd, London)*

The Powder Plot from 'A Thankful Remembrance of God's Mercie', George Carleton, 1630 *(Hulton Getty Collection Ltd, London)*

Victorian impression of Guy Fawkes being taken to the scaffold *(Hulton Getty Collection Ltd, London)*

Etching of Guy Fawkes laying his sinister trail, 1841 *(Hulton Getty Collection Ltd, London)*

The Papists' Powder Treason *(Henry E. Huntingdon Library and Art Gallery)*

A monument to the Plot's discovery, Tower of London, 1608, Sir William Waad *(Historical Royal Palaces © Crown Copyright)*

The search of the cellars of the House of Lords *(Times Newspapers Ltd, London)*

Bonfire Night, 1994, Lewes, Sussex *(Sussex Express, Lewes)*

The English Succession

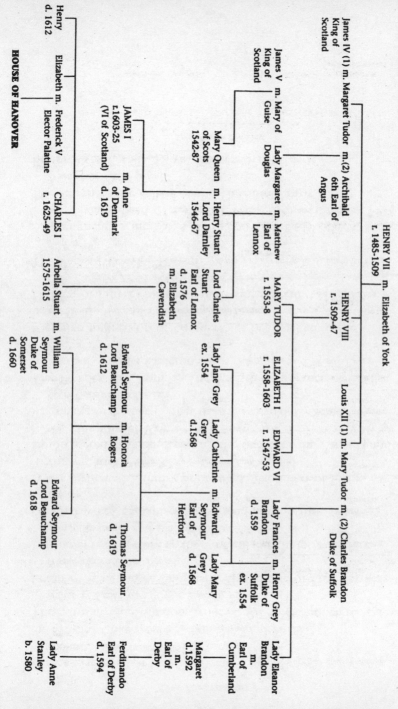

James IV (1) m. Margaret Tudor m.(2) Archibald 6th Earl of Angus
HENRY VII r. 1485-1509 m. Elizabeth of York
Louis XII (1) m. Mary Tudor m. (2) Charles Brandon Duke of Suffolk

James V King of Scotland m. Mary of Guise

Lady Margaret Douglas

Mary Queen of Scots 1542-87 m. Henry Stuart Lord Darnley 1546-67

Matthew Earl of Lennox

HENRY VIII r. 1509-47

JAMES I r.1603-25 (VI of Scotland) m. Anne of Denmark d. 1619

Lord Charles Stuart Earl of Lennox d. 1576 m. Elizabeth Cavendish

CHARLES I r. 1625-49

Arbella Stuart 1575-1615

MARY TUDOR r. 1553-8

ELIZABETH I r. 1558-1603

EDWARD VI r. 1547-53

Lady Frances Brandon d. 1559 m. Henry Grey Duke of Suffolk ex. 1554

Lady Eleanor Brandon m. Earl of Cumberland

Lady Jane Grey ex. 1554

Lady Catherine Grey d.1568 m. Edward Seymour Earl of Hertford

Lady Mary Grey d. 1568

Margaret d.1592 m. Earl of Derby

Edward Seymour Lord Beauchamp d. 1612 m. Honora Rogers

Thomas Seymour d. 1619

Ferdinando Earl of Derby d. 1594

Lady Anne Stanley b. 1580

Henry d. 1612

Elizabeth m. Frederick V Elector Palatine

HOUSE OF HANOVER

William Seymour Duke of Somerset d. 1660

Edward Seymour Lord Beauchamp d. 1618

CONSPIRATORS' RELATIONSHIPS

Plotter

Character in narrative

1 Tresham, Catesby, Wintour, Vaux connection

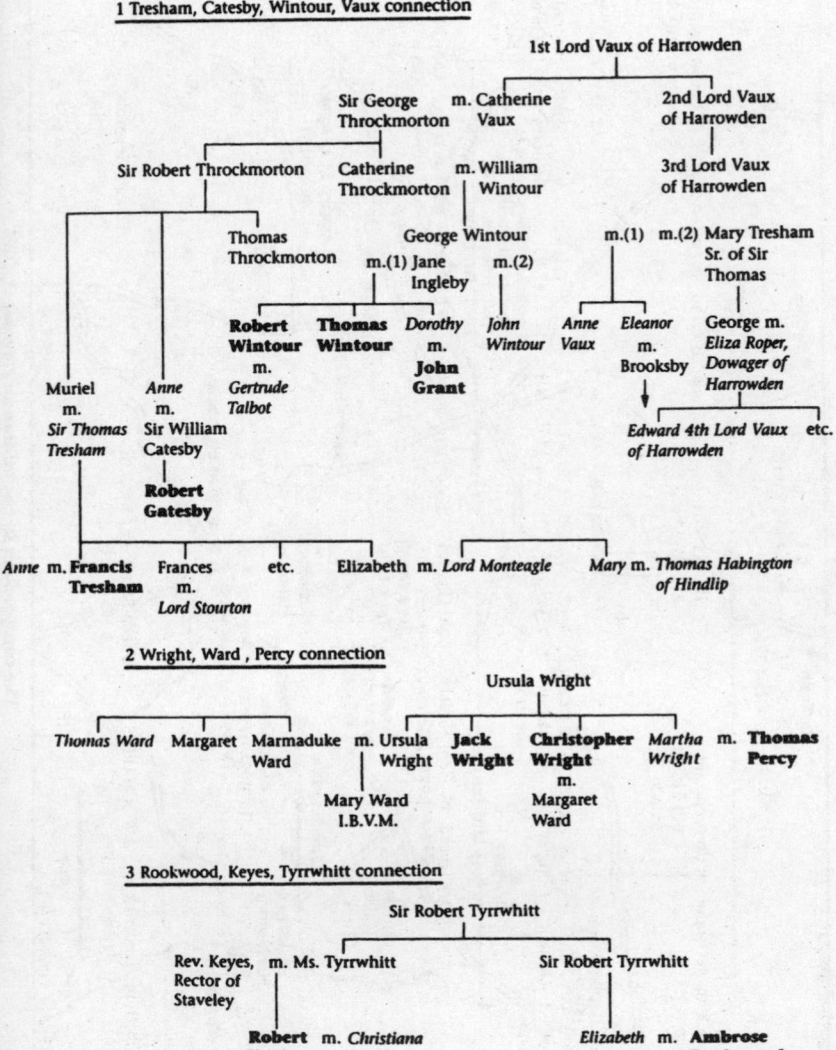

2 Wright, Ward , Percy connection

3 Rookwood, Keyes, Tyrrwhitt connection

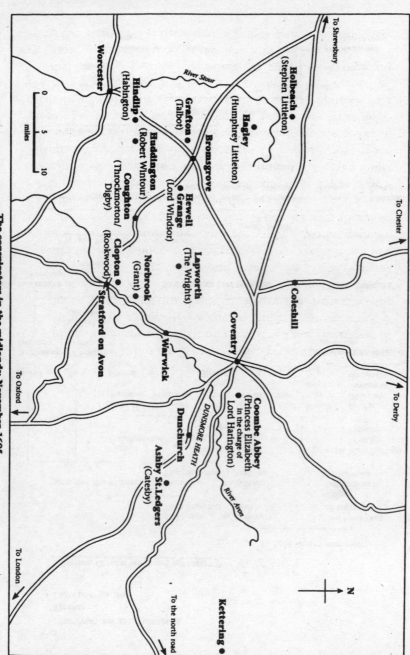

The conspirators in the midlands: November 1605

Author's Note

'That heavy and doleful tragedy which is commonly called the Powder Treason': thus Sir Edward Coke, as prosecuting counsel, described the Gunpowder Plot of 1605. It is a fair description of one of the most memorable events in English history, which is celebrated annually in that chant of 'Remember, remember the Fifth of November'. But who was the Gunpowder Plot a tragedy for? For King and Royal Family, for Parliament, all threatened with extinction by terrorist explosion? Or for the reckless Catholic conspirators and the entire Catholic community, including priests, whose fate was bound up with theirs? In part, this book attempts to answer that question.

Its primary purpose is, however, to explain, so far as is possible in view of imperfect records and testimonies taken under torture, why there was a Gunpowder Plot in the first place. The complicated details of this extraordinary episode resemble those of a detective story (including an anonymous letter delivered under cover of darkness), and, as in all mysteries, the underlying motivation is at the heart of the matter.

Obviously, to talk of providing an explanation begs the question of whether there really was a Plot. Over the years – over the centuries – dedicated scholars and historians have

divided into two categories on the subject. I have lightly designated these 'Pro-Plotters' – those who believe firmly in the
Plot's existence – and 'No-Plotters' – those who believe equally
firmly that the Plot was a fabrication on the part of the government. My own position, as will be seen, does not fall precisely into either of these categories. I believe that there was
indeed a Gunpowder Plot: but it was a very different 'Powder
Treason' from that conspiracy outlined by Sir Edward Coke.

By accepting that there was a Plot, I have also accepted that
the conspirators were what we would now term terrorists.
Certainly, the questionable moral basis for terrorism – can violence ever be justified whatever the persecution, whatever the
provocation? – is a theme which runs through my narrative.
And there is an additional problem: is terrorism justified only
when it is successful? These are awkward questions, but for
that reason, if no other, worth the asking.

Writers on the subject of the Plot have, naturally enough,
tended to draw their own contemporary comparisons. A
student of Catesby family history in 1909 referred to 'these
days of [Russian] Anarchist plots' as providing a suitable background for Catesby's own conspiratorial activities. Donald
Carswell, a barrister who edited *The Trial of Guy Fawkes* in 1934,
likened the Gunpowder Plot to the Reichstag Fire of February
1933: 'it turned out to be first-class government propaganda',
enabling the Nazis to suppress the Communists, as the
Catholics had been suppressed after 1605.

Graham Greene, providing an introduction in 1968 to the
memoirs of Kim Philby, the Briton who spied for Stalin's
Russia, compared Philby's Communist faith – 'his chilling cer-
tainty in the correctness of his judgment' – to that of the
English recusant Catholics, supporting Spain and its Inquisition.
Elliot Rose, in *Cases of Conscience*, published in 1975, the year in
which the Vietnam War ended, drew a parallel between
Catholics who refused to conform in the reign of Elizabeth and
James I, and protesters against the Vietnam War. More recently,
Gary Wills in *Witches and Jesuits: Shakespeare's Macbeth* (1995)
evoked the turbulent conspiratorial atmosphere in the United

States after the assassination of President Kennedy to explain the world in which the play first appeared. (First performed in 1606, the text of *Macbeth* is darkened by the shadow of the Gunpowder Plot.) Certainly, the events of 5 November 1605 have much in common with the killing of President Kennedy as a topic which is, in conspiratorial terms, eternally debatable.

It is appropriate, therefore, that in my case a book written towards the end of the twentieth century should be concerned with the issue of terrorism. This is an issue, for better or for worse, which has to be considered in order to understand the unfolding histories of Northern Ireland and Israel/Palestine – to take only two possible examples. Meanwhile we have a phenomenon in which a number of today's world leaders have in the past been involved – on their own recognition – in terrorist activities and have morally justified them on grounds of national or religious interest. It is for this reason I have given my book the subtitle of *Terror and Faith in 1605*.

One should, however, bear in mind that the word 'terror' can refer to two different kinds. There is the terror of partisans, of freedom fighters, or of any other guerrilla group, carried out for the higher good of their objectives. Then there is the terror of governments, directed towards dissident minorities. The problem of subjects who differ from their rulers in religion (have they the moral right to differ?) is one that runs throughout this book.

There is a similar contemporary relevance of a very different sort in the stories of the various Catholic women who found themselves featuring in the subterranean world of the Gunpowder Plot. At a time when women's role in the Christian Churches, especially the Catholic Church, is under debate, I was both interested and attracted by the role played by these strong, devout, courageous women. At the time Catholic priests compared them to the holy women of the Bible who followed Jesus Christ. Some were married with the responsibilities of families in a dangerous age; others chose the single path with equal bravery. Ironically enough, it was the perceived weakness of women which enabled them to protect the forbidden priests where others could not do so. Circumstances gave them power; they used it well.

Above all, throughout my narrative, I have been concerned to convey actuality: that is to say, a sense of what an extraordinarily dramatic story it was, with all its elements of tragedy, brutality, heroism – and even, occasionally and unexpectedly, its more relaxed moments, which sometimes occurred after unsuccessful searches for Catholic priests in their hiding-places. For this reason I have paid special attention to the topography of the Plot, including the details of these secret refuges, many of which are still to be seen today. Of course hindsight can never be avoided altogether, especially in untangling such an intricate story as that of the Gunpowder Plot: but at least I have tried to write as though what happened on 5 November 1605 was not a foregone conclusion.

In order to tell a complicated story as clearly as possible, I have employed the usual expedients. I have modernised spelling where necessary, and dated letters and documents as though the calendar year began on 1 January as it does now, instead of 25 March, as it did then. I have also tried to solve the problem of individuals changing their names (on receipt of titles) by preferring simplicity to strict chronological accuracy: thus Robert Cecil, 1st Earl of Salisbury, is known as Cecil and then Salisbury, missing out his intermediate title of Viscount Cranborne.

In writing this book, I owe a great deal to the many works of the many scholars acknowledged in the References. For further assistance, I would like to single out and thank the following: Mr Felipe Fernandez-Armesto for historical corrections and suggestions (surviving errors are my responsibility); Dr S. Bull, Lancashire County Museums, for allowing me to read his thesis 'Furie of the Ordnance'; Fr Michael Campbell Johnston S.J. for letting me see the Gunpowder Plot MS. of the late Fr William Webb S.J.; Dr Angus Constam of the Royal Armouries; Fr Francis Edwards S.J., whose friendship and support I value, despite our different conclusions on the subject of the Gunpowder Plot; Mr D.L. Jones, Librarian, House of Lords; Mr John V. Mitchell, Archivist, and Mr R.N. Pittman, then headmaster of St Peter's School, York; Mr Roland Quinault,

Honorary Secretary, Royal Historical Society, for allowing me to consult his thesis, 'Warwickshire Landowners and Parliamentary Politics 1841–1923'; Mr Richard Rose, editor of the unpublished diary of Joan Courthope; Mr M. N. Webb, Assistant Librarian, Bodleian Library; Mr Eric Wright, Principal Assistant County Librarian, Education and Libraries, Northamptonshire; lastly the ever helpful and courteous staff of the Catholic Central Library, the London Library, the Public Record Office and the Round Reading Room of the British Library.

It was, as ever, both a pleasure and a privilege to do all my own research, beyond the help which is gratefully acknowledged here. In particular, tracing the story of the Gunpowder Plot involved me in a series of historical visits and journeys. In connection with these, I wish to thank the Earl of Airlie, Lord Chamberlain, General Sir Edward Jones, Gentleman Usher of the Black Rod, and Mr Bryan Sewell, Deputy Director of Works, for making possible a visit to the House of Lords on the eve of the Opening of Parliament; Mr R. C. Catesby for our journey to Ashby St Ledgers and its church; Professor Hugh and Mrs Eileen Edmondson of Huddington Court for their hospitality; Mr and Mrs Jens Pilo for receiving me at Coldham Hall, and Mr Tony Garrett, who accompanied me there; Mr Roy Tomlin, Honorary Secretary, Wellingborough Golf Club, Harrowden Hall; Sr Juliana Way, Hengrave Hall Centre; Mr Dave Wood, Service Coordinator, and Mr David Hussey, Headmaster, RNIB Forest House Assessment Centre, Rushton.

Others who helped me in a variety of ways were Mrs K. H. Atkins, Archivist, Dudley Libraries; Professor Karl Bottigheimer; Mr Robert Bearman, Senior Archivist, Shakespeare Birthplace Trust; Mr Roy Bernard, Holbeche House Nursing Home; Fr Andrew Beer, St Pancras Church, Lewes; Fr M. Bossy, S.J., for the photograph of Helena Wintour's vestment at Stonyhurst; Mr Conall Boyle; Mrs Kathryn Christenson, Minnesota; Mr Donald K. Clark, Director, Hyde Park Family History Centre; Ms Sarah Costley, then Archivist, York Minster, and Mr John Tilsley, Assistant Archivist; Ms Caroline Dalton, Archivist, New College Library; Mr Charles Enderby; Mr Dudley Fishburn M.P.; Major-

General G.W. Field, Resident-Governor, Catherine Campbell, and Yeoman Warder Brian A. Harrison, Honorary Archivist, Tower of London; Ms Joanna Grindle, Information Officer, Warwickshire County Council; Father D.B. Lordan, St Winifred's Church, and Brother Stephen de Kerdrel, O.P.M. Cap, Franciscan Friary, Pantasaph, Holywell; the Very Rev. Michael Mayne, Dean of Westminster; Mr Jonathan Marsden, Historic Buildings Representative, Thames and Chilterns Regional Office, National Trust; Professor Maurice Lee, Jr; Mr Stephen Logan, Selwyn College, Cambridge; Miss K.M. Longley, former Archivist, York Minster; Mr Roger Longrigg for answering an enquiry about late-sixteenth-century horses; Mother John Baptist, O.S.B., Tyburn Convent; Mr Simon O'Halloran, Queensland, Australia; Sir Roy Strong; Mr Barry T. Turner, Guy Fawkes House, Dunchurch; Mrs Clare Throckmorton, Coughton Court; Mr Richard Thurlow, National Bibliographic Service, British Library, Boston Spa; Mr J. M. Waterson, Regional Director, East Anglia Regional Office, National Trust; Mr Ralph B. Weller.

Throughout, I have had great support from my publishers on both sides of the Atlantic: Nan Talese in the US, who, from the first, shared my vision of how the book might be; and Anthony Cheetham, Ion Trewin and Rebecca Wilson in England. Linda Peskin typed and retyped the MS with exemplary skill, matched only by her patience. My agent Michael Shaw counselled calm at the appropriate moments; Douglas Matthews, Indexer Extraordinary, not only performed his task with his accustomed dexterity but also supplied information about Guy Fawkes 'celebrations' in Lewes; Robert Gottlieb and Rana Kabbani offered editorial suggestions, as did my mother, Elizabeth Longford. Further family assistance included advice on the modern Prevention of Terrorism Act from my son-in-law Edward Fitzgerald Q.C. and my son Orlando Fraser. Lastly my husband Harold Pinter read a story which is, in part, about persecution, with his characteristic generous sympathy for the oppressed.

Antonia Fraser
St Nicholas Day, 1994 – Feast of the English Martyrs, 1995

Bountiful Beginnings

These bountiful beginnings raise all men's spirits, and put them in great hopes, insomuch that not only Protestants, but Papists and Puritans, and the very Poets ... promise themselves great part in his [James I] favour.

JOHN CHAMBERLAIN
to Dudley Carleton, 12 April 1603

On 21 March 1603 Father William Weston, a Catholic priest imprisoned in the Tower of London, was aware that 'a strange silence' had descended on the whole city. 'Not a bell rang out. Not a bugle sounded,' although ordinarily both bells and bugles were often heard, even in the tiny cell in which he had been held without fresh air or exercise for over five years.

The explanation for this silence was awesome. In Richmond Palace, the old Queen who had ruled England for over forty years 'lay dying beyond all hope of recovery'. Like so many of the beleaguered Catholics in England, men and women, the laity as well as the priesthood, nobles and serving people, Father Weston wondered whether a new reign might not bring relief.[1]

Elizabeth Tudor, daughter of Henry VIII and his ill-fated second wife Anne Boleyn, was in her seventieth year, a distinguished age for the time in which she lived. She had reigned alone, without consort or child, since the death of her half-sister Mary Tudor in 1558 – so long that a man would have to have been in his fifties to have any proper recollection of the age before Elizabeth.

She had outlived not only the Catholic Queen Mary Tudor, but Mary's erstwhile husband, England's arch-enemy Philip II of Spain, who had died in 1598. The pale Valois Kings of France of her youth (including Mary Queen of Scots' first husband, who had died young) had departed like shadows, leaving no heirs. The vigorous Henri IV of Navarre, married to Marguerite de Valois and now sitting on the throne of France, was twenty years her junior. Queen Elizabeth had in fact reigned longer than any previous adult successor to the throne.* On the one hand, common sense surely made her approaching death predictable; on the other, it was for most people unimaginable.

This element of disbelief owed something to the fact that it had long been forbidden, as in some twentieth-century dictatorship, to discuss the identity of the next ruler. For so doing in the House of Commons in 1593, the Puritan Peter Wentworth had been imprisoned in the Tower of London till his death. Ten years later, Elizabeth had still not indicated her successor (as we shall see, there were problems with a purely hereditary succession). Psychologically, this public void made the prospect of her demise seem unlikely, as though the Queen could not possibly let go of life until she had made proper arrangements for who was to follow her. It was a point of view the Queen herself had perfectly well understood in years gone by, when she had observed drily that she would not allow discussions of the succession, since men were always wont to worship the rising rather than the setting sun.

The Queen's surprisingly robust health had also encouraged foolish fantasies of her immortality in recent years. She might show a certain weariness on state occasions – at the Opening of Parliament in 1601 for example – or after riding her horse in the park. Critical eyes might note that the haggard, parchment-white face of the Queen in her late sixties was now plumped out with 'fine cloths' in her cheeks. Yet as late as March 1602 she was described as 'still, thanks to God, frolicky and merry', for all the signs of decay in her face. She continued

*Henry III, whose reign spanned fifty-six years, 1216–72, had succeeded to the throne as a child of nine.

to impress strangers by her sheer glittering presence. Her air of majesty elicited the cry of 'oh che grandezza!' from the lips of an emissary from the Spanish Netherlands. Only three months previously the Queen had danced a coranto at court, a complicated measure which demanded a good deal of energy.[2]

Melancholy seemed to be her chief enemy, that and the famous indecision which she had used so brilliantly in the past to manage (as well as madden) her male advisers, but which was now on occasion quite paralysing.[3] Much of this 'settled and unremovable' melancholy sprang from that unchanging tragedy of old age, the deaths of old friends. William Cecil, Lord Burghley, her faithful political servant, had died in 1598, leaving his brilliant, tireless son Robert to take his place. But the recent death of a close woman friend, the Countess of Nottingham (who as the daughter of Mary Boleyn was also the Queen's first cousin), was thought by many who knew Elizabeth well to have precipitated her decline.

The onset of what would be the Queen's last illness came at the beginning of March. The first allusion to it by her chief minister Robert Cecil was made nine days later in a highly secret letter to George Nicolson, his agent in Scotland. He wrote that his mistress had recently been 'much deprived of sleep', which was, as usual, making her impatient. Cecil went on to explore, in language that was cautious but unmistakable, the sombre possibility that she would not recover. 'Because all flesh is subject to mortality', as he delicately phrased it, Cecil had to confess that the Queen had been 'so ill-disposed' that he was fearful of her 'future weakness', leading to danger of that event 'I hope mine eyes shall never see'.[4]

In fact the insomnia did not improve and the weakness increased. In an age before newspapers, popular rumour had an especial role to play: a few years earlier, Shakespeare had personified Rumour as a character who wore a garment 'painted full of tongues'.[5] As stories of what was happening began to spread, the bells became silenced and the bugles stilled until even the prisoners in the Tower of London were aware of the crisis. The Councillors of State were by now

gathered at Richmond Palace in Surrey; it was understood that they would remain until that event so much dreaded by Cecil had actually taken place.

The old Queen's spirits further lapsed into an extraordinary depression which nothing seemed able to shake. For a while she refused to go to bed, lying upon cushions without eating as though nature could somehow be defeated by a strong will. Robert Carey, the grandson of Mary Boleyn and, like the Countess of Nottingham, a privileged courtier, visited her from the north of England, where he had been the Warden of the Middle March for the last five years. He was received by a Queen 'sitting low upon her cushions'. When he told her that he was delighted to see her well, the Queen took his hand and 'wrung it hard'.

'No, Robin, I am not well,' she said, and talked to him about her 'sad and heavy' heart, with more than forty or fifty 'heavy sighs'. Carey had only once known the Queen like this, and that was after the beheading of Mary Queen of Scots. It was an ominous precedent. Finally Lord Nottingham, widower of the Queen's old friend the Countess, managed to get her to bed: 'what by fair means, what by force'.[6] It was time for men to turn their eyes towards the rising sun.

To Robert Cecil and his fellow members of the Council surrounding the dying Queen, that sun was now represented by a man whose great-grandmother had been a Tudor princess: King James of Scotland (although this decision had been made comparatively recently). The agent Nicolson in Edinburgh had used his discretion to keep King James informed of the progress of Queen Elizabeth's illness. On 19 March, for example, the King had decided to postpone a visit to the remote Scottish Highlands, and merely journeyed as far as Stirling to see his elder son Prince Henry. The visit had some dynastic significance for very soon the handsome nine-year-old boy might find himself next in line to the English as well as the Scottish throne.

An extraordinary amount of traffic now sprang up between the English and the Scottish courts as the successful Elizabethan courtiers sought to devise methods of becoming

successful Jacobean ones. The most practical measure was that taken by Robert Carey. Sending word to Edinburgh to expect him without delay once the Queen was dead, he arranged to have fast horses posted all along the high road to Scotland. Carey intended to be the one who would break the news of his accession to the Scottish King. After all, he reasoned to himself, God helped those who helped themselves. Given that James had hitherto never shown him any particular favour, such a precaution was neither 'unjust nor dishonest'.[7]

By Wednesday morning, 23 March, the Queen was speechless and could communicate with her Council only by signs; later still a movement of the eyes had to suffice. When night came Elizabeth was in a coma, slipping away quietly towards that other realm, where, as the Archbishop of Canterbury frankly told her, 'for all that she had long been a great queen here upon earth...shortly she was to yield an account of her stewardship to the King of Kings'. At some point, when the Queen was still capable of making a sign, she was said to have indicated that James of Scotland should be her successor by putting her hand up to her head at the mention of his name.[8] The story, spread afterwards, was a convenient one to overcome the inconvenient fact that, for as long as Elizabeth had indeed been a 'great queen here upon earth' as described by the Archbishop, she had maintained her obstinate silence on the subject of the succession. Under the circumstances the Council was taking no chances.

There was a charged atmosphere inside the palace, and the porters were given a special command that no one was to leave, so that Rumour in his garment 'painted with tongues' should not escape. Outside, extraordinary precautions were being taken to ensure a smooth succession. For example the Council ordered that the wayward Lady Arbella Stuart, Elizabeth's cousin, one possible contender for the throne, should be brought south from Hardwick in Derbyshire. There, far from London, Papists might have kidnapped her and used her as a focus for some kind of coup since she was believed to have Catholic sympathies. Elsewhere 'the principal Papists'

were detained as the Queen's sickness worsened. Cecil's elder brother, Lord Burghley, in his administrative role of Lord President of the North, had a vital part to play in holding the peace in that troubled area between England and Scotland; he wrote that he was 'ready to defend the right'.[9]

The end for Queen Elizabeth came in the early hours of the morning on 24 March. At the last, only her women were with her. The members of the Council withdrew from Richmond to Whitehall to draft the vital document which would publicly proclaim James King of England later that morning. Long before this time, however, the enterprising Robert Carey was flying north on the first of his swift horses. His elder brother, George Carey Lord Hunsdon, who as Lord Chamberlain was a 'great officer' of the court, protected Carey from the indignant Richmond porter with the reassuring words: 'Let him pass, I will answer for him.' (Self-interest rather than family loyalty was at work, for all the Careys expected to benefit from Robert's derring-do.) There was some move from the Council to stop Carey but a friendly warning from another functionary, the Knight Marshal, enabled him to get clear of London shortly after nine o'clock.

Carey headed first for Doncaster, and by Friday night was at his own house at Widdrington in Northumberland. He was now ninety-seven miles from Edinburgh and would have been there for supper by starting 'very early' on the Saturday had he not suffered 'a great fall by the way' in the course of which his horse kicked him. So, weak with loss of blood, Robert Carey finally staggered into the royal palace at Holyrood and saluted James Stuart by his new four-fold title: King of England, Ireland, Scotland – and France (the mediaeval Plantagenet claim had never been formally discarded).

As proof of the old Queen's death, Carey told the King that he brought him 'a blue ring from a fair lady'. He then handed over a sapphire ring which James had sent south with specific orders that it be returned to him the moment Elizabeth was actually dead.*

---

* According to family tradition, preserved by Carey's great-granddaughter, this

'It is enough,' said the King. 'I know by this that you are a true messenger.' Far into the night, the sovereign of England sat up asking Carey questions about his new kingdom (having first considerately sent for a surgeon to tend Carey's wounds).[10]

The first proclamation of the new sovereign was made in London at 10.00am on 24 March – some seven or eight hours after the Queen's death. The drafting session in Whitehall, which took place, fittingly enough, as the sun was rising, was made unexpectedly easy by the fact that Robert Cecil produced a text. In his prudent way, he had no doubt been carrying it about with him throughout the last anxious weeks.* This proclamation, which referred firmly to 'the undoubted right' of James to succeed, was read first at Whitehall Gate at ten o'clock, then by the High Cross in Cheapside an hour later, where it was noted that Cecil spoke 'most distinctly and audibly'. Finally it was read at the Tower of London, where the prisoners of state, including the priests, rejoiced along with the others. Father Weston was able to watch from his window, listening to the 'crying out' and noting the pomp with which the ceremony was performed. He realised that the Council had calculated every detail 'with precision and thoroughness'.[11]

By nightfall, bonfires were burning brightly throughout the capital. Although the French Ambassador was shocked by the ungrateful behaviour of the Londoners in lighting fires to celebrate their sovereign's death, there is no doubt that these were flames of rejoicing, not lamentation. As John Isham, a law student from Northamptonshire, wrote to his father: the people were saluting 'a prince of great hope'. And throughout the country, not only in London, the sound of trumpets and other music was heard in the market-place. Spectators rent the air with shouts, their cries chiming with the bells, and an

precious ring could not be passed to Carey while he was still within Richmond Palace, but had to be thrown out of a window to him, by his sister Lady Scrope (Carey, p. 63 note).
* This draft, in Cecil's handwriting, still exists in his family papers (H.M.C. Salisbury, xv, p. 1).

enormous amount of liquor was consumed around each bonfire. In the north, at York and Kingston-upon-Hull, in the east at Norwich, in the west at Bristol, where the sheriffs in their scarlet had the new King's picture placed high over their heads, and in the south at Winchester, King James was proclaimed as 'being royally and in the right line from both Houses of York and Lancaster'.[12]

It was significant that the man who investigated the proclamation at Winchester, hastening there in advance of the Council's official notification with a speed worthy of Robert Carey, was a Catholic, Sir Robert Tichborne. Far from causing trouble as had been anticipated, the leading 'Papists' hastened to demonstrate their enthusiasm publicly, seeing in this moment an excellent opportunity to start the reign as they meant to go on, as loyal subjects of the new King, for all their dissident religious views. Even the Jesuit priests, whose mere presence in England was illegal and punishable by death, wanted to display their patriotism. Father Henry Garnet, Superior of the Jesuits in England, sent a letter to a prominent courtier, hoping that it would be shown to James, in which he expressed the Jesuits' wish to be 'dear and not unnatural subjects of the crown'.[13]

Catholics were ostentatiously among those who provided barrels of wine for public places and threw down money to the crowds from their windows. And no action was more presageful than that of the Catholic magnate Sir Thomas Tresham, who proclaimed King James at Northampton a mere day after the Queen's death. Born at the end of the reign of Henry VIII, long regarded as a leader in the Catholic community, which depended on him for 'advice, direction', Tresham had spent over twenty years of his life in prison for his refusal to conform to the Protestant religion, as well as suffering enormous fines.[14]

Married to a member of another distinguished Catholic family, a Throckmorton, Sir Thomas had a vast brood of children. One of these, Francis Tresham, his heir, was a scallywag who had been mixed up in the anti-government Essex

conspiracy of 1601. The charismatic Robert Catesby, Francis' first cousin on his mother's side, had also been involved. Francis Tresham had cost his father dear to buy him out of trouble, and Sir Thomas had helped too with Catesby's fine. The rest of Sir Thomas' children were more satisfactory and had made a variety of matches among the Catholic-oriented nobility and gentry. When he stood at the cross at Northampton to proclaim King James, barracked by the local Puritans, but not by the local Protestants, his family's rebellious tendencies curbed, Sir Thomas had reason to hope that he would enjoy a serene old age.

Some of that general English mood of rejoicing which had shocked the French Ambassador was due to the fact that the crown had passed to an adult male. James I, now aged thirty-six, had reigned since babyhood when his mother Mary Queen of Scots had been obliged to abdicate, and he had ruled since his majority. Such an experienced – masculine – hand at the helm had not been known since the death of Henry VIII over half a century previously. There was no doubt that for all the brilliant myth of Gloriana, for all the genius which Elizabeth had displayed at propaganda to turn her innate weakness of sex into a strength, a male ruler was regarded as the natural order of things.

Furthermore, that brilliant myth had itself begun to fade in the last years of Elizabeth's reign. And now that she was no longer alive to dazzle her subjects with splendour, it became easier to realise that the Queen had ended her life as an extremely querulous old woman. Popular ballads on her death tended to draw attention to her sex:

> Oh she bore the sway of all affairs
> And yet she was but a woman

or:

> A wiser Queen never was to be seen
> For a woman, or yet a stouter.[15]

The clear implication was that a male succeeding was a return to normality.

One must beware of hindsight in judging the relative popularity of Elizabeth I and James I in the first years of his reign. Just because the judgement of history has been to shower accolades upon the Queen rather than upon the King, it is important to realise how different the viewpoint was at his succession. There was now a great pack of Englishmen scurrying north: 'good news makes good horsemen', or, as James himself put it later, people ran, 'nay, rather flew to meet me'. They liked what they saw. Here was a man who, it was generally agreed, was 'of noble presence'. He was affable and intelligent, quick to get a point. What was more, for the patriotic English, it was important that he spoke their language perfectly (albeit with a strong Scottish accent). He also knew Latin, French and Italian.[16] At his side was his Danish wife, Queen Anne, a graceful blonde beauty in her late twenties who had already borne the King five children, three of whom survived, and was once more pregnant. How different from the home life of their departed spinster Queen!

What the English courtiers did not immediately realise was that an exceptionally harsh, unloving upbringing, beset with violent incident, and aristocratic feuds had made of the canny Scots King a consummate politician; and perhaps the only one the Stuart dynasty had ever produced (or ever would produce). Nowhere was his political astuteness seen to greater effect than in the King's presentation of himself as 'the son of Mary Queen of Scots'. The only child of the exquisite doomed Queen, who lost her head at Fotheringhay, and the charming wastrel Henry Lord Darnley, blown up at Kirk o'Field, hardly resembled either of his glamorous parents. But for many Catholics, the spiritual dimension was the one that counted. The first Supplication of the English Catholics to King James, in 1603, thought it especially shrewd to drag in a reference to 'Your Majesty's peerless ... martyred' mother.[17]

Even more bizarre, perhaps, was the Catholic belief, sincerely maintained, that 'the mother's merits' – that is, the spiritual merits gained by Mary Queen of Scots' martyrdom – would shortly win from God the grace of the King's

conversion to Catholicism.[18] This belief, for which there was absolutely no basis in reality, was encouraged by the subtle diplomacy of the King himself. It was a view that was widely held not only amongst the modest and perhaps naive Catholic laity but also in the counsels of the Catholic great. These included an august pair of Habsburg regents, the Archduke Albert and his wife the Archduchess Isabella, sister of Philip III of Spain, who ruled in the so-called Spanish Netherlands.* Here Protestant rebels had waged a thirty-year war against Spanish dominion. Despite English support (on religious grounds) these rebels had never succeeded in throwing off the Spanish yoke. Nor for that matter had Spain quelled them. The main result of this inconclusive contest was the financial exhaustion of all parties.

Nevertheless, King James received a friendly greeting from the Catholic Archduke in Brussels on his accession. The Archduke also informed Philip III that he had resolved to send an official envoy to James, without consulting his brother-in-law, so anxious was he to make friends with England (Albert had already released English prisoners following Elizabeth's death).[19]

One of the important provinces of the Spanish Netherlands was Flanders, which had a long seaboard, including the coastal town of Ostend, not many miles across the water from Dover and England's south-east coast. This geographical position made Flanders a kind of debatable land in the religious struggles of the times. From the vantage point of Flanders, Spain might contemplate the invasion of England; similarly England might despatch its own soldiers across the narrow crossing to support the Flemish Protestants.

Furthermore, the English Catholics might take refuge in Flanders against oppression at home. In this way, many young Englishmen, inspired by personal ambition and religious idealism, had become mercenaries in the Spanish armies in the Low

* The sixteenth-century Spanish Netherlands are to be equated, very roughly, with modern Belgium; the modern (Dutch) Netherlands were then known as the United Provinces or Holland, after the chief province.

Countries. It was for them liberating to seek advancement in an atmosphere where Catholicism was no bar to success, and there was always the question of restoring the True (Catholic) Religion to England. One day the all-powerful King of Spain might use his armies to bring about this restoration by force. Despite the failure of the Spanish Armada to secure an invasion of England in 1588, the Catholic expatriate soldiers continued to bear such a possibility in mind.

Typical of such adventurers, at once devout and aggressive, was Guy Fawkes. He was a native of York, who had been fighting in Flanders for the last ten years and who had at least once gone to Spain as part of an intrigue to raise military help for the English Catholics. But in the joyous atmosphere of the new King's reign, amid these rosy hopes of his conversion, and with the peace-loving Pope Clement VIII, who loved to mediate between great powers, making friendly overtures, maybe those days of lethal plotting had passed.

Moreover, unknown to Guy Fawkes, the slow-moving Byzantine council of Philip III had reached an important decision, even as Queen Elizabeth lay on her deathbed. There was to be no invasion, no imposition of a foreign Catholic sovereign of England: the English Catholics would reach their own solution to the subject of the succession. Thus Philip III approved instructions for a senior envoy Don Juan de Tassis to congratulate James even though Spain and England were still technically at war.[20] Tranquillity in the Netherlands and a treaty with England, which had for so long supported their infuriating Protestant rebels, were the new aims of the Spanish high command. They were hardly aims which fitted into any pattern of violent conspiracy against the new English King.

In this atmosphere of general benevolence, both national and international, the Scottish King set out on 5 April to travel south to take possession of his new kingdom. He was, wrote the playwright Thomas Dekker, 'our *omne bonum* [general goodness] from the wholesome north, Our fruitful Sovereign James'. In a further flight of the imagination, Dekker described

the King as accompanied by 'silver clouds of blissful angels'.[21] He might have been more accurate to describe the King's retinue as a grasping crowd of greedy Scots – at least from the English point of view. But the xenophobic English crossness about James' Scottish favourites had yet to find expression. For the time being, it was more significant that the host of English nobles who had rushed north had managed to join the triumphant procession south again.

Sir Robert Carey, his heroic feat underlined by the fact that he was still 'bebloodied and with bruises', was there. He was rewarded by being made a Gentleman of the Bedchamber of the King. It was, however, a position somewhat above his actual importance and he would indeed be demoted in the less sentimental atmosphere of the south, proving, alas, that the race was not after all to the swift. And not only the English were there: the French Ambassador came south from Edinburgh as a token of French friendship. He must, though, have seemed a dubious asset since his wife had to be carried all the way to London 'in a chair with slings' by shifts of perspiring porters.[22]

At the important stronghold of Berwick, the salutation was especially joyous. 'Happy day,' as a contemporary account had it, 'when peaceably so many English Gentlemen went to bring in an English and Scottish King, both included in one person.' They introduced him into a town that had for 'many hundred years' been 'a Town of the Enemy', or at the least held for one nation or the other. So much ordnance was shot off that the whole town lay in a mantle of smoke, as if there had been 'an earthquake'. There were ancient soldiers settled there – 'old King Harry's lads' – who must have been in their late seventies. These retired warriors vowed they had never seen a display to match this one.

So it was on to Newcastle (where the King admired the beauty of the Tyne Bridge), to Durham (after which, at a high spot outside Haughton-le-side, he enjoyed a 'beatific vision' of the country that was now his), and to York, where James was received by Lord Burghley, Lord President of the Council

of the North. Here the King insisted on walking to church: 'I will have no coach; for the people are desirous to see a King, and so they shall, for they shall as well see his body as his face.' Good cheer was universal – in the shape of red and white wine provided all day for the populace.

King James now passed on to those magnificent midland palaces, prosperous emblems of a powerful and settled nobility. The English lords were, as he believed, in marked contrast to the rough Scots lords who with their kidnappings, murders and threats to his person had made portions of his life a misery. The awkward fact that the old Queen had not yet been formally buried at Westminster Abbey (it was royal custom for this to happen a month after death) meant that the King was obliged to linger at this point. It would not do for his arrival to coincide embarrassingly with his predecessor's obsequies.

James dallied for four or five days at Burghley in Northamptonshire. This great Renaissance edifice had been erected by Elizabeth's servant, the first Lord Burghley, and had passed to his elder son. It could therefore be held to symbolise the rewards of loyal service in England, since the origins of the Cecil family were neither rich nor aristocratic. To the King from the north, however, the monumental exterior and the richly furnished interior 'like to an Emperor's', with its Turkey carpets, long galleries, huge floor-to-ceiling portraits, spelt luxury and leisure. Unlike Scottish castles of this date, Burghley was not fortified against attack.[23] There was no need.

The King's happiness was further increased by finding that he was able to indulge his obsessive love of hunting in the neighbourhood. This passion for a sport, in which the King tried to elude the cares of state while the stags tried to elude *him*, rapidly became a feature of the English courtiers' lives. It was first evinced to them on the royal journey. James suddenly caught sight of some deer outside Widdrington and, rushing out, killed two of them. He returned 'with a good appetite' to the house. It was not the only portent which might have provided a useful guide to the future. The other was the release of prisoners at the royal command *en route*.

The liberation of prisoners to celebrate an auspicious occasion had a long tradition, not only in English history but in antiquity too, the release of the robber Barabbas by Pontius Pilate to celebrate the Jewish Passover being one obvious example. At Newcastle the King had ordered all prisoners to be freed, and even paid up for those imprisoned for debt. The only exceptions were those held for treason, for murder – and 'for Papistry'. At York, too, all prisoners were released 'except Papists and wilful murderers'.[24]

It was at York on Sunday 17 April that a petition was presented on behalf of the English Catholics by 'a gentleman'. In fact this so-called gentleman was a Catholic priest in disguise, Father Hill. His petition, which asked for the full removal of all the penal laws against his co-religionists, unfortunately contained a tactless Biblical reference. King James was reminded that, when the Israelites sought relief from King Jeroboam and none was granted, they took 'the just occasion' to refuse to obey him in the future.

This kind of threat was exactly what the King did not want to hear. Hill's identity was rumbled and he was arrested. James' zest for theological discourse, another phenomenon to which his English subjects would have to accustom themselves, compelled him to have 'some conference' with the priest, after which Father Hill was put firmly in prison.[25]

Nevertheless the Catholic community felt perfectly justified in ignoring such minor unpleasantnesses, which could be regarded as hangovers from the previous reign. Hill was not a particularly savoury character, having led a dissolute life in Rome for some years before his return to England without permission. Besides, far more significant to the King was the fact that it was in York that he first encountered Robert Cecil. King James chose to celebrate their meeting with a royal quip, which he probably found more amusing than Cecil did: 'Though you are but a little man, we will shortly load your shoulders with business.' Cecil's appearance was certainly against him. In an age when the masculine leg, featured in tight-fitting hose, was the arbiter of elegance, his were

exceptionally short. He also had 'a wry neck, a crooked back and a splay foot', in the derisive words of one of his enemies.[26]

The King continued on his merry, sporting way on horseback, at least until a bruised arm from a hunting fall condemned him to a coach. At the approach to London, loud were the huzzas from the gathering crowds who threw their hats in the air at the sight of their new sovereign (many of these hats, unfortunately, vanished for ever into a multitude which turned out to be loyal but light-fingered). There were spectators 'in highways, fields, meadows, closes and on trees', so numerous that they 'covered the beauty of the fields'. This curiosity – among more intellectual types – had the unexpected if pleasing effect of making King James a best-seller. Thousands of copies of *Basilikon Doron*, a scholarly treatise which the King had written several years earlier on the art of government, were sold within the first weeks of his arrival.[27]

On Saturday 7 May, the Lord Mayor of London, accompanied by aldermen draped in velvet and gold chains, presented the King with the keys to the city of London, two miles outside its boundaries. Four days later, the King arrived at the Tower of London in a barge, the traditional method of access for monarchs. Here he admired such sights as the great armoury, the mint and the little zoo of lions within its precincts. All the way from Berwick, the King had been creating new knights – at least 230 of them. While he was at the Tower, he created new lords, chief among them Robert Cecil, who became Baron Cecil of Essendon.*

John Chamberlain, that percipient commentator, wrote to Dudley that 'these bountiful beginnings raise all men's spirits, and put them in great hopes, insomuch that not only Protestants, but Papists and Puritans, and the very Poets … promise themselves great part in his [King James'] favour'. As for the Poets – or rather the Playwrights – the favour was

---

* The swift progression of Robert Cecil's titles from 1603 onwards creates some problem of clarity during the period covered by this book. He became Viscount Cranborne in August 1604, and Earl of Salisbury in May 1605. To avoid confusion, he will be described as Cecil until he becomes Salisbury.

quick to come. A licence would be granted to a company, newly baptised the King's Servants, shortly after James' arrival in London. This enabled them to present 'comedies, tragedies, histories, interludes, morals, pastorals, stage-plays and such like' at 'their now usual place' the Globe Theatre.[28] This company included Richard Burbage and an actor–playwright called William Shakespeare.

Where the Papists were concerned, Father Henry Garnet, the Jesuit Superior in England, himself testified to the mood of optimism when he wrote in mid-April: 'a golden time we have of unexpected freedom…great hope is of toleration'.[29] Up until now, the proscribed priests had been crucially dependent on the support and hospitality of heroic Catholic women who concealed them in their households at great danger to themselves. Garnet derived especial support from a pair of courageous sisters, members of the Vaux family: Anne Vaux, who was unmarried, and her sister Eleanor Brooksby, who was a widow with children. Another Jesuit, the ebullient Father John Gerard, was protected over many years by their sister-in-law, another widow with a young family, Eliza Vaux of Harrowden. In all these refuges in the spring of 1603 there was an anticipation that the heavy yoke of penalties imposed upon Catholics under Elizabeth would soon be lifted.

Father Gerard, for example, came from a distinguished Lancashire family, preeminent in the past for its support of Mary Queen of Scots. So far, imprisonment and fines had been their only reward. In 1594 Father Gerard himself had been not only imprisoned but severely tortured. Now things had evidently changed. His brother Thomas was among the new knights created by James I at York.

The King – not for the first or last time – chose to allude to his relationship with Mary Queen of Scots, identifying himself with her supporters. 'I am particularly bound to love your blood,' said the King to Sir Thomas Gerard, 'on account of the persecution you have borne for me.' The news of such graciousness – surely prophetic of more favours to come – spread. Even more remarkable, even more exhilarating, was the

release of Father William Weston from his prison in the Tower of London on 14 May. The priest who had been struck by the silence which had marked the old Queen's passing had been informed shortly after the accession that his case had become 'obsolete with the passage of time'. However, his jailer insisted on a written release, so that it was not until 14 May, by which time the King himself had reached the Tower, that Weston at last gained his freedom on condition that he went abroad. His warder made up for the extra weeks of incarceration by giving Weston a magnificent dinner in his own lodgings.[30]

As Weston sallied forth, free after five years in the Tower and seventeen years altogether in prison, he found a crowd gathered to see him emerge. Various Catholics in its ranks then dropped to their knees and begged his blessing. No one hindered them. Yet, less than three years after these 'bountiful beginnings', the whole English Catholic world would be blasted apart by that conspiracy known to history as the Gunpowder Plot, and many Catholics would die bloodily at the hands of the state.

PART ONE

Before the Fruit Was Ripe

It were very small wisdom ... for pulling of unripe fruit to
hazard the breaking of my neck ...

KING JAMES
to the Earl of Northumberland

CHAPTER ONE

Whose Head for the Crown?

Thus you see this crown [of England] is not like to fall to the ground for want of heads that claim to wear it, but upon whose head it will fall is by many doubted.

THOMAS WILSON
The State of England, 1600

We now step back from the light of the new reign into the shadows of the 1590s: for that is where the story of the Gunpowder Plot begins. It is necessary to do so in order to explain how these significant Catholic expectations – the joyous 'Papist' welcome given to James I – came to be aroused.

The end of the sixteenth century was an uneasy time in England. Harvests were bad, prices were high. As the Queen grew old, men everywhere were filled with foreboding about the future. The execution of Mary Queen of Scots in 1587 had removed one focus of Catholic plotting; yet the departure of Queen Mary as a candidate did nothing to simplify the complicated question of the English succession. That subject which Elizabeth would not have publicly discussed was nevertheless secretly debated high and low, in England, in Scotland, elsewhere in Europe, throughout the last fifteen years of her reign.

Furthermore, the launching of the Spanish Armada against England the year after Queen Mary's death, with other armed Spanish intrusions during the decade, aroused an understandable paranoia on the subject of Spain and its Catholic monarch Philip II. In 1602 a play called *Alarum for London* recalled to

audiences the sacking of Antwerp twenty-five years earlier. Two small children ran on to the stage in a state of terror pursued by 'Spaniards' with drawn swords shouting 'Kill, kill, kill!'[1] From the Spanish point of view, the support which the Elizabethan government gave to the Protestant rebels in the Spanish-controlled areas in the Low Countries was intolerably subversive, given that England was geographically so well placed to make threats. But, as the English saw it, the narrow seas which divided England from the Low Countries could just as easily be crossed in the opposite direction by doughty Spaniards shouting 'Kill, kill, kill!' These same Spaniards might bring with them a Catholic monarch to succeed – or even replace – Elizabeth.

The reaction of the average English Protestant to Spain was well summed up by one of Cecil's agents resident there. It was, he wrote, an 'ill-pleasing country where a virtuous mind takes small delight, unless it be by learning to abhor vice by continually beholding the hideous face thereof'.[2] Of course English merchants continued to trade merrily with Spain, as merchants of all countries and all periods have defied ideological boundaries in the uplifting cause of commerce. Nevertheless, they shuddered, and with some reason, at the hovering vulture of the Spanish Inquisition, ready with its cruel claws to tear fine freedom-loving English Protestants to shreds.

In this context the unresolved subject of the English royal succession and the possibility of a Papist monarch proved a fertile field for anxiety, speculation and intrigue. Four hundred years later it is all too easy to suppose that the accession of James VI of Scotland, to be transformed into James I of England, was not only inevitable, but widely known to be inevitable, following the death of his mother.*[3] The truth is very different. The wise saying of the historian F. W. Maitland – that we should always be aware that what now lies in the past, once lay in the future – has never been more relevant.

---

* James was the sixth monarch of that name in Scotland (where he reigned from 1567 onwards) and the first in England. After 1603 he was thus technically King James VI and I; but since this term is confusing, he will be, where possible, described either as King James or James I.

4

A quick glance at the Tudor family tree (see p. xii) might seem to indicate that after the death of Elizabeth – the last of Henry VIII's offspring, all of whom were childless – the crown would straightforwardly pass to the descendants of Henry's sisters, Margaret and Mary, with the descendants of Margaret (the elder sister) having first claim. Alas, nothing was quite that simple.

The first complication was caused by the will of Henry VIII which had specifically barred the descendants of Margaret, who had married James IV of Scotland, from the throne on the ground that they were foreigners (that is, Scots). This meant that in the 1590s Queen Margaret's two greatgrandchildren, James of Scotland and Lady Arbella Stuart, descended from her second marriage to the Earl of Angus, had no legal claim to the throne. It was true that Arbella had actually been born in England and brought up there by her formidable maternal grandmother, Bess of Hardwicke, which perhaps annulled her 'foreign' descent. Unfortunately, Queen Margaret's marriage to Angus, in the lifetime of his first wife, had been of highly dubious validity.

What then of the descendants of Henry VIII's other sister, Mary? These were comparatively numerous for the unphiloprogenitive Tudors, all born, as well as living, in England. Regrettably, dubious marriages abounded here too, beginning with that of Mary herself to the Duke of Suffolk. Then Queen Elizabeth heartily disliked many of the Suffolk descendants. Perhaps that in itself would not have been a fatal handicap (sympathy for a putative successor was not a hallmark of the Queen's style – she detested Arbella Stuart and once described James as 'that false Scots urchin').[4] But it must be said that in this case the senior grandchildren of the ravishing Mary and the virile Duke of Suffolk were a sorry lot.

Was the disagreeable, pushy Lady Catherine Grey or the dwarf Lady Mary Grey – she was under four foot tall – to sit upon the throne of 'Great Harry's daughter', as Elizabeth persistently described herself right up to the end of her life? It was also the throne of Astraea, Cynthia, the Virgin Queen, to quote

other numinous titles Queen Elizabeth had gathered to herself. Fortunately, from Elizabeth's point of view, Lady Catherine died in the 1560s and Lady Mary ten years later. The latter had married far beneath her, a Sergeant Porter, and had had no children. But Lady Catherine left behind a legacy of trouble, with a secret marriage to Edward Seymour Lord Hertford that was probably not valid and a couple of sons of dubious legitimacy.

The Queen's continuing resentment of this branch of the family was fully displayed when she sent Catherine Grey's son Edward Seymour Lord Beauchamp to the Tower in 1595 for trying to prove that he was in fact legitimate. Beauchamp was not a particularly impressive character. Ferdinando 5th Earl of Derby, who descended through his mother from the junior Suffolk branch, was, however, a great territorial magnate, a man of noble stature as well as noble blood. There might have been something to be said for Lord Derby as a contender. But Derby himself showed no interest in pressing his claim; to do so, he believed, would be 'treasonous'.[5] He died in 1594, leaving only daughters. His royal rights, such as they were, passed to the eldest, Lady Anne Stanley, born in 1580 and thus a young woman of notionally marriageable age in the mid 1590s.

All of this meant that neither of Henry VIII's sisters – the direct Tudor line from Henry VII – provided potential successors with an untarnished claim to the throne. But if the English field was thrown wide open there were of course numerous noble houses in whose veins flowed a trickle of royal blood from previous dynasties, not least that of Edward III. These included the families of Huntingdon, Barrington and Rutland via Edward's fourth son, Edmund of York, as well as the Staffords, and the Earls of Essex and Northumberland via a younger son, Thomas of Woodstock. Such claims might seem remote: and yet English history had seen some remote claims to the throne succeed before now, notably those of Henry IV and Henry VII, and perhaps would do so again.

*

The Catholic point of view on the succession was equally complicated, but seen from the other side of the looking-glass. To begin with, Elizabeth herself was considered a bastard by foreign Catholics. (Neither Henry's divorce from Queen Catherine of Aragon nor his subsequent marriage to 'La Concubina' Anne Boleyn was recognised by the Pope.) Queen Elizabeth was understandably extremely sensitive on this issue, which for her raised questions of security – and English Catholic loyalties. As she herself pointed out concerning 'their chief pastor' the Pope, he had 'pronounced sentence against me while yet I was in my mother's womb'.[6]

That was bad enough. But in 1570 Pope Pius V had gone much further. In a bull *Regnans in Excelsis*, which was to have a catastrophic effect on the fortunes of English Catholics, he formally excommunicated the English Queen and released her subjects from their allegiance to her. However, the news of the Bull spread slowly if at all among the ranks of Elizabeth's humbler subjects, whose problems maintaining their religion to any degree were of a different nature.[7] Yet, if the Bull's commands were to be obeyed, Elizabeth could actually be deposed at the Pope's behest. She could even arguably – and there was indeed much argument on the subject – be assassinated as a kind of sanctified vengeance. In short, excommunication was a fearful weapon, but it was also a double-edged one. It might threaten Elizabeth with deposition or even death. But it also incised the message that all English Catholics, however lowly, however obedient, were potential traitors to their country at the orders of 'their chief pastor'.

In the 1590s, when efforts to dislodge Elizabeth by Spanish invasion had failed, the Pope and the other Catholic powers began to look beyond her lifetime just as the English themselves were surreptitiously doing. A Catholic successor to replace Mary Queen of Scots as a figurehead of the True Religion now became the desired aim. At this point the genealogical net was cast extremely wide, to an extent which seems extraordinary to the modern mind, but was much more plausible in the late sixteenth century. The concept of a

sovereign was essentially that of a human being with the appropriate *grandezza* – majesty – which Queen Elizabeth knew so well how to display. In this way, mightiness of royal command could finally count for more than nearness in royal blood. This, at any rate, was what the Catholic apologists, trawling for candidates, found themselves arguing.

In this connection *The Book of Succession*, published in 1595, was a seminal work.[8] It was allegedly by one R. Doleman, but the actual author was the leading English Jesuit (resident in Rome) Father Robert Persons. The book had the effect of infuriating King James of Scotland. He was also genuinely alarmed. Its preamble declared 'by many proofs and arguments' that a candidate's position as the nearest successor 'by ancestry of blood' was still not enough to guarantee him (or her) the crown. There had to be 'other conditions and requisite circumstances' in favour of his (or her) succession: this implied a paramount need for a strong Catholic monarch. James, a Protestant, clearly did not satisfy such conditions.

The Jesuit in his book brought into play such dignitaries as the Dukes of Parma and Savoy. Both these princes were of course Catholics, descended in the Lancastrian line from John of Gaunt, yet another son of Edward III. In the fashion of the time, it was understood that their somewhat remote claim could be reinforced by suitable marriages. In a sense, the Duke of Savoy had already done so, by marrying a daughter of Philip II who shared his Gaunt descent. When his wife died in 1597, the Duke became once more in royal terms an eligible bachelor, and there were suggestions that he might marry an English royal contender such as Lady Arbella Stuart or even Lord Derby's daughter Lady Anne Stanley. These names were also mentioned in connection with the Duke of Parma.

But the most desirable candidate according to *The Book of Succession* was the favourite daughter of Philip II, the Archduchess Isabella. First, she shared the ubiquitous Lancastrian blood of John of Gaunt. Secondly, through her mother, a French princess descended from the Dukes of

Brittany, she could advance an even more ancient claim. This was based on the pledge of feudal allegiance made by William the Conqueror of England five hundred years earlier to the Dukes of Brittany. Such daring excursions into the remote mists of royal history were, however, of much less importance than the fact that Isabella was a powerful Spanish princess, married to another Habsburg, the Archduke Albert of Austria.

To press the claims of Isabella meant of course advancing the cause of Spain. But the Catholic elements in Rome and elsewhere, who were more favourable to France than Spain, were hardly happy at such a development; any additional dimension to the Habsburg Empire worried them. Even the name of the French King, Henri IV, was introduced as a possible contender for the English throne, more because the French were in constant fear of encirclement by Spain than because they believed in his English blood.[9]

For all such challenges, the Archduchess Isabella had a great deal of genuine Catholic support to succeed Queen Elizabeth. This remarkable woman came of a long tradition of able and admirable Habsburg princesses who acted as deputies for menfolk sometimes less accomplished than themselves. Isabella Clara Eugenia was born on 12 August 1566 (she was two months younger than King James). She was named by her mother for St Eugenia, to whom the Queen had prayed; for St Clara, whose feast day it was; and for her great ancestress Isabella of Castile.[10] Perhaps the latter was the greatest influence, for Isabella displayed many of the same traits.

She was in her late twenties, still unmarried, when she came to the English Catholic seminary at Valladolid with her father, Philip II, and her half-brother, the future Philip III. Father Robert Persons raved over the entire family. The Spanish King was compared to Constantine the Great, and his children to Constantine's offspring Constans and Constantia, but Isabella in particular took his fancy: 'nay, the Infanta seemed to resemble not only the piety of Constantia, but even the very zeal, wisdom, fortitude and other virtues of our country woman St

Helena herself'.* Philip II was said to love Isabella with a special tenderness in memory of her mother, the wife he had adored, who died young. But even without the aid of sentimental recollection, Isabella was well equipped to be a father's favourite, being not only beautiful (in youth) but also clever enough to be Philip II's intellectual companion.

Isabella's celebrated piety did not prevent her having a strong practical streak which made her the generous patron of religious women, founding convents with a lavish hand. She became a benevolent helper of young English Catholic women in the Low Countries fleeing from the harsh religious laws of their own land. 'I will be a mother to you,' she said, arranging a vast banquet in their honour. But the Archduchess also knew how to enjoy the life of a royal. She made herself popular by attending national festivities and even confessed engagingly to a taste for wine. 'I am such a drinker,' she remarked on one occasion in Basle, accepting a glass. And she was an excellent horsewoman, not only presenting prizes but taking part in competitions.[11]

Her stamina showed itself when her father decided, shortly before he died, to appoint her as joint Regent of the Spanish Netherlands with her husband (and first cousin) the Archduke Albert. Isabella herself was well over thirty when she married, while Albert was nearly forty and had to be released from the religious vows he had taken in order to make this marriage of state and convenience. He was a serious, scholarly man who unlike Isabella was slow to laugh and relax; but the formal Habsburg mask concealed a kind heart and decent instincts.

Both Albert and Isabella took to their task with zest: indeed 'the Archdukes' as they were generally known (just as Ferdinand and Isabella had been known as 'the Catholic Kings') might be said to have gone native in Flanders. They quickly came to sympathise with the problems of the independent-minded population there, rather than with those of

---

* Helena, wife of the fourth-century Emperor Constantine and mother of Constantine the Great, discoverer of the True Cross, was believed to have been born a British (Celtic) princess.

Mother Spain, creating in the process what has been described as an 'embryonic national identity' which would reappear in modern Belgium.[12] Isabella was generous, gracious and good. Her youthful beauty, which had been the pride of the Spanish court, had faded and she had become rather stout. Nevertheless she bore herself with great dignity. In short, here was a princess who in her person and her quality was, unlike the feeble English Greys, well suited to occupy the throne of 'Great Harry'.

There were, however, a number of difficulties. An obvious one was that Isabella Clara Eugenia was a foreigner, a member of the Spanish race so detested by many righteous Englishmen. Yet although it was true, as the Archduke Albert observed, that there was a 'universal desire of all men to have a King of their own nation', this desire was not always fulfilled.[13] Once again, we must beware of hindsight. We must remember that European royalties frequently did come to occupy foreign thrones.* Furthermore, James himself, as a Scot, was also considered to be a foreigner. English prejudice against the Scots, although riddled with contempt rather than fear, was equally vituperative (it could be argued that contempt for a potential monarch was more of a drawback than fear).

As a potential Queen of England, however, Isabella did suffer from two distinct disadvantages. First, there was the question of her sex, given the disenchantment with female rule which grew towards the end of Elizabeth's life. Secondly, like Elizabeth, she was childless. Her inability to bear children seems to have been known or suspected in advance of her marriage to Albert.[14] The elaborate provisions drawn up for the rule of 'the Archdukes' in the Spanish Netherlands – by which they were not exactly independent of Spain, but not entirely dependent upon it either – laid down that Flanders was to

---

* Not only during this period. Less than a hundred years later a Dutchman came to rule England in the shape of William III; a few years after that a German hardly speaking English arrived in the shape of George I, who established the Hanoverian dynasty on the English throne, although he was by no means the closest relation in blood.

return to the Spanish crown if the Archdukes had no issue (and, if there was a child, it was to marry back into the Spanish royal family, which came to the same thing). Certainly by 1603 it was generally known among European royalties that 'so great a lady' had to endure the sorrow of 'not enjoying the sweet name of mother'. The prospect of another disputed succession on Isabella's death – or, worse still, direct domination by the Spanish crown – was a nightmare. In brief, Isabella would never be more than 'a temporary solution'.[15]

The third and perhaps most potent disadvantage was the ambivalent attitude of the Spanish Habsburgs themselves. Philip II had resigned his so-called rights to the English throne to his daughter as early as 1587 (he imagined these rights had been consigned to him in her last testament by Mary Queen of Scots). In the period leading up to Elizabeth's death, Philip's indecisive son Philip III never quite made up his mind what line to pursue on the subject and nor did his Council. Yet some official line had to be pursued, and official military support given, if a claim which was so genealogically vague was to be enforced.

Father Robert Persons' ecstasy on the subject of Isabella in *The Book of Succession* – 'a princess of rare parts' – was all very well. The Spanish Council and King Philip dithered on. Sometimes they indulged in pipe-dreams, imagining that once Isabella was Queen of England she would cede the Isle of Wight to her brother so that he could harbour his fleet there, in order to 'keep England (and even France) in subjection'. At other times, the Spanish Council, like the French, recognised the danger of Flanders being united with England – rather than Spain – in the future. In 1601 the Council suggested that Isabella should give Flanders back to Spain when she ascended the throne of England.[16]

But it was Isabella herself, backed up by Albert, who showed the most marked disinclination to have her rich and interesting life as a ruler of Flanders interrupted. She saw the whole matter in terms of Flemish, not English, independence: was Philip III trying to secure the return of the Spanish

Netherlands by this elaborate ritual of a royal claim elsewhere? English Catholics fantasised over the religious houses that this princess, 'both strong and mighty and also abounding in wealth and riches', would reestablish in their benighted country.[17] Isabella, however, nourished the more realistic ambition of a Flanders, virtually free of Spain, where there was peace and prosperity.

For all the royal lady's unwillingness, her mere presence among the contenders – a Catholic presence backed by a large army – had a profound effect on the policies and initiatives of King James. It is indeed impossible to understand his delicate finessing of the Catholic question while he was still in Scotland, his diplomatic treatment of the Pope, without bearing in mind the threat that the Archduchess Isabella represented to him.

In the final analysis, was this threat entirely in the mind? Speculations about what-might-have-been – what is now termed counterfactual history – are notoriously enjoyable. One might even conjecture that Queen Isabella of England would have made a remarkable, albeit Catholic sovereign, if she could have thrown off the Spanish influence. Like another great English Queen – Victoria – centuries later, she would have had an assiduous consort in the hard-working and supportive Albert.

Returning to the late 1590s, the reaction of the English court had to be brought into the equation. During this period, Robert Cecil and the Earl of Essex fought for position. Cecil's father instructed him: 'Seek not to be E and shun to be R' (standing for that other charismatic figure at the Elizabethan court, Sir Walter Ralegh), but Cecil did not in fact have much choice.[18] The respective weapons at his disposal and at that of Essex were very different: middle-class cunning on the one hand, aristocratic glamour on the other. Essex was the Queen's favourite, Cecil the Queen's servant; Essex charmed her, Cecil worked for her. During the reign of Elizabeth it was not clear which of them would prevail, still less was it clear who would prevail with the incoming monarch, whomsoever he or she might be.

Early on, Essex started to make the running with King James. He corresponded with him from at least 1598 onwards, showering him with those sentiments most calculated to gratify the Scottish King. Under the circumstances, it seems probable that Cecil did allow himself to contemplate the rival claims of the Archduchess Isabella. Rapid revisionism on Cecil's part after the fall of Essex in 1601 means that the subject is inevitably veiled in mystery. (No one knew better than Cecil how to cover his tracks when a change of direction was necessary.) Yet the affair of the royal portraits gives an interesting pointer to where Cecil's interests lay in the autumn of 1599: which he did not manage to suppress afterwards.

On 3 September 1599, Robert Cecil set about procuring portraits of Isabella and Albert, with the aid of Filippo Corsini, a foreign agent. Corsini promised not only to gratify Cecil's wish as soon as possible but also to respect his request for 'all secrecy and speed'. By 19 October the paintings were well in hand, and by mid-November Corsini was able to repeat his assurance to Cecil that the task had been carried out without anyone's knowledge.*[19]

Of course Essex, in his diplomatic war with Cecil, took care to see that rumours of Cecil favouring Isabella reached Scotland. Early in 1601 he instructed his Scottish ally the Earl of Mar to report to James that Cecil was persistently recommending Isabella's admirable qualities to Elizabeth in order to sway the English Queen in her favour.

In February, however, Essex attempted to mount an armed coup against the Queen's evil advisers – as he saw them – with a view to imposing his own authority. He gathered together a band of swordsmen, including certain youthful Catholics who saw in such a rebellion an opening to secure religious

---

* J. H. Hurstfield suggested that the portraits may have been intended for Queen Elizabeth rather than Cecil himself (in which case it is difficult to see why the great secrecy underlined by both sides was necessary); even so, Hurstfield admitted that the request for portraits was a sign that the English government took seriously claims being put forward on behalf of the Infanta (Hurstfield, 'Succession', p. 376).

toleration.[20] The rising failed almost before it began, meeting with little or no popular support; while force was certainly not the way to deal with Queen Elizabeth I. It was not a mistake that the thoughtful Cecil would ever have made with his sovereign. While some of Essex's Catholic accomplices – among them Lord Monteagle, Robert Catesby and Francis Tresham – were reprieved, Essex was tried and executed on 25 February 1601.

Significantly, Essex had still thought it worth while trying to blacken Cecil's name on the subject of the Archduchess Isabella at his trial. He accused him of telling a fellow councillor that her title to succeed was 'as good as that of any other person'. This would certainly be mortifying news for the King of Scots, who believed that his own title was clearly the best. Essex did not realise that Cecil was actually eavesdropping on the trial proceedings from a concealed position. Hearing this potentially damaging charge Cecil stepped into the open court. Falling to his knees, he begged permission to correct the record, and then challenged Essex to provide the identity of this Councillor: 'Name him, if you dare!'[21]

Essex consulted with Lord Southampton, and 'after a little hesitation' gave the name of Sir William Knollys. The drama was not over. Knollys was fetched and for his part declared that he had never heard Cecil 'speak any words to that effect'. But he did confirm that there had been a discussion of the book by Doleman – actually an alias for Father Persons – on the subject of the succession. Cecil, said Knollys, had described it as 'strange impudence' on the part of Doleman to give 'an equal right in the succession to the Crown' to Isabella as to any other. In short, Cecil's reaction to Doleman had been the exact opposite. So, supposing that Knollys (and Cecil) were telling the truth, something that could never be disproved in view of Cecil's new ascendancy, the matter was resolved.

In short, the fall of Essex gave Robert Cecil his opportunity. There were to be no more thoughts of the Archduchess. James must be the man if it could be brought about. In Scotland the Earl of Mar, preparing for an embassy south with instructions

from Essex, quickly backed off. Instead Robert Cecil initiated what was to prove two weary years of delicate correspondence between himself and the Scottish King. His conditions were that the 'greatest secrecy' (to spare Elizabeth's feelings) was to be maintained, and no other more open bargaining for the royal title was to take place.[22] Under these circumstances the two men cautiously grew to know and respect one another – by post.*

'Build up a party in England to aid your chances there and above all seek the favour of the Pope.' This strongly worded piece of advice was given to King James in 1600 by his relative Duke Ferdinand of Tuscany, who unlike James was a Catholic.[23] The relationship was not particularly close – their respective mothers descended from the Dukes of Lorraine – but it suited both men to address each other as 'cousin'. While Cecil hoped in time to establish the support of the English Council and build up a party for King James in England, as an outstanding Protestant, he could not solve the Catholic problem for him. Yet this the Scottish King must do, if he was to secure the great prize of England by peaceful means.

A tranquil accession was his dearest wish. By both temperament and experience, James disliked violent action. Why rob an orchard from over the wall before the fruit was ripe? That could be dangerous. 'By a little patience and abiding the season,' the King told the Earl of Northumberland, 'I may with far more ease and safety enter at the gate of the garden, and enjoy the fruits at my pleasure.'[24]

The Scottish King's first secret diplomatic overture to the Papacy had in fact occurred several years before the Duke Ferdinand's good advice. Apart from diplomatic moves abroad, in Scotland itself James was already showing personal favours to Catholics. He saw it as a means of balancing the more extreme form of Calvinism represented by the Scottish Kirk (as the reformed Church was known). The Earl of Huntly and his

* In the late sixteenth century this would be through a secret diplomatic form of post – trusted messengers riding between England and Scotland.

wife Henrietta Stuart, both Catholics, were members of the inner royal circle. Lady Huntly had a special place in James' heart, for her father Esmé Stuart had been his first love, when James was a neglected love-starved boy. As for her husband, James was inclined to address him as his 'good son'. Such accolades, reported to Rome and if anything exaggerated, could not help creating a good impression there.

Perhaps it was James' youthful crush on the personable Esmé Stuart which had given him a preference for his own sex where intimate relationships were concerned; perhaps homosexuality was natural to him. In either eventuality, James also found it perfectly possible to act the loving husband and father as he was expected to do. Indeed, King James in Scotland enjoyed a positively happy marriage to his Queen, Anne of Denmark; by the royal standards of that time, when arranged marriages to unknown foreigners were often bitterly unhappy, the union was a miracle of accord. It has been mentioned that the Queen was pregnant with her sixth child at the time of Elizabeth's death. All in all the King would beget a total of eight children over a period of eleven years – undeniable proof of marital assiduity.

Contemporary observers also bore witness to the King's affection outside the royal bedchamber for 'our Annie', as he called his wife. (More formally, in a poem to welcome her to Scotland, he addressed her as 'our earthly Juno ... the sweet doctor' who could heal his heavy heart.) Anne of Denmark's excellent royal comportment, her 'courteous behaviour to the people', made her a satisfactory consort in public, as well as a pleasing one in private.[25] A slight giddiness in character was no great disadvantage since James had a low opinion of women at the best of times and hardly expected in his wife the stability of a man.

In view of such public amiability, Anne's conversion to Catholicism in her twenties could not help being interpreted as another sign favourable to the Papal cause, especially in Rome itself. Anne had been brought up as a Lutheran and never took to the official religion of her husband's country. With time she

became 'most decidedly opposed to it' and she found Catholicism altogether more sympathetic. According to her confessor, the Jesuit Father Robert Abercromby, she had gone to Mass in the household of a certain anonymous 'great princess' as a girl. It is possible that her desire to convert was conceived as a child, as well as being in part a reaction to dour Scottish Calvinism. At all events, some time after 1600 but well before March 1603, Queen Anne was received into the Catholic Church in a secret chamber in the royal palace. By the summer of 1601, she was writing to Pope Clement VIII assuring him of her fidelity to the Church.[26]

King James showed himself tolerant of what he seems to have taken to be a feminine aberration. According to Father Abercromby's account much later, the royal couple discussed the matter 'one night, when they were in bed'. First of all, King James commented that his wife, inclined to be frivolous, had recently shown herself to be 'much more grave, collected and pious'. When Queen Anne revealed the reason, James in effect gave her his blessing in these wise husbandly words: 'Well, wife, if you cannot live without this sort of thing, do your best to keep things as quiet as possible, for if you don't our crown is in danger.'[27]

Genuine tolerance, where his own safety was not at stake, was one of the virtues of King James. Having been brought up to adhere to the strictest Calvinist doctrines as a child, he had come to see them as threatening the position of a sovereign. Elders of such a Church granted him no special 'divine right' or authority. A Church with a proper hierarchy of bishops and clergymen, on the other hand, had the monarch at its apex, duly supported by the whole structure.

It is true that James remembered with bitterness that the Catholic Church had supported his mother's claims to the Scottish throne over his own during her long English captivity. Yet James was personally pragmatic. Furthermore, in historical terms he was inclined to view Rome as the Mother Church, though much corrupted since. Not only were the Catholic Huntlys petted but Catholic priests such as Father Abercromby

were permitted at his court if suitably disguised as a keeper of hawks or something incongruous which did not challenge the Kirk. King James even enjoyed disputing with them. He was certainly not prepared to take issue over a mere woman taking comfort in Papist practices.

The Queen's conversion, details of which inevitably leaked out in Catholic circles, gave the King another excellent opportunity for the kind of ambivalent diplomacy at which he excelled. The Queen's letter to Rome of 1601 was ostensibly an answer to the Pope's communication to her husband. The King could not reply himself, Anne explained, since he had to be circumspect. Not only could the Pope be assured of the Queen's own devotion, and her care to educate her children in the Catholic Faith, but Anne went further and hinted that King James might soon grant liberty of conscience to Catholics. As for herself, if she publicly had to attend 'the rites of heretics', she asked for the Pope's absolution and blessing in advance. Such attendance was hardly her own desire, but due simply 'to the hostile times which we have to endure'.[28]

This letter was almost certainly written with James' knowledge, which made the reference to the royal children especially cynical. Anne had already clashed with her husband over the despatch of her eldest son Prince Henry away from her own care to the guardianship of the Earl of Mar, according to Scottish royal tradition which the Danish Queen greatly disliked. There was at the present time no question of these Scottish princes and princesses receiving Catholic instruction, much as the Queen would have liked it. But Queen Anne wrote out of wishful-thinking, an optimism based on a fantasy which came to be shared by Rome.

By July 1602, Pope Clement, already happy at the news about Queen Anne, was urging the conversion of her husband. There had in fact been a rumour of this conversion – which must have seemed a miraculous development – on the continent as early as 1599. A Scottish visitor to the Spanish court brought the glad tidings. In Spain in July 1600, King James was said to be on the verge of submitting to the Pope's religious

authority in order to have his English claim confirmed. In the following November even Father Robert Persons thought it a serious possibility that the Scottish King would be converted. In the summer of 1601, Henri IV of France joined in the act. He was after all an expert on the subject of royal conversion, having become a Catholic specifically to ascend the throne of France. As he put it with his usual light touch: 'Paris is worth a Mass.' Henri IV assured his new pastor the Pope that he would do everything in his power to assist in his brother monarch's conversion.[29]

The Pope now privately offered to champion King James against anyone who tried to deny him the English throne. Clement VIII, elected Pope in 1592, was, unlike Pius V, by temperament a conciliator. He prided himself on having mediated between France and Spain to bring about peace. Perhaps he could now repeat this triumph by securing peace between Spain and England, if only to bring succour to the beleaguered English Catholics.

King James' diplomatic manoeuvring with regard to the Papacy was certainly successful. It was also carefully calculated. The King wrote no letters of his own; it was better like that. On the one hand Queen Anne – with her repeated use of the royal 'we' – would be believed by the Catholics to speak for him; on the other hand he could deny to their opponents that he had any share in her views.

James' agents in Rome were able to have a field day along similar lines. They encouraged the tall tales, one of which reached as far as the Spanish King Philip III. Not only, apparently, was James becoming a Catholic but his son and heir would be brought up in Rome. When one particular letter did emerge later under James' own signature, addressing the Pope in Latin as 'Most Holy Father', and signed 'your most obedient son', the King was more than capable of dealing with the challenge. He blandly announced that he must have signed the paper quickly, without looking at it closely, on his way out hunting.[30]

From James' point of view there was no need to emulate

Henri IV and change his religion. It was far better to travel hopefully towards conversion – or to be seen to do so – than actually to arrive there. And, as we shall see, rumours of this famous conversion continued to circulate as late as 1605, the year of the Gunpowder Plot.

In 1600, Thomas Wilson wrote concerning the succession in *The State of England*: 'Thus you see this crown [of England] is not like to fall to the ground for want of heads that claim to wear it, but upon whose head it will fall is by many doubted.' He went on to list twelve competitors.* Yet by 1602 the picture had entirely changed. In the Spanish Netherlands, the Archdukes Albert and Isabella were working out ways of assisting James which would leave him under an obligation to them when he arrived in the south. As Don Baltasar de Zuñiga, the Spanish Ambassador in Brussels, wrote at the end of July: 'His [James'] game for the crown of England is almost won.'[31] It was therefore essential to give support to the monarch who 'would at the last, give liberty to the Catholics'.

This remarkable turnaround would allow the Archduchess Isabella to exclaim ecstatically over the accession of King James, in a letter of April 1603 to her brother's favourite, the Duke of Lerma. Surely the blood of the martyred Mary Queen of Scots must have 'cried out towards Our Lord' at the moment of her son's proclamation! The memory of Queen Mary's death would certainly spur on James' conversion to Catholicism: towards which Isabella felt 'strong signs' were already pointing. A Scot, resident in London, put the whole matter more phlegmatically in a report back to James in the winter of 1602: 'Wherever I passed and lodged they called your Majesty their young lord, which within a few years [back] no man durst speak.'[32]

So the crown fell at last upon the head of Scottish James. This peaceful accession was a political triumph for the King himself in terms of foreign relations, as it was for Robert Cecil in terms of English politics. But such triumphs are not always

---

* Wilson, as an author, was not without importance, since he was also (like a few others) employed from time to time by Cecil as a foreign agent.

secured without leaving hostages to fortune. In the case of King James, he would have to deal with those men and women, the Catholics of England, who were now expecting, after nearly half a century, that 'liberty' of which Zuñiga wrote.

The Honest Papists

Papists might be honest folks and good friends to
him, for his mother was a Catholic and yet he
behoved to say she was an honest woman.

KING JAMES
in Scotland

It is time to peer into the strange, hidden world of
Elizabethan Catholic England, in order to understand the
Papists' expectations from King James. 'Catholics now saw
their own country, the country of their birth, turned into a
ruthless and unloving land,' wrote Father Weston of the perse-
cutions they had endured. It was on the Catholics that all men
fastened their hatred: 'they lay in ambush for them, betrayed
them, attacked them with violence and without warning. They
plundered them at night, confiscated their possessions, drove
away their flocks, stole their cattle.' Lay Catholics, as well as
priests, filled every prison, 'no matter how foul or dark'. Father
Weston recalled a prophecy of utter desolation made in the
Bible: 'Whosoever killeth you, will think that he doth a service
to God.'[1] His lament is that of the outcast minority throughout
history who find a special cruelty in being persecuted in their
native land.

It is easy to understand Father Weston's despair if we consider what it was like – in purely legal terms – to be a Catholic
in England at the time of the death of Queen Elizabeth. In her
long reign penalties had increased, at a pace which was sometimes slow, sometimes violently accelerated, always destined to

make Catholic lives ever more painful, powerless and poverty-stricken.

Let us begin with the central tenet of a devout Catholic's life. The popular *Cathechisme of Christian Doctrine Necessary for Children and Ignorant People* by Laurence Vaux, a Lancashire schoolmaster turned monk, defined the commandments of the Church.[2] The first and greatest of these was to hear Mass every Sunday, and additionally on holy days, the official festivals of the Church. But not in England in March 1603. Nowhere in England could the Mass be legally celebrated, neither in public nor in private; not in the great cathedrals which had once been part of the Catholic fabric, not in secluded chapels in remote country houses, not in upper rooms in taverns nor in secret chambers hidden behind the breast of a chimney. To hear the Mass was for a layman (or woman) a felony punishable by heavy fines and jail.

For priests, the penalties were starker. If a Catholic priest was discovered, either in the act of saying Mass or otherwise compromised – in the possession of 'massing clothes' (vestments) or vessels – he would be flung into prison. If the charge was treason, the ultimate sentence was death: but not necessarily a straightforward death. He might be sentenced to be hung, drawn and quartered, which involved cutting down the living body, emasculating it, cutting out the heart and finally dividing up – 'quartering' – the limbs. Even before that he might be tortured in order to secure his confession that he was indeed a Catholic priest. As a result, priests often lived under perpetual aliases, not only to cover their tracks but to protect their families.

Lady Arundell was a Catholic widow who secretly housed Father John Cornelius, a priest renowned for his 'sweet and plausible tongue', in her manor at Chideock in Dorset. On Easter Sunday 1594 he was seized as a result of information laid by a treacherous servant. Father Cornelius was tortured before the Council until at last he admitted to being a Jesuit. He died with words invoking the Holy Cross on his lips. After the ritual dismemberment, Father Cornelius' limbs were posted

on the four gates of Dorchester town, until Lady Arundell boldly recovered them and gave them burial.[3]

Catholics could not have their children baptised legally in the Catholic rite by a priest, or even by a Catholic midwife, as sometimes illegally happened. These same children, grown to adulthood, could not be married according to the Catholic rite. At the moment of death, they would be denied the sacrament of dying, known as Extreme Unction. As the vice tightened, Catholics were explicitly forbidden to keep not only Catholic servants but a Catholic schoolmaster: since every master had to have a licence to teach. Moreover it was forbidden to send children abroad to the Low Countries to be educated in convents such as those patronised by the Archduchess Isabella, or in the new schools such as Douai, which were founded there in response to the general need.

It was a small mercy, but a mercy nevertheless, that a proposition put forward by Cecil's father, Lord Burghley, in a pamphlet of 1583 was rejected: this was to take children of known Catholic parents away from them at the age of seven. Even so, Catholic parents often voluntarily despatched their children at sixteen to a distant neighbourhood; this was the age at which these children would incur fines of their own for not attending church, thus increasing the family burden. Local churchwardens would be on the look-out for the sixteenth birthday of parishioners, but strange officials might be fooled for a year or two. In order to keep the Catholics under further control, an Act against Popish Recusants was passed in 1593 forbidding the convicted gentry from travelling more than five miles from their estates. The Catholic serving and labouring classes were already policed by the strong contemporary laws against vagrancy and unlicensed travel in general.[4]

These were all negatives, things that the law forbade Catholics to do. But there were also the positives: the things that the law obliged Catholics to do, if they were to keep clear of prison, or preserve themselves from fines. Babies had to be baptised in the Protestant church before they were a month old, just as adults had to be married in their local Protestant

church. By the Act of Uniformity, passed at the beginning of Elizabeth's reign, every person over the age of sixteen was compelled to attend his or her local (Protestant) church on Sundays or holy days. Protestant Communion had also to be taken at least twice a year. Failure to do so involved fines of a shilling a week in 1559, which was not an inconsiderable sum when the legal definition of a yeoman was someone who had forty shillings yearly at his disposal from his land. Continuous absence of a month or more led to heavier fines and finally to the seizure of goods in order to satisfy the courts. Such absentees were classed as 'recusants' – literally, those who refused (to attend Protestant services) and today might be termed *refuseniks*.

Under these circumstances, it may seem surprising that the Catholic community survived at all. The decision of Francis Swetnam, baker to Eliza Vaux and a good family man, is certainly understandable. For two years, he confessed, he had been a recusant, but then turned again to the Protestant Church, despite his personal convictions: 'for that he had rather adventure his own soul than lose his five children'. There were many more exalted than Swetnam the baker who preferred their own advancement and that of their family, to the practice of the Faith in which they had been brought up. The fines, as they mounted, weighed like lead. Only the rich could afford them and even their fortunes began to dip as they were obviously pursued with more enthusiasm than the poor. As A. L. Rowse has written, a family like the Arundells of Cornwall were paying a vast amount of money every year for 'the luxury of going to church'.[5] Meanwhile, in a sinister development, the Exchequer began to see the recusants not so much as heretics to be converted but as a prime source of revenue to be exploited.

And yet nothing was quite what it seemed. From the point of view of many Catholics, there were two worlds in England. One was the gallant world of the court, and those who ruled the country: a masterful, glittering world of honour where prizes were to be won, fortunes established. This was,

essentially, the world of the Protestant Church since, by the Act of Supremacy at the beginning of Elizabeth's reign, further tightened in 1563, allegiance to the sovereign as head of the Church had to be sworn by all office-holders and clergy. This Oath of Supremacy, specifically acknowledging that the (supreme) spiritual authority was vested in the crown, was one to which Catholics who acknowledged the spiritual authority of the Pope could not swear. Then there was the spectral world of their forbidden religion.

Catholics – pious Catholics – often slipped silently between these two worlds. They were like ghosts, freed by the darkness to worship as they pleased, but compelled to become conforming Protestants at cockcrow. Hypocrites? Not necessarily. Survivors? Certainly. These were the men and women of whom King James had spoken approvingly while in Scotland – with the obligatory reference to Mary Queen of Scots. 'Papists', he said, 'might be honest folks and good friends to him, for his mother was a Catholic and yet he behoved to say she was an honest woman.'[6]

These 'honest folks' included some who had connections to the leading luminaries of the Elizabethan court, many of whom were themselves suspected, not without reason, of Papist sympathies. It was helpful that the Queen herself made personal loyalty more of a touchstone than doctrinal orthodoxy. Besides, she 'was always slow to condemn without good proofs any man whatsoever'.[7] She came of a generation which understood how the heart might remain Catholic even if the mind was politically correct – and Protestant. Not only had she herself been born a Catholic (although denounced in the womb by the Pope) but she had lived through some extremely tricky periods of religious change. Many of her own devotional tastes were in essence Catholic, and she disliked married clergy, even if their marriages were officially permitted by the Anglican Church. The Queen was always prepared to smile graciously on those Papists or fellow travellers whom she considered to be her loyal subjects.[8]

The respected and apparently inviolable position of Magdalen Viscountess Montague was an example of how the most pious Catholic could survive if he (or she) did not challenge the accepted order. This remarkable and stalwart Catholic lady had as a girl walked in the bridal procession of Queen Mary Tudor when she married Philip II of Spain in Winchester Cathedral. Her husband died in 1592 but as a widow Magdalen Montague made no concessions where the practice of her religion was concerned. Her own mansion near Battle, in East Sussex, was so full of priests and chapels and secret chambers that it was known locally as 'Little Rome'. What was more, Lady Montague, a tall and striking figure, had the habit of walking in public, 'her gait full of majesty', in clear possession of rosary beads and crucifixes, although these were strictly forbidden objects. Most of her 'great family' of eighty persons – that is, her household – were Catholics, according to her chaplain Richard Smith, who compared her to the fourth-century widow St Paula, friend and supporter of St Jerome. In Southwark there was another great house, with another big household which was similarly honeycombed with Papists, including priests.[9]

None of this could have been unknown to the authorities. Nevertheless Queen Elizabeth chose to pay a ceremonial visit to Magdalen Montague at her Battle house in 1591. Afterwards the Queen sent a gracious message by a Lady of the Bedchamber to say that she was convinced 'she fareth much better for your prayers, and therefore desireth you ever hereafter to be mindful of her' in them.[10]

So this dignified old matriarch (she had eight children) managed to combine piety and loyalty – helped along by that famous obstinacy which her chaplain wrote could be seen in her actual face: a short sharp nose held high, and a very strong chin. But, at the same time as Magdalen Montague jangled her rosary in public, it was an offence of Praemunire, punishable by life imprisonment and confiscation of goods, to import such hallowed tokens, let alone display them in public. To the government officially, this was nothing but 'vain popish trish-

trash'. A servant found in possession of a brass crucifix became (unlike Lady Montague) an object of immediate suspicion; he was compelled to acknowledge the Queen's supremacy and declare that he abhorred 'all popish trifles'.[11] So thorough was the government detestation of the 'trish-trash' that during the searches gentlewomen were turned out of their beds in the middle of the night, in case anything of a subversive nature was concealed within the bedclothes.

When a priest named Cuthbert Mayne was seized at Golden in Cornwall in 1577, he was wearing an Agnus Dei round his neck. This was a little wax oval made from the remains of an Easter candle blessed at St Peter's by the Pope. At his trial, his Agnus Dei was one of the strong pieces of evidence against him.[12] Father Cuthbert Mayne's still-breathing body was hacked to pieces as the penalty for treason. For it was postulated by the English government that all Catholic priests were agents of a foreign power, either a spiritual one like the Pope (who had issued that Bull against their sovereign) or a temporal one like the King of Spain (who had attempted several invasions of their country).

With such an emphasis on patriotism, many Papists attempted to ensure their survival by taking particular trouble to demonstrate their loyalty to the Queen. One Cornish Arundell, in prison for his faith, announced boldly at the time of the Armada that he would support the Queen, not the Pope. Two Catholic peers, Lord Montague (Magdalen's husband) and Lord Dacre (her brother) attempted to make a subtle – and self-preserving – distinction. They declared that they had a duty to support the Pope if he came in peace, but would act against him in the field if he came in war. This division between the Pope's spiritual powers and his temporal powers might not be good theology in Rome, but the Holy City and the Holy Father were a long way off. Sir Thomas Tresham was another of the leading Catholics who were anxious to paint themselves as 'honest folks'. This Northamptonshire magnate spent many years in prison as a recusant. But, as he wrote in a petition of 1581 from the Fleet

prison, he did not wish 'to live one hour without her Majesty's grace, and favour'. He held 'nothing against her Majesty's person and dignity' – that is, her title to the crown – and, above all, nothing 'against my dear and native country'.[13]

How earnestly Henry Howard, who would be known to history as the Earl of Northampton, longed to be viewed as just such a patriot! It has to be said that the Howard/Norfolk family tree had some fearful blots on it where loyalty was concerned. His father, the poet Surrey, had been executed by Henry VIII for alleged royal pretensions when Howard was only six; his grandfather had been spared the axe only by the death of the King; his brother Thomas Duke of Norfolk had been executed by Elizabeth twenty-five years later for plotting the escape of Mary Queen of Scots. In Howard's opinion he had been unfairly demoted not once but twice from that high place 'by birth my due', thanks to the wrongdoings of others. That made him a slippery, ambitious man obsessed by his family heritage. But, although a Catholic by predilection – he thought it the natural religion for a gentleman – he was perfectly prepared to conform outwardly to the Anglican religion if he could worm his way back into royal favour.[14]

Howard was not generally trusted at court, and with good reason, since while he fawned on the Queen he maintained connections to the Spanish Ambassador in case the wind should blow in that direction. (Even the Spanish, who provided Howard with a secret income, did not exactly trust him: the Spanish Ambassador described him as being 'not as straight as he might seem in his speech'.) There is a story told of Howard's attendance at the Queen's chapel which sums up, albeit at the grandest level, the attitude of certain ambivalent Catholics. He could not, to be frank, endure the services there unless the Queen herself was to be present. Then Howard would hasten to arrive and ostentatiously 'continue at prayers'.[15]

A more edifying example of an Elizabethan Catholic who inhabited both worlds of sunshine and twilight is provided by William Byrd, described by Father William Weston as 'the very

famous English musician and organist'. Byrd's patrons were Henry Howard as well as the Catholic Earl of Worcester and another important peer with Catholic sympathies, the 8th Earl of Northumberland (Byrd taught Northumberland's daughter). Byrd was probably always a Catholic at heart, and his wife Juliana was indicted as a recusant as early as 1577.[16] But given his dulcet talent, as a musician – an organist – and a composer, he was able to maintain his position at court by adequate public conformity.

However, Byrd led simultaneously another secret life of music among his recusant friends, who included his neighbour Sir John Petre of Ingatestone Hall near Chelmsford (a house termed by Byrd in a dedication 'truly most friendly to me and mine'). Here and at other recusant centres, Byrd's Masses were sung. Given the occluded nature of these occasions, it was no coincidence that they were written for modest numbers, trios of sacred music, Masses for only four or five voices.

A young Frenchman happened to find himself at one of the country-house musical celebrations, a gathering to which numerous Papists of the gentry, both male and female, had come in their coaches. Byrd played the organ (as he had also done in the Queen's chapel). Father Henry Garnet, who had a 'rare and delightful' singing voice, may have been among others who took part. But the Frenchman was innocent of the significance of the occasion, 'not knowing them to be Jesuits on account of their disguises'.[17]

Howard and Byrd were in their different ways Church Papists, a term convenient for denoting those who attended Church of England services, as required by the state, but secretly considered themselves to be Catholics. (A definition of 1582 described them as 'Papists which can keep their consciences to themselves'.)[18] Some Church Papists also went to Mass in private. Others intended to be reconciled to the Catholic Church on their deathbed, when spiritual considerations would at the last predominate over more worldly ones. Not a few male Church Papists were heads of households who had an arrangement with their wives, whereby she would cling

to the Old Faith in private and might even raise her children in it, with the possible exception of the eldest son.

Dorothy Wiseman of Yorkshire, that stronghold of the Faith, was an outstanding example of a Catholic wife who stayed married to a Protestant.[19] She came from a pious Catholic background, her mother having been imprisoned as a recusant. However, Roger Lawson, whom Dorothy married in 1598 at the age of seventeen, was the Protestant heir to great estates. Dorothy did not let her husband's religion deter her: she immediately set about installing a priest clandestinely within her household so as to have Mass celebrated there at least once a month. Her husband was by profession a barrister and when he was away, Dorothy allowed in numbers of priests for the night to take refuge. 'Dexterously' she acquired Catholic servants.

She also acquired children, giving birth to at least fifteen. One became a Jesuit, one a Benedictine monk, one a Benedictine nun, and four followed the new order of the Institute of the Blessed Virgin Mary. With such an enormous family, it is comforting to read that her sweetness of disposition remained constant and converted some to Rome whom scholars could not win over 'by subtlety and learned argument'. Yet Roger Lawson himself converted to Catholicism only on his deathbed. This, given the devout nature of his children, was surely a last-minute release from a conformity which must have been practised for worldly reasons (including his own career as a barrister).

It is impossible to be sure of the numbers of similar marriages involved. But this counterfeit conformity – and there were other tricks – draws attention to one aspect of English Catholicism which was of crucial importance immediately after James' accession: the unreal perception of Catholic numbers in the minds of the government. How could the government know exactly who was and who was not a Papist at heart? A forbidden religion, like an ethnic minority whose existence and language are obliterated by government decree, does not advertise its numbers. In short, all recusants were Catholics, but not

all Catholics came out into the open, or were forced out into the open, as recusants.

In contrast to the vague numbers of Catholics, the names of actual recusants appeared, by definition, in government records.[20] Some five thousand names, for example, are listed as having paid fines between 1593 and 1600, thickest in Yorkshire and Lancashire but with other concentrations in the midlands and borders of Wales. When King James arrived in England, the Protestant bishops happily reported to him that, out of over 2 million Church of England communicants, there were only about 8,500 adult recusants.[21] This picture of a small, depressed, declining community took of course no account of the multitude of people – Church Papists – who would go to Mass if they could, the moment that conditions were more relaxed. There were the seeds of a dangerous misunderstanding here.

The estimable – but Catholic – lifestyle of Dorothy Wiseman draws attention to another aspect of English Catholicism which affected its entire fabric and frankly baffled the authorities. This was the comparatively privileged position of recusant women under the law. Ironically enough, this privilege arose out of a woman's absence of legal rights, based on the theory that she was inferior. The 'weaker vessel', as St Paul (translated in the Tyndale Bible) had memorably described the female, had no rights in common law. Any rights she might have had were assumed by her father before her marriage and her husband after it. Other categories – adult unmarried women and widows – somehow fell through the net of this theory: 'all of them are understood either married or to be married' (as we shall see, Catholic women of spirit took advantage of that too).[22] But this lack of rights, and thus of property, meant that it was extremely difficult to impose a fine upon a recusant woman – unless of course her husband was compelled to pay it.

But in a strange way this obvious solution was not deemed quite correct by the standards of the late sixteenth century.

What then was to happen to the propertyless female? One extremely old and extremely poor Catholic woman was condemned to be put in the stocks on market day in order to be displayed as 'a monster or an owl in daytime'. The local boys ran round her hissing 'a Papist, a Papist'. It can hardly have been a pleasant experience, and yet the poor old 'owl in daytime' was spared prison and fines, both exercises being evidently pointless. At the other end of the social scale, Queen Elizabeth had a low opinion of the female sex in general, counting herself as a 'Prince' or what would now be described as an honorary man. As a result, she did not believe that women should be the stuff of martyrs. In the time of Elizabeth, Parliament itself grappled with the awkward problem without ever quite coming to a hard and fast decision.[23]

As a result, the imposition of fines, as with so much to do with recusancy, largely depended on local administration. Here local vendettas might play their part in bringing about severe fines, but also local loyalties might cause them to be suspended. The husband with the 'costly' recusant wife who deducted the fine from her dress allowance may have been emulated elsewhere. Other husbands, wise in their generation, may have pretended to be henpecked by recusant wives to preserve their estates, even if the truth was somewhat different.

There were wives who did do time in prison for their refusal to attend services. Certain stout-hearted Catholic ladies in Yorkshire were offered a choice of twice-weekly Calvinist sermons in their homes or prison: they chose prison.[24] But even arrest was not necessarily the purgatory for women that it could have been, under the full rigour of the law. Sometimes women of quality were confined in the houses of aldermen, a form of house arrest. In other cases, a pious Catholic woman, confined in the same place as a number of Catholic priests, might find herself attending secret celebrations of the Mass with far greater ease than at home.

Home itself was not totally barred to a recusant wife during the term of her conviction. Contemporary opinion on a woman's role in society required that wives be released for

such conjugal duties as cooking the Christmas dinner or bearing children. A husband had the right to his helpmate's company – recusant or no recusant. The extent to which Catholic women took advantage of their alleged weakness is demonstrated by the angry exclamation of Robert Cecil's elder brother Lord Burghley. How 'pernicious' the female recusants were grown, he complained angrily in 1593.[25]

This sense of female immunity, due to fundamental female irresponsibility, meant that the Catholic women who ran large households had a vital role to play with regard to the priest-hood.[26] Within these households the priests might reside concealed as innocuous but necessary male servitors such as tutors, but their ultimate safety depended on the courage and wit of the lady of the house. It was an interesting role reversal. In all matters of the soul, these submissive ladies were utterly dependent for guidance on their spiritual pastors; but, when it came to the body, it was the pastors who were often utterly dependent for protection on the submissive ladies.

Furthermore, the idea that these ladies could – if absolutely necessary – defy their own husbands in the cause of religion was an extraordinarily subversive one. Conventional Catholic devotions of the time continued to hammer home the familiar theme of woman's weakness, suggesting – rather against the facts – that women were especially prone to heresy. But Catholic devotional writing and Catholic reality, in time of danger, were two different things. Father Henry Garnet, in *A Treatise of Christian Renunciation*, preached a very different message concerning recusant wives in dispute with Protestant husbands. It was in effect a revolutionary doctrine: 'your husbands over your souls have no authority, and over your bodies but a limited power', he wrote. The *Treatise* provided many helpful examples of families, in the days of the early Christian Church, broken asunder by religious differences.[27]

It was a point that the canny King James himself summed up. He pointed out that, where most women were concerned, their vows were 'ever subject to the controlment of their husbands'. Catholic women were however potentially different:

35

'their consciences must ever be commanded and overruled by their Romish God as it pleases him'.[28] To use a modern term, recusant women were empowered by the perils that all Catholics faced. (Just as women have throughout history been empowered in times of war when their services are seen to be vital to survival, only to lose it all when the national danger has passed.)

It was true that there were women, as there were men, who died for their Faith: three laywomen and fifty-eight laymen were put to death before 1603. In 1586 Margaret Clitheroe* endured the vile torment known as *peine forte et dure*. This (legal) punishment entailed being stripped before being, literally, pressed to death with weights to the value of seven or eight hundredweight because she would not plead either guilty or not guilty: 'Having made no offence, I need no trial.' Margaret Clitheroe may well have taken this extreme course in order to avoid betraying the whereabouts of priests, but by refusing to opt for trial by jury she also spared her servants and children the need to testify, which would have led to their own arrest (or to perjury). Her estates were not forfeit, since she had not been condemned for treason.[29]

But, for the vast majority of Catholic women, their role was both crucial and courageous – if not quite as testing as that of martyrdom. It was the women who taught the Catholic catechism to their servants and their children: mundane but crucial tasks which preserved the Faith. And as the zealous Jesuit missionaries began to come from abroad in the 1580s – to the horror of the government, which denounced them all as Spanish spies and responded with a special Act against them – the role of the female as nurturer and protector became all-important.

Two women stand out among the many who defied the government in defence of their priests. Both played a

---

* Canonised by the Catholic Church in 1970, along with other English martyrs including Anne Line, who was executed in London in 1601 for harbouring priests.

prominent part in the events surrounding the Powder Treason
(as the Gunpowder Plot was known to contemporaries). Eliza
Vaux was the sole head of a large Catholic household,
Harrowden Hall, in Northamptonshire, near Wellingborough.
She fell into one of those categories which allowed for a
certain independence of action on the part of women, for Eliza
was a widow, with a large family to organise and an estate to
guard for her eldest son, Edward. Her husband George Vaux,
heir to Lord Vaux of Harrowden, died in 1594 when she was
about thirty. But even before her marriage, as Eliza Roper,
daughter of Sir John Roper, she had demonstrated her spirit.*

The marriage had not pleased George's father Lord Vaux.
Above all, it did not please that great Catholic patriarch Sir
Thomas Tresham, a man who attempted to dominate everyone
within his far-reaching family circle. He certainly dominated
poor Lord Vaux, his close friend and brother-in-law.

Sir Thomas, despite his noble sufferings for the Catholic
Faith, was an intemperate man where inferiors including
women were concerned. He was disgusted to find that his
nephew George Vaux was about to make the classic mistake
(in late-sixteenth-century terms) of marrying for love. Sir
Thomas was determined to rip aside 'the guileful mask of
blinded fleshly affection' and put to an end what he called 'a
brainless match' to 'a creditless girl'.[30] Avuncular wrath lost out
to fleshly affection. George married his Eliza. It was, of course,
as such hotly contested matches often are, an extremely happy
union, with six children born in nine years, before George
Vaux's premature death.

Thereafter Eliza Vaux fell into an abyss of grief. She kept to
her room for a year, and for the rest of her life would not visit
the chamber in which her husband had actually died. It was
hardly surprising that she swore a vow against remarriage: 'As
she could not give God her virginity, she would offer him a
chaste life.' She also underwent a radical change of purpose.
Pursuing the interests of her eldest son and her other children

---

*The Ropers were connected to Sir Thomas More: they descended from William
Roper, whose brother married More's daughter Margaret.

was not to be enough for her, as it was for many women. She felt a call to protect and nurture the Catholic priesthood. As Father John Gerard wrote in his autobiography: 'I could see she was resolved, to fulfil as nearly as she could the role of Martha, and of other holy women who followed Christ and ministered to Him and His Apostles.'[31]

Eliza Vaux did not, however, lose her independence, still less her spirit. (After all, there is no reason to suppose that the Martha of the Bible was particularly submissive, given her outspoken complaint about her contemplative sister Mary.) With her large family in mind, and no doubt the interests of the hidden priests as well, Eliza successfully campaigned to get her ageing father-in-law to move to a smaller Vaux property for the last year of his life, leaving her with magnificent Harrowden. In no way did this successful petticoat dominance commend itself to Sir Thomas at neighbouring Rushton. In a postscript to a business letter, he made a bitter astrological joke, blaming Eliza for his old friend's failure to visit him: 'Commend me to the captive lord that dare not while the sign is in the dominating Virago to look upon poor Rushton.'[32]

It was a great advantage to Eliza's plans that extensive rebuilding at Harrowden, in the name of young Edward, who succeeded his grandfather as Lord Vaux in 1595, took place about this time.* A woman of 'talents of a high order', as Father Gerard described her, Eliza was able to have a kind of custom-built refuge constructed, since it was infinitely easier to conceal hiding-places at this point rather than insert them afterwards. So Eliza Vaux as the 'Dowager of Harrowden'†

* Harrowden Hall was rebuilt once more in the early eighteenth century. A Grade I scheduled building, it is now the site of the Wellingborough Golf Club; nevertheless within its walls lies at least one of the numerous late-sixteenth-century hiding-places. This is in the former stable block, now the caterers' flat, somewhere behind a thick wall at the top of a short staircase. If there are still hiding-places in the main house, which was largely refurbished in the 1970s, their location is unrecorded.

† Eliza Vaux was known as the 'Dowager of Harrowden' or the 'Dowager Lady Vaux' since she was the mother of the Lord Vaux of the day, although she never bore the actual title of Lady Vaux of Harrowden, given that her husband died before his father.

was able to maintain what has been described as 'a Jesuit college in the heart of England'.[33]

Unfortunately, even the most secure household could be penetrated by treachery. Harrowden, like other suspect Papist strongholds, was subjected to constant searches. On one occasion the ten-year-old Frances Burrows, Eliza's niece by marriage, showed that female spirit could start early, by defying the poursuivants (as the searchers were known). The priest was actually at Mass in an upper chamber when a great noise was heard in the house. Through the negligence, real or assumed, of the housekeeper, the poursuivants and constables had already entered with drawn swords. Frances ran down.

'Oh, put up your swords,' cried Frances, 'or else my mother will die, for she cannot endure to see a naked sword.' Frances pretended to fetch wine to revive her fainting mother, but actually gave the warning. On another occasion the intrepid Frances had a dagger put to her breast to make her reveal the secret hiding-places. When she declined, the poursuivant was sufficiently amused by the resolution of this small person – Frances was undersized for her age, and delicate – to offer a hundred pounds to buy her and present her to the Bishop of London: 'a maid of her courage should not be spoiled with Papistry'. The offer was declined. Frances was finally smuggled abroad to find, one hopes, greater tranquillity as a nun in Louvain.[34]

Father John Gerard, the dashing Jesuit priest who was Eliza Vaux's confessor, was one of those who had a narrow escape at Harrowden. Gerard's easy manner, his zest at hunting and hawking, his skill as a swordsman – the traditional pursuits of a gentleman – were all assets in covering up his true profession of priest. They also made him an attractive and persuasive proselytiser. Even his taste for 'very gallant ... apparel' was an advantage, since dress officially betokened the rank of the man. Criminals for example were wont to disguise themselves as gentlemen in order to have the same freedom of progress as the upper class – and of course priests were criminals according to the government. None of this had saved Gerard in 1594

when he was captured and held in the Tower of London, then severely tortured. But a dramatic escape from the Tower itself brought Gerard back into the clandestine Catholic community in time to exercise an important presence there at the accession of James I.

George Vaux's unmarried sister Anne* was the other member of the family who played a crucial part in the circumstances surrounding the Powder Treason. Mistress Anne Vaux was a 'maid' in the parlance of the time, but what we would call a spinster. She was born in 1562 and was therefore over forty at the time of James' accession: this spinsterhood was almost certainly a deliberate choice in that Anne Vaux held herself to be dedicated to the service of God. From the 1590s onward she saw this service as best performed by protecting and managing the affairs of Father Henry Garnet, the Superior of the Jesuits. Garnet's own sisters had gone abroad and became nuns at Louvain: this left Anne Vaux able to pose as his sister 'Mistress Perkins' in order to avoid awkward questioning about the priest's precise status. In private Garnet called Anne his 'sister in Christ'.

Father Henry Garnet had been born in 1555, some seven years before Anne, at Heanor in east Derbyshire. His family antecedents were not quite so glamorous as those of Father Gerard, but he did have a notable taste for scholarship. He was a brilliant linguist, expert in Hebrew, Greek and Latin. Having been educated at Winchester, he acted as a corrector in a legal press, and then went abroad, becoming for a while Professor of Hebrew at Rome. As a priest, his scholarly bent made him a natural devotee of theology and theological debate. He also had a great love of music: he had a 'rare and delightful' voice, already mentioned in connection with Byrd, he had an ability

---

* Anne Vaux was in fact the step-sister of George Vaux, her own mother having died as a result of her birth, after which Lord Vaux married Sir Thomas Tresham's sister Mary; but the term 'step' was never used during this period, nor the distinction made, at a time when so many women died young in childbirth leaving their babies to be brought up by their husband's next wife as their 'mother'.

to set songs extemporarily, and was skilled with instruments, especially the lute.[35]

Certainly Garnet was the opposite of a man of violence, believing with 'his usual modest cheerfulness', in the words of one who knew him well, that things were best settled by submission to the will of God. This applied to the reconversion of England to the Catholic Faith: political manoeuvres, let alone armed risings, were much less likely to be efficacious than prayers, the maintenance of Catholic rituals and the celebrations of Masses. Contemporaries also bore witness to Garnet's kindheartedness and compassion. He thought it his duty to attend (in disguise) the hideous public executions of his priests in order to administer the last rites to them if he could. Such ordeals filled this sensitive and scrupulous man with apprehension: would he be able to act so bravely if and when his own turn came?

Anne's father Lord Vaux once reflected wistfully: 'St Paul admonisheth that women should learn in silence and subjection: in their houses they themselves should learn by demanding of their husbands; who doth not permit them to teach in their presence, but to be silent.' But Anne Vaux (like her widowed sister-in-law Eliza) did not have a husband from whom to learn. Buoyed up by her Faith, in the words of Father Henry Garnet, 'this brave Virgo became a veritable Virago'.[36]

Father Garnet, unlike Sir Thomas Tresham, meant the word 'virago' as a compliment. Nevertheless, for all her piety, Anne did, like Eliza, take on Sir Thomas himself, suing him in the Court of Wards as a trustee for her marriage portion. Since she had not married and had no intention of doing so, it was a bold gesture undoubtedly provoked by her desperate need of funds to help the priests. Sir Thomas was once again furious and this time managed to fight back by forcing Anne Vaux to come to Rushton, to beg for the money personally. If she showed herself 'stomachful' (uppish), she still would not receive it. Anne was in her turn extremely angry. Hauling along her widowed sister Eleanor Brooksby (equally pious but much

more timid), Anne Vaux indulged in 'verbal combat' with Sir Thomas in his own house from noon until four in the afternoon, stopping him from eating his dinner. She got her money.[37]

As a single woman with a handsome fortune at her disposal and a convenient widowed sister to provide domestic respectability, Anne was able to play a crucial part in renting houses in which Jesuits might gather in safety. The Jesuit rule required priests to meet at least once a year – hopefully twice – in order to give an account of their conscience to their Superior and renew their vows. Such a congruence of Jesuits inevitably presented dangers which single priests, operating alone, did not face. For this purpose Anne Vaux rented Baddesley Clinton in Warwickshire from the antiquarian Henry Ferrers.

Baddesley Clinton was a secluded early Tudor mansion, with a moat, set amid woods about a hundred miles from London. The situation was perfect for the purposes of retreat and Anne immediately set about having a talented lay brother called Nicholas Owen (who will play an important part in this story) devise enough hiding-places to conceal twelve or more priests.* By using the moat and the levels of a sewer, together with secret turret trapdoors and stairways, Owen was able to ensure that Father Garnet and others survived a notorious search in 1591. They stood for four hours, half immersed in water. But they were not captured.

Not all the houses Anne Vaux and Eleanor Brooksby occupied were in the midlands. White Webbs, rented in 1600 on behalf of Father Garnet, was deep in Enfield Chase, on the borders of Hertfordshire and Essex. This was another 'spacious house' – but nearer to London – which could be honeycombed with escape routes and refuges. And of course not every visitor to White Webbs would actually be a priest. There would also be members of the vast Catholic cousinage to which Anne Vaux belonged by birth.

---

* Baddesley Clinton, now a National Trust property, still retains its air of romantic mystery; and the hiding-places so skilfully constructed by Nicholas Owen can still be inspected.

In this small world, which for security's sake perpetuated itself by intermarriage, it is perhaps simplest to state that almost everyone was related to almost everyone else. This was certainly true of Anne Vaux, with a Throckmorton grand-mother as well as a Tresham step-mother. Thus visitors to White Webbs who were her relatives included the two first cousins, children of Throckmorton sisters, Robert Catesby and Francis Tresham. They were respectively ten and six years younger than Anne and they regarded her with that affection which kindly maiden-aunt figures are inclined to inspire in their juniors.

It would be some years before the interweaving in time and place of these rash Elizabethan gallants with the forbidden English Jesuits would prove to have terrible consequences for the latter. In the meantime, it was understandable that with such women as Eliza and Anne Vaux at work, Father Robert Persons should conclude that the continuance of the Faith in England was due to the courage of its women.

So the sombre picture of ruthless persecution painted by Father Weston was not in fact unrelieved by light. First, there was the way in which Catholics managed to survive, their Faith more or less intact, by leading a kind of schizophrenic exis-tence. Secondly, while there were 'honest' Papists in King James' phrase, there were also brave priests and their coura-geous helpers, often female.

There was hope for the future, not only practical hope but also spiritual hope which Robert Southwell, the Jesuit put to death (after torture) in 1595, described in his poem *The Burning Babe*:[38]

> As I in hoary winter's night stood shivering in
>   the snow
> Surprised I was with sudden heat which made my
>   heart to glow.

In the last year of Queen Elizabeth's life, it began to be whispered among English Catholics that King James had

already made them promises of genuine toleration to be redeemed when and if he came to the throne.

Diversity of Opinions

I will never allow in my conscience that the blood of
any man shall be shed for diversity of opinions in
religion...

KING JAMES VI
to Robert Cecil

What, if anything, did King James, while in Scotland,
promise to the Catholics in England? The question is
of crucial importance in understanding the Powder
Treason. And there is a supplementary question: if such
promises were made, were they verbal or written?
Unfortunately, the various personalities involved complicate
rather than simplify the issue: none of them is particularly
satisfactory from the point of view of honest record.

There was King James' own way with hints, protestations
and the like – the superb diplomatic skill by which he raised
but did not satisfy religious hopes. His dealings with the
Papacy were certainly not sincere since, whatever his feelings
about Rome as the historic Mother Church, King James never
had any plans to become a Catholic. The granting of toleration
for other Catholics was rather different, and makes estimating
the King's sincerity a much subtler problem.

In the course of his secret correspondence with Robert
Cecil, which began in the spring of 1601, King James gave vent
to a number of opinions on the subject, although we should
bear in mind that these letters, written and received without
the old Queen's knowledge, were emphatically not destined for

publication, and nor were they dated. For example, on one occasion he saw fit to warn 'my dearest and trusty 10' as Cecil was known in their private code, of 'the daily increase that I hear of popery in England'. King James, who enjoyed giving a good lecture, ended his warning on a kindly if condescending note. He admitted that it might be argued that Cecil (actually in England) knew all this much better than James (in Scotland) did: 'yet it is a true old saying, that another man will better see a man's game than the player himself can do'.[1]

Cecil responded with an interesting account of his personal credo. Much as he loathed the Catholic priests and the peril they represented – 'I condemn their doctrine, I detest their conversation' – nevertheless he confessed that he shrank to see them 'die by dozens' when 'at the last gasp' they came 'so near loyalty'. (Cecil's compassion, however, specifically excluded the Jesuits, whom he designated 'that generation of vipers' trading in 'the blood and crowns of Princes'.) On another occasion James similarly dissociated himself from the shedding of blood. And where the priests were concerned, he believed that exile was a better solution than execution: rather than have their heads separated from their bodies 'I would be glad to have both their heads and their bodies separated from this whole island and transported beyond seas.'[2]

This letter from King James probably comes near to expressing what he actually felt on the subject: 'I will never allow in my conscience that the blood of any man shall be shed for diversity of opinions in religion, but I should be sorry that Catholics should so multiply as they might be able to practise their old principles upon us.' Although he would never agree that men should die for 'errors in faith', a pronounced rise in the numbers of Catholics was another matter. Such a Catholic increase would have serious consequences 'as by continual multiplication they [the Catholics] might at last become master'.[3]

When King James wrote these words, he suggested at the least that English Catholics might one day enjoy the tolerated minority status of the Protestant Huguenots in France. Yet

This engraving shows eight of the thirteen conspirators: missing are Digby, Keyes, Rookwood and Tresham.

Both Ben Jonson and William Shakespeare had connections to Catholics on the periphery of the Gunpowder Plot; *Macbeth* contains allusions to the fate of the 'equivocating' Jesuit, Henry Garnet.

Henry Percy, 9th Earl of Northumberland, by Van Dyck: although Northumberland's actual involvement in the plot remains controversial, he was fined heavily and sentenced to prolonged imprisonment as a result.

Robert Cecil, 1st Earl of Salisbury, attributed to John de Critz: equipped with a prodigious intellect, and a capacity for hard work, Salisbury was short and physically twisted at a time when the outer man was often thought to be a key to his inner nature.

Sir Everard Digby: the darling of the court for his handsome looks and sweetness of character, Digby's fate caused universal consternation even among those who condemned him.

Two contrasted signatures by Thomas Wintour: one indubitably his, in the habitual form in which he signed his name; the other, using a different spelling, on his so-called 'Confession', possibly forged by the government.

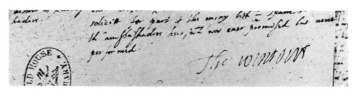

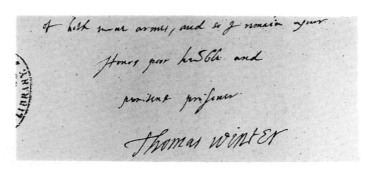

from persecution for religious reasons: 'I would be sorry to punish their bodies for the error of their minds.' But in another sense the speech – by totally discarding those promises he was supposed to have made – could only cause the most frightful dismay among his Catholic subjects.

It was all very well to be told that the King would be a friend to them so long as they conducted themselves as good subjects. But what were they to make of the stern sentiments which followed? The Papists were admonished not to presume too much upon the King's leniency. They should not think it lawful for them 'daily to increase their number and strength in this Kingdom', whereby, if not in his time, at least in the time of his successors, 'they might be in hope to erect their Religion again'. The King was emphatic on this point: there was to be absolutely no increase or 'growing' of their religion, otherwise he would consider that he had betrayed himself and his own conscience. Then the King in his speech addressed the Protestant bishops and urged them henceforward to be more 'careful, vigilant, and diligent than you have been to win souls to God...where you have been in any way sluggish before, now waken yourselves up again with a new diligence in this point...'

It was the firm opinion of Father Gerard in his *Narrative* that this directive by the King was responsible for the renewed persecution of the Catholics which followed. The Puritans were bound to bay for Catholic blood, or at any rate for Catholic penalties. Nevertheless the King could easily have stayed their fury by saying that he would consider the matter, instead of confirming the most rigorous laws and statutes of the previous reign. In short, 'all hopes were foiled on which Catholics did build their comforts'. Father Tesimond took the same line. He also drew attention to the King's brutal denial of those very promises on which the Catholics had built their expectations. In Tesimond's words, the King 'protested most vehemently that he would take it as an extreme insult if anyone imagined that either then or at any time in the past, he had entertained the slightest intention of tolerating their religion'.[14]

In 1591 John Florio had written a poem on the 'Ten Pains of Death'. These included 'To serve well and not to please' and 'To stand at the door that none will open'.[15] These two pains the Catholics could now claim that they were suffering, the last one especially agonising since it had been believed now for several years that the door of toleration was actually going to open.

Both Father Tesimond and Father Gerard, in their accounts, used equestrian metaphors, perhaps elicited by the royal mania for hunting, to illustrate the effects of the King's change of heart. Father Tesimond saw the (Protestant) horse of St George as being quickened in its intolerant pace by the King's pressure: 'These words dug spurs into the steed he was coursing and gave unbounded delight to Bishops and Puritans alike,' he wrote. Father Gerard, on the other hand, saw the pricks as being administered to the Catholics themselves. It was generally thought by wise men, he wrote, that these events and those of a repressive nature which followed were 'the spurs' that set the conspirators 'upon that furious and fiery course which they afterwards fell into'.[16]

Both priests could justify the sharp image. On 27 March, a week after the King's speech, Lord Sheffield told Cecil with relish about 900 recusants, new names and old, who had been brought before the assizes at Normanby in Yorkshire. There would have been more but for the slackness of the Archbishop. Sheffield's glee at being empowered to quell a growing menace is understandable from his own (strongly Protestant) point of view. The accounts of recusants in Yorkshire for this period do show that over a quarter of those accused had broken the law only since the accession of King James. On 24 April a bill was introduced into the House of Commons to class all Catholics as outlaws. It was also 'about this time' – late April – that according to Lord Chief Justice Popham the Gunpowder Plot was 'set on foot as the only means to relieve that [Catholic] party'.[17] Both sides had indeed been spurred forward.

The prince of darkness at the centre of the Gunpowder Plot

was Robert Catesby, not Guy Fawkes. A historical accident of discovery led, as we shall see, to Guido carrying the popular odium for the conspiracy down the ages. But Guido, although heavily involved in the action, was not at the heart of the strategy. He was the outsider in the band. With the single exception of Fawkes, the plotters formed a tight-knit circle of interlocking relationships which was a vital protective element in their dangerous and secret game. And it was Catesby who was 'the first inventor and the chiefest furtherer' of that game.[18]

Catesby as a harbinger (if not a prince) of darkness would be the government's own image in the future when he was termed 'a second Phaeton'.[19] Phaeton, son of Phoebus Apollo, was a mythical bringer of night, who by upsetting his chariot had threatened to parch and blacken the whole world until Zeus destroyed him with a thunderbolt. Shakespeare, in a play written towards the end of the previous reign, had Juliet call for Phaeton the 'waggoner' to whip up his fiery-footed steeds towards the west 'And bring in cloudy night immediately' – the night which would bring Romeo to her. But the Catesby of 1604 was to his contemporaries more Phoebus Apollo than Phaeton, more shining sun god than destructive charioteer.

Among his family and friends, including Catholic priests and devout ladies, 'Robin' Catesby was adored. To Catesby's contemporary Lord Monteagle (who was married to his first cousin, Elizabeth Tresham), he was 'my loving kinsman ... dear Robin' whose person was 'the only sun that must ripen our harvest'.[20] Charm and a special kind of personal radiance are qualities notoriously hard to transmit across the ages, to societies with very different preoccupations and values. And yet such qualities in individuals may play just as important a part in defining the course of history as more visibly enduring talents.* Certainly, it is impossible to understand the course of the Powder Treason from now on unless one takes into account the magnetism of Robert Catesby.

---

* A comparison might be made to Adam von Trott, one of the plotters to blow up Hitler in 1944, who also exercised an extraordinary personal influence on his contemporaries.

Father Tesimond, writing in the wake of the terrible retribution which Catesby had brought down upon the whole Catholic world, still dwelt nostalgically upon his erstwhile friend, because of the love that he inspired as well as his generosity and sweetness. Obviously Catesby's handsome appearance was part of his glamour. He was six foot tall and 'more than ordinarily well proportioned', bearing himself splendidly.[21] In short, for many people this fine figure of a man represented the contemporary male ideal.

Robert Catesby was probably born at Lapworth in Warwickshire. That was the main place of residence of his father, Sir William Catesby, although he also had properties around Ashby St Ledgers, in Northamptonshire. The Catesbys had a long pedigree, and one ancestor had already made his mark on English memories. Robert was sixth in descent from that Sir William Catesby who was the 'Cat' in the satirical rhyme constructed round the three supporters of Richard III (whose crest was a hog or boar):

> The Cat, the Rat and Lovell our Dog
> Rule all England under the Hog.

But the 'Cat' had backed the wrong side and was put to death following Richard's defeat at Bosworth Field.

Robert's father could also be said to have backed the wrong side since he suffered long imprisonment for his Catholic Faith. He married Anne Throckmorton from Coughton, also in Warwickshire, to whom he was already connected by his mother's second marriage to a Throckmorton. There were the usual liberal helpings of recusant blood on both sides, including Vaux. But the crucial link, from the point of view of their son Robert, was the Tresham one. It has already been mentioned that Catesby and the Wintour brothers were related; and Tom Wintour in particular bore 'a great love' for his cousin 'Robin'. But Robin and Francis Tresham, as the sons of two sisters, were even closer. Quite apart from other consanguinities, they had been brought up from childhood together.[22]

On the one hand this brought Robin into the orbit of his authoritarian but generous uncle Sir Thomas Tresham, who had helped bail him out of the Essex crisis in 1601; it also emphasised his closeness to members of the Vaux family such as Anne. On the other hand, it put the weaker, less stable Francis under the influence of the magnetic Robin. As with the Wintour brothers, where Robert followed his younger brother Thomas, it was generally agreed that Francis Tresham was dominated by Robin Catesby rather than the other way around. Since Francis was several years older than his cousin, this pattern, inculcated in childhood, would seem to be the first example of Robin Catesby's natural ability to command.

Catesby should have been a rich man. The fact that by 1604 he was a poor one was due to his own recklessness at the time of the Essex conspiracy. In youth he had made all the right moves (or they had been made for him). After early life in Warwickshire he may have been educated for a while at Douai in the Netherlands, the new English Jesuit College for young Catholic men. But he certainly spent time at Oxford University, at Gloucester Hall (now Worcester College). He left, however, without taking his degree, presumably in order to avoid swearing the Oath of Supremacy.[23]

At this point, however, whatever his earlier ambivalence, Catesby moved resolutely down the worldly path. At the age of nineteen, he married a wealthy girl from a Protestant family, Catherine Leigh of Stoneleigh in Warwickshire. At one stroke he liberated himself in official eyes from the recusant taint and also secured her prodigious dowry (by contemporary standards) of two thousand pounds a year. By Catherine, Catesby had two sons. William died in infancy while the other, Robert, was baptised in November 1595 in the Protestant church at Chastleton, Oxfordshire. Here the young Catesbys lived on a property inherited from his grandmother.[24]

Fifteen-ninety-eight was a crucial year of change for Catesby. His father died, leaving his mother with the Ashby St Ledgers properties for her lifetime, while Robin continued to live at Chastleton. Then Catesby's young Protestant wife Catherine also died after only six years of marriage. To this loss has been attributed Catesby's return to the Catholicism of his forefathers: to the Church in its fanatical form.[25] Given the timing, it seems a reasonable supposition, even if the depths of despair he experienced at the tragedy (or guilt at his own earlier lapse into apparent Protestantism) cannot be known. For the rest of his short, terrifyingly hazardous life, Robin Catesby was noted for his religious dedication.

His involvement with Essex, in which Catesby publicly wielded his sword in the vain hope of ameliorating the Catholic lot, resulted in a hefty fine of four thousand marks (approximately three thousand pounds). Sir Thomas Tresham did assist, but Robin Catesby himself was obliged to sell Chastleton to a local wool merchant from Witney called Jones. His name had been noted as a rebel, and what was more a Catholic rebel. As a result, Robin Catesby was probably among those recusants briefly imprisoned in advance of the death of Queen Elizabeth. In the new reign, Catesby's country home was with his widowed mother at Ashby St Ledgers, a property in which he had more than a passing interest since it would revert to him on her death.*

By April 1604, Catesby's mentality was that of the crusader who does not hesitate to employ the sword in the cause of values which he considers are spiritual. At the same time, his was not the straightforward unexamined piety of, for example, the soldier Guy Fawkes. Catesby had a passion for theology, for testing his actions and arguments against the precepts of the Church rather than acting first and hoping for justification afterwards. He was a man who wanted to go to work – destructive work – with his eyes open to the moral consequences of what he was doing. How ironic, then, that it was exactly this honourable analytical trait of Catesby's which

---

* This makes sense of the traditional claim that Catesby and others plotted the Powder Treason in the half-timbered Tudor gatehouse which leads to the great mellow brick pile which is Ashby St Ledgers itself (still in private hands). The pretty twelfth-century church beside it, with its Catesby brasses, can however be visited. Chastleton in Oxfordshire is now National Trust property.

would cause the most damage to the English priesthood in the whole sad saga of the Gunpowder Plot.

Father Thomas Strange was a Jesuit who came back to England in 1603 and fell under Catesby's spell at the house of Anne Vaux. He was an affable fellow, in his late twenties, who had been born in Gloucestershire, and liked 'using the tennis court and sometime having music in his lodging', gentlemanly tastes which made it easy for a priest to pass in polite society without discovery. He began writing a religious manual, 'a compendium of all the sciences', on Palm Sunday (1 April) 1604 and finished it appropriately enough on 23 May, the eve of the feast of St Robert. It was dedicated to Catesby, his 'most distinguished and beloved' friend: *vir ornatissime atque charissime.*[26] The priest would have been horrified if he had known the schemes which were beginning to obsess his distinguished and beloved friend at roughly the same period and as a result of which the affable Father Strange would be utterly ruined in mind and body.

Catesby, the second Phaeton, bringer of darkness, was on his way.

PART THREE

That Furious and Fiery Course

These things were the spurs that set those gentlemen upon that furious and fiery course which they afterwards fell into.

FATHER JOHN GERARD
A Narrative of the Gunpowder Plot

CHAPTER SEVEN

So Sharp a Remedy

He [Catesby] told me the nature of the disease
required so sharp a remedy, and asked me if I would
give my consent. I told him Yes, in this or what else
soever, if he resolved upon it, I would venture my
life...

Confession of Thomas Wintour, 1605

Sunday 20 May 1604 was the fateful date. On this day a
meeting was held between Robin Catesby, Tom Wintour,
Jack Wright, Thomas Percy and Guido Fawkes. Although
the band of conspirators would eventually amount to an ill-
omened thirteen, these five were regarded as the prime movers
of the plot that followed, with Catesby as their inspirational
leader and Wintour as adjutant. This meeting, which kick-
started the Powder Treason into life, was held at an inn called
the Duck and Drake, in the fashionable Strand district, where
Tom Wintour stayed when he was in London.

The background to this meeting is as follows.*[1] Catesby first
sent for Wintour, who was in Worcestershire with his brother
Robert, in late February. Tom Wintour was however ill, and
could not at first answer Catesby's summons. When he did
arrive at Catesby's house in Lambeth he found his cousin

---

* This narrative is pieced together from the various contemporary accounts,
although there is scarcely any piece of surviving evidence concerning the
Gunpowder Plot which has not, by one authority or another, been considered
dubious. This is hardly surprising in an episode which included interrogation after
torture, as well as government revisionism after the event. As for the Plotters,
obviously they did not always tell the truth, whether to protect themselves, their
associates or their families.

together with the swordsman Jack Wright: he may have wished he had stayed at secluded tranquil Huddington instead of answering Catesby's summons.

The proposition put by Catesby was simple and it was blood-curdling. A scheme would be devised to blow up 'the Parliament House with gunpowder' in order to destroy the King and his existing government. Catesby justified his choice of Parliament for this deliberate holocaust with equally shocking simplicity. 'In that place', he said, 'have they done us all the mischief'; perhaps God had designed that place for their punishment.

When he first heard of Catesby's deadly plan, which he called 'a stroke at the root', Wintour demurred. If the stroke succeeded it would certainly bring about 'new alterations' in religion, but, if it failed, the scandal surrounding Catholicism would be so great in England that not only their enemies but also their friends would with good reason condemn them. This was an eminently sensible judgement. Unfortunately Wintour did not hold to it. The Catesby spell continued to work on him. Wintour was won over.

When Catesby told his cousin that 'the nature of the disease required so sharp a remedy' and asked Wintour if he would give his consent, Wintour agreed. 'I told him Yes, in this or what else soever, if he resolved upon it, I would venture my life ...'

Catesby still had not quite given up on the idea of foreign help, that pipedream which had obsessed the English Catholics for so long. In order to leave 'no peaceable and quiet way untried' Tom went back to the continent yet again, where the Constable of Castile was holding court before sailing for England. The Constable was, as it happened, a great deal more interested in the affairs of Flanders than in those of the Anglo-Spanish Treaty he was supposed to be concluding (he would not actually arrive in England until August). When the Constable did meet Wintour, he was friendly rather than forthcoming. As for Hugh Owen and Sir William Stanley, they poured cold water on the idea of Spain providing assistance, or for that matter the Archdukes ruling Flanders, Albert and Isabella: 'all these parts were so desirous of peace with England'.²

But Owen did provide the necessary introduction to Guido Fawkes. Guido's name had already been supplied by Catesby as 'a confidant [discreet] gentleman' suitable for their business, but Wintour had evidently not yet encountered him. Fawkes' name could have been mentioned to Catesby by anyone in recusant circles, including his schoolfellow, Catesby's friend and ally, Jack Wright; he would have been recommended as a staunch and courageous soldier. Although the English government, who feared and detested Hugh Owen, tried to pretend later that he had been directly involved in the Plot, there was at this point no plot. Owen, an expert on the Flanders scene after so many years, simply put Wintour in touch with Fawkes; Stanley (who had been Fawkes' superior) also commended him. An advantage of introducing Guido into this secret plot was that, while his name was known, his face was not, as he had not been in England for many years.

Tom Wintour's first encounter with Guido was the satisfactory part of his trip abroad. They were after all two people of a similar outlook, contemporaries, men of action, who had both experienced first hand the dilatoriness of the Spanish and the empty nature of their promises. Wintour told Guido that if the peace with Spain really gave no assistance to the beleaguered Catholics, 'we were upon a resolution to do somewhat in England', although as yet there were no firm plans. Finally the two men sailed back together, landing on or about 25 April.³ Together they went to find Catesby in his Lambeth lodging, on the south bank of the river. Wintour broke the news that, although the Constable had spoken 'good words', Wintour very much doubted whether his deeds would match them. In this way, Catesby could consider himself thrown back on his original, radically violent plan. Four conspirators were now in place.

The fifth member of the inner caucus, Thomas Percy, joined them a few weeks afterwards. Percy, like Guido, was immediately attracted by the idea of taking some action in England itself. Percy was a vigorous character and he had shown already in Scotland his wish to be part of the solution to his co-religionists' woes. He was also working for Northumberland, 'one of the great Peers of the kingdom' as Tassis described him.[4] Furthermore, there was a family connection to bind him to the conspirators: not only was Percy Jack Wright's brother-in-law but it seems that his young daughter (by Martha Wright) had been betrothed to Robert Catesby's eight-year-old son the previous year.

'Shall we always, gentlemen, talk and never do anything?' were Percy's first words. Whatever his moral failings as an individual, he spoke for so many in that frustrated cry. It was in this way that the 20 May meeting at the Duck and Drake was convened. All the Plotters – Catesby, Wintour, Wright, Guido and Percy – swore an oath of secrecy upon a prayer book in a room 'where no other body was'. Afterwards, since it was a Sunday, Father John Gerard celebrated Mass in another room, in ignorance of what had taken place. The five men all took the Sacrament of Holy Communion.

At the time this Mass merely seemed like a silent personal endorsement of what had been decided earlier. Guido, Catesby and Wintour were, of course, conspicuous by the frequency with which they went to the Sacraments, at a time when recourse to them was not necessarily made all that often. Father Gerard and Catesby were friends. One of their links was Eliza Vaux, the Dowager of Harrowden Hall, who was the priest's chief protector in the country and an important part of Catesby's family network, Catesby himself being a frequent visitor to Harrowden. The presence of Catesby and his companions at the Mass was not exceptional, nor, for that matter, was Father Gerard's presence in London.

London, said to be the largest city in Europe, was at this date a vast sprawling conurbation of teeming tenements and slums, as well as palaces and mansions. The population had swollen so alarmingly in the course of the previous century that King James himself observed that 'soon London will be all England'. Under the circumstances, recusants often stood a better chance of preserving their anonymity here among the 'dark dens for every mischief worker' (including priests) than in the isolated state of a country house, which gave servants the chance of prolonged inspection leading to betrayal.[5] But there was no question of Father Gerard being let in to the secret of the oath which had just been sworn.

Much later the coincidence of the oath and the Mass, including the taking of the Sacrament, would become a big stick with which the government beat the hated English Jesuits. Lancelot Andrewes, in an official sermon on the subject, described how the plot was 'undertaken with a holy Oath, bound with the holy Sacrament'. It was a favourite slur that Catholic confessors gave absolution for crimes in advance, thus using their sacramental authority to legitimise a crime. In the case of Father Gerard it was suggested that he had purposefully sanctified the enterprise of destruction which lay ahead. But Tom Wintour was quite clear in his confession that the priest knew nothing. Even Guido, while admitting to the oath and receiving the Sacrament upon it, 'withal he added that the priest who gave him the sacrament knew nothing of it'. In a subsequent examination, Guido specifically exculpated Gerard.[6] The only conspirator who implicated the Jesuits at his interrogation was Catesby's wretched servant Thomas Bates, who, being small fry, had some expectation of saving himself if he gave the government what they wanted: 'the considerable hope of life which they held before him'. Even Bates retracted his charge on the eve of his death, when he was conscious that he was about to appear before what Father Gerard called 'that dreadful tribunal' of God's own judgement.[7]

Eliza Vaux declared eloquently that she would pawn her whole estate – 'yea, and her life also' – in order to answer for Father Gerard's innocence.[8] She was of course quite as passionately partisan as the government. More cogent therefore is the surviving correspondence of the Jesuits with Rome in the summer of 1604. The Plotters had decided on 'so sharp a remedy', but the English Jesuits were in contrast manifestly holding on to their previous hopes of liberalisation in the wake of the Anglo-Spanish Treaty. As Father Garnet expressed it, in the high summer of 1604 'no one with any prudence or judgement' found the idea of peace 'displeasing'. But he added in cipher that, if the expected moves for toleration did not go well, it might be impossible to keep some of the Catholics quiet.[9]

Father Garnet spent a great deal of 1604 in travels throughout England which have been recorded (others of his peregrinations remain unknown to this day because of the constant need for secrecy). At Easter, for example, he was reported to have said Mass at Twigmoor, the house of Jack Wright in Lincolnshire, which was a notorious haunt of seminarians. In the following November, he was at White Webbs, with Anne Vaux as hostess, when the Jesuits made their annual renewal of their vows on the Feast of the Presentation of Our Lady. This may have been the musical occasion cited earlier, witnessed by a Frenchman, when Father Garnet, with his fine voice, sang and William Byrd played. The Jesuit Superior was therefore all too well qualified to make his anxious prediction about the instability of certain lay people. 'The Pope must command all Catholics not to make a move,' Father Garnet pleaded to his Superior in Rome.[10] It was a point to which he would return with increasing desperation over the next twelve months.

Although still without a detailed plan, one of the Plotters now received a lucky promotion. On 9 June Thomas Percy was appointed a Gentleman Pensioner – one of fifty special bodyguards – by his kinsman and patron the Earl of Northumberland, who commanded them.[11] This meant that Percy had an unassailable reason to establish himself with a London base. The conspirators were moving closer to some kind of proper organisation. A small dwelling in the precincts of Westminster – more of an apartment than a house – was chosen.* In May 1604 the house belonged to John Whynniard, by right of his office as Keeper of the King's Wardrobe, but it was leased to a distinguished recusant, the antiquarian Henry

---

* The topography of this dwelling and that of 'the Parliament House' itself will be considered later.

Ferrers, who owned Baddesley Clinton, that house in Warwickshire where Anne Vaux had formerly entertained the Jesuits. Here Guido was installed as a kind of caretaker, passing himself off as one John Johnson, servant to Thomas Percy.

Gentlemen Pensioners were supposed, as a matter of the law, to swear the Oath of Supremacy, which sincere Catholics found so uncomfortable to take because, by implication, it denied the spiritual authority of the Pope. But Lord Northumberland did not impose the oath upon his cousin Percy, whom he supposed to be a Catholic. It was a gesture, rather like Father Gerard's coincidental celebration of Mass, which was to have most unfortunate consequences for Northumberland himself. In the hectic atmosphere of post-Plot accusations, the omission, as we shall see, was construed in a sinister light. But in the summer of 1604, when the Plot was in its very earliest stages, Northumberland was doing no more than behaving in his usual generous manner towards Percy.

As that summer wore on, events did nothing to persuade the conspirators to abandon their lethal project. Until Parliament was formally adjourned on 7 July, to meet again on 7 February 1605, anti-Catholic legislation continued to go through. Priests were put to death including Father John Sugar, who, with his servant Robert Grissold, was executed at Lancaster shortly after the adjournment of Parliament. The priest died heroically, confident of his soul's salvation as his body was cut into pieces. Pointing to the sun he remarked, 'I shall shortly be above yon fellow,' and later, 'I shall have a sharp dinner, yet I trust in Jesus Christ I shall have a most sweet supper.'[12]

The persecution was not likely to abate, for in mid-September King James issued a commission to Lord Ellesmere to preside over a committee of Privy Councillors 'to extermi-nate' Jesuits, other priests and 'divers other corrupt persons employed under the colour of religion' to withdraw his subjects from their allegiance. As to the laymen, by the end of the year the recusant fines were back in full force, and would shortly net three thousand pounds. 'Ancient' recusants complained of the new severity, but without success. It may well be that arrears of the fines already remitted were also sought, bringing an additional hardship (and injustice). Although the point has been debated, at least one leading recusant, Sir Thomas Tresham, was charged with paying arrears. His accounts reveal that the charge was made, following a year of paying nothing, thanks to the 'relief' of 1603. In fact the so-called relief cost Sir Thomas nearly £200 in bribes; that was the amount which he had dispensed that summer as a sweetener, in order to secure 'the pardon concerning recusancy money' – of which £120 had gone to Sir Edward Coke.[13]

Even the long-awaited visit of the Constable of Castile in August was nothing more than a ceremonial interlude of banquets and processions which left behind an Anglo-Spanish Treaty – but absolutely no promise of toleration. Papists who listened to this magnificent peace being proclaimed at Cheapside by a herald on 19 August may have wondered at the secret agenda which lay behind it. But there was none. It was simply the conclusion of years of fighting between nations, a conclusion which suited the great men concerned. Owen and Stanley in Flanders had been right when they warned Tom Wintour that the peace was too precious to all parties to be disturbed by any other enterprise.

The conspirators (with the exception of Guido) left London some time after their initial pact. The adjournment of the government from the targeted 'Parliament House' gave them, as they thought, until early February to get their plans in place. They went to the country, to those various family houses which made up a stately map of recusancy. They left, having decided on a course of action which would cause them, in the late twentieth century, to be described as terrorists. The words terrorist and terrorism were not then in use. Nevertheless the Gunpowder Plot does satisfy a modern definition of terrorism: 'the weapon of the weak, pretending to be strong'.[14]

Like the Irish men and women involved in the Dublin upris-
ing of 1916, they saw themselves as a small band, whose
actions would lead to great change.* The Plotters also believed
that they had left no peaceable and quiet way untried, as
Catesby put it to Wintour. In face of continuous persecution,
theirs was the violence of last resort. Furthermore, they took
on board what Bakunin, the nineteenth-century Russian anarchist, would call 'the propaganda of the deed'.† That is to say,
the blowing up of Parliament by gunpowder was to be a deliberately sensational and indeed outrageous action. In this way
not only the government but the outside world would be
alerted to sufferings which were in themselves outrageous.

Of course Elizabethan and Jacobean state justice itself was
conducted along these same lines. When the public gazed with
morbid fascination at the disembowelment of living Catholic
priests, they were supposed to draw the conclusion that the
victims must have deserved such cruel treatment. In other
words, the crime which *had* taken place must have fitted the
appalling punishment which *was* taking place. Catesby's
showman instinct to blow up the place where all the mischief
had taken place had something of the same propagandist logic.

Violent opposition in the historical period under consideration was conducted not by terrorism but by tyrannicide, both
methods being justified by their proponents by doctrines of the
right to resistance. The demerits (or merits) of tyrannicide had
been debated for centuries. It is important to realise that, in
the course of the debate, tyrannicide – to bring about the overthrow of an existing government – had never been condemned
outright by the Catholic Church. On the contrary, there was a

* Paul Wilkinson, in *Terrorism and the Liberal State*, points out that the Dublin
Rising, by a 'small band of dreamers', although ostensibly a failure at the time,
alerted the world to the cause of Irish national freedom and led to the foundation
of the Irish Free State: 'Violence can act as a dramatic revelation and catalyst not
only for the destruction of the established regime, but also for the forging of a
new political community' (p. 86).
† The Oxford English Dictionary suggests a nineteenth-century origin for the
word terrorist: 'Anyone who attempts to further his views by a system of coercive
intimidation; specially applied to members of the extreme revolutionary societies
in Russia.'

long tradition of discussion about whether an evil ruler could be removed. (That begged the question, naturally, of exactly what constituted an evil ruler.) In the thirteenth century St Thomas Aquinas, the doctrinal Father of the Church, had held that the overthrow of a tyrannical government was not necessarily an act of sedition, unless the community concerned suffered more from the overthrow than from the previous tyranny. In the sixteenth century, not only Catholics but Protestant Huguenots discussed it in their polemical literature. The discussion spilled from theology into art, where the bloodthirsty description of (holy) Judith slaying (unholy and tyrannical) Holofernes was a significantly popular one.[15]

The furthest position on such an overthrow was that taken by the Spanish Jesuit Mariana in *De Rege et Regis Institutione*, published in 1599. Written in the form of a dialogue, Mariana answered the question 'Whether it may be permissible to oppose a tyrant?' in the affirmative. There could be 'no doubt' that the people were able to call a king to account, since there was a contractual element in their relationship. Ideally a public meeting should be held, but if that proved impossible a tyrant might be destroyed by 'anyone who is inclined to heed the prayers of the people', and the assassin 'can hardly be said to have acted wrongly' by serving as an instrument of justice.[16]

This notorious passage aroused the frenzy of Protestants, and was the basis of accusations about 'Queen-killing' and 'King-killing' Jesuit policy in the English state trials of 1606. All one can say with certainty is that on the edges of Catholic political thinking what one authority has called 'an ultimate right of tyrannicide' was reserved for the oppressed, based on an idea of a broken contract. (It is an ultimate right which has after all been reserved by many of those who see themselves as oppressed throughout history.) Against this ultimate theoretical right, at the turn of the sixteenth century lay the heavy weight of practice, under which lawful governments could in fact expect the obedience of their citizens, whatever their religious persuasion. This was a point of view expressed vividly by Erasmus in 1530 in a book designed for the instruction of the young. 'Even if the Turk (heaven forbid!) should rule over us,' he wrote, 'we would be committing a sin if we were to deny him the respect due to Caesar.'[17]

The distinction between a lawful and an unlawful ruler was crucial. After that, debate could still rage over what constituted such a ruler (debates which may be compared to modern arguments about what constitutes a democratically elected government in considering the legality of the coup which overturns it). However, to many English Catholics, led by priests such as Father Garnet, there was a vital difference between Queen Elizabeth and King James. The former had been a bastard by Catholic rules, had usurped the throne rightly belonging to the Catholic Mary Queen of Scots, and had been subject to a bull of excommunication by the Pope. None of these blemishes marred King James. He was legitimate and he was not a usurper, having inherited the throne as next in blood. Above all he had never been excommunicated – thanks to that cleverness with which he handled the Papacy while still in Scotland. What was more, since James had never been a Catholic, he could hardly be accused of apostasy. Father Garnet himself would make a careful distinction between King James and the Catholic backsliders, those who reneged on the religion into which they had been born.[18]

Thus the Plotters were going against the profoundly held loyalties of many of their co-religionists when they decided to remove 'a king who had succeeded lawfully to his kingdom'. And yet there was enough in the contemporary Catholic political literature on the overthrowing of tyrants – which they had probably not read themselves, but had simply imbibed at second or third hand – to convince men of their particular temperament, frustrated men ('Shall we always talk and do nothing?' Percy had asked), that their course was virtuous.[19]

It was Father Tesimond who commented that such gentlemen as these would not have staked their whole future on a conspiracy 'if they had not been convinced in their utmost consciences that they could do so without offence to God'. The conspirators ordered for their endeavour special swords of

Spanish steel, their blades richly engraved with scenes from the life of Jesus Christ; these swords would bear the legend, 'The Passion of Christ'.[20] In their own estimation, these men were not assassins; they were fighters in a holy cause (which they found to be an absolutely different concept).

For all the wild language of horror after the Plot's discovery – one Biblical comparison was made to the 'Passover' massacre of the first-born of Egypt – both the killing of rulers and the killing of the innocent were endemic in the times in which Catesby and his companions lived.*[21] But if the Plotters' consciences were at ease with the killing of rulers, there is evidence that they were greatly anguished over the killing of the innocent. Blowing up the King was one thing, and the Royal Family – his wife and heirs – another. But the extinction of the Parliament house by gunpowder at the Opening would inevitably result in many more deaths than that.

It was the possible deaths of Catholic peers which aroused this fierce anxiety. These conspirators were terrorists, but it is too simple a view of human nature to suppose that they were immunised from all weakness or regret. Father Garnet later described Catesby's split mind. On the one hand he planned to save 'all the noble men whom he did respect' and on the other he was determined not to spare his own son if he were there 'rather than in any sort the secret should be discovered'. For these men to envisage the deaths of co-religionists who had borne the heat and burden of the day might prove to be 'cruel necessity'. But it could never be a light decision.

In general, Parliament had been responsible for anti-Catholic legislation: hence the choice of the site for the explosion. The prospect of the death of Robert Cecil, a member of the House

---

* There have been few periods of history when this has not been true. Leaders killed since the Second World War include President John F. Kennedy and his brother Robert Kennedy, President Sadat of Egypt and Prime Minister Rabin of Israel. Attempts have been made on the lives of numerous leaders including Fidel Castro, Ronald Reagan and Margaret Thatcher. As to the killing of the innocent, since the Second World War (when the bombing of Dresden and its civilian population caused a controversy not yet extinguished) the bombing of Baghdad, with its civilians, in the Gulf War has aroused similar questions.

of Lords since the granting of his first peerage in May 1603, could no doubt be accepted with equanimity. But was the devout young Lord Montague to die? He had spoken up bravely on behalf of 'the religion of our fathers' in the House of Lords this very summer in a bitter attack on the Act against recusants, and as a result had spent four days in the Fleet prison.[22] Was he to be sacrificed? Then there were the two prominent peers who were married to the daughters of Sir Thomas Tresham (Catesby's first cousins). Lord Stourton, husband of Frances, was some twenty years older than Catesby, but the men were close friends. Lord Monteagle, husband of Elizabeth, belonged to the Catesby generation – he was born in 1575 – and he had been involved like Catesby, Jack Wright and Tom Wintour in the Essex Rising. Wintour now acted as his secretary.

In the light of what happened later, there is a question mark, to say the least of it, over Monteagle's subsequent commitment to Catholicism. He had in fact privately made a grovelling submission to Cecil while in the Tower in April 1601. He had also described himself as a born-again Protestant in a letter to the King, in order to establish his right as Lord Monteagle (it was a title that came through his mother) so that he could sit in the House of Lords in the lifetime of his father, Lord Morley.[23] But these kinds of ambiguities and compromises were far from uncommon at the time, especially at court, where Monteagle had an appointment in the household of Queen Anne.

In the summer of 1604 Monteagle would have been seen as a member of the recusant family ring, not only through his Tresham marriage, but through his brother-in-law Thomas Habington (his sister Mary's husband). Habington had been involved in one of the plots to free Mary Queen of Scots and had spent six years in the Tower as a result. In the recent Parliamentary election, Habington had been among the prominent Worcestershire recusants who supported a Catholic candidate, Sir Edward Harewell. Although it was not yet technically illegal for a Catholic to sit in Parliament if he swore the Oath of Supremacy, an armed guard on the gates of Worcester against Harewell's supporters had proved an effective if brutal deterrent.[24] Habington's house, Hindlip, like neighbouring Huddington, was another important recusant centre, a maze of hiding-places where priests could linger – it was hoped – for months with impunity.

Was Monteagle, was Stourton, to die? And finally, what of the great Earl of Northumberland, Thomas Percy's patron?

On such an agonising question as the death of the innocent the doctrine of the Catholic Church was far more clearly established than over the murky question of tyrannicide. It was a matter of what was called 'double-effect'. A single action might have two quite separate effects. There were, however, three conditions which had to be fulfilled for the double-effect principle to operate. First of all, the good effect had to be disproportionately important compared to the bad effect; secondly, the bad – harmful – effect had to be involuntary, rather than in any way desired; thirdly, both good and bad effects had to be so closely linked as to be brought about more or less simultaneously.*[25]

The Powder Treason, as planned by Catesby, easily fulfilled the second and third conditions of the double-effect principle. No 'innocent' deaths were desired – absolutely to the contrary – and yet they would certainly be brought about simultaneously with those of the 'guilty' in the general combustion. The question of the fulfilment of the first condition – was the enterprise of sufficient worth to 'countervail' these innocent deaths? – entirely depended, as in all terrorist actions, on the standpoint of the individuals involved. Nevertheless, the theological clarity of the issue did not prevent each new conspirator, as he joined the band, from suffering the same doubts and anguish.

The Plotters returned to London in early October. Around this time, a sixth conspirator, Robert Keyes, was admitted to their

* The principle of double-effect remains in place today in Catholic theology. The example of Dresden bombed in the Second World War was cited earlier. According to the double-effect principle, the bombing of a legitimate (industrial/military) target which incidentally causes unplanned civilian deaths would be in a different moral category from the deliberate bombing of the civilian population to strike terror and lower enemy morale.

ranks. They needed someone to take charge of Catesby's house in Lambeth, where it was intended that the gunpowder and other necessary stores such as firewood should be kept for the time being. Keyes was nearly forty in 1604, a 'trusty and honest man', tall and red-bearded; he too, like Guy Fawkes, could be relied on to show courage *in extremis*. His father had been the Protestant Rector of Staveley in North Derbyshire, but Keyes had clearly always favoured the religion of his mother, who came from the well-known recusant family of Tyrrwhitt in Lincolnshire.[26]

From the point of view of the Powder Treason, it was important that Keyes' first cousin, the beautiful Elizabeth Tyrrwhitt, was married to a wealthy young Catholic with money and horses to spare, Ambrose Rookwood of Coldham Hall in Suffolk. This golden couple was thus brought within the general orbit of the conspirators. In the autumn of 1604 it was Ambrose Rookwood who was asked to acquire some gunpowder by Catesby and bring it to the Lambeth house. At this point, the acquisition of the gunpowder was presented as merely being for the use of the English regiment in Spanish service in Flanders, no longer of course an illegal operation, thanks to the Anglo-Spanish Treaty.[27]

Keyes was not particularly well off. His wife Christiana, a widow when he married her, was a clever woman who acted as governess to the children of Lord Mordaunt at Drayton in Northamptonshire. Keyes received horses and other amenities in return for his wife's teaching services. Mordaunt was another prominent Catholic peer and his safety in Parliament would obviously be a matter of much concern to Keyes. As for Drayton, Cecil described the great house as 'a receptacle of most dangerous persons', meaning 'the foreign seminaries' he believed to flock there. Nevertheless King James was happy to stay at Drayton for the hunting near by, good sport glossing over a multitude of Popish sins: an example of the double-think which existed in court circles on the subject of grand Papists.[28]

A few months later, a seventh conspirator was recruited. This

was Catesby's servant Thomas Bates, who according to his confession joined the Plotters in early December 1604. Bates must
surely have had his suspicions about a Plot already. He was not
a menial, since he was allowed his own armour and his own
servant at Ashby St Ledgers. Bates, born at Lapworth, was
more of a retainer, part of Catesby's 'family' or intimate household; and he was known to be absolutely devoted to his
master.[29] Bates' own family consisted of an independent-minded
wife called Martha. (The conspirators' wives constituted a
remarkable group: but then they were part of the larger, resolute
and often intrepid body of Catholic women.)

However, Bates' confession is one of the more unreliable
pieces of evidence surrounding the events of the Plot. His
lower social standing was relevant here for it meant that he
could be subject to special pressures from the authorities. On
the one hand he might – conceivably – hope to get off where
the other more senior Plotters could not, or be induced to
believe that such a chance existed. On the other, the ultimate
threat of torture was routinely seen as a matter of social hierarchy: people without proper rank in the estimation of the gov-
erning class were much more likely to be subject to it than
their superiors. Nor should too much attention be paid to
Bates' so-called revelations concerning the priests, including
Father Tesimond.

In the context it is unsurprising to find Bates claiming to
confess his sin in advance to Tesimond (that persistent
Protestant smear on Catholics and the Sacrament of penance).
In Bates' official version he was not only absolved but encouraged by Tesimond with the words 'that it was no offence at all,
but justifiable and good'. What Bates probably did say under
duress was much less incriminating: 'he thought Father
Tesimond knew something about this plot but he could not be
certain'.[30] Bates of course recanted at the last and apologised to
those he had traduced.

At the time, Bates' recruitment made every sense in view of
his close, dependent relationship to Catesby. He was a practical
man, his loyalty could be taken for granted and so could his

silence. The circumstances where this might no longer be true – twelve months ahead – were, perhaps fortunately, beyond the conspirators' imagining. In any case, their plans were shortly to meet with a startling reversal, as it must have seemed at the time.

This reversal took the form of a postponement of Parliament, and in the event would be creatively used by the Plotters to elaborate and expand their plans. Nevertheless the announcement on Christmas Eve that Parliament would not after all sit again in early February, owing to renewed fears of the plague in London, must have come as a shock. The new date was 3 October 1605. That left many months of secrecy and planning ahead – months in which more help, either at home or abroad or both, might be recruited. Alternatively, of course, these were months in which news of the conspiracy might leak out, first in the secret recusant world, and then by degrees elsewhere through spies or covert governmental well-wishers high and low.

The prosecution in its account of the conspiracy had the Plotters involved in an amazing and daring venture at this period. This was the digging out of a mine beneath the Palace of Westminster, which was intended to convey the gunpowder from the cellar of the Whynniard house within Westminster to a cavity under the House of Lords. The digging was supposed to have been begun on 11 December and abandoned as impractical on 25 March, because the foundation walls were in places eleven feet thick.

This mine was most likely a mythical invention, used by the government to spice up the official account of the narrowly averted danger.* For one thing, no traces of this famous mine were ever found – nor have any traces of it ever been found

* Much ink was spilt in the late nineteenth century over the question of the mine, part of the ongoing controversy as to whether there really was a Gunpowder Plot, between the historians S. R. Gardiner and Father John Gerard (sic). Gardiner, who was a Pro-Plotter, defended its existence and Gerard, who was a No-Plotter, attacked it as part of the general picture of governmental fabrication; perhaps more ink was spilt than the subject deserved, since it is perfectly possible to have the Plot without the improbable mine. (Gardiner, *Plot*, pp. 34–5, 63–5, 41–2; Gerard, *What Plot?*, pp. 58ff.).

since. If dug, it was quite brilliantly shored up. The sheer logistics of digging out such a subterranean passage would have been horrendous – particularly since none of the conspirators had any mining experience or knowledge and no move was ever made to import an experienced tunneller from the mining communities that had existed in England since ancient times. Catesby and Percy were both exceptionally tall men: Tesimond in his *Narrative* was astonished that they had been able to stoop to the work. Furthermore, the mind boggles at the problems of disposal within the busy Palace of Westminster. Some of the stones would have been enormous (far too big to lose in the little garden next door) and, if the Thames was used, it must be remembered that the river was at this date the main highway of a capital city.[31]

None of these obvious questions about the working of the mine was answered in any way by the prosecution. Nor was a real attempt made to do so. Sir Edward Coke, prosecuting, by admitting that the mine was 'neither found nor suspected' by the government until the danger was past, was able to tell a tall tale without risk of contradiction. It is notable that Guy Fawkes did not mention the subject at all until his fifth interrogation. By this time, he had been put to the torture and was in no position to quibble about such unimportant details as a mine which had played no part in the action and had subsequently vanished into the ground from whence it came. Even so, someone thought it necessary to add – in handwriting other than Fawkes' own – a clarifying detail to his deposition. It was a mine leading 'to the cellar under the Upper House of Parliament'.[32] The wretched Guido obviously did not know the precise notional whereabouts of the phantom mine.

Why did the government bother? The answer must lie in the special sinister element which is introduced by the very idea of a subterranean tunnel occupied by wicked men, working away in the darkness like moles beneath the feet of the righteous. It is noticeable that in government propaganda the mine of itself made an excellent focus for shock, horror. 'Lord, what a wind, what a fire, what a motion and commotion of earth and air would there have been!' exclaimed Coke. The conspirators were regularly termed the 'Miners' in debate in Parliament. Its members had only to look down to be reminded of the great peril which had once threatened them all. One of their number, Sir Roger Wilbraham, wrote in his diary of 'hellish practices under the earth', while the playwright Thomas Dekker would wax eloquent on the subject of Lucifer's devilish assistant, the Mouldwarp: 'Vaults are his delight.'[33]

New Year 1605 was celebrated by the court with enthusiasm, all unknowing of the Plot which – mine or no mine – was being devised to blow so many of their number to smithereens. The proliferation of the Royal Family had been further emphasised by the arrival of Prince Charles from Scotland in October to join his brother and sister. The puny little boy was greeted glumly at first by the English courtiers, who hesitated to apply for his household in case he died and the household vanished.[34] But things looked up when he was created Duke of York at Twelfth Night. Besides, Queen Anne was visibly pregnant and would in fact bear her fourth (surviving) child in April.

The subject matter of the 'entertainment' which crowned the Twelfth Night revelries had an unconscious aptness. Written by Ben Jonson and designed by Inigo Jones, this was entitled *The Masque of Blackness*. Queen Anne and her ladies, representing 'the daughters of Niger', were conventionally swathed in azure and silver, decorated with pearls. But they blacked up their faces, and their arms up to the elbow, something which made the task of the French Ambassador in kissing the royal hand somewhat tricky.[35] A year which began with darkness as its official theme could not, perhaps, have been expected to pass without catastrophe threatening to engulf it.

CHAPTER EIGHT

Pernicious Gunpowder

The world has no instrument or means so pernicious
as gunpowder, and capable of effecting such mischief.

THOMAS BARLOW
The Gunpowder Treason, 1679

Twenty-fifth of March, known as Lady Day in honour of the Feast of the Annunciation, was the date on which the new year started officially in the contemporary calendar.* It was a time of new beginnings, and on 25 March 1605 the Powder Treason took on a new dimension. It was considerably enlarged when Robert Wintour, John Grant and Kit Wright were let in to the secret. All three made strategic sense, continuing the feeling of family which pervaded the whole Plot. Not only was Robert Wintour of Huddington the elder brother of Thomas, but John Grant of Norbrook had married their sister Dorothy, and Kit Wright was the brother of Catesby's close ally Jack.

John Grant, like Jack Wright, was a man of few words, with a general air of melancholy. But, unlike the famous swordsman Wright, Grant was something of an intellectual who studied Latin and other foreign languages for pleasure. Beneath the melancholy surface, however, and the air of scholarly withdrawal lay an exceptionally resolute character. Grant refused, for example, to be browbeaten by the local poursuivants, and

* 1 January was not employed until 1752; although it is used in the dating of this narrative to avoid confusion.

defied them so often and so forcibly that they began to flinch from searching Norbrook (despite the fact that the house was more often than not sheltering Catholic priests). It was a steadfastness, based on a belief in God's blessing on what he did, which John Grant 'obstinately' maintained to the very last.[1]

Crucial to John Grant's admission, beyond his Wintour marriage and his own strength of purpose, was the geographical position of Norbrook. Grant's house, near Snitterfield in Warwickshire, a few miles north of Stratford-upon-Avon, was excellently situated from the conspirators' point of view. First, it belonged in the great arc of Plotters' houses which now spread like a fan across the midlands of England: from Harrowden and Ashby St Ledgers near Northampton to Huddington and Hindlip by Worcester – not too far from the Welsh Marches, wilder terrain which offered a prospect of escape. It was vital to be able to evade searches by fleeing to a safe – or at least recusant – house. In the past priests had often been saved by making their way under cover of darkness to a neighbouring refuge until the search was over, and then returning when the coast was clear. One of Salisbury's intelligencers referred to such elusive prey as having the cunning of foxes: 'changing burrows when they smell the wind that will bring the hunt towards them'.[2] The town which lay at the centre of this recusant map was Stratford-upon-Avon.

Grant's house, Norbrook, was not far from Lapworth, the house where Catesby had been born and brought up, which now belonged to Jack Wright.[3] Then there was the Throckmorton house, Coughton Court, a few miles to the west, owned by Catesby's uncle Thomas but equally for rent if necessary since the Throckmorton fortunes were heavily depleted by recusancy. Baddesley Clinton lay to the east.

In order to understand how the midlands of England could constitute, with luck, a kind of sanctuary for recusants, it is necessary to project the imagination back to Shakespeare's country (and Shakespeare's native Forest of Arden) and away from the idea of an area dominated by the huge proliferating mass of today's Birmingham, England's second city. If

Birmingham is removed from the mental map,* it will be seen that gentlemen could hunt (and plot) in this area, priests could take part in gentlemanly pursuits such as falconry, women could conduct their great households, including these priests as musicians or tutors, just so long as local loyalties remained on their side.

The reference to Shakespeare's country is an appropriate one. We shall find the Gunpowder Plot providing inspiration in a series of intricate ways for one of Shakespeare's greatest plays – *Macbeth* – and that again is not a coincidence. Stratford, celebrated as Shakespeare's birthplace, was also the focus of his family's life. The playwright's father received a copy of *The Spiritual Testament of St Charles Borromeo* from Father Edmund Campion at Sir William Catesby's Lapworth house. Shakespeare's mother, from the recusant family of Arden, had property at Norbrook where John Grant lived and Shakespeare himself bought property at New Place in the centre of Stratford, in July 1605, in anticipation of his eventual retirement back to his birthplace.[4]

In London, the circles in which Shakespeare moved also meshed with those of the conspirators. This was the world of the Mermaid Tavern, where Catesby and his friends were inclined to dine and which was hosted by William Shakespeare's 'dearest friend' (he witnessed a mortgage for him) William Johnson. This meshing had been true at least since the time of the Essex Rising, which had involved Shakespeare's patron Lord Southampton, who went to prison for it, as well as Catesby, Jack Wright and Tom Wintour.

The figure of Sir Edward Bushell, who had worked for Essex as a Gentleman Usher, provided a further link – in this case a family one. Ned Bushell was a first cousin of the Wintours. As he admitted, the conspiracy included 'many of my near kinsmen': he would eventually become the guardian of young Wintour Grant, son to John Grant and Dorothy, which put him in control of Norbrook. But Bushell was also

* It was a small market town of some fifteen thousand inhabitants as late as 1700 and began to develop only in the late eighteenth century.

connected by marriage to Judith Shakespeare, the playwright's daughter. Shakespeare's familiarity with the environment of the Plotters both in London and in the country – and his own recusant antecedents – are certainly enough to explain his subsequent preoccupation with the alarming events of 1605, so many of which took place in 'his country'.[5]

John Grant's house at Norbrook had a further advantage since it was close to Warwick as well as Stratford. Horses – so-called 'war-horses' – would be an essential part of the coup. John Grant was to be in charge of their provision from the stable of Warwick Castle. War-horses of the continental type, strong, heavy 'coursers', about sixteen hands high, able to bear a man and his weaponry into battle, were rare in Tudor and post-Tudor England. The Spanish had blithely believed in their existence during the earlier invasion plans: but in fact the Tudors had tried in vain to breed this continental strain at home. The decent saddle horses of this time were Galloway 'nags' or native Exmoor ponies, a considerably smaller breed. When push came to shove – as it was expected to do – the 'war-horses' of Warwick Castle would be a valuable asset. The need for good horses of any type led directly to the induction of further conspirators later on in the year.

Finally, this natural focus on the midlands would, it was hoped, facilitate one of the plotters' most important objectives. This was the kidnapping of the nine-year-old Princess Elizabeth.

The King's daughter was housed at Coombe Abbey, near Coventry, not much more than ten miles north of Warwick and west of Ashby St Ledgers. Here, under the guardianship of Lord and Lady Harington, with her own considerable household, the Princess resided in state. If the little Prince Charles, with his frail physique, had disappointed the English courtiers, and Prince Henry, with his air of command, had enchanted them, Princess Elizabeth fulfilled the happiest expectations of what a young female royal should be like.

She was tall for her age, well bred and handsome according to a French ambassador who was eyeing her as a possible bride for the French Dauphin. (The canonical age for marriage was twelve, but royal betrothals could and did take place from infancy onwards.) The previous year she had already proved herself capable of carrying out royal duties in nearby Coventry. Following a service in St Michael's Church, the young Princess had sat solemnly beneath a canopy of state in St Mary's Hall and eaten a solitary dinner, watched by the neighbouring dignitaries.[6] The Princess was therefore far from being an unknown quantity to those who lived locally – as royalties might otherwise be in an age without newspapers. On the contrary, the conspirators knew that she could fulfil a ceremonial role despite her comparative youth.

The ceremonial role which the Powder Treason Plotters had in mind was that of titular Queen.[7] The location of the King's nubile daughter was a critical element in their plans, for her betrothal was an immediate practical possibility and her marriage could be visualised within years. The Princess was currently third in succession to the throne, following her two brothers. But from the start it seems to have been envisaged that Prince Henry would die alongside his father (he had after all been markedly in attendance at all the state ceremonies of the two-year-old reign). On the subject of the four-year-old Prince Charles, the thinking was rather more confused. This was probably due to the fact that he was a latecomer to the royal scene. This, with his notorious feebleness (he had only just learnt to walk) made it difficult to read the part he would play at the Opening of Parliament. In the end the Plotters appear to have settled for improvisation in this, as in many other details.

If the little Prince Charles went to Parliament, then he would perish there with the others. If he did not, then it was Thomas Percy who was deputed to grab him from his own separate household in London. The birth of Princess Mary on 9 April 1605 introduced another potential complication. Although fourth in the succession to the throne, following her elder sister, the new baby had in theory the great advantage of being born in England. Remembering the xenophobia of

Henry VIII's will – foreign birth had been supposed to be a bar to the succession – there seems to have been some speculation about whether the 'English' Princess Mary was not a preferable candidate.[8]

The baby was given a sumptuous public christening at Greenwich on 5 May. Her tiny form was borne aloft under a canopy carried by eight barons. Her two godmothers were Lady Arbella Stuart and Dorothy Countess of Northumberland.*[9] But the talk about the baby, even the plans for the little Duke, do not seem to have had much reality, compared to the practical planning concerning the Princess Elizabeth.

In the total chaos which the 'stroke at the root' would inevitably bring about, the conspirators would need a viable figurehead and need him – or her – fast. No mere baby or small child would suffice. Princess Elizabeth, keeping her state in the midlands, was ideally placed for their purposes. As Catesby said, they intended to 'proclaim her Queen'. Although a female ruler was never an especially desirable option, the memory of Queen Elizabeth, dead for a mere two years, sovereign for over forty, meant that it could scarcely be described as an unthinkable one. There was also the question of a consort, who might prove eventually to be the effective ruler: the Princess could be brought up as a Catholic in the future and married off to a Catholic bridegroom.[10] (They were unaware – perhaps fortunately – that the Princess was completely unaffected by her mother's romantic Catholicism and was already, at her young age, developing that keen Protestant piety which would mark her whole career.)

Such plans for a young girl did, however, pose the problem of an immediate overseer or governor. Once chaos had been brought about, a Protector would be needed urgently to restore order – and bring about those 'alterations' in religion which

---

* The day before, letters patent were issued to transform Robert Cecil, currently known as Viscount Cranborne, into the Earl of Salisbury, the name by which he will henceforth be known.

were the whole purpose of the violent enterprise.*[11] Who was this Protector to be? The obvious answer was the Earl of Northumberland. At forty-one, he was a substantial and respected figure: the sort of man 'who aspired, if not to reign, at least to govern', in the words of the Venetian Ambassador.[12] Northumberland was a Catholic sympathiser, and Thomas Percy, one of the chief conspirators, was both his kinsman and his employee. Compared to Northumberland, none of the overtly Catholic peers – not the outspoken Montague, not Stourton, not Mordaunt – because of their long-term depressed position as recusants, had the necessary stature. As for that untrustworthy Church Papist from the past, Henry Howard, Earl of Northampton, age was creeping up on him – he was sixty-five. His main Catholic activity these days was trying to persuade the King to have a splendid monument made to Mary Queen of Scots in Westminster Abbey (she was currently buried in Peterborough Cathedral in modest conditions which dissatisfied the aesthetic Earl).

It would certainly have made sense for the conspirators to reach a decision in Northumberland's favour and, having made it, to alert him via Percy in some discreet fashion, if only to prevent his attendance at the fatal meeting of Parliament. Yet, curiously enough, the conspirators do not seem to have made any final decision on the subject. Once again there was an area of improvisation in their plans. Certainly, Northumberland's behaviour around the crucial date in early November, which will be examined in detail in its proper place, gives no hint that he had been alerted to his glorious – or inglorious – destiny. Guy Fawkes never gave any information on the subject, presumably because he had none to give. Tom Wintour denied any knowledge of 'a general head'.[13]

Father Tesimond's explanation to Father Garnet, that the choice of the Protector was to be 'resolved by the Lords that

* The office of Protector was a familiar – if not exactly popular – one in English history from the reign of Edward VI who succeeded to the throne at nine; while Scotland under King James, crowned king at thirteen months, had needed a series of regents.

should be saved', is probably the true one. And who these would be no one of course knew for certain in advance. As Father Tesimond added: 'They left all at random.' This was indeed the line taken by Coke at the trial: the Protector was to be chosen after the 'blow' had taken place from among those nobles who had been 'reserved' by being warned not to attend Parliament – a clever line to take, since it left open the important question of who had been warned and who had not.[14] In short, the same policy was pursued as with the members of the Royal Family: they would wait and see who survived, with Northumberland as the front-runner.

Under the circumstances, there was a certain unconscious irony in an allusion to Princess Elizabeth made by King James in the spring of 1605. Increasingly he was venting his spleen on the subject of the Papists, who had been 'on probation' since his accession. Now he was irritated by their refusal to recognise how truly well off they were under his rule. Why could they not show their gratitude by remaining a static, passive community? John Chamberlain heard that King James had ranted away along the lines that, if his sons ever became Catholics, he would prefer the crown to pass to his daughter. In the meantime the recusancy figures were rising. As the Venetian Ambassador reported in April, the government was now beginning to use 'vigour and severity' against the Catholics.[15]

Some English Catholics were still exploring the option of 'buying' toleration with hefty amounts of cash, possibly obtained from Spain, and came to talk to the envoy Tassis about it. Meanwhile Pope Clement VIII, who died in the spring after a seventeen-year Papacy, went to his grave still believing in the imminent conversion of King James to Catholicism. In part this was due to the diplomatic manoeuvres of a Scottish emissary in Rome, Sir James Lindsay, whether sincere or otherwise; in part it sprang from the soulful communications of Queen Anne, which were certainly sincere but not necessarily accurate.[16] From the point of view of the conspirators, however, both hopes were equally unrealistic. 'The nature of the disease required so sharp a remedy,' Catesby had told Tom Wintour, pointing to the need for terrorism. A year further on, plans to 'do somewhat in England' were at last taking practical shape.

Twenty-fifth of March, the date on which the new Plotters were admitted, was also the date on which a lease was secured on a so-called cellar, close by the house belonging to John Whynniard. This house itself, it must be emphasised, was right in the heart of the precinct of Westminster: and yet there was nothing particularly exceptional about that. The Palace of Westminster, at this date and for many years to come, was a warren of meeting-rooms, semi-private chambers, apartments – and commercial enterprises of all sorts.* The antiquity of much of the structure helped to explain its ramshackle nature. There were taverns, wine-merchants, a baker's shop in the same block as the Whynniard lodging, booths and shops everywhere. In short, modern notions of the security due to a seat of government should not be applied to the arrangements at Westminster then.

The Whynniard house in 1605 lay at right angles to the House of Lords, parallel to a short passageway known as Parliament Place. This led on to Parliament Stairs, which gave access to the river some forty yards away. There was also a large open space bordering on the Thames known as the Cotton Garden. One authority has compared the plan of the relevant buildings 'for practical purposes' to the letter H.[17] If an H is envisaged, the House of Lords occupied the cross-bar on the upper floor, with a cellar beneath. The left-hand block consisted of the Prince's Chamber, used as a robing-room for peers, on the same level as the House of Lords; Whynniard's house, and the lodging of a porter, Gideon Gibbon, and his wife, lay below it. The right-hand block housed the Painted Chamber, used as a committee room, on the upper floor.

Most houses of the time had their own cellar for storing the

* The diaries of Pepys, sixty years on, bear ample witness to the success of these enterprises: Westminster Yard was a favourite rendez-vous, where he shopped for prostitutes among other goods on offer.

endless amount of firewood and coals required for even the most elementary heating and cooking. The cellar belonging to Whynniard's house was directly below the House of Lords and it seems to have been part of the great mediaeval kitchen of the ancient palace. However, this area, which was to become 'Guy Fawkes' cellar', where in the popular imagination he worked like a mole in the darkness, was actually on ground level. It might, therefore, be better described as a storehouse than a cellar. Over the years it had, not surprisingly, accumulated a great deal of detritus, masonry, bits of wood and so forth, which quite apart from its location made the 'cellar' an ideal repository for what the conspirators had in mind. It had the air of being dirty and untidy, and therefore uninteresting and innocuous.[18]

Just as the cellar was really more of a storehouse, the house, on the first floor, was so small that it was really more of an apartment. Certainly two men could not sleep there at the same time. Thus while Guy Fawkes, alias John Johnson, was ensconced there, Thomas Percy used his own accommodation in the Gray's Inn Road. A convenient door from the lodging – which, it will be remembered, was leased in the first instance to Whynniard as Keeper of the King's Wardrobe – led directly into the House of Lords at first-floor level. This meant that it could be used on occasion as a kind of robing-room, and even for committee meetings (the shifting employment of the rooms around the Palace of Westminster for various purposes demonstrates the casual nature of the way it was run).*

Thomas Percy's excuse for needing this 'cellar' – so crucially positioned – was that his wife was coming up to London to join him. Mrs Susan Whynniard appears to have put up some resistance on behalf of a previous tenant, a certain Skinner, but in the end money talked: Percy got the lease for £4, with an

---

* The Palace of Westminster was redesigned in 1840 by Sir Charles Barry, following the fire of 1834. Fortunately William Capon, an enthusiast for architectural research, had made an elaborate survey of the old palace in 1799 and 1823, illustrating it with a map which was eventually acquired by the Society of Antiquaries (see plate section).

extra payment to Susan Whynniard. A Mrs Bright who had coals stored there was probably paid off too.[19] Using the customary access from the river (with its easy crossing to Lambeth – and Catesby's lodgings – on the opposite bank) a considerable quantity of gunpowder was now transported to the cellar over the next few months.

Guy Fawkes revealed that twenty barrels were brought in at first, and more added on 20 July to make a total of thirty-six. According to Fawkes, two other types of cask, hogsheads and firkins, were also used, with the firkins, the smallest containers, generally employed for transport. While there would be some divergence in the various other accounts of exactly how much gunpowder was transported and when – between two and ten thousand pounds has been estimated – the amount was generally agreed to be sufficient to blow up the House of Lords above the cellar sky high.*[20]

The gunpowder was of course vital to the whole enterprise. As Catesby and his companions lived in an age when the deaths of tyrants (and of the innocent) were observable phenomena, they were also familiar with the subject of gunpowder, and explosions caused by gunpowder. Although the government had a theoretical monopoly, it meant very little in practical terms. Gunpowder was part of the equipment of every soldier: his pay was docked to pay for it, which encouraged him to try and make the money back by selling some under cover. The same was true of the home forces – the militia and trained bands. Similarly every merchant vessel had a substantial stock. Proclamations on the part of the government forbidding the selling-off of ordnance and munitions, including gunpowder, show how common the practice was.

In any case, the Council encouraged the home production of gunpowder in the last years of Elizabeth's reign. There were now powdermills at various sites, many of which were around

* There can be no doubt that a substantial amount of gunpowder was placed in the 'cellar', as the recent publication of the official receipt for it, on its return to the Royal Armouries at the Tower of London, has demonstrated (Rodger, pp. 124–5).

London, including Rotherhithe, Long Ditton in Essex, Leigh Place near Godstone, and Faversham. In 1599 powdermakers were ordered to sell to the government at a certain price, while any surplus could go to merchants elsewhere at threepence more in the pound. The diminution of warfare and the disbandment of troops in the context of the Anglo-Spanish peace meant that there was something like a glut. Access was all too easy, so that anyone with a knowledge of the system and money to spend could hope to acquire supplies. Furthermore, conditions of storage were alarmingly lax. Although powder was supposed to be kept in locked vaults, it was often to be found lying about, as official complaints to that effect also demonstrate.[21]

When two Justices of the Peace for Southwark had gone to search the London house of Magdalen Viscountess Montague in 1599, it was significant that they had been looking for gunpowder. They reported that it was supposed 'to have been lately brought hither', but although they searched 'chamber, cellar, vaults' diligently their efforts met with no success. (Either the gunpowder was well hidden – like the many priests this distinguished recusant habitually concealed – or the Justices were acting on false information.)[22] The formula for gunpowder mixed together sulphur, charcoal and saltpetre, which by the end of the fifteenth century were, with added alcohol and water, being oven-dried and broken into small crumbs known as 'corned-powder'. In this form gunpowder was used for the next four centuries. In many ways it was the ideal substance for explosive purposes. It was insensitive to shock, which meant that transport did not constitute a problem, but was extremely sensitive to flame.*[23]

The Plotters might have been original in the daring and scope of their concept, but they were certainly not original in choosing gunpowder to carry out the 'blow'. In 1585 five hundred of the besiegers of Antwerp had been killed by the use of an explosive-packed machine, invented by one

* With elements of potassium, nitrogen, oxygen, carbon and sulphur making it up, gunpowder ignited at between 550 and 600 degrees Fahrenheit.

Giambelli. Then there were accelerated explosions, comparatively frequent, testifying to the lethal combustion which the material could cause. To give only one example, there was an enormous explosion on 27 April 1603 while the King was at Burghley. This took place at a powdermill at Radcliffe, near Nottingham, not many miles away. Thirteen people were slain, 'blown in pieces' by the gunpowder, which 'did much hurt in divers places'.[24]

There was only one problem: gunpowder did, after a period of time, 'decay' – the word used. That is to say, its various substances separated and had to be mixed all over again. 'Decayed' gunpowder was useless. Or to put it another way, decayed gunpowder was quite harmless, and could be safely left in a situation where it might otherwise constitute an extraordinary threat to security.

While the logistics of the 'blow' were being worked out, foreign aid in the form of majestic Spanish coursers and well-trained foreign troops to supplement the slightly desperate cavalry which would be constituted by the English recusants was still the desired aim. Guy Fawkes went back to Flanders to swap being John Johnson for Guido again, where he tried to activate some kind of support in that familiar hotbed of Catholic intrigue and English espionage. About the same time, the grand old Earl of Nottingham set off for Spain to ratify the treaty. Approaching seventy, Nottingham (yet another Howard) had been married to Queen Elizabeth's first cousin and close friend whose death had set off her own decline. However, age had not withered Nottingham, since he had quickly remarried into the new dynasty: a girl called Margaret Stewart, kinswoman of the new King. Unfortunately Guido and his colleagues did not share the same appreciation of diplomatic and dynastic realities as this great survivor.

At some point in this trip, Fawkes' name was entered into the intelligence files of Robert Cecil, Earl of Salisbury. The King's chief minister had of course an energetic network of spies everywhere, not only in Flanders but in Spain, Italy,

Denmark and Ireland. Furthermore, Salisbury was able to build on the famous Elizabethan network of Sir Francis Walsingham. The number of 'false' priests abroad – treacherous intriguers who either were or pretended to be priests – constituted a specially rich source of information, as Salisbury admitted to Sir Thomas Parry, the Ambassador in Paris. They were all too eager to ingratiate themselves with such a powerful patron. The rewards could include permission to return to England for one who actually was a priest or straightforward advancement for one who was not. In the autumn of 1605 George Southwick (described as 'very honest' – which perhaps from Salisbury's point of view he was) returned to England in the company of some priests he had secretly denounced. The plan was that he should be captured with them, so as to avoid suspicion.[25]

After the official – and dramatic – discovery of the Plot, there would be no lack of informants to put themselves forward and claim, as did one Thomas Coe, that he had provided Salisbury with 'the primary intelligence of these late dangerous treasons'. Not all these claims hold water: Southwick for example was still busy filing his reports about recusant misdeeds on the morning of 5 November, with a manifest ignorance of what was to come.[26] The person who seems to have pointed the finger of suspicion at Guido Fawkes – and even he did not guess at the precise truth – was a spy called Captain William Turner.

Turner was not a particularly beguiling character. He was heartily disliked by the man on the spot, Sir Thomas Edmondes, Ambassador to Brussels, who considered him to be a 'light and dissolute' rascal, someone who would say anything to get into Salisbury's good books. Rascal or not, Turner certainly had a wide experience of the world, having been a soldier for fourteen years, in Ireland and France as well as the Low Countries. His earliest reports on the Jesuits had been in 1598. Now he filed a report, implicating Hugh Owen (always a good name to conjure with where the English government was concerned) in a planned invasion by émigrés and Spanish, to take place in July 1605.[27]

There was, however, no mention of the conspiracy which would become the Powder Treason. Moreover, when Turner went on to Paris in October and passed papers to the English Ambassador there, Sir Thomas Parry, about 'disaffected [English] subjects' he still knew nothing of the projected 'blow'. Parry, however, took his time in passing all this on. Turner's report on the dangerous state of the stable door did not reach England until 28 November, over three weeks after the horse had bolted. In essence, Turner's information belonged to a diffused pattern of invasion reports, rather than anything more concrete.[28]

Nevertheless, Turner had picked up something, even if he had not picked up everything. In a report on 21 April, he related how Guy Fawkes – who was of course a well-known figure in the Flemish mercenary world – would be brought to England by Father Greenway (the alias of Father Tesimond). Here he would be introduced to 'Mr Catesby', who would put him in touch with other 'honourable friends of the nobility and others who would have arms and horses in readiness' for this July sortie.[29] There are clear omissions here. Invasion reports had been two a penny for some time – as, for that matter, had unfulfilled plans for such an invasion, including those of Wintour and Fawkes himself. Apart from the specific lethal nature of the Powder Treason (which we must believe Turner would have relished to reveal, had he known it) Guy Fawkes' alias of John Johnson is missing, which is an important point when we consider that he was not about to leave for England, but had been installed as Johnson in a Westminster lodging for nearly a year. Yet Turner had established Guy Fawkes, if not John Johnson, as a man to be watched and he had connected his name to Catesby's – already known as one of the Essex troublemakers – and to that of Greenway/Tesimond. This information must have taken its place in the huge mesh of other reports which Salisbury received, even if its significance was not immediately realised.

Turner's alarm about a July invasion-that-never-was leads on to the far more crucial question of who knew about the

Powder Treason in England. For it was in England, where the conspiracy was actually being hatched, that betrayal was infinitely more likely to take place.

Who knew? First of all, there were the servants, that ever present body of the 'inferior sort', in the Privy Council's dismissive phrase, which nevertheless all through history has had unrivalled opportunities for keyhole knowledge. The hierarchical nature of society meant that servants nearly always followed the views of their masters with fanatical loyalty, since they would probably be casually condemned for them anyway (witness the number of servants, like Robert Grissold of Lancaster, who died with their masters, the priests). Then there was that other body, the faithful Catholic gentlewomen of recusant England, the women already trusted with the lives of their pastors, the wives and close relations of the conspirators. There must be a strong presumption that, in whispers conducted in corners, in veiled allusions in innocent domestic correspondence, the news spread.

At Easter 1605, a very odd incident had taken place involving Eliza Vaux which was never satisfactorily explained.[30] (It goes without saying that the conspirators' wives, notably the admirable Gertrude Talbot Wintour of Huddington, would deny having any scrap of foreknowledge, but with a family's future at stake such a denial may not have represented the whole truth; what a wife knows privately about her husband's plans is in any case unquantifiable.) Eliza Vaux herself was at this time properly concerned with her duty to marry off her eldest son Edward, 4th Baron Vaux of Harrowden, who was seventeen. Lord Northampton, who took on the duty of arranging a suitably worldly match, selected Lady Elizabeth Howard, one of the numerous daughters from the brood of his nephew the Earl of Suffolk and the avaricious but beautiful Catherine.

Lady Elizabeth Howard was on paper an excellent choice. She was well connected due to her parents' position at court and, like all the Howard girls, she was extremely pretty. It is clear from what happened afterwards that the young Edward

Vaux fell deeply in love with her. Unfortunately the advantageous marriage hung fire, and Eliza Vaux, getting increasingly impatient at the delay, correctly assessed the reason. It was because she and her son were both considered to be 'obstinate Papists'.

Eliza had a close woman friend, Agnes Lady Wenman, who was the daughter of Sir George Fermor of Easton Neston, not so far away from Harrowden, and yet another cousin of the family (her grandmother had been a Vaux). Since her marriage Agnes Wenman had lived at Thame Park, near Oxford. Eliza Vaux expected to get a sympathetic hearing from Agnes on the subject of the delayed match, not least because she had influenced her friend in the direction of Catholicism during Sir Richard Wenman's absence in the Low Countries, or, as that gentleman preferred to put it, Eliza Vaux had 'corrupted his wife in religion'. Father John Gerard himself taught Lady Wenman how to meditate, and she began to spend up to two hours a day in spiritual reading. At Easter – 31 March – Eliza Vaux indiscreetly confided to Agnes Wenman in a letter that she expected the marriage would soon take place after all, since something extraordinary was going to take place.[31]

'Fast and pray,' wrote Eliza Vaux, or words to that effect, 'that that may come to pass that we purpose, which if it do, we shall see Tottenham turned French.' (This was contemporary slang for some kind of miraculous event.) What Eliza Vaux did not expect was that this letter would be opened in Agnes Wenman's absence by her mother-in-law Lady Tasborough. The latter, who interpreted the reference as being to the arrival of Catholic toleration, showed the letter to Sir Richard. Even though he remembered the phrase slightly differently – 'She did hope and look that shortly Tottenham would turn French' – the hint of conspiracy was salted away in his mind. The letter itself vanished before November, leaving Eliza to take refuge in the traditional excuse of a blank memory. She claimed she had no recollection of the phrase or what she meant by it.[32]

Tottenham did not turn French, and the compromising Wenman letter was exposed only by chance, aided perhaps by the malice of a mother-in-law. It conveys, however, in a private communication from one woman to another, an atmosphere of excitement and Catholic hope, even if its precise meaning remains mysterious. (But it is surely unlikely that the reference was to toleration, given the Anglo-Spanish situation.) How many other hints were dropped at this period can only be suspected, given that in the dreadful aftermath of 5 November such incriminating letters would, where possible, have been quickly destroyed.

There was, however, a third body in England, beyond the mainly silent servants and the mainly discreet gentlewomen, who might on the face of it have known about the Plot and remained quiet on the subject. These were the hidden, watchful priests. At the beginning of the summer, Father Henry Garnet reported unhappily to Rome that the Catholics in England had reached 'a stage of desperation' which made them deeply resentful of the ongoing Jesuit commands to hold back from violence.[33] At this stage, he too was acting on suspicion rather than direct information.

Meanwhile, the secret Catholic community tried to maintain those rituals which were so precious to it. One of the chief of these was the Feast of Corpus Christi (the Blessed Sacrament) following Trinity Sunday, celebrated this year on 16 June. Although instituted comparatively recently in ecclesiastical terms, it had become a great feast of the late mediaeval Church, involving a procession, banners and music. All of these things were far more conspicuous, and thus difficult to conceal, than a Mass said in an upper room at 2.00 a.m. (a popular hour for the Mass, when it was hoped that the searchers would not intrude). This particular Corpus Christi was celebrated at the home of Sir John Tyrrel, at Fremland in Essex. Involving 'a solemn procession about a great garden', it was watched by spies, although the priests managed to get away safely afterwards.[34] What the spies did not know was that a week earlier Father Garnet had found himself having a conversation, seemingly casual, yet uncomfortably memorable all the same, with his friend Robin Catesby.

The conversation took place in London on 9 June, at a room in Thames Street, an extremely narrow lane which ran parallel with the river west from the Tower of London. In the course of a discussion concerning the war in Flanders, Robin Catesby threw in an enquiry to do with the morality of 'killing innocents'. Garnet duly answered according to Catholic theology. It was a case of double-effect, as Garnet propounded it to Catesby. In ending a siege in wartime 'oftentime ... such things were done': that is, the assault which ended it would result in the capture of an enemy position, but at the same time it might cause the death of women and children. From Catesby to Garnet, there was certainly no mention of 'anything against the King', let alone gunpowder. As Garnet confessed later concerning Catesby's enquiry: 'I thought the question to be an idle question': if anything, it referred to some project Garnet believed Catesby entertained, to do with raising a regiment for Flanders.[35]

If we accept Garnet's version to be the truth, then he was still in genuine ignorance of any specific design when Father Tesimond sought him out in the Thames Street room, shortly before 24 July. Oswald Tesimond was a lively northerner whose bluff appearance – his 'good, red complexion', black hair and beard – owed something to these origins. But Tesimond, who had been trained in the English College in Rome, after years abroad was now a sophisticated fellow, as indicated outwardly by the fact that his clothes were 'much after the Italian fashion'.[36] He had been back in England for about seven years. An intelligent and thoughtful man, he was a great admirer of the calm wisdom of the Superior of the English Jesuits, Father Garnet.

What he now told Garnet could in no way be shrugged off as 'idle'. For Father Tesimond had recently heard the confession of Robin Catesby. In a state of extraordinary distress, Tesimond now sought out his Superior in order to share the appalling burden of what he had heard. Like Catesby, he proposed to impart what he had to say under the seal of the confessional.

CHAPTER NINE

There Is a Risk...

There is a risk that some private endeavour may
commit treason or use force against the King.

FATHER HENRY GARNET
in a letter to Rome, 24 July 1605

'I would to God that I had never heard of the Powder
Treason,' Father Garnet cried 'very passionately' eight
months later.[1] But from late July 1605 he *had* heard of it.
The question was, under what circumstances, and with what
obligations to those whom the conspiracy threatened? The revelation from Father Tesimond to Garnet provided one of the
most anguishing aspects of the whole episode. Certainly Father
Garnet's secret knowledge was enough to make the rest of his
life a torment, first of uncertainty, later of horrified certainty.
When he first heard the news, however, it represented the
nightmare scenario, which he had so long dreaded, come true
– or threatening to come true.

Father Tesimond makes it quite clear in his *Narrative* that
Catesby had for some time been expressing his impatience with
Father Garnet's lukewarmness and 'excessive patience'. The
previous summer, they had all been together, the two priests
and Catesby, sitting over a meal when Father Garnet took the
opportunity to speak a few 'grave words' on the subject of the
Pope. It was his 'express order' that the English Catholics
should live in peace and leave the reconversion of their
country to Providence. But Catesby refused to accept the

message in silence. Instead, as they got up from the table, he referred pointedly to those who had grown weary of putting up with persecution. People were saying openly that such doctrines of non-resistance took away from the Catholics their spirit and energy, leaving them 'flaccid and poor-spirited'. Making it clear that he was speaking for others as well as himself, Catesby said that the English Catholics were now in a worse situation than slaves, despised by their enemies as 'God's lunatics'.[2]

Perhaps all of this could have been dismissed, or at least tolerated, as the outpourings of an active, frustrated, but fundamentally sound son of the Church. But Catesby's final defiant remarks could hardly be construed in this light. Whatever the Pope's words, said Catesby, people were asking whether any authority on earth could take away from them the right given 'by nature' to defend their own lives from the violence of others. It was a point of view, of course, with which Garnet profoundly disagreed. He continued to argue with Catesby – when he had the opportunity.

Father Tesimond bears witness that the conspirator began to avoid Garnet's company after their meeting so as not to receive this 'prohibition', which evidently made Catesby uneasy. In early July, Father Garnet, backed up by a letter from Aquaviva, went back to Fremland, where he found Catesby with his cousin Francis Tresham and his cousin by marriage Lord Monteagle. Yet again he preached against them 'rushing headlong into mischief'. As a result, a compromise was reached by which it was agreed that Sir Edmund Baynham should go to Rome and present the desperate plight of the English Catholics. Father Garnet was under the impression that he had managed to avert disaster.[3]

In late July – shortly before the Feast of St James, on 25 July – Father Garnet discovered that he had failed. He had learnt of the existence of a plan which was 'a most horrible thing, the like of which was never heard of'. He had failed to prevent the inception of the conspiracy. Whether he could or would prevent the implementation of this plan remained to be seen.[4]

Everything Catesby told Father Tesimond was under the seal of the confessional. It was afterwards strongly maintained by both Father Garnet and Father Tesimond that Tesimond also consulted his spiritual adviser (and his Superior) under the same seal. But what he had to say was likely to be long drawn out, as well as distressing in its content. In a fit of kindness, Father Garnet suggested that instead of kneeling, as would have been customary, Father Tesimond should continue his own confession as they walked together in the garden. It was one of those small gestures which seemed unimportant at the time but was to have terrible unforeseen consequences.

Tesimond came 'to confess and ask advice'; he also received permission in advance from 'his own penitent' (Catesby) to do so. As to the validity of the conditions under which Tesimond made his own confession, neither priest ever gave up on this point. The most that Garnet conceded – under appalling pressure – was that, if the consultation had not actually taken place 'in confession', nevertheless 'he conceived it to be delivered in confession'.[5] This, from the theological point of view, came to the same thing, since Garnet would then, in good faith, consider himself to be bound by the confessional rules.

Catholic rules concerning confession were perfectly clear. Under canon law, all information received under the seal was privileged: that is, it could not be divulged under any circumstances (unless, of course, the penitent concerned gave permission). However, this rule would not apply to information received in a more generalised way, nor to a 'confidence', provided the seal itself was not invoked. According to Father Garnet, writing to Tesimond afterwards – who never contradicted him – Tesimond was unquestionably making a confession, not imparting a confidence, in spite of the unusual circumstances in which he made it.[6]

It is extremely difficult for the non-Catholic mind – and even perhaps a Catholic one – to grapple with the question of Garnet's foreknowledge, if it is put in the baldest terms. A priest hears in advance that Parliament is to be blown up, with appalling loss of human life; is he really to say nothing, and allow this horror to proceed?* The heart of the matter was what action Garnet should have taken thereafter. Catesby and his companions were terrorists – or terrorists by intention; their terrorism had its own internal dynamic by which it was either justified or not. None of that was anything to do with the priests, who neither then nor thereafter ever claimed any justification for the conspiracy and were genuinely appalled by it. Where then did their duty lie?

Perhaps the correct priestly reaction was expressed most clearly by Father Garnet himself: 'The confessor himself is bound to find all lawful means to hinder and discover the treason.'[7] Even if Garnet could not use the knowledge specifically gained in the confessional, that did not mean he would have to remain passive and allow events to unfold.

What Father Garnet did next made perfect sense under the Catholic rules. Immediately he wrote to his own general, Aquaviva, in Rome. He said that he had prevented violence or 'serious trouble' breaking out on four separate occasions already, but that he remained perturbed on two counts. First, that those 'in another country' might 'fly to arms' which could cause others in England to join them in open rebellion. Secondly, and much more seriously, he wrote: 'there is a risk that some private endeavour may commit treason or use force against the King'. In this way all the Catholics might be obliged to join them in the fighting, to the ruin of the community. Yet again Father Garnet urged that the new Pope, Paul V, elected on 29 May, himself might issue a public brief against the use of 'armed force'. In order not to mention his own heavy burden of knowledge, Father Garnet carefully suggested that the pretext for the Pope's action could be the recent troubles among the recusants in Wales who formed a notoriously turbulent community.[8]

---

* The consequences of the seal of the confessional, where a priest must not divulge what he has learnt even to save an innocent person/people, have always been seen as having great dramatic potential; of the various works in which it has been put to use, the most notable is the film *I Confess* (1953), with Montgomery Clift as a priest who hears the confession of a murderer and is subsequently himself accused of the crime; he cannot clear himself by breaking the seal of the confessional.

But Garnet did not leave his 'hindering' of the treason at that. He also asked the English Catholic emissary to Rome, Sir Edmund Baynham, to emphasise the need for the papal declaration. The government later delivered a two-pronged attack on the Baynham mission.[9] It was made out that Garnet had deliberately despatched Sir Edmund too late to produce any effective restraint. A picturesque sporting analogy was used: Garnet was like a thief going to steal partridges with the aid of a dog, who takes care that his animal (Baynham) does not go too near the birds too soon, before the net is fully over them, 'for fear the game should be sprung and the purpose defeated'. By contrast, it was also suggested that Baynham had been sent in order to justify the plot in advance, an absolutely contradictory thesis.

The real truth about Baynham seems to have been somewhat different. He was a wild young man, who had been imprisoned around the time of the Essex Rising for some outspoken speeches against the King of Scots. He had then had some peripheral involvement in the Bye Plot. But he was a master of languages, with the unusual accomplishment of being able to pass as a Frenchman or an Italian, and his mission across the whole of Europe – remembering the perils of travel at this period – would therefore attract less attention.[10]

On 28 July Parliament was prorogued by proclamation yet again. It would not now meet on 3 October as had been intended for the last six months, because it had been decided that 'some dregs of the late contagion' (the plague) still lingered in the capital. Since people were accustomed to return to London around All Hallows – 1 November – the new date chosen, which was in fact the third projected date, was Tuesday 5 November.[11]

In the course of the next fourteen weeks, Father Henry Garnet allowed himself to be lulled into a sense of false security. Everything was in abeyance until the results of the Baynham mission were known. The nightmare scenario was not going to take place. But in the popular imagination, forever after, Father Garnet's activities at this point were as presented in a well-known rhyme, *Mischeefes Mysterie… The Powder Plot*:

Yes, impious Garnet for the traitors prayed
Pricked and pushed forward those he might have stayed
Being accessory to this damned intent
Which with one word this Jesuit might prevent.[12]

There was a deceptive placidity about English life in the high summer of 1605. This outward normalcy existed at many different levels. The King busied himself with his hunting. He was quite convinced that the prolonged violent exercise (away from London) was essential to the royal health. Since this was in fact 'the health and welfare of us all', as he had pointed out to his Council in January, he asked his Councillors to take charge of 'the burden of affairs' and see that he was neither interrupted nor troubled with too much business.[13] It was an insouciant request which meant, of course, that his Councillors, led by Salisbury, now had the freedom to decide what was or was not sufficiently important to trouble their master. And there was another kind of freedom. His absence from the centre of affairs gave them freedom to plot and plan without royal interference.

The anniversary of the Gowrie Conspiracy of 1600 against King James, so miraculously foiled, was once again celebrated with a solemn thanksgiving on Tuesday 5 August. The Archbishop of Canterbury, Dr Bancroft (formerly Bishop of London), seized the opportunity to preach an extremely anti-Papist sermon at St Paul's Cross in the course of which he quoted the King. So resolute, he said, was King James to sustain the Protestant religion that he was quite prepared to pour out the last drop of blood in his body.[14] Obviously, there was no perceived contradiction between this kind of bold statement and the fact that King James, on his sporting tour, continued to stay with prominent Papists, as and when convenient. James even spent the night at Harrowden Hall, where he was entertained not only by Eliza Vaux, but also by that aspiring bridegroom, the young Lord Vaux, whose match to the lovely Elizabeth Howard was still hanging fire for religious reasons.

On 27 August, King James, Queen Anne and Prince Henry arrived in Oxford for a three-day visit. King and Queen lodged together at Christ Church and the eleven-and-a-half-year-old Prince at Magdalen College. Elaborate preparations on behalf of the University had also included instructions to the undergraduates to behave themselves and dress decently. Streets were swept, much new paint was applied. Varying intellectual pleasures were on offer. As for Queen Anne, she was impressed when an official of the University made a speech in front of her at the city centre in ancient Greek, a language which, as the Queen said, 'she had never before heard'.[15]

The King for his part enjoyed a Latin entertainment by Matthew Gwinn, entitled *Tres Sybillae*. Two aspects of it gave him special pleasure. First, the sybils' prophecies made flattering allusions to his Scottish ancestry: his royal descent in a line of kings from a certain Banquo was praised while a certain Macbeth was described in contrast as having no descendants. Secondly, the Gwinn play was short. William Shakespeare, in Oxford at this time, had the opportunity to take note of both things in the development of his own play on the historical theme of Macbeth. At the Bodleian Library, King James observed genially: 'Were I not a King, I would be a University-man.'[16] Immediately after this, however, despite the lure of academe, King James went back to his hunting again.

At another, much less public level, Papist life also continued, revolving, so far as was possible, with the year's religious cycle, just as it had done in happier times gone by. The Feast of St Bartholomew on 24 August found Father Garnet at White Webbs, near Enfield, with the Catholics to whom he was closest – Anne Vaux, her sister Eleanor Brooksby, her nephew William Brooksby and his wife Dorothy. The decision was reached to take a great pilgrimage through the midlands to the shrine of St Winifred, at Holywell on the north coast of Wales.

Convinced that 'as far as we can ascertain, the Catholics live quietly at peace' – at least until the return of the Baynham mission – Father Garnet announced his intention to depart for the pilgrimage, accompanied by his loyal supporters, on 28

August.[17] On 30 August, the day that King James left behind the cheers of Oxford, these pilgrims also set forth. It was a journey which took them across the whole recusant arc from Enfield in the east, just north of London, via John Grant's house at Norbrook near Stratford, Huddington Court near Worcester, a tavern at Shrewsbury and finally into Wales itself.

Afterwards Sir Edward Coke made great play with the fact that this pilgrimage was a cover-up for more serious matters. 'By colour thereof', Father Garnet intended to call a conference of the conspirators.[18] In fact, if the pilgrimage had a specific individual purpose, it is more likely to have been the cure of Anne Vaux, who, now in her forties, was persistently troubled with some kind of female disorder. Apart from that, the recusants in England had plenty to pray for, given the deepening severity of their persecution. As for Father Garnet himself, he may have wished to keep an eye on his restive midland flock along the way, but he would scarcely have ventured as far as remote Holywell if he had had any idea that the dreaded 'private endeavour' continued to develop for all his prohibitions. In retrospect, the pilgrimage to St Winifred's shrine appears as an elegy for a certain kind of old Catholic England, where spiritual people, however sorely tried, really did live 'quietly at peace'.

Around thirty people made the pilgrimage, and then, as ever, there were the servants. Eliza Vaux joined her relations, bringing with her two priests, habitués at Harrowden, Father Gerard and Father John Percy. The latter, like Gerard, had been captured and tortured (in Bridewell prison), but like Gerard had also managed to escape. Father Tesimond came and the lay brother who attended him, Ralph Ashley. Then there was a young pair, Sir Everard Digby and his wife Mary, who came from Gayhurst in Buckinghamshire. They brought with them their secret chaplain, the Jesuit Father Edward Oldcorne.

This son of a Yorkshire bricklayer (with a devout mother who had been imprisoned for her faith) had been educated at St Peter's, York, like Guy Fawkes, the Wright brothers, and also Father Tesimond. In school terms, however, Father

Oldcorne was more of an age with his fellow priest: Tesimond and Oldcorne were in their early forties, while the conspirators were on average five years younger. Father Oldcorne had studied medicine before he went abroad; but he had become so strict a punisher of his own health through penances such as scourging that he had, according to Father Gerard, developed cancer of the tongue. Since he was a talented preacher, this constituted a special penance in itself. But Father Oldcorne had been cured by a visit to the shrine of St Winifred four years earlier. His own participation in the pilgrimage was in the nature of a thanksgiving.

One lowly figure in Father Garnet's entourage, a little man with a limp, would not have attracted much attention. Nor for that matter would he have attracted much sympathy: this was a time when a 'crooked' body was often believed to denote a similarly twisted nature. Yet the great soul and measureless courage of Nicholas Owen would provide in themselves, if such a thing was needed, the strongest possible refutation of the contemporary prejudice. This inconspicuous lay brother, not much higher than a dwarf, actually held within his craftsman's hands all the vital secrets of the Catholic hiding-places. Nicknamed Little John (Father Gerard in contrast was Long John of the Little Beard), Nicholas Owen was one of the four sons of an Oxford carpenter. Two of his brothers, Walter and John, were Jesuit priests. A third brother, Henry, ran a clandestine press for Catholic literature in Northamptonshire whose publications were falsely stamped 'printed in Antwerp'. At one point, when he was convicted for recusancy, Henry even set up a secret press in prison.[19]

Little John found his vocation in his work as combined architect, mason and carpenter of innumerable hiding-places.* His various constructions have been described by his biographer

* They are literally innumerable; Owen was a genius at his work and it is likely that some of his hiding-places still remain uncharted today (discoveries were made both in the late nineteenth century and in the twentieth). It is remarkable that Father Richard Blount, who spent forty years in England (and for twenty-one years was Superior of the Jesuits) had some hiding-places whose whereabouts are still unknown (Morris, *Troubles*, 1st, p. 192).

Margaret Waugh as 'wordless prayers'.[20] He probably worked for Father Edmund Campion in the 1580s, and was certainly imprisoned for championing him in 1585. In 1586, however, he joined Father Garnet and henceforth accorded him his complete devotion.

In 1599 Little John suffered an accident which crippled him, giving him a further handicap beyond his small stature. A packhorse fell on top of him, severely damaging his leg: 'ill-setting' of the bone did the rest. But when it came to working in the cramped conditions needed to construct a hideaway – a chimney, a drain – Little John's tiny size was a positive asset. He nearly always worked alone, praying silently as he toiled away, in the covering darkness of the night hours. This solitude was Little John's deliberate choice. He wanted no one else to share the danger at the time – nor the threat of interrogation, including torture, afterwards. Since Little John was among those who had been tortured in a London prison in 1594 (hung up for three hours on end 'with their arms pinioned in iron rings' and their bodies distended), he knew exactly the risk that he was taking.[21]

'How many priests, then, may we think this man did save?' enquired Father Gerard rhetorically. Father Garnet for his part described how Little John travelled all over the country making hiding-places for priests and other Catholics so that they could conceal themselves from the 'fury' of the Protestant searchers.[22] His clientele included Sir Everard Digby at Gayhurst, Eliza Vaux at Harrowden, and preeminently Thomas Habington at Hindlip in Worcestershire, where Little John constructed about a dozen hiding-places.

Owen did his chosen work 'free of charge'; if any money was forced upon him, he gave it to his brothers. It was essential that each hiding-place should be different, lest the uncovering of one should lead to the uncovering of many others. Working in the great thickness of Tudor masonry – a problem in itself – Little John had nevertheless to make a solid construction of his own, lest the tapping of the searchers be met with a hollow sound. (It was dangerous to use the space provided by chimneys because fires might be lit by the searchers.) Over the years Little John developed certain trademarks. He passed feeding or communicating tubes into the hiding-places for the longer sojourns of the priests, and he worked out a trick by which an outer hiding-place concealed an inner one in order to delude the searchers into going away when they found the outer hiding-place empty.* As the pilgrims wended their way across England to Holywell in North Wales, Owen took the opportunity of their various stopovers to render new hiding-places, and renovate the old ones yet more securely.[23]

The shrine of St Winifred with its well of healing waters was one of great antiquity. It took its inspiration from the legend of the seventh-century virgin Princess – Gwenfrewi in Welsh – described by Father Gerard as 'a saintly and very beautiful girl' whose faith and love of chastity made her more beautiful still. When Winifred's head was struck from her body by a suitor, Caradoc, whose advances she resisted, a spring of water welled up where the head had hit the ground: that was the first miracle. The second occurred when Winifred's uncle St Beuno managed to reunite the severed head and body, leaving only a white mark round her neck as a reminder of what had occurred. The murderous would-be ravisher Caradoc vanished into the ground, leaving the triumphant Winifred to become the patroness not only of virgins but also of problems of female infertility and allied illnesses. Her two special feast days were 22 June (her martyrdom – or rather her apparent martyrdom) and 3 November.[24]

The cult of St Winifred grew during the middle ages, when pilgrimages to St Winifred's Well became increasingly popular. In 1415 a statute ordered the feast-days of St Winifred to be officially celebrated throughout England along with those of St George and St David. Margaret Beaufort, mother of Henry

---

* These trademarks help to establish which of the surviving hiding-places in England are the work of Nicholas Owen. In addition to those named above, holes at Sawston Hall, near Cambridge (the home of the recusant Huddleston family), Baddesley Clinton and Huddington Court are generally rated as his work; Owen was also most probably responsible for the surviving hiding-places at Coughton and Coldham Hall.

VII, had an especial devotion to the saint, and to Holywell itself. She was responsible for the first printed life of St Winifred (by William Caxton) and was a substantial benefactress of the Holywell chapel and surroundings. Winifred was one of those saints, beloved by ordinary people, who was demoted in 1536 as a result of the Reformation; her feast-day was no longer to be regarded as a holiday. Nevertheless St Winifred's Well and its pilgrimages – a very long way from Parliament – continued to flourish regardless of governmental prohibitions and inclement weather. Father Gerard described how the mass of the people crossing the stream on 3 November once had to break the ice on the water. He himself prayed, immersed in the waters, for fifteen minutes; yet he took no cold afterwards, in spite of leaving on his dripping shirt under his other clothes.[25]

The ladies of this 1605 pilgrimage made the last part of the journey, as was customary, barefoot. The priest whom they found in charge was a remarkable man in his own right. John Bennett, who had trained at Douai, had arrived in Holywell nearly thirty years before. He had been imprisoned in 1582 for three years, and banished thereafter (the actual sentence was death but it was presumably commuted due to local feeling in his favour). In spite of his banishment, however, Father Bennett managed to get back to Holywell in 1587, operating there under a series of aliases for the rest of his life. In total, he served the chapel for nearly fifty years. Once again, the loyalty of the Welsh people to the pastor they loved must have protected him.*[26]

* In the late nineteenth century, the shrine and St Winifred herself inspired the Jesuit priest and poet Gerard Manley Hopkins:

> As sure as what is more sure, sure as that spring primroses
> Shall new-dapple next year, sure as tomorrow morning,
> Amongst come-back-again things, things with a revival, things with a recovery,
> Thy name ...

It is pleasing to report that Hopkins' prophecy has come true; St Winifred's shrine, today owned by Cadw (Welsh Heritage), is still a centre of devotion and

The way back from the pilgrimage turned out to be distressing and disquieting in equal parts. At Rushton Hall, Father Garnet and Anne Vaux found a house of mourning. Sir Thomas Tresham, the august, self-willed and devout patriarch, had died on 11 September, after a long sickness. His widow Muriel was still keeping to her chamber, according to custom. Francis Tresham reported that his father's last hours had been spent in great suffering, 'tossing and tumbling from one side and from one bed to another', and said that he himself would rather choose a 'death the pain whereof could not continue half an hour' than to die in such an agonising manner as his father.[27] Francis meant death by hanging. Before the year was out, Francis Tresham would discover that very few get to choose the manner of their own death, and he would not be among them.

The death of Sir Thomas at this precise moment had a profound effect on the development of the Powder Treason as it introduced Francis Tresham into the equation in quite a different light. Theoretically, the thirty-seven-year-old Francis was now a man of substance, with properties (and responsibilities, including his widowed mother, unmarried sisters and financially reckless brother Lewis). Unfortunately, Sir Thomas, the Catholic Moses, once colossally rich, had left enormous debts. These debts – including those where Francis had been bound up with him in a bond – provided a further cause for bitterness for his son.[28] Francis Tresham was now in the position of a man who has long awaited his inheritance, and at the last

pilgrimage, maintaining its unbroken record. The shrine is open all the year round, but the 'Well Season' is less spartan than it was in Father Gerard's day, lasting only from Whit Sunday, through the 22 June feast, till the end of September. There are grateful inscriptions in the chapel such as 'TW' for 'Thanks Winifred'. A pilgrimage on the part of James II and his second (Catholic) wife Mary of Modena in August 1686 was believed – for better or for worse – to be responsible for the birth of their son James Edward, known to history as the 'Old Pretender', after fifteen childless years of marriage. (*Hopkins*, p. 165; Br Stephan de Kerdrel, O.P.M., Franciscan Friary, Pantasaph, and Fr D. B. Lordan, St Winefride's, Holywell, to the author; David, *passim*.)

minute finds that the overflowing cup is poisoned. Furthermore, the Tresham family entail of 1584 meant that Francis was only a life tenant of a greater part of the estate, which at the time seemed yet another disaster.

The best of Francis Tresham was in his steadfast relationship with his wife Anne, daughter of Sir John Tufton of Hothfield in Kent. This devoted and resourceful woman – as events would prove her to be – had borne two daughters in the previous five years, Lucy and Eliza; no doubt the male child necessary for the family entail would soon follow. In all other respects, Francis Tresham's character was generally considered unsatisfactory in recusant circles. The priests did not rate his Catholicism very highly: he had none of the passionate – if fanatical – piety of a Catesby or a Guy Fawkes. He was clever enough, but 'not much to be trusted', in the words of Father Tesimond. At the same time Francis Tresham knew how to look after himself. An example of this was his reaction to the accession of King James. On a visit to his brother-in-law Lord Monteagle, he was frank with Tom Wintour (who was acting as Monteagle's secretary): henceforth he was resolved 'to stand wholly for the King'. All former plots were done with and he asked Wintour 'to have no speech with him of Spain'.[29]

Nevertheless Francis Tresham's new affluence – at least he had access to horses and could borrow money – meant that he could not be altogether ignored by the Plotters as a potential supporter. Besides, Robin Catesby had been accustomed to dominating his wayward cousin since their shared boyhood and he had a blithe confidence in the unchanging nature of their relationship.

Leaving Rushton in mourning Father Garnet and Anne Vaux went on to Gayhurst, the seat of their fellow pilgrim, the glamorous Sir Everard Digby. Here was a young man whom everyone adored and everyone trusted. He was only twenty-four, but had already been married to his heiress wife Mary Mulshaw (who brought with her Gayhurst) for nearly ten years. Theirs was an ideally happy match: she was 'the best wife to me that ever man enjoyed', he would say later, while he himself was by common repute 'the goodliest man in the whole court'.[30] His handsome face, athletic figure and height – he was over six foot tall – had indeed caught the eye of the King when he knighted Digby on 23 April 1603. Everard Digby was not politically ambitious – why should he be? He was wealthy, beloved by his wife and, being passionately interested in every kind of field sport, had quite enough to occupy his time. He had his horses (he was an expert horseman), his gun-dogs and his falcons. He was also a Catholic convert, whose life had come to be defined by his recusancy, but at this point it was the kind of religion of which Father Garnet would have approved: acquiescing in the status quo, trusting in God to bring about the conversion of England in His own good time.

Everard and Mary Digby had both been converted by Father John Gerard – but separately. It was a measure of the secrecy which obtained that for some time Mary Digby had absolutely no idea that the elegant gentleman hunting by day, playing card-games by night – who was introduced to her by a neighbour – was in fact a priest. 'The man lives like a courtier,' she exclaimed in astonishment when she learnt the truth, 'he never trips in his terms.' Then Everard Digby became seriously ill, which gave Father Gerard the opportunity to catch him too 'in St Peter's net'. Gerard and Digby became extremely close, 'calling each other "brother" when we wrote and spoke', and Father Gerard acted as godfather to Digby's first son.[31] Meanwhile the Digbys installed a secret chapel and sacristy at Gayhurst.

At hospitable and easy-going Gayhurst, Anne Vaux came to Father Garnet and expressed her extreme disquiet about what she had noted in the course of their recent journey. The suspicions of this shrewd and observant woman, whose life had been lived centrally in the recusant world for over twenty years, had been aroused by what she had seen. She was disturbed that there were so many fine horses being collected in the various stables of her cousins and relations. Anne Vaux, much perturbed, told Father Garnet that she 'feared these wild heads had something in hand'. She begged him, for God's sake, to talk to Robin Catesby.[32]

A little later Father Garnet felt able to reassure her. There was nothing to concern her unduly. Her cousin Robin was actually aiming to obtain a military commission under the Archduke Albert in Flanders, which in the wake of the Anglo-Spanish peace was no longer an illegal venture. Catesby even showed Anne Vaux a letter of recommendation for this enterprise written for him by Father Garnet – a document, we may believe, that Father Garnet must have penned with exquisite if unspoken relief, believing that this was the shape things were now taking. But of course this relief was quite unjustified. The risk of the destruction of the King and Royal Family, which on the other side encompassed not only the conspirators themselves, but their relatives, the Catholic community as a whole and above all their fugitive pastors, was as great as ever.

Although there is some conflict of evidence about when Guido Fawkes returned from the continent, slipping back into his personality of John Johnson, he was certainly in London again by late August, as the King went back to his hunting and the pilgrims set forth for St Winifred's Well. At this point Fawkes and Wintour discovered that the gunpowder in the so-called cellar, which had been there for some time, had 'decayed' – that is, the elements had separated. So the conspirators transported more gunpowder and more firewood, as a cover and to conceal it. During the summer also John Grant seems to have installed a quantity of weaponry at Norbrook, including muskets and powder.

The rising tempo of the conspirators' plans was further demonstrated at a secret meeting at Bath in August, at which Catesby, Percy, Tom Wintour and possibly some others were present. An important decision was taken that, 'the company being yet but few', Catesby should be given the authority 'to call in whom he thought best'.[33] It was a decision which was perhaps inevitable, given the wildly ambitious nature of their terrorist project, but it only increased the further risk of the plan – the risk of discovery.

CHAPTER TEN

Dark and Doubtful Letter

The means was by a dark and doubtful letter...

SIR EDWARD COKE
1606

There was a double eclipse in the early autumn of 1605 – a lunar eclipse on 19 September followed by an eclipse of the sun in early October. Such celestial phenomena were traditionally held to 'portend no good'. The sequence of these astronomical events with the political cataclysm of the Powder Treason was remarked on afterwards. Shakespeare probably commemorated the coincidence in *King Lear** when he had Gloucester express a series of gloomy predictions as a result of the late eclipses of the sun and moon: 'friendships fall off, brothers divide ... in countries, discord; in palaces, treason...' Second of October, the date of the solar eclipse, was just over a month before Parliament was to reassemble in the Palace of Westminster. But there would be not much more than three weeks before the first betrayal occurred, and friendship fell off, as brothers divided. The means by which this took place was described later – with perfect truth – as 'a dark and doubtful letter'.[1]

In the early autumn, Robert Catesby recruited three more

---

* *King Lear* was performed at court on 26 December 1606 when the Powder Treason, and the terrible threat it had constituted to the state, had been allowed to fade from no one's memory (*King Lear* (Muir), p. xviii).

conspirators, as he had been deputed to do. At Michaelmas –
29 September – he let the young, wealthy and staunchly
Catholic Ambrose Rookwood into the secret. It is sometimes
suggested that Rookwood had been enlisted earlier, but this is
improbable, given that Thomas Percy, as late as November,
had no idea that Rookwood was part of the group.[2] Rookwood
had of course already supplied gunpowder the previous year,
apparently for Flanders, and he may therefore have had his
own suspicions about the 'private endeavour'; similarly, his
wife's relationship to Keyes (and Keyes' wife Christiana) left
open the possibility of rumours having spread on the distaff
side. This is unverifiable, but what is clear is that Rookwood
immediately became an enthusiastic member of the conspiracy.

Ambrose Rookwood was in his mid-twenties, that is, considerably younger than the Plotters; already, however, he had the
reputation of a brave man, one that would dare anything for 'a
cause that was good'. He was the child of staunchly Catholic
parents, Robert Rookwood and his second wife Dorothea
Drury (both were imprisoned as recusants). Robert Rookwood
had considerable estates, including Coldham Hall, near Bury St
Edmunds in Suffolk, and Ambrose had been educated abroad,
among the first of the pupils at the Jesuit school at St Omer,
near Calais, which had been founded in 1593. Since it mainly
attracted the children of the wealthy, St Omer was beginning
to create a new kind of Catholic elite, consisting of well-
educated and pious young men.

Even without this influence Ambrose Rookwood had many
recusant connections. His cousin Edward was the kind of
affluent Papist who was allowed to entertain Queen Elizabeth
at his great house, Euston Hall, in Norfolk, but who also spent
ten years in prison for his Faith. One half-sister Dorothea
became a nun at St Ursula's, Louvain – 'the talk of the place
for her holiness' – and another, Susanna, also a nun, was one
of the earliest and closest associates of Mary Ward.[3]

On his father's death in 1600, Ambrose Rookwood inherited
Coldham. With his wife Elizabeth, he proceeded to make the
house 'a common refuge of priests' as it had been in his

father's day.* This devout young man had however his lighter side: his manner in public was 'easy and cheerful'. Being handsome, but rather short, he found compensation in a taste for extravagant, showy clothes, and was generally rated a dandy – perhaps too much so for 'his degree', when clothes were supposed to denote rank rather than money. There was, for example, his 'fair scarf' with figures and ciphers upon it, his 'Hungarian horseman's coat' entirely lined with velvet.[4]

But horses rather than clothes were Rookwood's abiding passion, after his religion. And it was for his celebrated stable of horses at Coldham that Ambrose Rookwood – among the many who were under the charismatic spell of Catesby – was drawn into the net. It was necessary to have Rookwood and his horses close by the other midland conspirators. He was persuaded by Catesby to rent Clopton House, adjacent to Stratford. At Clopton, where Rookwood took up residence after Michaelmas, we know from government records later that he introduced at least two chalices, two or three crucifixes, vestments of different colours for the various feasts of the Church (including red for martyrdom and black for a Requiem Mass), Latin books and 'praying beads' made of bone. To conceal all this, Little John constructed a large cellar stretching under the garden, which could be reached by an underground passage.[5] Ambrose Rookwood was the eleventh conspirator.

On 14 October, Catesby recruited a twelfth, Francis Tresham. The encounter took place at the home of Lord Stourton, Tresham's brother-in-law, in Clerkenwell. Afterwards Tresham gave a highly partial account of the whole affair.[6] By this time he had every reason to minimise his own participation (and guilt), not only for his own sake but for that of his wife and children.† Throughout this exculpatory confession

---

* Coldham Hall is still in private hands. Although considerably altered since the Rookwood days, it nevertheless still contains the three hiding-places in all likelihood constructed by Nicholas Owen; the attic-room which was the chapel is also extant.
† State prisoners would do much to avoid outright condemnation for treason for the sake of their innocent dependants after their death; a conviction for treason meant that all their property and goods would be forfeit, which was not necessarily so in the case of lesser crimes.

Tresham emphasised his own belief that he had at the very least secured a 'postponement' of the Powder Treason until the end of the Parliamentary session when the full extent of the new anti-Papist laws would be known.

In conversation with Catesby, Tresham raised at once the moral issue of whether the conspiracy was 'damnable', that is, leading to their spiritual damnation. When Catesby said it was not, Tresham replied: 'Why then, Robin...you must give me leave to censure it myself.' With the perfect accuracy of hindsight, Tresham presented himself as having foreseen correctly the dreadful effects of the Powder Treason. If Parliament was blown up, what could the Catholics do afterwards? 'What strength are they of, as of themselves?' he asked, having no foreign power to back them. Even if the government were confused at first, they would quickly rally, in order to run down and kill all the Catholics in England. To this Catesby simply answered: 'The necessity of the Catholics' was such that 'it must needs be done'. These last words, with their ring of authenticity, represent Catesby's unswerving view on the subject since the spring of 1604, when he had despaired of securing that toleration, once promised by King James, by peaceful means and had called for 'so sharp a remedy'.

Catesby pressed his cousin for two favours. First he wanted a large sum of money – two thousand pounds – and then he begged Francis to keep Rushton open. According to Francis, he carried out neither request. He was not in possession of the kind of money Catesby wanted, given the tangled state of his father's affairs, although he did give a hundred pounds to Tom Wintour, on the understanding he was taking a ship for the Low Countries. Secondly, Francis did shut up Rushton, bringing his mother and unmarried sisters to London, which, he pointed out, he would hardly have done if he had believed he was carrying them into 'the very mouth and fury' of the coming action.

In short, Francis Tresham, while admitting that from the government's point of view he was 'guilty of concealment', maintained that he had never in any sense been an active

Plotter. Furthermore he believed he had brought Tom Wintour and even Thomas Percy to see the wisdom of postponement. Lastly, he had actually been planning to tip the wink to Sir Thomas Lake, the King's Latin Secretary (but he planned to talk of a Puritan conspiracy in order to save his friends and relations), when events forestalled him.

It is questionable how much of all this should be believed, beyond the characteristic do-or-die attitude of Catesby, given the circumstances under which the story was told. It seems unlikely that Tresham, so clever and so close to Catesby, really thought he had secured this famous postponement, but the matter is finally unprovable. The most important point which emerges from Tresham's narrative is his sheer unreliability. Whether he believed the Plot to be postponed or not, he was contemplating betraying his companions – among them his closest friends – to the authorities. For it was hardly likely that the assiduous Lake, who had the King's ear for his championship of the Scots at court, would be long fooled by the prospect of a phantom Puritan rising, when emerging evidence of a real Catholic one was at hand. It was a man of this dangerous calibre that Catesby, with the reckless confidence of one who knows himself to be a natural leader, had introduced into the Powder Treason.

A week after Tresham's meeting with Catesby – on Monday 21 October – the Feast of St Luke was celebrated at Harrowden. This was a day on which the Jesuits in England traditionally tried to gather together to renew their vows.* Everard and Mary Digby rode over from Gayhurst for the occasion, returning that night. Father Garnet went with them, and so did Anne Vaux. It was at Gayhurst on this visit, while out riding, that Robin Catesby took the opportunity to let Everard Digby in on the secret.[7]

Sir Everard Digby was the thirteenth and last conspirator. But, whoever was to be the Judas in their midst, it was not

---

* Since the actual feast-day was on 18 October, the celebration had been postponed a few days – presumably to allow for a Sunday Mass as well for those who had to make a secret journey of some distance.

Digby. He was twenty-four and like the other junior member of the band, Ambrose Rookwood, was recruited for two practical reasons. Digby was wealthy, and he also had the essential horsemanship, as well as the equally essential stable of horses.

Digby, unlike Rookwood, was never involved in the grim London end of the proceedings. On the contrary, he was asked to install himself at Coughton Court, near Alcester in Warwickshire, which he was to rent from the current head of the Throckmorton family, Thomas, who had gone abroad in 1604. This move was, in Catesby's words, to make Digby 'the better to be able to do good to the cause'. He was to take Coughton for a month, 'purporting to take it longer... if his wife should like to live there'.[8] Near by, Digby was to organise a meeting of gentlemen, ostensibly for a hunt, but actually armed and on horseback ready for some great deed.

What was that great deed to be? There are some grounds for thinking that Digby, unlike Francis Tresham, was for the time being left in ignorance about the heart of the treason, the plan to blow up Parliament. It makes sense that Digby should have been entrusted with the vital midlands operation to abduct the Princess Elizabeth. Not only his horsemanship but his famous chivalric presence made him an excellent and even, it could be argued, reassuring figure. It is also likely that Digby believed that this abduction was the English side of some Flanders-based project of the sort which had beguiled Catholic intriguers for so long. Furthermore, he was informed – quite wrongly – that the Jesuits had given the venture their blessing.[9] So, far from being a Judas, the thirteenth conspirator may well have been at this stage an innocent, or comparatively innocent, figure in the whole affair.

There was certainly a sweetness, even a naivety, about his character, which with his handsome looks charmed all those who knew Everard Digby. The mere memory of him would later cause Father Tesimond intense grief.[10] Digby had not had a wild or dissolute youth like many of the older Plotters: nor had he endured the trauma of a recusant childhood. (Although now part of the Catholic world, he was one of the three conspirators who had no place in the close network of blood relationships which bound ten of them together, the others being Guy Fawkes and the servant Bates.) As a ward of Chancery, following his father's early death, he had been brought up a Protestant, before his conversion by Father Gerard. His teenage marriage to a young – and rich – girl whom he adored meant that his private life was similarly stable. In all his twenty-four years, Digby had never really had cause to feel himself to be an outlaw, and he was perhaps emotionally ill-equipped to deal with those who, for good reason, did.

October 1605 was a time of extraordinary tension, as rumours continued to spread, not altogether damped by the conspirators with their jittery consciences. It was now barely a month before the explosion was planned to take place and some people, inevitably, tried to assuage their guilt in advance. Others, less sympathetically, saw in the tense and tricky situation an opportunity for advancement.

In October Anne Vaux had another troubling interview with Father Garnet. This took place either at Gayhurst or at Harrowden. Anne told the priest that she feared 'some trouble or disorder' was brewing, since 'some of the gentlewomen had demanded of her where they should bestow themselves until the brunt was passed in the beginning of Parliament'. This news must have filled Father Garnet once again with apprehension. But Anne refused to divulge any names: 'she durst not tell who told her so, she was charged with secrecy'.[11] The likelihood, however, was that the question came from the wives of the conspirators – from Gertrude Wintour of Huddington or her sister-in-law Dorothy Grant of Norbrook. Outside the direct circle of conspiracy, there was also Mary Habington of Hindlip, wife of loyal recusant Thomas and sister to Monteagle and Eliza Vaux, who already in April seems to have anticipated some extraordinary event when 'Tottenham would turn French'. Father Garnet remained reassuring, emphasising the importance of Flanders as a sphere of action – and, we may assume, still hoping profoundly that he was right.

More serious in its implications for security than the secret talk of recusant women was the conversation which Catesby obviously engineered with Viscount Montague. This took place in London on 15 October, the day after he had recruited his cousin Francis.[12] Montague encountered Catesby in the Savoy, a district off the Strand. The two men exchanged 'a few words of compliment' and then Catesby casually asked: 'The Parliament, I think, brings your lordship up now?' Montague, mainly based at Cowdray in Sussex, replied that he was actually visiting his aunt, Lady Southampton. But, as to Parliament, 'he would be there' in a few weeks' time, unless he got the King's permission to be absent, which he was in some hope of doing.

'I think your Lordship takes no pleasure to be there,' commented Catesby. To this Montague could only agree. He had already suffered a short spell in prison for speaking out against anti-Papist legislation in the House of Lords and, given his sense of honour, had every reason to wish to be absent when the next round of penalties was announced, so as not to have to approve them. Catesby had done what he could.*

It was in October, in London and the country, that the final details of the plan were worked out: how Guy Fawkes was to light the fuse in the cellar, and then, swiftly making his way out to avoid the explosion, escape by boat across the Thames. There would be a rising in the midlands, coincidentally with the explosion in London, and the person of the Princess Elizabeth would be secured for a puppet queen. At the same time, back on the continent, Guido would be explaining what had happened – and why – to the Catholic powers such as Albert and Isabella, and how it had been a holy duty to blow up the King, the Royal Family and the English government. This mission of explanation 'to present the facts in the best light possible' was certainly a necessary task in an age when

---

* Maybe Catesby had done a little more than this, more than Montague subsequently admitted: this account was proffered to the government by a reluctant Montague after the discovery of the plot, when the heat was turned on him, as one of the leading Catholic peers. He may have discreetly edited it, in the absence of Catesby to contradict him.

authority respected authority. Acts of radical terrorism such as tyrannicide were in principle frowned upon by those who might one day suffer themselves.[13]

A series of supper parties in various taverns – the Mitre in Bread Street in the City of London, the Bull Inn at Daventry – mark this final stage of plotting. These parties sometimes included unsuspecting guests as a cover. There was, for example, the party which Catesby gave on 9 October at the Irish Boy in the Strand at which Ben Jonson was present. The playwright, who had been in trouble for his satire on the Scots, *Eastward Ho!*, was in the habit of associating with recusants and was in fact himself charged with recusancy the following year.

At the same time, Ben Jonson was developing a useful client/patron relationship with Salisbury and had greeted the latter's elevation to an earldom in May with some obsequious verses:

> What need has thou of me, or of my Muse
> Whose actions so themselves do celebrate?

After the discovery of the plot, Ben Jonson, as we shall see, laboured hard to remove the taint of his association with the conspirators by aiding the Council.[14] He was by no means the only recusant-sympathiser to do so. But the question of who knew what on these occasions would never be fully resolved, in view of the catastrophe which enveloped the major players.

Then on Saturday 26 October, apparently thanks to an obscure and ill-written letter delivered under cover of night to Lord Monteagle, everything changed.

The text of this 'dark and doubtful letter', as it would be later termed, was as follows:*

> My Lord, out of the love I bear to some of your friends, I
> have a care of your preservation. Therefore I would advise

---

* Given here in modernised spelling and punctuation.

you, as you tender your life, to devise some excuse to shift of your attendance at this Parliament; for God and man hath concurred to punish the wickedness of this time. And think not slightly of this advertisement, but retire yourself into your country [county] where you may expect the event in safety. For though there be no appearance of any stir, yet I say they shall receive a terrible blow this Parliament; and yet they shall not see who hurts them. This counsel is not to be condemned because it may do you good and can do you no harm; for the danger is passed as soon as you have burnt the letter. And I hope God will give you the grace to make good use of it, to whose holy protection I commend you.[15]

Unlike many controversial manuscripts – for example, the so-called Casket Letters, which thirty years earlier were used to condemn Mary Queen of Scots – the document itself has not vanished from sight.* Its survival in its original form has not, however, prevented the Monteagle Letter from being argued over fiercely for, in effect, the last four hundred years. Candidates for its authorship have included almost all the main players in the drama of the Gunpowder Plot.[16]

The official account, as related by King James, was mysterious enough.[17] Monteagle was at this point in his house at Hoxton, in the northern suburbs of London, a house which had come to him at the time of his marriage to Sir Thomas Tresham's daughter. About seven in the evening, his servant, named Thomas Ward, was accosted in the street by a stranger – 'a man of reasonable tall personage' – and given a letter to place before his master. At first Monteagle found the letter difficult to read and called for help to make it out. Once it had been deciphered he found himself in a quandary. Was it 'some foolish devised pasquil' (piece of nonsense) intended to stop him doing his duty at the coming Parliament? Or was it something more serious, a heavy warning? In spite of the lateness of

* The Monteagle Letter is still to be seen in the Public Record Office; it is reproduced in the plate section.

the hour and the darkness of the night, Monteagle decided to take his problem to Salisbury, at his house in Whitehall.

Salisbury, by his own account, took the whole matter seriously from the start. He had after all already been fed those rumours about the Papists' intentions to deliver the King a petition for toleration, and probably back it up with force. They were to be like 'sturdy beggars' who begged for alms with one hand outstretched, while carrying a stone in the other in case of refusal. Nevertheless he did not choose to alert the King, busy at his usual 'hunting exercise' near Royston in Cambridgeshire. James was not expected back until the Thursday – 31 October – before the solemn Opening of Parliament. In the King's absence, Salisbury did tell the other members of the Council, including the Catholic Lord Worcester and the Church Papist Lord Northampton, about the warning that had been received. But he did not at this point take any steps to keep the King himself in touch.

It was on the surface a surprising decision. One possible explanation would be the King's own instructions not to bother him with trifles while away hunting. So Salisbury was content to wait until his master's return, in order to consult him and benefit from his celebrated good judgement in clearing up and solving 'doubtful mysteries'. Another explanation, mentioned casually afterwards by Salisbury, was that waiting would afford more time for the plot 'to ripen'. A third explanation might be, of course, that Salisbury with the Monteagle Letter between his fingers now felt confident of commanding the situation.

Meanwhile, amid the network of the conspirators, matters were proceeding in a way which was neither placid nor yet leisurely. It so happened that Thomas Ward, Monteagle's servant, had close family connections with his fellow Yorkshire Catholics, the Wright brothers. Kit Wright's wife, Margaret Ward, may actually have been Thomas Ward's sister, but in any case recusant Wards and recusant Wrights were tightly interwoven (Ursula Wright the younger, sister of the conspirators, had also married a Ward).[18] While Monteagle went to see Salisbury in London, Thomas Ward availed himself of the information which had come the way of his master and sent a vital message to Catesby, then at White Webbs, about the betrayal.

Ironically enough, Catesby had been talking to Anne Vaux about joining the King out hunting at Royston the next day, which, if a serious project, was an extraordinary example of nerve. However, the conversation between the cousins, the one suspicious, the other blandly determined to keep her off the scent, is more likely to have been a diversion on Catesby's part. Now Catesby knew that somewhere in their midst was a traitor. His immediate reaction, shared with Tom Wintour, was that this traitor must be his cousin, Francis Tresham.[19]

This instinctive response concerning Tresham, the twelfth conspirator recruited so very recently, is crucial in assessing the affair of the Monteagle Letter. First, it demonstrates the way Tresham was esteemed among his contemporaries, even those who loved him: he was a man who might betray them, even those he loved. Secondly, it means that a great deal of weight must be attached to the fact that Tresham now managed to convince both his cousins Robin Catesby and Tom Wintour that he was not guilty.

Catesby and Wintour bearded Tresham, saying they would 'hang him' unless he exonerated himself. Tresham then swore his innocence 'with such oaths and emphatic assertions' that the pair of conspirators were convinced. Tresham reiterated his denial concerning the letter the next day – although he did urge them to abandon their plan and flee. Tresham has always been a popular choice of villain (or saviour) in the perennial historical guessing game of who wrote the Monteagle Letter: but there is surely some foolishness in disregarding the judgement of his lifelong intimates.

This exoneration by Catesby and Wintour is in fact only one of three pieces of evidence which point away from Tresham as the actual author; the two others will be considered in due course. Before that, however, the letter itself must be scrutinised.

*

Why and for what purpose did the Monteagle Letter come into existence? It is a useful maxim that these two questions should always be asked when examining any primary source.[20] Where this byzantine letter is concerned, there are two separate – and radically different – purposes for which it might have been written. The first, although still constituting a betrayal of sorts, as shall be explained later, is fairly straightforward. The letter was exactly what it purported to be: a genuine warning from a well-wisher to Lord Monteagle. His informant knew the outlines of the Plot – 'a terrible blow this Parliament' – but did not know enough (or was too frightened) to give details beyond a conceivable, if far-fetched, hint on the subject of fire in the penultimate sentence: 'the danger is passed as soon as you have burnt the letter'.

Prime suspect as the author of such a well-meant if risky communication must be Monteagle's sister Mary Habington of Hindlip or someone acting on her behalf. There was an eighteenth-century tradition in the county of Worcestershire that she had done so personally to save her brother, which may represent oral confidences handed down from generation to generation. Equally, Mary Habington might have passed the news – 'dark hints of the business', garnered along the recusant network – to a priest. It has been suggested that Father Edward Oldcorne might have written the letter or once again caused it to be written. Anne Vaux herself is another candidate.[21] This seems unlikely not so much because the handwriting is totally at variance from her own (she too could have employed a scribe) as because she had already followed a different procedure over these rumours: she had consulted with her revered Father Garnet.

If the Monteagle Letter was written in good faith to save the man to whom it was addressed, it was nevertheless a betrayal, for no one could have supposed that Monteagle would keep this news to himself. (Nor, of course, did he.) The young, ambitious peer had already demonstrated his wish to get on in the Jacobean court, and, on both a worldly and a human level, he was unlikely to quit London for the country – 'to expect [await] the event in safety' – as instructed, leaving his fellow peers and his sovereign to perish. Therefore this secret well-wisher must also have intended to scuttle the Plot before it started. The whole conspiracy would be aborted, with no one blown up, no one kidnapped, no one even harmed on the government's side, while among the Catholics no one would be hunted down, no one killed. Since the recusant community, especially the priesthood, was trembling with apprehension at what the reckless among them might do, not only Mary Habington but any priest would have had a strong motive to halt things there.

All this is to take the Monteagle Letter at its face value. But there is, to be blunt, something very fishy about the whole episode which makes it difficult, if not outright impossible, to accept this straightforward explanation. One is bound to ask why a sister needed to use an anonymous letter, delivered at dusk, to warn her brother not to attend Parliament. It is true that Mary Habington was heavily pregnant at the time (she would in fact give birth to a son at Hindlip on 5 November) but there were many discreet ways of delivering the necessary information. It seems extraordinary that anyone should need to use such a melodramatic method on a matter of such vital importance to both the individual and the state. It was not only melodramatic, it was also clumsy, since the style was vague to the point of obscurity.

It seems far more plausible to see the Monteagle Letter as certainly 'dark and doubtful' but also deliberately concocted. This is where, in order to unravel the truth about the authorship of the letter, one must ask another question, famously posed by Cicero, but since become a staple enquiry of crime-detection: *Cui bono?* To whose profit? Who benefited from the disclosure of the Monteagle Letter?

Francis Tresham did not benefit but in the end suffered a miserable fate. Nor for that matter did Thomas Percy benefit, another man generally felt to be capable of double-dealing at the time. Percy's wife was owed money by Monteagle, on which the latter paid £50 interest yearly. This might have provided a motive for Percy to seek the debtor's 'preservation' (Sir William Waad, Lieutenant of the Tower, suspected Percy, for this reason).²² But if Percy wrote any letter he would have written it, surely, to his patron Northumberland, and no such letter was ever found, rummage as the government might. There was, however, a clear beneficiary, after the event, and that was the hero of the hour: Monteagle himself.

It was Monteagle who was saluted with fervour after the event: 'saviour of my country, thee alone' wrote Ben Jonson. It was Monteagle, too, who received a financial reward – lands worth £200 a year and an income of £500 – as an acknowledgement of the part he had played in averting a national peril.²³ All this gratitude – not only the lyrical but also the financial, for Monteagle was not a rich man – must have come sweetly to one who had, only a few years previously, been imprisoned for his part in the Essex Rising.

Contemporary suspicions of Monteagle's role were not slow to develop. Cynical observers spotted Monteagle's need to dissociate himself from the Plotters, who included his closest friends and relatives. A fortnight after the discovery of the Plot, Sir Edward Hoby wrote to Sir Thomas Edmondes in Brussels: 'Such as are apt to interpret all things to the worst, will not believe other [than] that Monteagle might in policy cause this letter to be sent.'²⁴ The 'discovery' of the letter, at one stroke, prevented Monteagle from being suspected as a villain, and transformed him into a hero.

Mischeefes Mysterie, that political poem which denounced Father Garnet for his connivance in the treason, suggested that it was 'heaven's finger' which directed Monteagle's attention to the letter 'as the best means to have this fact detected'.²⁵ Whether Monteagle wrote the letter himself or (as seems more prudent) got another to do so, there was certainly nothing miraculous about the process. Someone had let Monteagle into the secret of the Powder Treason. Who was his source? In this case the obvious suspect, Francis Tresham, is surely the right one. Although Tresham did not use the means of an anonymous letter, he did warn his brother-in-law. After all, Tresham did not need to *write* to his brother-in-law. The kind of confidence he had to make was far better delivered face to face, since it was not so much a warning as a betrayal of what was about to take place.

There is reason to believe that Tresham's warning fell upon fertile ground where his brother-in-law was concerned. A loving letter from Monteagle to Catesby, which is generally dated September 1605, has been supposed to make some allusion to the impending conspiracy. 'If all creatures born under the moon's sphere cannot endure without the elements of air and fire,' he wrote, 'in what languishment have we led our life since we departed from the dear Robin whose conversation gave us such warmth as we needed no other heat to maintain our healths?' Monteagle went on to bid Catesby to make an appearance at Bath, 'and let no watery nymphs divert you, who can better live with the air and better forbear the fire of your spirit and vigour than we'. If the precise meaning of this flowery communication remains hidden, the ominous repetition of words such as 'warmth', 'heat' and 'fire' in a missive to Catesby at this juncture is surely suspicious. It indicates that Monteagle probably knew far more in the months leading up to the Powder Treason – long before the mysterious letter appeared – than he would afterwards ever admit.[26]

Returning to Tresham's part in warning Monteagle, he must have been aware that a verbal communication stood much less chance of being exposed than a written one. For Tresham could easily predict that he would be suspected afterwards, as indeed he was. This is the second piece of evidence which points away from Francis Tresham as author of the Monteagle Letter (even if he was ultimately responsible for the betrayal of the Plot), the first being Catesby's conviction that he was innocent.

The third piece of evidence, the most cogent of all, is the fact that Tresham never boasted of his loyal/disloyal achievement on his deathbed. Since he was at this point hell-bent on securing the maximum advantage for his descendants, it is inconceivable that he would not have mentioned the celebrated

THOMAS HABINGDON Esq.
Confined to WORCESTERSHIRE on account of the
GUNPOWDER TREASON PLOT;
The first Collector of Antiquities for that County;
died Oct! 1647, aged 87.

Mary Wife of Thomas Habingdon;
DAUGHTER of LORD MORLEY and Sister to LORD MONTEAGLE;
to whom she is supposed to have wrote the Letter which discovered
the Gunpowder Treason Plot.

Thomas Habington of Hindlip and his wife Mary; she was the sister of Lord Monteagle and local tradition has named her as the author of the anonymous Monteagle letter.

Vestment embroidered by Helena Wintour, daughter of Robert and Gertrude, and presented by her to the Jesuits (the legend *Ora pro me Helena Wintour* can be seen at the bottom); it is still at the Jesuit college, Stonyhurst.

(below) The Browne Brothers by Isaac Oliver: members of a leading recusant family, including Anthony, 2nd Lord Montague who for a short period employed Guy Fawkes as a footman.

Life in a recusant household, illustrated by a scene from the childhood of Mary Ward, founder of the educational religious order, the Institute of the Blessed Virgin Mary, who was a niece of the conspirators, Jack and Kit Wright; on the left can be seen Margaret Garnet, sister of Father Henry Garnet, who became a nun.

Rushton Hall, Northamptonshire; seat of Sir Thomas Tresham, the great Catholic patriarch and builder who was the father of the conspirator Francis Tresham.

Hindlip House in Worcestershire: a celebrated Catholic safe house, with over a dozen hiding-places for priests, where Father Garnet was captured; it was burnt down in the early nineteenth century.

Baddesley Clinton, Warwickshire, rented by Anne Vaux as a refuge for priests; Nicholas Owen, known as 'Little John', constructed hiding-places here, using the moat, the levels of a sewer and secret turret trapdoors.

Coughton Court, Warwickshire, home of the leading recusant family of Throckmorton, which was rented by Sir Everard Digby, at the time of the Gunpowder Plot, allegedly for hunting.

Huddington Court, Worcestershire; home of Robert and Gertrude Wintour, it contains hiding-places probably constructed by Nicholas Owen.

HUDDINGTON COURT, NR. DROITWICH

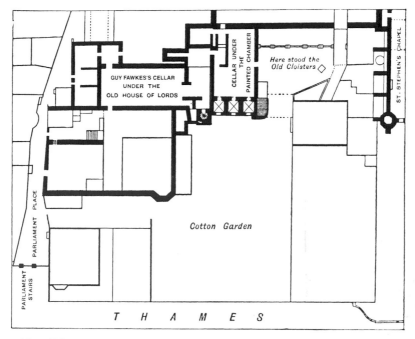

Map of Westminster, showing Parliament and the old House of Lords, beneath which gunpowder and firewood were stored.

Tower of London, *c.* 1615 by Van Meer; it was both a royal residence and a prison. Guy Fawkes, together with other conspirators and priests, was held and tortured here.

Ashby St Ledgers, Northamptonshire, owned by Lady Catesby, mother of Robert: it is said that the conspirators used this gate-house to plot their treason.

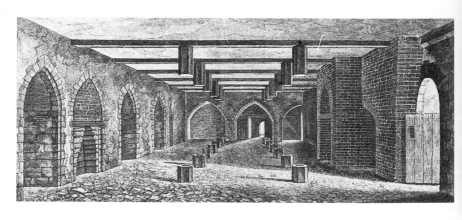

Although the old Palace of Westminster burned down in 1834, this drawing by William Capon of 1799 gives an impression of how the cellar beneath the House of Lords must have been in 1605.

(right)
An interpretation of Guy Fawkes entering Parliament.

A·PLOT·WITH·POWDER 1605
OVEMBER 5th
LD STILE
Opus tenebrarum
A deed of darkenes
BLACKE DEED S. WEST
DIGITVS·DEI·HIC·CONS
FAVX why
THVS SAY THE LORD BEHOLD
I WILL RAYS AGAYNST THEE OVT
OF THINE OWNE HOVSE
2 SAMV

Europe took a keen interest in the Gunpowder Plot: a contemporary Dutch print.

The anonymous letter delivered to Lord Monteagle on 26 October 1605; the authorship of – and motive behind – this notorious document, described later as 'dark and doubtful', now in the Public Record Office, have never been conclusively established.

The gallant *Eagle*, foaring vp on high :
Beares in his beake, *Treafons* difcouery.
MOVNT, noble EAGLE, with thy happy prey,
And thy rich *Prize* to th' *King* with fpeed conuay.

Woodcut showing the delivery of the Monteagle letter to Salisbury, from Vicar's *Mischeefes Mystery*, 1617.

letter if he had actually penned it. As it was, Tresham could not even get away with falsifying the record, since the actual author – or at any rate the actual begetter – of the Monteagle Letter was alive and well, petted by the government: his brother-in-law Monteagle himself.

The Monteagle Letter, then, was a fake and not only Monteagle but Salisbury knew it was a fake. It was brought into being for a special purpose. Nothing else makes any sense of Salisbury's extraordinary urbanity – one might even call it complacency – in the days following. There was certainly no sense of impending danger in his conduct, such as might have been expected if the letter had presented him with a genuine mystery.

It is no wonder that Salisbury remained so calm. There was nothing astonishing to him, in principle, about the Powder Treason. As he said himself, he had already heard of a 'stir' from his sources. Now he had been presented with another piece – an important piece – in the puzzle. He did not as yet know everything, for the information which had come to Salisbury from Tresham via Monteagle was limited. Not every detail about the conspirators themselves had been passed on; nor had the connection with the sinister Flanders-based Guy Fawkes yet been made. Furthermore Salisbury must have been troubled by the lack of clues to the identity of the prospective Protector to the young Queen-to-be Elizabeth (Tresham could not have passed this on because it had not been decided). He needed to know what great noble at the court was secretly plotting against his sovereign. This lack alone would have provided Salisbury with a strong motive for letting the Plot develop instead of blasting it apart immediately. It must have been a vital factor in his otherwise mysterious delay in making arrests.

What Salisbury did know about, on or just before 26 October, was the nature of the 'blow' which was to be struck at the House of Lords. Let us be clear: Salisbury did not manufacture the Powder Treason out of thin air for the very good reason that he had no need to do so. The conspiracy already existed, belonging to that long tradition of Catholic activism, plans for foreign invasion and the rest, with the aim of securing toleration. It was a violent conspiracy involving Catholic fanatics.

But this was Salisbury, the crafty statesman *par excellence*, as his past history showed: the man who had masterminded among other things King James' accession to the British throne. From his point of view, it was his positive duty, as a patriotic royal servant, to promote as much counter-espionage and provocative action as he could successfully inspire: it was all in the cause of public safety. Nor was Salisbury unique in this. The history of the late-Elizabethan plots (like many modern conspiracies) is chequered with so many agents and counter-agents that the truth of them is often impossible to unravel. Thus Monteagle's whispered warning gave Salisbury an opportunity to do what he did best. It was not an opportunity that he intended to miss.

The next move was to involve the King. Whoever thought up the dramatic ruse of the anonymous letter with its mysterious warning was aiming it specifically at one man. For most people (then as now) it was not even a particularly convincing story: and yet it was calculated to intrigue King James by playing upon two of his most marked characteristics, his intellectual vanity and his concern for his own safety. The precise authorship of the strategy cannot be known with certainty. It may have been Monteagle, hence the lavish official gratitude expressed in the preamble to his grant. This stated that by his perspicacity over the letter 'we had the first *and only* means to discover that most wicked and barbarous plot'. (The italicised words were inserted afterwards, presumably to distract attention from the government's prior knowledge of the treason which would have robbed it of much of its horror in the public imagination.) Or it may have been Salisbury, who knew so well how to manipulate his royal master.[27]

This matters less than the fact that the Monteagle Letter, obscure and ill-written as it might be, was in no sense a genuine document but was part of a plan of entrapment.

Thanks to information received, Salisbury could now sit calmly for the next ten days waiting, in his own words (which for once were perfectly sincere), for the plot 'to ripen'.

This ten-day period was also the time when the conspirators had their last chance to save themselves. Tom Wintour said afterwards that he had tried to persuade Catesby to abandon the Powder Treason, when Monteagle's servant Thomas Ward broke the news of the letter. But Catesby, like Phaeton, characteristically reckless (or foolhardy or fanatical), refused to listen.[28] He was by now at White Webbs, along with the Wright brothers. Taking the line that the letter was far too vague to constitute a serious danger in itself – which in a sense was true – Catesby decided that they must press on. On Tuesday 29 October, Mary Lady Digby moved ahead of her husband to Coughton Court in Warwickshire, in order to celebrate the great Feast of All Saints on the Friday. Father Garnet, Father Tesimond, Little John, Anne Vaux and her sister Eleanor Brooksby went with her. Sir Everard remained a few extra days at Gayhurst before setting out for his 'hunting party' in the neighbourhood.

On the Wednesday, 30 October, Guy Fawkes inspected the cellar in Westminster and satisfied himself that the gunpowder was in place (he did not check whether it was 'decayed', since with Wintour he had recently replaced any damaged gunpowder with new material). The next day Ambrose Rookwood travelled down from Clopton and joined his wife's cousin Robert Keyes at his London lodging. Thomas Percy was on his way back to London.

None of these men knew that the conspirators, who had been the hunters, were now the hunted.

PART FOUR

Discovery — By God or the Devil

The devil, and not God, was the discoverer.

GUY FAWKES

CHAPTER ELEVEN

Mr Fawkes Is Taken

Catesby sent for me into the fields...So I went to
him, who told me that Mr Fawkes was taken and the
whole plot discovered.

CONFESSION OF ROBERT WINTOUR
1606

Salisbury put the Monteagle letter in front of his royal
master on Friday 1 November. The King had returned
from hunting the previous day, but Salisbury evidently felt
no need to quicken his pace and waited until the afternoon to
give it to him. The King was alone in his gallery at Whitehall.
Salisbury handed him the letter without comment and let the
King read it in silence. Having read the letter once, James took
'a little pause', then he re-read it all through.*[1]

Salisbury said that the letter must have been written 'by a fool'.
This was a deliberate ploy, Salisbury explained afterwards. He
wanted to be sure to get his master's true reaction. Salisbury drew
particular attention to the phrase 'the danger is passed as soon as
you have burnt the letter', which, he said, he found quite mean-
ingless. It was his sagacious master – so experienced in the ways
of conspiracies in both England and Scotland – who puzzled out
the answer. James believed that something to do with 'powder'
was being suggested – in other words an explosion.

---

* These and the following details are taken from King James' own account, published in the so-called *King's Book* (printed as *King's History* in S.T., II, pp.
195–202). We therefore have his point of view, but Salisbury's point of view, of
course, only in so far as he communicated it to the King.

At this point, one might have thought that Salisbury – a sincerely concerned Salisbury – would have dropped his pretence of bafflement. If he had been in genuine ignorance about the meaning of the anonymous letter, surely this was the occasion to reveal at the very least the intelligence reports he had been receiving over the past year about Catholic unrest. But still Salisbury thought it best to 'dissemble' to the King; he did not tell James that there was already 'just cause' for apprehension about the Catholics' future behaviour. The King's fine questing intellect was to be allowed to flourish in a vacuum; its triumph when it pointed brilliantly to the solution would be all the greater. This at least was the gist of Salisbury's explanation afterwards to the King.

One may suppose that the true explanation was rather different; Salisbury was still in the dark about many details of the Plot, especially about the involvement, if any, of the leading nobles. He wished to lead his master to discover it more or less single-handed (with a little help from Monteagle), but he did not wish to embroil him in the murkier details of Salisbury's counter-plotting. Above all, Salisbury had no wish to arouse in King James those ever lurking fears for his personal safety which might have led to him insisting on springing the trap too soon. Thus Salisbury carefully managed the elaborate ritual of his consultation with the King.

On this same Friday a very different kind of ritual was taking place in far-off Warwickshire. While Salisbury nonchalantly conversed with the King in Whitehall, the Feast of All Saints was being solemnly marked at Coughton Court. If the pilgrimage to St Winifred's can be seen as an elegy to the recusant way of life, so this festival at Coughton may be viewed with similar nostalgia as the last great celebration of the English Catholic world: a world which was essentially loyal despite harassment, peace-loving despite suffering, and, where persecution was concerned, submissive to the will of God. They were all of them, the priests, the gentlemen and the gentlewomen, the faithful servants, about to see this world blown apart.

Coughton Court was an appropriate setting for such a solemnity.² It had belonged to the Throckmortons since the early fifteenth century and had been extended in Elizabethan times into a spacious and beautiful house with its 'stately castle-like Gate-house of freestone', in the words of the seventeenth-century antiquary Dugdale. Coughton also commanded from its flat roofs amazing views of the surrounding countryside. This was a perspective which would be useful in perilous times of searches by eager poursuivants.

For the staunchly recusant Throckmortons, these perilous times had lasted since the Reformation. A Throckmorton cousin had been executed in 1584 for a plot to free Mary Queen of Scots. Thomas Throckmorton, the present head of the family, like his brothers-in-law Sir William Catesby and Sir Thomas Tresham, had been persistently fined and had spent many years in prison. It was hardly surprising that by 1605 Coughton's gracious structure had its secrets, including a hiding-place in the north-eastern turret of the so-called Tower Room, with its inner and outer compartments, which was most probably the work of Little John, and there may well have been others.*

At High Mass on All Saints' Day, in front of a great gathering of Catholics, Father Garnet preached a sermon on the theme of a Latin hymn from the Office of Lauds: 'Take away the perfidious people from the territory of the Faithful.' The government prosecutor, Sir Edward Coke, afterwards used this text to suggest that Garnet had 'openly' prayed for 'the good success' of the Powder Plot, four days before it was due to happen. Such a prayer supporting treason, declared Coke, counted far more than mere consent, which he suggested Garnet had also given. In fact Garnet's correspondence around this time provides ample evidence of a concern for Catholic

---

* When this hole was broken into in 1858, a palliasse bed, a rope ladder, a small piece of tapestry and a folding leather altar were discovered within. Coughton Court is today leased to the National Trust, although the direct Throckmorton descendants are still closely involved with it. Coughton is proud of its connection to the Gunpowder Plot: a special exhibition has been mounted to commemorate it.

suffering which would justify the use of such a text. In October he wrote to Rome to say that the persecution was now 'more severe than in [Queen] Bess' time', with the judges openly saying that 'the King will have blood'. He later explained publicly that the text referred to the prospect of 'sharper' anti-Catholic laws in the coming Parliament.*[3]

The next day, 2 November, the Coughton party turned to the more melancholy rituals of All Souls Day, feast of the dead. This protracted sojourn of the Digby household at Coughton – Lady Digby and her small sons, of whom the elder Kenelm was only two – did not however pass unremarked. Also on 2 November, Father John Gerard came over to Gayhurst from Harrowden (presumably to say Mass). He was disconcerted to find the household vanished, with only Sir Everard remaining, making visible preparations for his 'hunting party'. Father Gerard then had a long conversation with Digby in which he asked some searching questions. Was there 'any matter in hand'? And, if so, did 'Mr Whalley' (an alias for Garnet) know about it?

'In truth, I think he does not,' replied Digby. There was 'nothing in hand' that he, Digby, knew of, 'or could tell him of'. This was of course disingenuous, to put it mildly, since Digby had been assured of Jesuit approval of the treason less than a fortnight earlier. Digby's honourable intention was to protect Gerard from implication in the Plot, and in a sense he did so successfully since Gerard afterwards called the conversation to witness as proof of his innocence. But Father Gerard, who was extremely averse to such 'violent courses', would always regret that he had not had an opportunity to try to dissuade Digby from his dreadful purpose.[4] So Digby was left to his own devices – or rather to those of his hero, Robin Catesby.

Saturday 2 November was also the day on which the

---

* Father Garnet has been called 'unwise' for using such a text (although it formed part of the Office of Lauds for that day): but it is likely that whatever text he used for a sermon so close to the chosen date of the Powder Treason would have been twisted in some way by the government (Anstruther, *Vaux*, p. 281).

Council resolved to take some action on the question of the threat to Parliament reported to them by Salisbury. Various Privy Councillors came to see the King in his gallery in his Whitehall palace. They told him that it had been decided that the Lord Chamberlain, Lord Suffolk, should 'view' the Houses of Parliament 'both above and below'. Yet, once again, urgency was scarcely the key-note of the proceedings. This expedition would not take place until the Monday, partly to prevent unlawful rumours spreading, and partly because it would be best to make the search 'the nearer that things were to readiness'.[5]

This decision, along the same lines as Salisbury's wish to let the Plot 'ripen', makes little sense if the Councillors were really in complete ignorance of what was being planned. By Saturday a full week had passed during which Salisbury and selected Councillors had been aware, thanks to the Monteagle Letter, that 'a terrible blow' might be struck at Parliament. To leave things as they stood for another forty-eight hours was reck-lessly irresponsible – unless Salisbury had taken his own steps to secure the safety of the building.

On Sunday evening, 3 November, Thomas Percy, back from the north, had a conference with Catesby and Wintour in London. By now Catesby and Wintour had been urged more than once by Francis Tresham to abandon their venture and flee because of the sinister omen of the Monteagle Letter. But Catesby would still have none of it. Percy, similarly resolute, declared himself ready to 'abide the uttermost trial'.[6]

It is possible that some rearrangement of the plans for a royal abduction was discussed at this late stage. There was a story afterwards about a visit to the young Prince Charles, Duke of York, by Percy: this at a time when everyone was trying to get in on the act (and please the government) by offering helpful information. According to the deposition of one Agnes Fortun, servant, Percy came to the little Duke's lodgings on or about 1 November and 'made many enquiries as to the way into his chamber', also 'where he rode abroad' and with how many attendants. But by the time this deposition was given it was too late for Percy to confirm or deny it. Wintour's version in his confession has the London conspirators getting word indirectly that Prince Henry was not after all going to the Opening of Parliament: which would have made the kidnapping of the second son pointless.[7] (This was hardly the line taken by the government subsequently. There were few references to the Powder Treason which did not drag in the fact that the royal heir – the kingdom's hope for the future – had been in the same appalling danger as his father.)

Events were now moving at such a pace that one cannot be absolutely certain what Catesby, Wintour and Percy discussed at this meeting. Guy Fawkes' statement that after 'sundry consultations' it was considered easier to abduct the Princess Elizabeth in the midlands rather than the Duke in London 'where we had not forces enough' remains, however, more convincing. (As for the fourth royal child, Princess Mary, aged six months, Guido admitted her kidnapping was discussed – but they 'knew not how to come by her'.) Sir Everard Digby's departure for Dunchurch, south of Rugby, the next day reinforces Fawkes' testimony. The point of Dunchurch, Digby stated later, was that it was only eight miles from where the Princess was housed at Coombe Abbey, so that she could be 'easily surprised'.[8]

Monday 4 November, therefore, saw Sir Everard Digby and seven servants installed at the Red Lion in Dunchurch, near Dunsmore Heath, where the 'hunting party' was to take place.* He travelled as the gallant he was, taking with him not only servants but a trunk of clothes which included 'a white satin doublet cut with purple' and other satin garments thickly encrusted with gold lace. Digby was joined by his uncle Sir Robert Digby and two Littletons, 'Red Humphrey' and his very tall, very dark nephew Stephen. These men were not conspirators but they were recusants or had recusant sympathies (Humphrey Littleton, like Thomas Habington, had been among those who had tried to get a Catholic MP elected locally in 1604).[9]

* The Red Lion at Dunchurch is now a private residence, known as Guy Fawkes House.

The whole party had a convivial supper at the inn. Later, a message was sent to John Wintour, step-brother of Robert and Tom from their father's second marriage, who happened to be at Rugby. He was invited to join them in order 'to be merry' together. Later still, John Grant and a friend, Henry Morgan, who had been sworn to secrecy at Grant's house, also joined them.[10] There was a Catholic priest in the party, Father Hammond, who said Mass early the next day, before the hunt moved off.

At eleven o'clock on the morning of Monday 4 November, Thomas Percy appeared at Syon House, the great house on the Thames, to the west of London, which belonged to his patron the Earl of Northumberland. This foray, which would bring about the downfall of Northumberland, was actually a fishing expedition on Percy's part. For all Catesby's bravado and Percy's own resolution, the Monteagle Letter could not be dismissed entirely. Percy decided to go down to Syon to find out what rumours, if any, had reached Northumberland (a member of the Privy Council). 'If ought be amiss,' he told Wintour and Catesby, 'I know they will stay [detain] me.' He used the excuse that he wanted a loan from Northumberland. Percy encountered his patron, talked to him, found to his great relief nothing out of the ordinary about his reception, and set off back to London about one o'clock.[11]

The timing of this visit was extraordinarily damaging to Northumberland. It was characteristic of the ruthless and self-centred Percy, a middle-aged man without any of the impetuosity forgivable to youth, that he did not seek to protect the man who had treated him so generously. He might at the very least have avoided Northumberland's company, but Percy did not even warn Northumberland to avoid Parliament next day, as his patron's subsequent moves demonstrate.

Afterwards Northumberland desperately tried to exculpate himself. Unfortunately he was in the position of a man who, all unawares, has had an encounter with a plague-carrier – and finds out too late to avoid suspicion of having caught the plague himself. He remembered the conversation in the hall at Syon, denied that it had had any treasonable content whatsoever, declared merely that Percy had asked him 'whether he would command any service' before going on his way. Yes, he had sent a message after Percy, but that was purely to do with the audits of the northern properties for which Percy collected the rents.[12]

What Northumberland did not know was that Thomas Percy on his return to London also paid a visit to Northumberland's London home, known as Essex House. There Percy saw his nephew Josceline, who was in the Earl's service.[13] No doubt Percy was also testing the waters at Essex House. But the double visit would ensnare Northumberland still further. As for Northumberland himself, he stayed at Syon till after dinner, when he sent for his horses to take him to London, where he would spend the night at Essex House. He had not applied for leave of absence from Parliament, and showed every sign of intending to go there – he had his servant bring up 'the necessaries for Parliament' from Syon – apart from one spasm of fatigue which passed.* Even the King, in a handwritten note directed to Salisbury, afterwards drew attention to the innocence of Northumberland's behaviour: 'as for his purpose of not going to Parliament, he only said at dinner that he was sleepy for [because of] his early rising that day, but soon after changed his mind and went.'[14]

About five or six o'clock in the evening, Thomas Percy assured Wintour, Jack Wright and Robert Keyes that 'all was well'. After that compromising visit to his nephew at Essex House, Percy went to his own lodging in the Gray's Inn Road, where he left orders for his four horses to be ready for an extremely early departure the next day. Late that night Robin Catesby set off for the midlands, to take part in the rising, the vital second stage of the Plot, and it seems that Jack Wright, his faithful henchman, and his servant Thomas Bates went

---

* There were ten bishops and forty peers eligible to sit in the House of Lords, of whom twenty-nine had appointed proxies; but Northumberland was not among them (Anstruther, 'Powder', p. 457).

with him as well. This public display of armed rebellion was intended to rally Catholics everywhere to the cause. At 10.00p.m. Guido Fawkes visited Robert Keyes and was handed a watch which Percy had left for him to time the fuse. An hour later John Craddock, a cutler from the Strand, brought Ambrose Rookwood the finest of all the engraved swords with the words 'The Passion of Christ' upon them.

But Thomas Percy was quite wrong. All was not well. For the hunters who were themselves being hunted, the last stage of the chase was beginning.

Monday was also the day on which members of the Council, headed by Lord Suffolk as Lord Chamberlain, were due to make their long-delayed search of Parliament, 'both above and below'. The official story told afterwards was of two searches, with a visit to the omniscient King in between. Nevertheless, Salisbury's first report of these tumultuous events (to the English ambassadors abroad) mentioned only one search – and that around midnight. Salisbury, however, may have been at this point concerned to simplify, for the sake of foreign consumption, what was certainly a very elaborate tale.[15] What is quite clear is how the search (or searches) ended.

Accepting the King's version, Lord Suffolk made the first search on Monday, accompanied by among others Lord Monteagle, whom he sent for from Monteagle's house in the Strand. Suffolk deliberately conducted himself in the most casual manner possible. He took care not to arouse the suspicions of a tall man standing in or near the cellar who appeared to be some kind of servant. In the words of the King, Suffolk merely cast 'his careless and his rackless [reckless] eye' over the scene. But his eye was not so careless that it did not observe an enormous amount of firewood – piles of faggots – heaped up in the cellar. Yet the lodging it served was quite small.

That was one surprise. The second came when the party was told by John Whynniard, owner of the house, that his current tenant was none other than Thomas Percy, kinsman and employee of the Earl of Northumberland.[16] That made the unusual quantity of firewood even more astonishing, since

Percy was well known to have his own house elsewhere in London and seldom slept at Westminster. The news also provoked from Monteagle a histrionic flash of revelation. Surely Percy must be the author of the anonymous letter? Monteagle told Suffolk that, as soon as he heard the name, he knew Percy must be his man. There was not only Percy's 'backwardness' in religion, that is his Catholicism, which pointed to him, but there was also that 'old dearness of friendship' which Percy felt for Monteagle, to explain the warning.

Monteagle – and Salisbury – were of course bound to produce an author, or at least a suspected author, of the letter which they themselves had actually concocted. Percy's was a convenient name: as tenant of the cellar, there was no question about his involvement in the conspiracy (all the details of which were not yet revealed). But, for the members of the Privy Council not in the know, the name of Percy was somewhat of an embarrassment. On the one hand they were anxious to secure the safety of Parliament. On the other hand, the whole matter – anonymous letter and all – might be 'nothing but the evaporisation of an idle brain'. Percy's connection to Northumberland, 'one of his Majesty's greatest subjects and councillors', was well known. They would be 'loath and dainty [reluctant]' to interfere unnecessarily in such a way as to cast aspersions on such an august figure.

The King was not content with this dainty approach. When he heard what had taken place, he pointed out sensibly enough that either a proper search must be made, or he would 'plainly ... go next day to Parliament' and leave the outcome of the day 'to fortune'. It seemed right that 'a small party' under Sir Thomas Knevett, a member of the King's Privy Chamber but also, conveniently, a Justice of the Peace for Westminster, should make a further discreet investigation.

Thus a search party, headed by Knevett, went back to the Westminster cellar. It was there, around midnight on Monday 4 November or perhaps in the small hours of 5 November, that a figure in a cloak and dark hat, booted and spurred as though for flight, was discovered skulking beneath the precincts of

Parliament. This 'very tall and desperate fellow' was immediately apprehended and bound fast. He gave his name as John Johnson, servant to Thomas Percy. It was a story that Guido Fawkes would maintain steadfastly for the next forty-eight hours.

The government's first warrant for arrest was issued in the name of Thomas Percy. He was described as a tall man with stooping shoulders, having 'a great broad beard' grizzled with white, and near-white hair: 'privy to one of the most horrible Treasons that ever was contrived'. It was stated to be essential 'to keep him alive' so that the rest of the conspirators could be discovered.[17] But Percy was mistakenly sought at Essex House rather than at his own lodging. It was then supposed that he had headed back to the north.

By this time the hubbub and commotion in the capital was swelling – not only in the Westminster area where the arrest had been made (and 'John Johnson' was being held in the King's chamber) but also in the Strand neighbourhood of the great lords' houses. These men were being turned out of their beds to fulfil their public responsibilities in a time of crisis. Thus Kit Wright overheard Lord Worcester, a Councillor, summoning Monteagle to go with him and 'call up' Northumberland. He rushed round to Tom Wintour at the Duck and Drake, crying 'the matter is discovered'. Wintour ordered him to make a further check and, when the hue and cry at Essex House was confirmed, correctly deduced that Percy was the man they were seeking. Wintour then told Kit Wright to hasten to Percy's lodging and 'bid him begone'. According to his confession, Tom Wintour added: 'I will stay and see the uttermost.'[18]

As news of the calamity which had befallen Guido spread among the conspirators still in London, a desperate dispersal commenced. Men fled on sweating horses, urged on by their panic-ridden masters. Fresh mounts would be needed along the way for in fleet horsemanship lay their only hope of eluding their pursuers. Kit Wright and Thomas Percy now went together, Percy dramatically saying to a passing servant as he went: 'I am undone.' At daylight Robert Keyes took to his horse. At this point Rookwood and Tom Wintour were the only conspirators left in London.* Rookwood was the next to depart. He set out on an epic ride, thanks to his famous horsemanship and the unparalleled quality of his steeds he had arranged along the way (he managed to ride thirty miles in two hours on one horse: an amazing feat for both man and animal). As a result he overtook Keyes, who had only got as far as Highgate, and then Kit Wright and Percy at Little Brickhill, north of Dunstable in Bedfordshire. Finally he caught up with Catesby, Jack Wright and Bates further along the same road. It was thus Rookwood who broke the news of the disaster to Catesby, the man who had planned it all.

In the meantime Catesby and Jack Wright had had an encounter of their own, with a recusant who was returning from London called Henry Huddlestone. The young man's father lived at Sawston Hall near Cambridge, but Henry, who was related to the Vaux family, had installed his heavily pregnant wife at one of their houses near Harrowden. The meeting was a most unfortunate chance from Huddlestone's point of view, since although he was friendly with many of the conspirators – and had recently seen them in London – it is clear that he knew nothing of what was being plotted. But he now rode cheerfully along with Catesby and Wright. When Catesby's horse lost a shoe at Dunstable and had to be reshod, Huddlestone stayed with him. It was not until they met up with Percy that Catesby bade Huddlestone 'go home to his wife'.[19] From the point of view of the authorities, however, Huddlestone had already been fatally contaminated by this short, innocent journey.

With Rookwood reintegrated into the group – which included Catesby and Bates, the Wright brothers and Percy – six of the Plotters now rode on together in the direction of

---

* No one seems to have thought of contacting Francis Tresham, who since his vain pleas that the action be abandoned was evidently no longer regarded as part of the conspiracy.

Dunchurch. They were aided by horses sent out to them by Digby by prearrangement, Percy and Jack Wright throwing off their cloaks into the ditch to make for greater speed. At this point, however, Keyes hived off in the direction of Lord Mordaunt's house at Drayton where he used to live with his wife the governess, and went to ground in the neighbourhood.

Still the intrepid Tom Wintour lingered. With remarkable cool, he decided to go down to Westminster and find out for himself what was going on. He was, however, checked in King Street by a guard in the middle of the road who would not let him pass. He then overheard someone saying: 'There is a treason discovered in which the King and Lords were to have been blown up.' At this point Wintour really did know that all was lost.[20] He went to the stable which housed his gelding, and headed after his comrades. Unlike the superbly mounted Rookwood, however, he knew he had no chance of catching up with them before the rendezvous arranged by Catesby at Dunchurch. He therefore made for his brother Robert's house at Huddington, taking in Norbrook, home of his sister Dorothy Grant, on the way.

Catesby and his companions reached the family home at Ashby St Ledgers, on the road to Dunchurch, at about six o'clock in the evening. His mother Lady Catesby was at dinner, and Robert Wintour, who had ridden over from Huddington on his way to Dunchurch, was there too. According to Robert Wintour's testimony, Catesby sent a message that he should join him in the fields, at the edge of the town, bringing his horse: 'but that I should not let his mother know of his being there'. Robert Wintour duly kept the rendezvous. Catesby told him that 'Mr Fawkes was taken and the whole plot discovered.'[21]

This was the reality of it all. It says something for Catesby's courage, the fabulous misguided courage which had buoyed him up since the beginning of the whole mad enterprise and had acted like an elixir on his companions, that even now he had no idea of giving up. It was on to Dunchurch, where Catesby proceeded to persuade Digby, in the words of Milton's Lucifer: 'what though the field be lost, all is not lost'. Catesby admitted to the full dreadful details of the conspiracy, which, it is suggested, Digby did not know before. He admitted that the plan had been discovered and that they were all on the run. But, he stoutly maintained, they were still ahead of the game.

Even in his darkest hour, he fantasised of victory, Catesby announcing that the King and Salisbury were both dead. This must be their opportunity: 'if true Catholics would now stir, he doubted not that they might procure to themselves good conditions'. To Warwick for arms! To Norbrook where their own armaments were also stored! To Hewell Grange, home of Lord Windsor! To Grafton Manor, home of Robert Wintour's wealthy father-in-law John Talbot who would surely join them! Finally to the west and to Wales, where the restive Catholics would happily join with them...

Digby, whatever his private shock, was won over. He may not have believed in what Catesby said, but he still believed in Catesby, his hero. Digby succumbed once again to Catesby's double evocation of their 'bonds of friendship' and the needs of the 'Cause'. But the party which now clattered on through the November darkness to carry out Catesby's grand plan at Warwick and so to the west was not much more than fifty people. It included the Wintours' step-brother, John, and Stephen Littleton, as well as Grant's friend, sworn to secrecy, Henry Morgan. The rest of Digby's hunting-party were appalled by the news that Catesby brought, and deeply resistant to any involvement with him. They correctly estimated his venture to be both treasonable to the state and ruinous to themselves. Then there were the 'lesser sort'. One of Digby's innocent servants, helpless in the face of his master's declared treachery, spoke for many when he asked what was going to happen to all of them, those who had never known the secret of 'this bloody faction' but now looked like being ruined by it.

Sir Everard Digby answered simply. No, he believed his servant had not known what was going on, 'but now there is no remedy'. George Prince, servant at the Red Lion Inn, remembered overhearing words of similar pessimism spoken

by one of the conspirators at an open window. 'I doubt not
but that we are all betrayed.'[22]

The London which the conspirators had left behind was in a
state of confusion and apprehension. In the words of a contemporary observer: 'the common people muttered and imagined many things', and, as for the nobles, they knew not what
to say or who to exonerate (or who to suspect): for a time 'a
general jealousy possessed them all'. Running through all of
this was a strain of wild if mindless rejoicing, for although it
was certainly not clear who had been trying to do what and for
why – except that the King had been saved from death – the
crowd was not disposed to forego its traditional and exhilarating pastime of lighting bonfires in celebration. The Council
made a virtue of necessity: there could be bonfires so long as
they were 'without any danger or disorder'.[23] So the very first
flames in commemoration of 'gunpowder, treason and plot',
flames that would flicker on down the centuries, were lighted
on 5 November 1605.

Obvious precautions were taken. The Lord Mayors of the
City of London and of Westminster were ordered to set a civil
watch upon their gates. The ports were all closed and did not
reopen until 16 November. An embarrassing situation arose
when the enthusiastic mob was found to be demonstrating
outside the house of the Spanish Ambassador, assuming that
the hated Spaniards were at the bottom of it all. The Council
issued a hasty order that the Spanish Ambassador must not be
'touched with this horrible practice of treason', which was fair
enough, given that he had planned to be present at the
Opening of Parliament and would have perished with the
others. In general the foreign ambassadors thought it politic to
light their own bonfires of thanksgiving and throw money
down into the crowd.[24] This went not only for the beleaguered
Spaniard, and the Ambassador of the Catholic Archdukes, but
also for the emissary of the Protestant Dutch: it was no time
to be taking chances.

The Council, with Northumberland present, met in the

morning in an atmosphere of deepening perplexity concerning the Earl's position. He left the meeting believing that no restrictions had been placed upon his movements, while many of the lords believed equally strongly that he had been advised to rest quietly in his own house for the time being.*[25]

Northumberland's man Thomas Percy was the only name known for sure to be associated with the treason, other than that of the prisoner 'John Johnson'. Nothing illustrates the bizarre nature of this particular day better than two contrasting measures. On the one hand, someone sent off to Simon Foreman, the celebrated astrologer, to get him to work out the probable whereabouts of the fugitive, Percy. On the other hand, a search was put in hand for a collaborative Catholic priest who would persuade the prisoner Johnson that it was his duty to spill the beans.[26]

Parliament met briefly in the afternoon. The entry in the Commons' Journal for 5 November (crammed into a small space in the margin) was as follows:[27]

This last Night the Upper House of Parliament was searched by Sir Thomas Knevett; and one Johnson, Servant to Mr Thomas Percy was there apprehended; who had placed 36 Barrels of Gunpowder in the Vault under the House with a Purpose to blow the King, and the whole company, when they should there assemble.

Afterwards divers other Gentlemen were discovered to be of the Plot.†

Parliament was then prorogued until Saturday 9 March.

As the conspirators scattered and the Londoners wassailed, 'John Johnson' was being interrogated.[28] He had so far given away nothing beyond the bare facts that he was a Catholic

* Possibly Northumberland's deafness was responsible for this unfortunate mix-up at such a manifestly delicate moment in his fortunes.
† The original entry has been framed and today hangs in the 'Noes' voting lobby of the House of Commons, commemorating what might well have been the most dramatic day in Parliament's history. There is always a large circle of curious tourists and schoolchildren round it at times of public access (see plate section).

from Netherdale in Yorkshire and that his father was called Thomas and his mother Edith Jackson (this at least was true) and that he was thirty-six years old (he was actually thirty-five). Certain scars noted on his body – presumably wounds received during his time as a soldier – he claimed to be the effects of pleurisy. A letter addressed to Guy Fawkes, and found in his possession, he explained neatly away by saying that Fawkes was one of his aliases.

Guido's composure was astonishing. Yes, he had intended to blow up the King and the Lords. No, he had no regrets – except the fact that he had not succeeded. 'The devil and not God', he said firmly, was responsible for the discovery of the Plot. No, he had not sought to warn the Catholic peers, he would have contented himself with praying for them. When the King asked 'Johnson' how he could 'conspire so hideous a treason' against the royal children, and so many souls which had never offended him, Guido did not attempt to deny the charge. He simply answered that a dangerous disease required a desperate remedy (an echo of Catesby's original words to Wintour, which suggest that the comforting catchphrase had been in general use among the conspirators).

Guido even had the ultimate bravado to tell some of the Scots present that his intention had been to blow them back into Scotland: his xenophobia remained unswerving. From time to time during the interrogation he smiled sorrowfully at his examiners, and told them they had not authority to examine him.

This iron self-control even evoked the admiration of King James. He described the prisoner as seeming to put on 'a Roman resolution': he was so constant and unshakeable in his grounds for action that the Councillors thought they had stumbled upon 'some new Mucius Scaevola born in England', comparing him to a legendary hero of Ancient Rome, who intended to assassinate the city's Etruscan enemy Lars Porsena, but slew the wrong man by mistake. Captured and hauled in front of Lars Porsena, Scaevola deliberately held his hand over the fire and let it be burnt off without flinching, in order to demonstrate that he would not give way under torture. In the legend, Lars Porsena was so impressed by Scaevola's endurance that he ordered his release and made peace with Rome.

The fate of Guy Fawkes, whatever the King's respect for his fortitude, was to be somewhat different.

CHAPTER TWELVE

The Gentler Tortures

The gentler tortures are to be first used unto him
[Guy Fawkes] ...
... and so God speed your good work. – James R

LETTER OF KING JAMES I
6 November 1605

The decision to apply torture to 'John Johnson' was taken by the King on 6 November.

Throughout the day the veteran Lord Chief Justice Sir John Popham pursued his investigations. Now in his mid-seventies, Popham was 'a huge, heavy, ugly man'. He was also implacable and 'inordinately cruel' in his hatred of the Catholics. His main line of attack was to go for those known Catholic subversives who had precipitately vanished from their usual haunts. Thus the servants of the extravagant, showy Ambrose Rookwood were examined on this day and his goods at Clopton – those incriminating crucifixes, beads and vestments – were seized.[1]

It is of course impossible to be certain how much of this process was helped on by Tresham's confidences to Monteagle, which were relayed forward. By the evening, however, the Lord Chief Justice had discovered enough to tell Salisbury that in addition to Percy he had 'pregnant suspicion ... concerning Robert Catesby, Ambrose Rookwood, one Keyes, Thomas Wynter [sic], John Wright and Christopher Wright and some suspicion of one Grant'.[2] Apart from Tresham, it will be seen that three names were missing at this stage: Digby, Robert

Wintour and Bates. The omission of Bates may be due to his inferior status, which made him less immediately interesting to the government. But the omission of Digby and Robert Wintour, both of whom operated in the midlands, suggests that the original source may well have been Francis Tresham, who from his London base would not necessarily have known of their involvement.

For all these advances, the obduracy of 'John Johnson' continued to enrage and baffle the authorities. Who on earth was he, with his scarred body and his mysterious past? Catholic subversives were supposed to be known to the government and closely watched, in an England which in its supervisory aspects met the criteria of a modern police state. But Guido stoutly maintained his false identity, allowing his comrades, as he hoped – if only it had been true! – time to get clear of the country.

Guido was now transferred to the Tower of London. The King himself drew up a list of questions that were to be put to him there, headed by the vital question *'as to what he is,* For I can never yet hear of any man that knows him'. After that, there followed many others including 'When and where he learned to speak French?' and 'If he was a Papist, who brought him up in it?' (There was evidently a strong suspicion that this 'John Johnson' was a Catholic priest.)[3]

The decision to put Guido to the torture was one that needed the authority either of the King or of the Privy Council, using the royal prerogative. King James himself took an active interest in the whole topic and his rights of decision in the matter. When Ralegh had been arrested in 1603 for possible conspiracy in the Main Plot, it had been the King who 'gave charge no torture should be used'. In the case of 'John Johnson', he reached a different decision.

Torture as such was contrary to English common law, or, as Sir Edward Coke in his capacity as a jurist would write in his *Third Institute*: 'there is no law to warrant tortures in this land'.*

* In 1215 Magna Carta, that cornerstone of English liberties, had expressly forbidden torture (Jardine, *Torture*, p. 48).

Coke, who was now in his fifties, had been the Attorney-General since 1594. (Before that, he had been in turn Solicitor-General and Speaker of the House of Commons.) He was a man who thoroughly understood the ways of the world, having married two extremely rich women. The second of these, Lady Hatton, twenty-six years his junior, was rich in connections too, being a member of the Cecil family. Immensely skilful – if at the same time pitiless and unscrupulous – he would in the words of Aubrey 'play with a case as a cat would with a mouse'.[4]

What Coke blandly ignored, in his emphasis on the rule of law, was that use of torture, supported by the royal prerogative, had actually been on the increase in England under the Tudors. Far from being a mediaeval survival, torture was one of the novel weapons in the armoury of Henry VIII's servant Thomas Cromwell, who had seemingly learnt much about this useful European practice during his travels abroad for Cardinal Wolsey.[5]

Torture was in theory reserved for exceptional circumstances, but, since these special circumstances included any suggestion of treason, a long list of Catholic priests had suffered frightfully in the time of Queen Elizabeth. (They were subject to torture, the government was careful to point out, not for their religion but for their supposed treason.) Among the leading characters in this narrative, both Father John Gerard and Little John had been tortured in the 1590s.

The uncovering of any conspiracy – and there had been a great number of them under Elizabeth, connected to the rescue of Mary Queen of Scots – was bound to be followed by the avid use of torture. Francis Throckmorton, a cousin of Catesby and Tresham, had been 'often racked' for his part in a plot of 1583. Then there were the servants of great men, such as those of the Duke of Norfolk, whom Burghley discreetly had tortured, under 'the Queen's signet'. Thomas Norton, the rackmaster, was said to have boasted of pulling one unfortunate fellow, called Alexander Briant, 'one good foot longer than ever God made him'. Sometimes there was not even the excuse of treason. Gypsies were tortured in Bridewell in 1596 to answer the truth about their 'lewd behaviour'; a boy Humfrey was 'lightly tortured' (no arms to be dislocated) in Nottingham for suspected complicity in a burglary.[6]

Such indiscriminate use – and the fact that it was against common law – made for a lingering popular uneasiness on the subject of torture. In 1592 the 'often exercise of the rack in the Tower' was said to be 'odious and much spoken of by the people'.* This uneasiness was not of course shared by the authorities, who were in the business of extracting information as fast as possible. Another method of applying pressure was by starvation, known as 'pinching'. Prisoners – including priests – would be incarcerated without food or water in dark subterranean dungeons, the only moisture being drops falling from the dank roof.[7]

This method took time to produce results. For those who were investigating a genuinely treasonable conspiracy, speed might be of the essence in probing its depths, as was undoubtedly the case with the dangerous criminal 'John Johnson'. Yet it is notable that Thomas Norton finally got into trouble for going beyond the permissible limits regarding torture and was forced to explain that he had not actually carried out his grotesque boast about lengthening Alexander Briant, but had only *threatened* to carry it out. In any case he had admired the 'poor unlearned' fellow's courage. (Briant was in fact not so poor and unlearned: he was a disguised priest.)[8]

Torture of course had its rules. No one was supposed to be tortured to death: this would have been counter-productive apart from anything else. For this reason, maimed or mutilated people – such as Little John since his accident – were not supposed to be subjected to it because they might be too weak to survive. If a session failed to provide the desired information,

---

* It should be pointed out that England was not alone in the practice. The Spanish Inquisition – the 'Holy Office' – employed torture: this was one of the aspects of England's hereditary Catholic enemy, Spain, which had aroused disgust and horror among the English, especially those merchants who might fall foul of the Inquisition, during the reign of Elizabeth I.

the victim should not in theory be tortured over and over again, on the reasonable assumption that he might not have had the information in the first place, and therefore had no truthful means of ending his torment. This was a rule which was generally ignored, especially in the case of priests. Lastly, torture was supposed to be increased gradually.

The letter which the King signed on 6 November specified that for 'such a desperate fellow' as John Johnson, if he would not otherwise confess, 'the gentler Tortures are to be first used unto him *et sic per gradus ad ima tenditur*' – and so by degrees proceeding to the worst. He concluded, 'and so God speed your good work', signing himself 'James R' (see plate section).[9] The gentler tortures referred to the manacles and the worst to the rack. By the 1590s, the manacles had become the method most favoured by the authorities, as they were inexpensive and easy to operate for those who applied them. The traitor – or suspect – was hung up by his wrists against a wall, using iron gauntlets which could be gradually tightened; wood supports beneath the feet would be removed and the prisoner would be left dangling for several hours, sometimes longer. As the vicious Richard Topcliffe observed of Campion (whom he tortured more than ten times): 'it will be as though he were dancing a trick or figure'. There were survivors of the manacles – notably Father Gerard – but there were also those such as his fellow Jesuit Father Henry Walpole whose hands were permanently maimed.[10]

There was only one rack in England, housed at the Tower of London. The rack was a large open frame of oak, raised from the ground. The prisoner was laid on it with his back to the floor, his wrists and ankles attached by cords to rollers at either end. Levers were operated which stretched the prisoner, quite slowly, while he was urged to confess. The rack, inevitably, caused permanent damage and dislocation to the prisoner. So feared was the instrument, indeed, that sometimes the mere sight of it was enough to cow the prisoner into giving information.[11]

It is not absolutely certain that in the case of Guy Fawkes

the authorities proceeded from manacles to the rack, although the King's letter clearly envisaged that it might be necessary to move on to 'the worst', in order to break this iron man. Sir Edward Hoby, a well-informed observer and a Gentleman of the Privy Chamber, wrote to Brussels that only the manacles had been used. 'Yet the common voice', in the words of Father Gerard, 'was that he was extremely racked in the first few days.' Priests subsequently held in the Tower certainly heard that Fawkes had been racked, and observers who saw Guido on the next occasion he was displayed in public witnessed a sick man, utterly broken in body.[12] Thus the balance of probability is in favour of the rack. Men did manage to hold out against the manacles – and Guido was nothing if not strong – but against the rack never, or hardly ever.

What is certain is that some time on 7 November, following the application of torture, they broke him – they broke Guido's body and in so doing they broke at last his spirit.* Hoby had a meaningful phrase for it: 'Since Johnson's being in the Tower, he beginneth to speak English.' His courage was still high the night before, as Sir William Waad, Lieutenant of the Tower, reported to Salisbury.[13] (As Lieutenant, Waad was always present at these sessions of torture.)

Guido's conversation with Waad was revealing. Here was no common criminal but, in a certain warped way, an idealist – or perhaps fanatic was the appropriate word: 'He [Johnson] told us that since he undertook this action he did every day pray to God he might perform that which might be for the advancement of the Catholic Faith and saving his own soul.' To explain his silence, Guido revealed that he had taken an oath to say nothing in company with his (so far nameless) comrades, and they had all then partaken of the Sacrament. But he

---

* There is a lack of documentary evidence to show conclusively where Guy Fawkes was held and tortured; traditionally he was held in the Bloody Tower, but tortured in the White Tower, in rooms below the present wooden (ground) floor; he may also have been held in a room, now vanished, in what looks like the thickness of the wall. Prisoners, in general, were tortured in subterranean areas and often held near by in advance to maximise the terror (Geoffrey Parnell, Keeper of Tower History, to the author; Yeoman Warders to the author).

was careful to add that the (similarly nameless) priest who gave them the Sacrament 'knew nothing about it'.[14] This oath had been sworn, and this illegal Sacrament administered, in England, which of course whetted the appetite of his interrogators. Nevertheless Guido still hoped to be able to endure long enough not to have to break his vow.

To Waad's amazement, Guido even managed to pass the night of 6 November resting peacefully 'as a man devoid of all trouble of mind' – although he had been warned of what lay in store for him. Waad told the prisoner that 'if he held his resolution of mind to be so silent', he must realise that the state was equally resolved to proceed with that severity which was necessary in a case of such great consequence. 'Therefore I willed him to prepare himself.'[15]

Having held out with a staunchness which did indeed recall the legendary determination of Scaevola, Guido cracked. He began to talk, probably late on 7 November, and continued on the 8th and 9th.

There was only one problem with all this. As the historian Tacitus had wisely observed fifteen hundred years before Guido was taken to that dark, underground chamber in the Tower, torture tended to bring about false witness.*[16] In order to alleviate his sufferings, the tormented man was more likely to give the Council the details it wanted to hear, rather than a strictly truthful account of what had taken place.

On 6 November, with Guido still holding out, Catesby and his confederates in the midlands must be judged to have had at least a chance of escape, although they would no doubt have left a wake of destruction behind them when the innocent – wives, families and uninvolved recusants – were picked up to pay for the crimes of the guilty. In any case it was not an option that Catesby considered. The mad scramble for further arms, further horses and further adherents continued, but it continued without success.

* Torture was a judicial procedure that had been known among the Romans, when slaves were frequently subjected to it.

The raid on Warwick Castle did secure some horses, but it also provoked the second public proclamation by the government, which was issued the next day. This named as wanted men, in addition to Percy: Catesby, Rookwood, Thomas Wintour, the two Wrights, John Grant (misnamed Edward Grant) and Robert Ashfield, servant to Catesby (probably a mistake for Bates). Rather touchingly under the circumstances, Robert Wintour had denounced the raid on Warwick because it would make 'a great uproar' in the county. Rookwood was against it for quite a different reason and skirted the town: with his magnificent equestrian cortège, he had no need of further horses.[17]

After a visit to Norbrook to pick up the stored arms, the conspirators headed in the direction of Huddington. At this point Catesby ordered Thomas Bates to make a detour and break the news to Father Garnet and his fellow priests at Coughton Court. In his letter to Garnet, Catesby once again showed that blind faith in the rightness of what he was doing – and had done – which was singularly out of touch with the reality of the recusant position. Catesby, together with Digby, asked Father Garnet to excuse their rashness, but then proceeded to solicit Garnet's assistance to raise a party in Wales where, far from the centre of government, Catholic support was believed to be vigorous. Garnet was appalled. With the arrival of Father Tesimond, Bates overheard the despairing words: 'we are all utterly undone'.[18]

The priests understood quite well what was going to happen, and so did poor Mary Digby. When Father Garnet tried to comfort her she burst out weeping, as well she might, with her glorious young husband a traitor and, almost worse, her two little boys as traitor's sons. Garnet's reply to Catesby and Digby begged them to desist from their 'wicked actions' and listen to the preachings of the Pope.[19]

Eliza Vaux, at Harrowden with Father Gerard and two other priests, Father Singleton and Father Strange, had got wind of the catastrophe the night before. It was brought to her by her young cousin (and tenant) Henry Huddlestone, who had had

that ominous encounter with Catesby and others on the road
as they fled. At the time it was thought safer to pretend she
had heard it via the servants' network, from one of Sir Griffin
Markham's men to one of hers. Eliza was still intent on the
marriage of her son Edward to Lord Suffolk's daughter. She
had been about to send him up to London to further the protracted negotiations when she heard that there were some 'gar-
boils' (disturbances) in the capital and held him back.[20] With a
sinking heart, Eliza realised that there was now little point in a
Catholic Romeo trying to further his suit with Lord Suffolk's
Juliet.

A more immediate problem was the plight of the priests.
Harrowden, like any known recusant centre, might expect to
be searched imminently. There was also the general Harrowden
concern for Father Garnet, at Coughton. So Father Singleton
and Father Strange, accompanied by Henry Huddlestone (who
left his pregnant wife behind at Harrowden), set out on the
morning of 7 November. On reaching Warwick, however, they
found it heavily patrolled following the raid of the night
before. Attempting to make a circuit, they were stopped and
arrested at Kenilworth by Sir Richard Verney.

Since Sir Richard was uncle to Eliza's new son-in-law, Sir
George Symeon, Eliza was full of hope that she could get the
prisoners released. But the situation was too serious for cosy
family connections to operate – and recusant connections
could in any case be an embarrassment. Furthermore Eliza, in
sending desperate messages to Sir Richard, naively issued full
physical descriptions of her friends – since she had no idea
under what aliases they were being held (while fervently
denying that any of them could possibly be priests).[21] Coolly,
Verney passed all this on to Salisbury. Huddlestone and Father
Strange were taken to the Tower, and Father Singleton to
Bridewell prison. Meanwhile the household at Harrowden –
including Father Gerard – awaited the inevitable arrival of the
poursuivants. At least Father Garnet managed to vanish from
the authorities' sight for the next few weeks into the thin recusant air. Anne Vaux was able to join him, posing as his sister

Mrs Perkins.[22] The Superior of the Jesuits was safe – or so it seemed at the time.

The leading conspirators – those who were left – and their diminishing band of helpers continued on their route to Huddington, where, according to Gertrude Wintour's subsequent testimony, they arrived at about two o'clock in the afternoon on 6 November.* Here they were joined by Tom Wintour. Even among the Wintours' closest relations and neighbours, there was no sympathy for the cause, only horror at the past and fear for the future. Thomas Habington of Hindlip, who had his wife Mary and their new-born son William to protect as well as priests, refused to have anything to do with the fugitives, and forbade his household to show any sympathy. Father Edward Oldcorne, among those he was sheltering, was equally horrified. Only Father Tesimond, the lively 'cholerick' Yorkshireman, seems to have had some concern for his friends' plight, even if he did not share their objectives. He came back with Bates from Coughton to join Catesby at Huddington for a while. (Danger did not however diminish his sense of style: Henry Morgan would later testify that Tesimond had been wearing 'coloured satin done with gold lace' on this occasion.)[23]

On 7 November the Archpriest Father Blackwell issued a passionate public statement which was far more in keeping with the sentiments of these honest Catholics than the wild do-or-die statements the conspirators were still making. Blackwell denounced the Plot against the King, the Prince and the nobility as 'intolerable, uncharitable, scandalous and desperate'. He was horrified by the news that a Catholic – he meant Guido – had been privy to 'this detestable device'. Father Blackwell hastened to point out that according to Catholic doctrine it was

---

* There are various traditions at Huddington associated with this dramatic arrival: Gertrude Wintour is supposed to have stationed herself at her window, waiting for the messenger from London: if he waved his hat when he came into view, all was well, but if he rode with his head covered, all was lost. An inscription on a windowpane in the main bedchamber, 'past cark [hope], past care', may refer to Gertrude's despair. 'Lady Wintour's Walk' in the woods is said to be haunted by her restless ghost. (Huddington owner to the author; Hamilton, I, pp. 182–3.)

not lawful for 'private subjects, by private authority, to take arms against their lawful king', even if he turned into a tyrant. He hammered home the message still further by referring to the duty of priests to instruct their flocks that 'private, violent attempts' could never be justified; Catholics must not support them in any way.[24]

For the conspirators, even if they had time to be aware of the Archpriest's proclamation, all this was the useless language of passive endurance which they had long ago rejected. In the small hours of the Tuesday morning, 7 November – as early as three o'clock – all those left at Huddington Court including the servants went to confession before taking the Sacrament at Mass. It was an indication, surely, that none of them now expected to live very long. Then they rode out into the rainy darkness, thirty-six of them all told. At midday they were at Hewell Grange, the house of the fourteen-year-old Lord Windsor (Northampton's ward), who was not there. It was still raining heavily. They helped themselves to arms, gunpowder and a large store of money. But the local villagers gazed at them with sullen hostility. On being told that the conspirators stood for 'God and Country', the reply came back that round Hewell Grange, men were for 'King James as well as God and Country'. Digby admitted later that 'not one man' joined them at this stage.[25] Their expectations of gathering support had been moonshine.

At ten o'clock that night, the band arrived at Holbeach House, near Kingswinford, just inside Staffordshire. It was the home of Stephen Littleton, one of those from the hunting-party who had actually stuck with them, and it was a house they believed could be fortified. For some time the Plotters had been aware of being followed. For a moment a hope sprang up that these were reinforcements, but it was a wild hope. It was in fact the *posse comitatus* (vigilante force) of the High Sheriff of Worcestershire, Sir Richard Walsh, accompanied by 'the power and face of the county'.

Tom Wintour now elected to beard the venerable John Talbot of Grafton, Gertrude Wintour's father, and see if there might not be some help forthcoming from that source. (Robert Wintour had pointedly refused to do so while they were still at Huddington, saying that everyone knew that John Talbot could not be drawn away from his loyal allegiance to the King.) Stephen Littleton went with Tom. None of this did any good. John Talbot was at his Shropshire home of Pepperhill about ten miles from Holbeach. He repelled them angrily, saying that the visit 'might be as much as his life was worth', adding, 'I pray you get hence.'[26] It was while these two were away on their fruitless mission that a horrible accident took place at Holbeach House, which in the taut and eerie atmosphere seems to have changed the mood there from one of bravado to despair.

The gunpowder taken away from Whewell Grange, conveyed in an open cart, had suffered from the drenching rain. It was now spread out in front of the fire at Holbeach to dry, which was an extraordinarily rash thing to do. One gets the impression that the Plotters were by now all so tired, as well as desperate – they had been riding on and on and on, some of them, like Catesby himself, seeking not only arms but sanctuary for the last three nights – that they were hardly aware of what they were doing. At any rate a spark flew out of the fire and the gunpowder ignited. So Catesby got his powder explosion at last. It was a quick violent blaze which engulfed him, together with Rookwood, John Grant and the latter's friend (from the Dunchurch hunting-party), Henry Morgan. The night before Robert Wintour had had a dream of premonition: 'He thought he saw steeples stand awry, and within those churches strange and unknown faces.' When he saw the scorched faces of his comrades, he recognised them as the faces in his dream.[27]

As Wintour and Stephen Littleton were on their way back to Holbeach, a man brought them a message, which suggested that these conspirators were dead, and the rest of the company 'dispersed'. At this point Littleton's determination gave out – he had after all been a latecomer to the enterprise. He encouraged Tom Wintour to fly 'and so would he'. Wintour, however, showed his usual stubborn resolve. He refused to turn away. 'I told him I would first see the body of my friend [Catesby] and bury him, whatsoever befell me.' Wintour went on alone.[28]

When he arrived at Holbeach, however, he found that the messenger had exaggerated the disaster. It was true that Digby had vanished – in fact he went with the intention of giving himself up – and so had Robert Wintour, who would eventually join up with Stephen Littleton. John Wintour, the stepbrother, who felt he had blundered into the conspiracy by mistake, slipped away during the night hours and gave himself up. The servant Thomas Bates had gone: no pressure was now being put on the Plotters to remain together. But Catesby at least was 'reasonably well' and so was Rookwood, although John Grant had been so badly disfigured by the fire – 'his eyes burnt out' – that he was blind. Morgan had also been burnt. The remainder of the company consisted of the two Wright brothers, Jack and Kit, stalwart to the last, as they had been among the first of the Plotters, and Thomas Percy. Wintour asked them what they intended to do.

'We mean here to die,' was the unyielding reply.

Wintour answered with equal firmness: 'I will take such part as you do.'

It would not be long now. Sir Richard Walsh and his two hundred men were closing in on Holbeach. On the morning of Friday 8 November, as Guido in the Tower prepared painfully to make the first of his major confessions, his erstwhile comrades readied themselves for the end. The devastating chance of the explosion had convinced them that their deaths were fast approaching, and so they all started to pray: 'the Litanies and such like'. Then Catesby, taking the gold crucifix which always hung round his neck, and kissing it, said that he had undertaken everything only for 'the honour of the Cross' and the True Faith which venerated that Cross. He now expected to give his life for that same cause, since he saw it was not God's will that they should succeed as they had planned. Yet he would not be taken prisoner: 'against that only he would defend himself with his sword'.[29]

The company under Walsh arrived in front of Holbeach

about eleven o'clock to besiege the house. Walsh was after-wards criticised for keeping himself 'close under the wall' for safety's sake, although such a quantity of men, armed with muskets, could hardly be said to be in any great danger, nor could the issue of the siege be in much doubt. Almost immedi-ately Tom Wintour, crossing the courtyard, was shot in the shoulder, which cost him the use of his arm. The second shot dropped Jack Wright; Kit Wright was hit next. Their famous swordsmanship had availed them little against the muskets' fire. After that, Ambrose Rookwood, still suffering from the effects of the fire, was also hit.

There were now left, as possible defenders, Catesby and Percy, as well as the wounded Tom Wintour, the blinded John Grant and the burnt Henry Morgan.

'Stand by me, Mr Tom,' said Robin Catesby, 'and we will die together.'

'I have lost the use of my right arm,' answered Wintour, 'and I fear that will cause me to be taken.' Even so, the two stood close together for their last stand, along with Percy, at the door of the house by which their assailants would enter. Robin Catesby and Thomas Percy were then brought down together by the same lucky shot. (John Streete of Worcester, who fired the shot, later petitioned for a thousand-pounds reward for this feat, although it was certainly by chance rather than design.)[30] Then the besiegers rushed in. What happened next was a macabre kind of rout, in which common sense – these men were wanted criminals – and even humanity, took second place to brutish greed.*

The Wright brothers and Percy were clearly *in extremis* but might just possibly have been kept alive, despite their 'many and grievous wounds', if there had been a surgeon available. Instead, their moribund bodies were crudely stripped: the Ensign of the posse himself pulled off Kit Wright's boots and

---

* According to local tradition, Stephan Littleton's young groom, Gideon Grove, managed to mount a horse and break out of the courtyard in the confusion of fire and smoke; he got as far as some fenland near Wombourne where the sol-diers caught and killed him. His ghost, as commemorated in a ballad by the nine-teenth-century Rhymer Greensill, is said to haunt the spot as a 'Phantom Rider'. (*Black Country Bugle*, October–November 1972; local information to the author.)

fine silk stockings. It was a distasteful scene. Sir Thomas Lawley, who was assisting Walsh, commented on it afterwards to Salisbury, when he referred to the unpleasant lack of discipline of 'the baser sort'. Percy died fairly quickly, thus fulfilling the explanation of Simon Foreman, the astrologer consulted after his flight: 'Saturn, being Lord of the 8th house [of death] sheweth that the fugitive shall be taken by the commandment of the Prince, and in being taken, shall be slain.'[31] If the Wrights lingered longer, it was not to any purpose; lying there naked on their way to death, they had neither the voice nor the energy to explain why and what they had done.

Grant and Morgan, both damaged by the fire, were easily captured, as was Ambrose Rookwood, who was not only scorched but wounded by musket fire. Tom Wintour, the first to fall, seems to have been saved by the action of the Sheriff's assistant, Lawley, and Lawley's servant. Afterwards there was a squabble about Wintour's horse, which the rival Sheriff of Staffordshire tried in vain to claim. But at the time Lawley at least had some practical sense of duty, realising that the conspirators, taken alive, would do 'better service' to the King than their speechless bodies.[32] Wintour was at first manhandled and beaten and probably stabbed in his stomach by a pike. Then someone came from behind, caught his arms, including the wounded one, and made him prisoner.

Robin Catesby survived long enough to crawl painfully inside the house. There he managed to find a picture of the Virgin Mary, and it was clutching this in his arms that he finally died. Lawley, who had denigrated the plunderers, saw himself in a different light when he collected up Catesby's gold crucifix and the picture of the Virgin, together with any other religious items he could find. Naturally, these were not despatched to the bereaved Lady Catesby at Ashby St Ledgers, the mother to whom Robin, on his fiery course, had not wished to say goodbye. To Lawley, these were not devotional emblems but valuable trophies. He sent them up to London to demonstrate just the kind of 'superstitious and Popish idols' which had inspired the rebels.[33]

So Tom Wintour's worst fears had come about. He had not died with his beloved Robin Catesby and he had lived on, in whatever lacerated state, to tell the tale of the Powder Treason. But Catesby, whose gallantry and rashness had dazzled and seduced a generation of young Catholic men, had had his last wish fulfilled. He had died without being 'taken'. Not for Catesby the Tower of London and its rigours, nor for him the pitiless indignities of a traitor's death. Of the two of them, Robin and Tom, it was Catesby who was the lucky one.

In London, the confused frenzy which had gripped almost everyone from King to commoner in the first two days after the discovery of the Plot was beginning to subside. Even before the news of the Holbeach shoot-out reached the capital, the general feeling of actually being endangered – where would they strike next? – was fading. Yet the government made it clear that no chances were being taken. On 7 November, while Percy was still at liberty, his patron the Earl of Northumberland was placed under house arrest, in the care of the Archbishop of Canterbury at Lambeth Palace.

On the same day, the gunpowder 'from out the vault of the Parliament House' was transported to the Tower of London. Here it was deposited in 'His Majesty's Store within the office of Ordnance', not very far from where Guido was incarcerated in his subterranean chamber. The gunpowder was described in the official receipt in the Debenture Book of the Royal Ordnance as having been 'laid and placed for the blowing up of the said house [Parliament] and the destruction of the King's Majesty, the nobility, and commonality there assembled'. Together with a couple of iron crowbars, eighteen hundredweight of powder was received.[34]

Interestingly enough, the powder was described officially as 'decayed'. A cynical clerk in the Royal Ordnance might have reflected that the danger to the King and all the rest of them had not really been so great after all. This powder (unlike the wretched stuff which had burnt up the conspirators at Holbeach) would not have exploded anyway. The straightforward explanation for this failure in the Plotters' arrangements is that the powder had once again separated in its elements – as had happened previously – and that Guido had simply not realised the fact (unless of course the 'decay' had taken place in the two days following 5 November). A rider to this, of a more Machiavellian nature, involves the Earl of Salisbury. One may question whether he really tolerated with equanimity the presence of a substance such as gunpowder in the vault at Westminster, in such large quantities and for so long. Perhaps a discreet search had established that the powder no longer constituted a real threat to anyone – except of course to Guy Fawkes himself by incriminating him.

Now that the government was so demonstrably on the winning side, an amazing quantity of people of all sorts, high and low, stepped forward to flag their loyalty by providing information. One of the first to do so was Lady Tasborough, mother-in-law to Agnes Lady Wenman, the bosom friend of Eliza Vaux. She thought it helpful to communicate the contents of that fatal letter of April which, it will be remembered, she had opened in her daughter-in-law's absence. On 5 November itself Lord Chief Justice Popham was already able to communicate to Salisbury details of Eliza's unfortunate prophecy – 'we shall see Tottenham turn French' – which proved that she 'expected something was about to take place'. Popham's comments on this were not encouraging for Eliza's future. Since two Jesuits, Gerard and Whalley (an alias for Garnet), made Harrowden 'the chiefest place of their access', therefore 'she may know somewhat'.[35] All this was in advance of Henry Huddlestone's capture and Eliza's frantic efforts to free the priests, which scarcely improved her chances of eluding the attentions of the Privy Council.

Others rapidly discounted any connection to the traitors. There were, for example, those who stepped forward gratuitously to point out – in case there was any doubt – that they had not seen the conspirators for at least ten years. Where Catholicism was concerned, Ben Jonson reflected cynically that immediately after the Plot's discovery there were 'five hundred gentlemen less' professing that religion. On 7 November, Jonson himself, uneasily aware of his known connection to the Plotters, came before the Privy Council. He had tried to contact an undercover priest who wanted a safe conduct in exchange for information but had failed to find him, in spite of the help of the (Catholic) chaplain to the Venetian Ambassador.

Two days later Sir Walter Ralegh (whose wife, Elizabeth Throckmorton, was a first cousin of Lady Catesby) utterly denied any connection with the recent treason, which he said he would have given his life to uncover. He recalled to mind his many services to his country, and desperately tried to distance himself from a plot which he termed 'this more than devilish invention'. On the same day, the Earl of Dorset, father-in-law of Viscount Montague, asked him anxiously whether he had known anything 'either directly or indirectly' which would have stopped him coming to Parliament.[36]

All the while Guy Fawkes sweated in the Tower, first to resist his torturers, then to give them in some measure what they wanted – or at any rate enough to relieve his torment. So far as the evidence can be pieced together, he revealed his true identity on 7 November and said that the Plot was confined to five (unnamed) people. His important confession was that on 8 November.[37] This confession named at last names, although it did not identify any Catholic priests. Nor for that matter did Guido incriminate prominent English Catholics or reveal the identity of the Protector, although he did talk at length about the plans for the proclamation of the Princess Elizabeth.

The third confession of 9 November, attested in front of Commissioners on 10 November, must be assumed to be the product of prolonged bouts of torture, growing increasingly severe.[38] Guido named Francis Tresham at this point, although he ascribed to him a comparatively minor role, and he named the priest who had administered the Sacrament following the oath as Father Gerard (but Guido stuck to his point that Gerard had not known what was going on). It is quite possible that Salisbury was present at this session since Waad wrote to him, saying that Fawkes wanted to see him. At all events, one new revelation was exactly what Salisbury wanted to hear. Here at last as a result of torture was the name – or so Coke would pretend later – of the government's *bête noire*, Hugh Owen of Flanders.

The signatures of Fawkes, declining in strength and coherence as the interrogation proceeded, provide, even today, their own mute testimonial to what he suffered (see plate section). The last 'Guido' – his chosen name, his name of exile – was scarcely more than a scrawl, and little helpless jabs of the pen beside it showed what it had cost Fawkes even to write as much as this.

CHAPTER THIRTEEN

Fire and Brimstone

It may well be called a roaring, nay a thundering sin
of fire and brimstone, from the which God hath so
miraculously delivered us all.

KING JAMES
to Parliament, 9 November 1605

King James' speech to Parliament on Saturday 9
November was a fine flowery piece of oratory. As the
discoverer of the Plot, he certainly blew his own
trumpet royally.[1] At the same time, he showed courage – he
did after all believe that he had been the intended victim of an
explosion only four days earlier. Even more admirably, James
showed himself merciful towards the English Catholics who
had not been involved in the Powder Treason as it did not
follow 'that all professing the Romish religion were guilty of
the same'. The 'seduced' Papists could still be good subjects.
He expressly mentioned the fact that the souls of some
Catholics would be saved and criticised the harshness of the
Puritans 'that will admit no salvation to any Papist'.

Although this policy of mildness and conciliation faded, as
the extent of the Jesuit priests' involvement – their alleged
involvement – was signalled by a vengeful government, it is as
well to remember that the Powder Treason was in the early
days seen by the King for exactly what it was: the work of a
few Catholic fanatics.

Naturally King James recalled his own troubled history.
Monarchs, 'like the high Trees', were subject to more tempests

than ordinary mortals, and the King himself had suffered from more tempests than most monarchs: he had been first threatened 'while I was yet in my mother's belly'. Now God had miraculously delivered them all from 'a roaring, nay a thundering sin of fire and brimstone'.

Then the King outlined the various unique elements which went to make up this particular treason. First, there was the sheer cruelty of the Plot itself which had threatened to destroy so many innocent people with no distinction made 'of young nor of old, of great nor of small, of man nor of woman'. Considering the various ways of putting mankind to death, he had no hesitation in picking on fire as the 'most raging and merciless', because there was no pity to be expected and no appeal against it. (A man might pity his fellow man at the last moment, and in any case a defence could be mounted; as to the 'unreasonable' wild animals, even the lions pitied Daniel...)*

The second element was one on which some might have had other views. The King insisted that there were small grounds if any to justify the conspiracy – only religion, and that was scarcely enough. The third element was the truly miraculous one, and on this the King really let himself go. This was his own unequalled brilliance in discerning what was about to happen. Regardless of his own trusting nature – 'I ever did hold Suspicion to be the sickness of a Tyrant' – he had been inspired to interpret the Monteagle Letter as indicating 'this horrible form of blowing us up all by Powder'.

The King solemnly told the assembled peers that he would have had one consolation if the Plot had succeeded. At least he would have died 'in the most Honourable and best company', rather than in 'an ale-house or a stew' (a brothel). Concerning the conspirators, he quoted another King, the Biblical David:

---

* This, the King's preeminent point, makes it clear that it was the fact of the terrorist plan being both random in its effect and inexorable in its execution which was found specially shocking, in exactly the same way as it is found shocking today about terrorist activities, which are usually pointed out to be cowardly as well as wicked.

'they had fallen into the trap which they themselves had made'. Moving on from the Bible to Ancient Rome he emphasised the need for thanksgiving. For if Scipio, 'an Ethnic [that is, neither Jewish nor Christian] led only by the light of Nature', had called on his people to give thanks for his victory over Hannibal, how much more necessary was it for Christians to express their gratitude! 'The Mercy of God is above all his works,' said the King.

In the House of Commons, the point was well taken. Sir Edward Hexter moved that the Speaker of the House 'should make manifest the thankfulness of the House to God, for his [the King's] safe Deliverance'. For the future, 'they would all, and every one of them be ready with the uttermost Drop of their Blood'. Parliament was now once more prorogued – until 21 January 1606 – since, as the King pointed out, all their energies would be needed in the unravelling of the recent wicked conspiracy. The chosen day was, incidentally, a Tuesday, like 5 August 1600 and 5 November 1605. Since the King had twice been 'delivered' on this propitious day of the week, he thought it 'not amiss' that the experiment of meeting on a Tuesday should be repeated.[2]

Salisbury was left to write to the English ambassadors abroad an elaborate letter of explanation of what had occurred. These included Edmondes in Brussels, Parry in Paris and Cornwallis in Spain. Fortunately King James had taken pains in his speech to establish that the Catholic foreign powers were not suspected of complicity – 'no King or Prince of honour will ever abase himself so much'. The government proclamation against the conspirators had indeed ended with the most slavish defence of the Catholic powers' integrity: 'we cannot admit so inhumane a thought as their involvement'. The way was open for these rulers to send back to London formal expressions of sheer horror at what had been so grossly plotted.[3]

Of course the powers and potentates revealed their own preoccupations. The Duke of Lerma, the Spanish King's *privado* (favourite), while describing the conspirators as 'atheists and devils', hoped to hear that there were also Puritans 'in the mixture'. Zuñiga, the Spanish envoy in London (he who had prudently lit bonfires and thrown money to the crowd on 5 November), believed that Thomas Percy had been in charge of the operation and that he was 'a heretic', in other words a Protestant, who was known to favour France over Spain. With equal conviction and equal inaccuracy the French King was quite sure that the Spanish ministers must have had a hand 'in so deep a practice'.[4]

On Sunday 10 November, Salisbury, armed with Guido's confession, was able at last to set in motion proceedings to extradite Hugh Owen from Flanders. Owen angrily rebutted the charge: 'I would take my oath', he wrote to Lerma in Spain, that he had known nothing about the conspiracy. The cautious Archdukes, worried by the lack of proof, contented themselves with putting Owen and his secretary under house arrest.[5]

Much more gratifying for the government was the sermon of the Bishop of Rochester, Dr Barlow, at Paul's Cross on this same Sunday. It was to be the first in a long line of such exhortatory sermons on the subject of the Powder Treason. Described as 'one of the ripest in learning', Barlow had been part of the team associated with producing the Authorised Version of the Bible after the Hampton Court conference. Since he, like the King, would have been present in the House of Lords at the moment of the explosion, his awareness of his own narrow escape must have lent him a particular fervour. In any case Barlow, a man who had already given two sermons at Paul's Cross, one praising Essex on his return from Ireland in 1596, and another justifying his execution five years later (with detailed instructions from Salisbury), had surely been primed over what to say.[6]

Yet again the party line was to vilify Guy Fawkes, and to see the Plot as the work of fanatics. In contrast to many, many subsequent sermons, the English Catholics were not attacked as such, just as King James had been careful to distinguish good Papists from bad. But the main thrust of Barlow's sermon was an extraordinary panegyric of his sovereign in terms which made even James' own self-glorification seem rather flat. The King was not only a 'universal scholar, acute in arguing, subtle in distinguishing, logical in discussing', he was also 'a faithful Christian': and so forth and so on, in what has been described as an evocation of the King as 'something of a Christ figure'.[7]

An awareness of having had a narrow escape was not of course confined to the King and Dr Barlow. Queen Anne, that famously fruitful vine, found herself being congratulated all over again on her fecundity in every loyal address. Yet, in her case, once sheer relief – for she would certainly have been present at the Opening – had given way to a more sober consideration of the future, she could appreciate the shadows falling over her Catholicism. As James' Queen Consort, she had attended Protestant services (although without taking the Sacrament); she had agreed to the baptism of the Princess Mary in the Protestant rite in May, while she herself had similarly undergone the ceremony of 'churching' (the purification of a woman after childbirth) in the Protestant rite. At the same time, she maintained her position as a closet Catholic – literally so, since her Mass had to be heard extremely privately in her own apartments.

This graceful ambivalence might not survive in the post-Plot atmosphere of England, and in fact Queen Anne was careful to evade meeting the emissaries of the Catholic powers. She declined to meet Baron Hoboken, envoy of the Archdukes, for two years, thanks to their laggard response to the Hugh Owen business. A convenient fever also caused her to cancel an audience with Zuñiga immediately after the Plot's discovery, lest the Queen's patriotism be suspect. When she did meet the Spaniard, towards the end of November, she spoke at length about her grief at the unfortunate plight of Catholics, and her desire to help them.[8] But in the future her active Catholic sympathies found their expression chiefly in trying to secure grand Catholic marriages for her children.

Another member of the Royal Family who became aware of her own escape as details of the Plot emerged was the nine-year-old Princess Elizabeth. When the alarm came from Warwick, she had been bundled off to Coventry, which was thought to be safer than Coombe Abbey. In her case, she had escaped abduction rather than death, but she made it clear to her guardian Lord Harington that what had been proposed for her by the conspirators would have been a fate *worse* than death. Lord Harington reported: 'Her Highness doth often say "What a Queen should I have been by this means? I had rather been with my Royal Father in the Parliament-house, than wear the Crown on such condition".' Not surprisingly, the shock of it all left the little girl 'very ill and troubled'.[9]

If Queen Anne was justified in bewailing, however ineffectively, the unfortunate plight of the English Catholics, that of the conspirators was infinitely worse. Those at Holbeach – Thomas Wintour, Ambrose Rookwood and John Grant, all in bad physical shape – were taken first to Worcester in the custody of the Sheriff and then to the Tower of London. Meanwhile the bodies of Robert Catesby and Thomas Percy were exhumed from their midland graves by orders of the government, and their heads cut off. The intention was to exhibit the decapitated heads at the corners of the Parliament House which they had planned to blow up. (The blacksmith who forged the ironwork to make this possible was paid 23 shillings and 9 pence.) Among those who inspected these grisly relics *en route* to London was Lord Harington himself, who thought that 'more terrible countenances were never looked upon'. He discerned a special evil mark on their foreheads, a description one suspects that he passed on to his royal charge to fuel her understandable fears still further.*[10]

Thomas Bates, Catesby's servant, was taken prisoner in Staffordshire, and Robert Keyes, who had broken away from the Dunchurch meeting, was also caught. Sir Everard Digby,

---

* This ghoulish practice was not special to the dead Gunpowder Plotters; the heads and limbs of traitors were commonly so displayed; these relics might survive *in situ* for a considerable time as an awful warning of the perils of betraying the state.

who had intended to turn himself in to Sir Fulke Greville at Warwick, was discovered by a small posse of pursuers with two servants concealed in 'a dry pit'. Excited cries of 'Here he is! Here he is!' were met by the imperturbable reply of the gallant horseman: 'Here he is indeed! What then?' Since Digby did not intend to surrender to such small fry, he advanced his horse 'in the manner of curvetting' – that is, in an expert equestrian leap.[11] He would have broken out of the encirclement had he not spied reinforcements of several hundred men coming up behind the posse. He then gave himself up to the most senior-looking man among them. These conspirators, also, were eventually taken to London.

By December, only Robert Wintour, of the surviving comrades, was still at liberty. In London, Francis Tresham was arrested, following Guido's denunciation on 12 November, and taken to the Tower three days later. Three leading Catholic peers, Lord Montague, Lord Mordaunt and Lord Stourton, who all had embarrassing connections to the abortive Plot, were also taken to the Tower. Lord Montague had not only briefly employed Guy Fawkes, but had probably been tipped off by Catesby not to attend Parliament; Lord Mordaunt was Keyes' patron as well as being connected to him by marriage and had planned to be absent because he disliked the coming legislation; Lord Stourton was Tresham's brother-in-law, and Guido had said he would have been detained from the Opening by some kind of accident. The prisoners in the Tower were joined on 27 November by the Earl of Northumberland, transferred from Lambeth.

While plans for the intensive interrogation of the Plotters and their presumed allies were being worked out by the government in London, the English recusant community was suffering exactly that kind of relentless investigation which it had feared for so long. There was now no reason for the authorities to let sleeping recusants – and their priests – lie. On the one hand, further information about the recent wicked conspiracy must be sought, and on the other hand old scores might be paid off (there was always a degree of vindictiveness about the poursuivants' action, nor were they above making a financial profit from it). The desire to make a good thing out of the Powder Treason was not however confined to one rank in society. One of the communications on this subject to Salisbury was that of Susan Countess of Kent who was quite sure – on no particular grounds – that a certain Mr William Willoughby must have been mixed up in the conspiracy. As a result of his presumed villainy, she suggested that she might have his £200 living in Suffolk.[12]

White Webbs, in Enfield Chase, was searched on 11 November and found to have 'many trap doors and passages'. Anne Vaux, alias Mrs Perkins, was of course absent and had been for some time, since Father Garnet judged the house too dangerous a refuge. But four servants were found there: James Johnson, who was about forty, Elizabeth Shepheard, the wife of the coachman, Margaret Walker, in her twenties, who had been in the service of 'Mrs Perkins' for three years, and Jane Robinson, aged fourteen, who was known as the 'Little Girl'. While all admitted to being 'obstinate Papists', they denied at first that the Mass had ever been said at White Webbs.[13]

Then the terrified Jane Robinson gave the game away. She said that there had been a Mass said within the last month but she could remember nothing about the priest except he was 'apparelled like a gentleman'. Father Garnet, the alleged brother of Mrs Perkins, had been known as Mr Meaze there; and yes, in answer to questioning, he had had quite separate apartments from Mrs Perkins. This was probably intended to establish that Mr Meaze was in fact a priest, not a bona-fide brother of Mrs Perkins, whose true identity was not at this point known. But the question marked the beginning of officialdom's prurient interest in the relationship of 'Mr Meaze' and 'Mrs Perkins', which would continue till the day of the former's death, and cause him great pain. James Johnson was now taken up to London and held in the Gatehouse prison.

The long-anticipated search of Harrowden took place over nine days beginning on 12 November. Father Gerard, an unseen, well-hidden presence throughout, was a veteran of such searches, and knew, like all the recusants, the importance of absolute attention to detail. Candles could not even be lit in the kind of dark hole where a priest was concealed, lest the characteristic smell of snuffed-out wax gave the game away. During one search, at Braddocks near Saffron Walden in the 1590s, Gerard had had to exist for four days on two biscuits and a pot of quince jelly which his hostess, Mrs Wiseman, happened to have in her hand as the poursuivants burst in and he was bundled away.

At Harrowden, Gerard was able to sit down but not to stand up in his refuge. But on this occasion he did not starve, since this hiding-place contained one of Little John's characteristic devices, a tube through which he could receive food. After about four days, Eliza Vaux distracted the attention of the authorities by prudently revealing a hiding-place which contained 'many Popish books' and other objects of devotion, 'but no man in it', said the disgruntled government report. The search let up a little after this. Thus Gerard could be brought out at night and warmed by the fire. On 21 November, the searchers finally departed, quite convinced that no one could have survived their inspection.[14] Father Gerard was safe.

By the time the search was abandoned, Eliza Vaux had already been taken away to London under arrest, and had undergone her first interrogation. She was, after all, in deep trouble already with her unfortunate letter to Agnes Lady Wenman and her ill-timed efforts to suborn Sir Richard Verney into releasing her friends. Even her father, Sir John Roper, who was Clerk of the Common Pleas, wrote her an angry letter of remonstrance over her behaviour. Now over seventy, he was determined not to die without acquiring the peerage he believed to be his due. All Roper's succulent presents to Salisbury, including fruit, falcons, game and 'a great standing bowl', were likely to go to waste if his own daughter let the side down by recusancy. And maybe – with the news of this frightful treason – she had let the side down with something worse than that... But Eliza Vaux, as a widow with a cause, was perfectly capable of standing up for herself: as Sir Thomas Tresham and the late Lord Vaux had discovered.

She responded to Sir John with equal indignation. In a letter addressed to 'my loving father' and signed 'your obedient daughter', she craved her father's blessing, but the text between these conventional salutations was anything but submissive. Eliza professed her absolute amazement that her father could for one moment believe that she had had anything to do with the recent conspiracy. As it was, it would be another eleven years and a colossal amount of money expended before Sir John Roper finally got his peerage; he spent the last two years of his life gratifyingly entitled Lord Teynham.[15]

In front of the Council, Eliza Vaux was equally spirited.[16] She refused to admit a number of things. Most importantly, she absolutely refused to give way on the subject of Father Gerard's priesthood. She swore she had not known that Gerard and the others were priests, since they looked 'nothing like priests'; she had taken them for Catholic gentlemen. (This was a vital denial since the penalties for harbouring priests could include death.) She also absolutely refused to admit that Father Gerard had been or was now at Harrowden. She said she had no idea of his whereabouts, but, if she had, she would not give them away to save her own life or anyone else's.

One of the Councillors who had always been friendly to her – probably Northampton – now escorted her courteously to the door. 'Have a little pity on yourself and your children,' he said in a low voice. 'And tell them what they wish to know. If you don't you will have to die.'

But Eliza answered in a loud, bold voice: 'Then I would rather die, my Lord.' Her servants listening outside the door burst into tears. Northampton's words had of course been intended purely to cow her – which they did not succeed in doing – and Eliza Vaux did not die.

She was put into the custody of an alderman, Sir John Swynnerton, in London, and made to remain with him for many months until a plea to Salisbury got her bail. At this point Eliza cunningly manipulated the contemporary image of a female as both frail and indiscreet. How on earth could she have been entrusted with the details of the treason? Who would dream of putting 'their lives and estates in the power and secrecy of a woman'?[17] Her questions were wonderfully disingenuous for someone who had been breaking the law with courage and consistency for years. The truth was that the discovery of Father Gerard (or any other priest) at Harrowden could have destroyed her and her family, but the secret structures of Little John preserved them all. The only inevitable casualty was the match between Edward Lord Vaux and Lady Elizabeth Howard. Within two months, the girl had been married off to a grand old widower, forty years her senior.

Eliza Vaux had handled herself and her secrets well. The wives of the actual conspirators were in far more parlous situation, from which bravery and bluff could not rescue them. Six wives, among other women connected to minor figures in the Plot, were brought up to London, and housed, like Eliza Vaux, by the City aldermen. Martha Wright Percy and Dorothy Wintour Grant, sisters as well as wives of Plotters, were in a specially fraught situation. Then there were Dorothy and Margaret Wright, wives of Jack and Kit, Christiana Keyes, the governess wife of Robert, and Elizabeth Rookwood (Martha Bates does not seem to have been rated worthy of arrest). Notification from the Sheriff to the government following these arrests drew attention to one poignant aspect of the wives' removal to London. He had, he said, 'taken care and charge of these women's children until your honours' pleasures be further known'.[18]

The conspirators' homes were searched and in many cases looted. Goods sought were seized at Ashby St Ledgers, although this was the property of Lady Catesby rather than of her son. Huddington Court was similarly treated. By 17 November, nothing of any real value was said to be left there, since so much had been taken away every day; although some devotional objects and books to do with the Mass were discovered in a hollow in the wall a few weeks later.[19] Even John Talbot, Robert Wintour's staunchly patriotic father-in-law, had his house searched and arms and papers removed. (These papers, not surprisingly, revealed nothing to do with the treason.)

One of the most piteous situations was that of Mary Lady Digby. Brought up as a wealthy young woman, she found that great possessions now made her an outstanding target for rapacity. Gayhurst was ransacked. 'Base people' were everywhere. Even the servants' belongings (which were certainly not forfeit) were simply transported away. The cattle and grain were sold at half price.

As for Mary herself, the Sheriff would not let her have 'apparel' to send to her husband in the Tower, nor for herself 'linens for present wearing about my body' (underwear). In a desperate plea to Salisbury, Mary wrote that the Sheriff – who would probably make over a thousand pounds profit 'underhand' – was dealing in all the properties at Gayhurst 'as though they were absolutely his'. As a result, she was utterly destitute, having nowhere for herself and her children 'to abide in' and nothing for their maintenance. Judging from the official records, it does not seem that Mary Digby exaggerated. The Sheriff himself wrote proudly: 'All goods are carried away, even to the very floor of the great parlour.'[20]

In the Tower of London, that fire and brimstone which had been so miraculously averted from Parliament was being brought down upon the heads of the erstwhile conspirators. Coke afterwards said that the interrogations had taken 'twenty and three several days' altogether (in a ten-week period), with a separate commission set up to examine the lesser folk – not only minor people who had become involved at Dunchurch but serving people and bystanders who could act as witnesses.[21]

The Lieutenant's Lodgings, under the control of Sir William Waad, were used for the important interrogations. Waad, now in his sixties, had been made Lieutenant of the Tower in August. The appointment marked a long career of diplomacy and intrigue in the service of Salisbury's father Burghley, and it was Waad who had first ransacked, then skilfully rearranged the papers of Mary Queen of Scots in 1586. It was also Waad, involved in the discovery of all the major conspiracies of late Elizabethan and early Jacobean times, who was responsible for the interrogations centring on the Main and Bye Plots of 1603. Significantly 'that villain Waad' was later accused by Lord Cobham of tricking him into signing a piece of blank white paper so that Waad could forge his confession. Like Sir Edward Popham, Waad had a vindictive dislike of Catholics beyond the call of duty, and as Clerk of the Privy Council had been ardent in the pursuit of priests and recusants.[22]

In October 1608 he erected a monument to his work on the discovery of the Powder Treason, which ended by quoting, in Hebrew, the Book of Job: 'He discovereth deep things out of darkness, and bringeth out to light the shadow of death.'* Where the Catholics were concerned, bringing deep things out of darkness was certainly the aim of Sir William Waad.

Only two of the 'confessions' which resulted from these numerous interrogations were ever made officially public. These appeared in the so-called *King's Book*, printed for the general edification about the end of November.[23] The *King's Book* had a wide circulation, stimulating popular interest in the recent dramatic – and potentially horrifying – events still further. (Among those stimulated by it may well have been Shakespeare as he worked on his new play, *Macbeth*.) The two statements printed in the *King's Book* were a version of Guy Fawkes' original full confession of 8 November, revised on 17 November, and the confession of Thomas Wintour signed on 23 November. Otherwise, the state papers provide various versions of the numerous interviews, while Coke quoted from them, freely adapted according to the needs of his prosecution, at the coming trials.

---

* The monument – still extant today – begins with a tribute to King James ('most renowned for piety, justice, prudence, learning, courage, clemency and the other Royal virtues …'), then names the Councillors who helped uncover the Plot, before listing the Plotters themselves, including Sir William Stanley, Hugh Owen and Father William Baldwin (see plate section). But the Council Chamber where it lies cannot literally have been the site of the interrogations, since it was carved out of the Great Hall only in 1607. (Parnell, *Tower*, p. 61.)

Was torture used once more? There was no further official sanction for torture given this year, other than the King's letter of authorisation concerning Guido and 'the gentler tortures' already quoted. The eager recommendation to Salisbury by Lord Dunfermline, the Lord Chancellor of Scotland, that 'the prisoners should be confined apart, in darkness, and examined by torchlight, and that the tortures be slow and at intervals, as being most effectual', is no proof that Salisbury actually followed his suggestion, although it does indicate the kind of atmosphere then prevailing.* More concrete evidence of the use of torture is provided by a letter from Salisbury himself, dated 4 December. In a document which is difficult to interpret in any other sense, he complained of the conspirators' obstinate refusal to incriminate the priests, 'yea, what torture soever they be put to'.[24]

It suggests that some at least of the Plotters had been subject to the manacles, or perhaps they had simply been shown the rack to terrify them: a method of interrogation which could be construed as needing no authorisation. The same technique may have been used over the trial of Ralegh. Coke denied that a certain witness had been threatened with the rack, answering smoothly: 'we told him he deserved the Rack, but did not threaten him with it'.[25] Since Salisbury and the government were now trying to entrap men who were innocent – the priests – in the same net as the guilty – the conspirators – they were no longer engaged in simply laying bare the truth. In order to achieve false or partially false confessions, torture and its threat might indeed be necessary.

A candidate for torture may have been the young recusant Henry Huddlestone, who made a series of confessions about that fatal meeting on the road with Catesby, and his expedition thereafter with the priests. Father Strange, captured with him, was certainly tortured at some point ('grievously racked'), although probably not until the next wave of interrogations in 1606.[26]

---

* As for King James' personal attitude to torture, it should be borne in mind, given his Scottish Lord Chancellor's words, that the practice certainly did not come to him as an English novelty; he had grown up with its use.

Yet the first confessions, those of November, did not provide that precise, strong link between the priests and the Plot which would have been convenient for the government. In his declaration of 13 November (the day after his arrest) Francis Tresham, while generally exculpating himself, did implicate Father Garnet in the abortive negotiations with Spain of 1602 – the so-called Spanish Treason.[27] This was helpful so far as it went, because the Spanish Treason was otherwise a somewhat tricky subject for the government to handle. It was undoubtedly a treasonable venture, whether described by Wintour or Guy Fawkes, for it was certainly treason to seek the armed assistance of a foreign power in order to overthrow the existing government of England. However, times had changed and there was absolutely no advantage, and a great deal of possible disadvantage, in berating the Spanish King in the new warm climate following the Anglo-Spanish Treaty. To make the Spanish Treason a Jesuit-inspired enterprise was the tactful solution.

In exactly the same way, the government were concerned to impose the names of their enemies Hugh Owen, Sir William Stanley and Father William Baldwin upon the conspiracy. Since the Plot already contained quite enough genuinely treasonable material, this imposition was for their own wider purposes. It has been noted that Salisbury had been quick off the mark in demanding the extradition of the detested Owen from the Spanish Netherlands. In the two published confessions of Guido and Tom Wintour, if collated with the various drafts and versions still in existence, there is evidence that these names were deliberately introduced. Salisbury let himself go about 'that creature Owen' in a letter to Sir Thomas Edmondes of 2 December. He instructed the Ambassador in Brussels carefully on the version of the Plot which must be spread among Owen's friends. It should be 'as evident as the sun in the clearest day' that Stanley, Father Baldwin and Owen were all involved 'in this matter of the gunpowder'. Furthermore, Baldwin, via Owen, and 'Owen directly of himself' had been 'particular conspirators'.[28]

In short, a Cold War was being conducted (and had long been conducted) with the Catholic intriguers across the water. This meant that matters of veracity were less important than the wider issue of ensuring Protestant success.

Tom Wintour's confession was supposedly signed by him on 23 November. He added to it further details of the so-called Spanish Treason on 26 November.[29] Wintour's account became the basis for most other subsequent narratives, including that of Father Tesimond himself. This was not only because the confession was published at length, but also because Wintour, uniquely among the survivors, had been in on the Powder Treason since the beginning. Guido, battered and tortured as he might be, could still not provide the full details of those early days with Catesby, the season before he himself was recruited.

It is, however, a document which cannot be taken purely at its face value. This is because Wintour's signature at the bottom – 'Thomas Winter' (sic) – is quite impossible to reconcile with any signature that had been made by him in the past. The version 'Wintour' was the one invariably used by him – whereas the version 'Winter' (or 'Wynter') was generally used by the government.[30] There is a further difficulty posed by the signature, which, whatever its spelling, is not noticeably shaky. Yet this was the alleged signature of a man who had been seriously wounded in the shoulder, losing the use of his right arm, less than a fortnight previously. Nor does Waad's report to Salisbury on 21 November inspire confidence: 'Winter' (sic) now found his hand so strong that he would write down after dinner what he had already declared to Salisbury verbally; the prisoner would then add 'what he shall further remember'. The implication is that Tom Wintour by now was remembering what he was told to remember.[31]

Wintour, since his confession was so vital, may well have been exposed to the awesome sight of the rack. But perhaps, wounded and helpless as he was, it was not necessary. The implicit threat of his situation – the despair of the prisoner cut off in the darkness described by Lord Dunfermline – may have been enough for the government to produce from him the confession they wanted. At all events, a surviving draft marked in Coke's handwriting shows how carefully the text was monitored: wording has been altered in places, and underlined in others. The main drift of these markings is to hammer home the involvement of the Jesuits, especially Gerard, and of course the guilt of Owen.[32]

Then there was the question of the famous mine under the House of Lords, which had not been mentioned in Guido's first confession, but featured, by a strange coincidence, in both the confessions which were published. It was suggested earlier that this mine – for which no independent corroboration exists and of which no trace remains – was a myth promulgated by the government. Its importance in the *King's Book* was as an artistic effect intended to emphasise the sheer horror of what had happened – or rather, what had nearly happened. Having elaborated the kind of confession they wanted from Wintour – both for evidence and for publication purposes – it is scarcely surprising that the government then went further and appended his signature to it. Wintour was completely in their power: the forged signature – by 'that villain Waad' yet again? – was only the culmination of the process.

If the Council had not got all the information it wanted about the priests, it had also not succeeded in probing that worrying matter of the future Protector's identity. The Earl of Northumberland was not, of course, tortured or even threatened with torture. He was a great man, not an obscure recusant. He was, however, subjected to intensive questioning by the King among others. James was preoccupied with the idea that Northumberland had had his horoscope – and that of the royal children – drawn up: casting the horoscope of a reigning monarch was always seen as a threatening and thus treasonable activity. Northumberland's problem, as he himself would point out to the King a few years later, was that he could not prove a negative. On 15 November, in front of the Council, he had argued that he should be presumed innocent on the grounds of

his lifestyle, which was 'unambitious and given to private pleasures, such as gardening and building'.[33] Unfortunately this
touching picture was not the whole image of the man.

It was Northumberland who had acted as the Catholics'
advocate in the previous reign, something the Earl might loftily
dismiss as 'an old Scotch story', but others did not forget so
easily. It was Northumberland who had employed Thomas
Percy (a dead man who could tell no tales, even to exonerate
his patron) and it was Northumberland who had been visited
by Percy at Syon on 4 November, before the latter went back
to Essex House, Northumberland's London home. Against
this, Northumberland, denying over and over again any complicity in the Plot, could only point to the practical arrangements he had made to attend Parliament on 5 November.
Even Salisbury admitted to Edmondes: 'it cannot be cast
[charged] that he was absent'.[34]

It was not enough. Northumberland remained in the Tower,
although he lived in comfort compared to the prisoners in
their dungeons below.[35] Nevertheless he was not a free man.
Assuming that he was innocent, Northumberland, like the
Plotters' wives, was among the numerous tangential victims of
the Powder Treason.

The rest of the prisoners held in connection with the Plot –
with one key exception – did not provide the government with
anything very much in the way of fresh information. Men like
Ambrose Rookwood and Sir Everard Digby had been brought
into the conspiracy too late to have much detailed knowledge.*
Rookwood's main contribution beyond attesting to his enduring feelings for Catesby, whom he 'loved more than his own
soul', was to state that he had been promised that the Catholic
lords would be spared.†[36]

---

* The fact that the majority of the principal Plotters – Catesby, Percy and the
Wright brothers – died at Holbeach House on 8 November meant that their
version of the conspiracy would never be known; this complicated its unravelling
for the government in 1605, and has continued to complicate it for historians
ever since.
† There is the etched name 'Ambrose Rookwoode' still to be seen in the upper
Martin Tower (R.C.H., p. 83b (no. 12)).

As for Digby, he suffered from the delusion, pathetic under the circumstances, that he could explain everything to King James if only he could meet him face to face, and put the Catholic case.[37] Of course the once petted darling of the court was not allowed this luxury. One can hardly blame King James for not wishing to entertain further a young man who had recently planned to murder him and his family in such a ruthless fashion. Nevertheless Digby's conduct either raises a doubt about the full extent of his implication, or suggests that Digby was astonishingly naive and trusting of his sovereign's forgiveness.

Digby had been involved in the conspiracy a mere fortnight before its discovery. It is possible that he learnt the full dreadful nature of what had been planned for the Parliament House only at Dunchurch when the London conspirators arrived to disband the meeting, by which time the Plot had already failed. Digby was not the kind of man to desert his friends at this juncture, and so he pressed on with them (although his reaction to the servant at the inn – 'there is no remedy' – suggests he did so with a heavy heart). But he did of course leave Holbeach, when the cause was evidently lost, to surrender himself to the authorities, and he was the only major conspirator to do so.

Denied an interview with the King, Digby took refuge in a kind of Christian defiance, as family papers discovered after his son's death revealed. 'If I had thought there had been the least sin in the Plot,' he wrote, 'I would not have been of it for all the world, and no other cause drew me to hazard my life but zeal to God's religion.' As for the reaction of the Pope and the English priesthood, he had been assured that they would not hinder any 'stirs' (risings) that should be undertaken 'for the Catholic good'.[38] Apart from writing, he occupied himself, like Rookwood, with carving an inscription in his cell at the Broad Arrow Tower.*

* This inscription is still extant, although it is currently (1996) covered by a panel to allow for an exhibition connected to the Peasants' Revolt of 1381 (R.C.H., p. 82b (no. 15); information to the author from Yeoman Warder B. Harrison.).

The key confession which forged the link between priests and Plot so much desired by Salisbury was that of Thomas Bates on 4 December.[39] This confession constituted something of a breakthrough, because Bates directly implicated Father Tesimond (something he would apologise for at the last). This false witness was born almost certainly as a result of his being threatened with torture on the one hand and promised a pardon on the other: that is certainly what Father Tesimond himself believed, accepting in effect Bates' ultimate apology. But by then it was of course too late to save the Powder Treason from its transformation into the Case of the Conspiring Jesuits.

Bates, unfortunately, was in all too good a position to give the kind of testimony which would be lethal in the hands of an agile prosecutor. In his capacity as Catesby's servant, he had been present at so many of the crucial scenes of the conspiracy. His great loyalty had been to his master, but now Catesby was dead, and he at least was beyond the government's vengeance. Thus, in a subsequent examination of 13 January 1606, Bates was able to describe the mission he had made to Father Garnet at Coughton on 7 November, on Catesby's instructions, to break the devastating news of the Plotters' flight. He could report the fatal exchange between the two priests, Father Garnet and Father Tesimond, and that exclamation – all too accurate, as it turned out – 'we are all undone!' It was Bates who had ridden with Father Tesimond to Huddington, before Tesimond went to the Habingtons at Hindlip. Bates also spoke of a meeting between three priests, Garnet, Gerard and Tesimond, at Harrowden, some time in mid-October.[40]

Putting Bates' testimony with that of Francis Tresham on 29 November which linked Father Garnet with the earlier Spanish Treason of 1602, Salisbury was rapidly developing the case he wanted against the Jesuits, one which specifically connected them to the recent treason. (As Catholic priests, their presence in England was of course already contrary to the law.)

Then in December there was an unexpected complication. Francis Tresham, held in the Tower of London, went into a rapid physical decline. The condition he was suffering from, known as strangury, was caused by an acute and painful inflammation of the urinary tract. This was no sudden out-of-the-blue attack. The condition had evidently been with Tresham some time before the current crisis, since he already had a doctor in charge of him. This was a distinguished man, Dr Richard Foster, who had recently been President of the College of Physicians. Tresham preferred him to the regular Tower doctor, Dr Matthew Gwinne, because Foster knew all about his case.[41]

By mid-December Tresham was being described by Sir William Waad as 'worse and worse'. Indeed, Waad wondered gloomily whether Tresham would survive long enough to meet the death he deserved. In addition to Foster, three more doctors were being called, and a woman – a nurse – was also admitted to attend him. Tresham already had his own man in attendance, one William Vavasour, who acted more as a confidential assistant than as a servant, as was Thomas Bates to Robert Catesby. Vavasour was supposed to be an illegitimate son of the late philoprogenitive Sir Thomas, and thus Francis Tresham's half-brother.[42] This would have made sense of their intimacy by the standards of the time, when the 'base born' were often provided with just this kind of family employment. (Rumours that Thomas Percy was an illegitimate half-brother of Northumberland were in fact untrue, but demonstrate how frequently contemporary patronage had its roots in this kind of relationship.)

While Waad squabbled pettishly with the Lord Mayor of London about who was in charge of what (the latter had the irksome habit of parading about 'the greatest part of the Tower' with a ceremonial sword carried in front of him to assert his authority), Francis Tresham groaned in his cell. Anne Tresham, another gallantly supportive wife, joined him two days before the end came. But it was in fact left to Vavasour to take down Francis Tresham's deathbed confession, since

Anne was by this time too upset. Vavasour also wrote an affecting account of his master's last hours.*[43]

Tresham died slowly, agonisingly and inexorably. This wayward, treacherous and perhaps ultimately self-hating character was however, like many such, intending to do better in the next world than in the one he would shortly leave. Above all, he wanted to make restitution to Father Garnet for implicating him in the Spanish Treason of 1602. In the statement he dictated to Vavasour – 'because he could not write himself, being so weak' – Tresham referred to Garnet (under the name of Mr Whalley) as someone whose safety he respected and tendered as much as his own, adding 'many words' on 'the virtues and worthiness of the man'. Tresham desired that his former confession might be called in and that 'this [new one] may stand for truth'. He then pledged 'his Salvation' that he had in fact no idea whether Tom Wintour had had any letter of recommendation from Garnet for his visit to Spain 'about the latter end of the Queen's days... for he did not see Mr Whalley [Garnet] at that time, nor had seen him in fifteen or sixteen year before...'.[44]

This was a vital piece of exculpation – how vital would not be totally clear, of course, so long as Father Garnet remained securely in hiding. (He had gone to ground at Hindlip at the beginning of December.) It is, though, proof that Tresham, even as he was dying, understood the value of what he had said and that he specifically commanded a copy of the document to be got to Garnet even before it reached Salisbury. As Vavasour wrote: this was 'my Master's special desire'. But it did not happen. Anne Tresham was prostrate with grief after her husband's death, and in her own words 'altogether unfit', while Vavasour himself was held prisoner.[45] So Garnet was never to know exactly what Tresham had said. The omission is

* This account by Vavasour is of special importance since it lay for three hundred years unknown to, and thus untouched by, the government – among the muniments at Deene Park, the home of Thomas Brudenell; he had married one of Francis' numerous sisters, Mary, in the summer of 1605 and would assist his mother-in-law Muriel Lady Tresham in her administrative duties after Francis' death, so the document's presence at Deene makes sense (Wake, p. 31).

understandable, given the desperate circumstances in which they were all living; but in this world of governmental manipulation such a failure of communication was to prove extremely dangerous.

The rest of Tresham's deathbed confession repeated the protestations of virtual ignorance and thus practical innocence which had occupied him on 13 November. He had, after all, his two little daughters' future to protect. He commended Lucy and Eliza to his brother Lewis as Christ had commended his mother to St John. He never, however, referred to the Monteagle Letter at any point, which makes it virtually certain that Tresham did not write it. He would hardly have failed to claim the credit for it at a time when Monteagle, for his contribution, was being hailed as the saviour of his country.

When Tresham refused to add to his statement, in answer to the questions of the hovering Waad, saying that he had nothing heavy on his conscience, the Lieutenant of the Tower went away angry. Significantly, the son's obsession with the father continued to the last. Francis observed, as he read *De Imitatione Christi*, that he hoped to make a better death than old Sir Thomas, who had died tossing and turning only three months before.

Francis Tresham did make a holy death: if not the short half-hour of agony which he had wished for himself.[46] The Litany and Prayer of the Virgin Mary and St John were said around his bedside by Anne Tresham and William Vavasour as Francis gradually became too weak to join in. Vavasour was asked to remind him to call upon the Name of Jesus (a Catholic devotion) at ten o'clock, but when Vavasour went to wake him Tresham looked 'ghastly', did not recognise Vavasour and tried to shake him off. About midnight, more Litanies, the Confiteor and the Mea Culpa were recited; at two o'clock in the morning on 23 December, Francis Tresham died.

Thereafter the government tried to treat the dead man as a traitor, despite the fact that he had never been indicted as such, in order to confiscate Tresham's goods and lands, along with those of the other conspirators. Ironically enough, the entail in the male line made by Sir Thomas in 1584, which had proved such a burden to Francis in his lifetime, now turned out to be a blessing in disguise, as did the fact that Francis left only daughters. Since Francis Tresham proved to be a mere life tenant in much of the estate, a great deal of it was able to pass to his brother Lewis. As for his mortal remains, we must assume that Francis Tresham, like Catesby and Percy, was indifferent to the fact that his decapitated head was posted up in Northampton, since he died, by government standards, impenitent. His headless body was tumbled into 'a hole' on Tower Hill.[47]

Unfortunately, Francis Tresham left a further legacy, one which would justify the words of Shakespeare in *Julius Caesar*, a play first performed about five years earlier:

> The evil that men do lives after them,
> The good is oft interred with their bones...

CHAPTER FOURTEEN

These Wretches

[The Powder Treason] shameth Caligula, Erostratus,
Nero and Domitian, who were but each of them fly-
killers to these wretches.

LORD HARINGTON
6 January 1606

I n the new year of 1606, the popular mood concerning the
recent Powder Treason was one of mingled revulsion and
relief, but also that secret delight which the contemplation
of horrors narrowly averted inevitably produces. The opening
of a poem appearing on 3 January, entitled *The Devil of the
Vault*, captures this particular mood of gleeful shuddering:*

> So dreadful, foul, chimera-like
> My subject must appear:
> The Heaven amaz'd and hell disturbed
> The earth shall quake with fear.[1]

But the King himself was not gleeful: he was sour and
angry. The courage and statesmanship he had shown in his
speech to Parliament of 9 November had given way to something a good deal less attractive and a good deal more vengeful. With time, the memory of his kindnesses to the Catholics
– the ungrateful Catholics – was beginning to loom large in his

---

* The phrase 'Devil of the Vault', which took a hold on the popular imagination,
was originally used by Bishop Barlow in his sermon of 10 November (Nowak,
p. 41).

own mind, while the important distinction between the guilty and the innocent Papists was beginning to blur. To the Venetian Ambassador, Niccolò Molin, he ranted for an hour on the subject of 'this perfidious and cursed doctrine of Rome' which produced English subjects who believed they could plot against their lawful Prince. James told Molin that the Catholics threatened to 'dethrone him and take his life' unless he gave them liberty of conscience. In consequence of their behaviour: 'I shall, most certainly, be obliged to stain my hands with their blood,' although, with his reputation as a merciful sovereign to maintain, he added: 'sorely against my will.'[2]

The blood with which the government was hoping to stain the King's hands – in addition to that of the Plotters – was Jesuit blood. By 15 January, it was decided that enough material had been accrued to proceed against certain priests. The official proclamation listed Father Garnet, Father Gerard and Father Greenway (Tesimond) and issued the usual meticulous descriptions employed in these circumstances. Father Garnet, for example, was said to be a man 'of middling stature, full faced, fat of body, of complexion fair, his forehead high on each side, with a little thin hair coming down...the hair of his head and beard grizzled'. His age was reckoned to be between fifty and sixty (life in hiding had aged Father Garnet: born late in 1555, he was only just fifty). At least his gait was said to be 'upright and comely' for a man who was so weak.[3] This proclamation marked a radical and ironic shift in the direction of the prosecution. From now on, with tragic irony, the names of the Jesuits headed the list of conspirators in the Plot which they had so desperately attempted to circumvent.

In London, Father Tesimond had the unnerving experience of reading details of his 'good red complexion' and his tendency to wear showy clothes 'after the Italian fashion' when the proclamation was posted up. Then the priest's eyes met those of a man in the crowd and he realised that his appearance was being checked out. When the stranger suggested that they go together to the authorities, Tesimond with seeming docility allowed himself to be led away, until they reached a quiet street, where the priest took to his heels and ran off. Tesimond then rapidly and discreetly left London, managing to smuggle aboard a cargo of dead pigs headed for Calais. From there he went to St Omer and finally on to Rome. Here a long and comparatively happy life awaited him: Father Tesimond survived for another thirty years after these tumultuous events. Most importantly he was one of those who lived to tell the tale from the Catholic angle.[4]

The escape of Father Tesimond was one ray of light in the rapidly encircling gloom of the Catholic situation. On 9 January, two months after their flight from Holbeach, Robert Wintour and Stephen Littleton were captured. It had been a time of great hardship, as well as fear, for these fugitives, who had to camp out in barns, or at best in poor men's houses, in midwinter. They were discovered in one hiding-place, in the outbuildings belonging to a tenant farmer of Humphrey Littleton, by a drunken poacher whom they had to imprison in order to make their escape. Since New Year's Day they had holed up at Hagley, the Worcestershire house where 'Red Humphrey' Littleton lived with his widowed sister-in-law Mrs Muriel Littleton. The treachery of a cook, John Finwood, led to the fugitives' arrest: the man suspected the extraordinary amount of food being sent up for his mistress's consumption. It was a feat for which Finwood would be rewarded with an annual pension.[5]

When the authorities arrived, Red Humphrey, who was not personally being sought by the government, since he had left Dunchurch without joining the conspirators, tried to prevent their entrance. Fatally for his own cause, he denied the presence of Wintour or his nephew. Another servant, David Bate, knew better and led the searchers round to the back door. Wintour and Stephen Littleton were captured in the adjoining courtyard. Humphrey Littleton then jumped on his gelding and rode away; he had got as far as Prestwood in Staffordshire, before he was seized.

Red Humphrey was imprisoned first at Stafford, and then at Worcester, where he was condemned to death. At this point, his morale collapsed – not all the recusants were heroes. He 'offered to do good service' if his execution might be reprieved. Father Tesimond later commented contemptuously on Littleton's behaviour: here was a man 'who had no further hope of life but was desperately anxious to save it'.[6] Tesimond's contempt is understandable, for Red Humphrey's testimony played its part in the last act of the drama currently being enacted, not far away from Worcester, at Hindlip. Here Father Garnet, together with two lay brothers, Little John and Ralph Ashley, had retreated at the beginning of December. Father Oldcorne, the regular chaplain there, better known under his alias of Hall, was also in residence.

Hindlip was traditionally one of the safest Catholic houses, in spite of the known recusancy of Thomas Habington, himself a convicted conspirator in the previous reign. Like Coughton, it occupied a good position, with views of the surrounding countryside. In addition, it had been custom built by Habington's father in the middle of the last century, to act as a labyrinth of refuges when necessary. (It was infinitely easier to construct these holes and secret closets at the start because there were no tell-tale signs of renovation – sawdust, brick-dust, fresh plaster – to be detected.) An early-nineteenth-century description of Hindlip referred to 'its every room' as having 'a recess, a passage, a trap door, or secret stairs; the walls were in many places false. Several chimneys had double flues, one for a passage for the smoke, the second for the concealment of a priest.'*[7]

All in all, there were at least a dozen hiding-places in use at Hindlip by this date. A search was always a game of cat and mouse. Father Garnet's decision to desert Coughton for Hindlip was based on the premise that at Hindlip the cat might

---

* Hindlip House burnt down shortly after this description was written and was totally rebuilt. No trace of its exotic unlawful past remains: its reincarnation has in fact brought it strictly within the law, for it is now the Headquarters of the West Mercia Police Authority. However, the Church of St James, close by, contains a fine and colourful memorial to the Habington family of Hindlip, including coats of arms.

suspect that there were mice to be found, but could not place the precise whereabouts of the mouseholes.

It was 'at break of day' on Monday 20 January that a local Justice, Sir Henry Bromley, and his retainers arrived outside the house. Sir Henry was the eldest son of Sir Thomas Bromley, who as Lord Chancellor had presided over the trial of Mary Queen of Scots. Yet Muriel Littleton, one of his many sisters, was a recusant, which illustrates the remarkable mixture of religious loyalties which any large family could show at this period. Sir Henry carried with him a commission from the Privy Council. The promise of a 'bountiful reward' for the capture of the miscreant priests meant that he and his men set about the task with enthusiasm. He also had detailed practical instructions on how the search was to be conducted, from the use of a gimlet to pierce panelled walls, to the inspection of any lofts under the roof, 'for these be ordinary places of *hovering*'.[8]

As it happened, Thomas Habington was absent from Hindlip on business when Bromley arrived. When, on his return, Habington was shown the official proclamation for the arrest of the three Jesuits, and Bromley's commission, he strongly and passionately denied the presence of the priests. Indeed, he volunteered to die there and then at his own gate if any Catholic priests were to be found lurking under his roof. This 'rather rash' speech cut no ice with Sir Henry.[9] So for the next three days the most thorough search possible was mounted, regardless of the family's protests.

In this way, a series of hiding-places was uncovered, including two cavities in the brickwork in the gallery over the gate, and three others in the chimneys, where planks of wood had been darkened with soot to match the brick. Altogether eleven 'secret corners and conveyances' were probed, all of them containing 'Popish trumpery' – vessels and books necessary to the celebration of the Mass – except for two which had been uncovered at an earlier date and thus left empty. Thomas Habington, with admirable sang-froid, continued to maintain his stance of absolute ignorance. The revelation of each hiding-place in turn was greeted by him with great surprise. It was only when the vital title deeds to his lands were discovered lodged in one hole for safe-keeping – which might argue for a certain degree of knowledge on the owner's part – that Habington had to waver in his denials.[10]

Then on Thursday morning 24 January there was a breakthrough of sorts, or so Sir Henry hoped. Two stealthy figures emerged from the wainscot in the gallery. The figures were in fact Nicholas Owen and his fellow lay brother Ralph Ashley and they were starving, having had nothing but one apple between them to eat since the search began on Monday. (Before that, lying in 'a lower chamber descending from the dining-room', they had been able to get food.)[11] It is possible that Owen and Ashley intended to give themselves up, to distract attention from the presence of their superiors Garnet and Oldcorne, concealed elsewhere. But it seems more likely that the two men were attempting to make a bold getaway, choosing a moment when the gallery was, as they thought, empty. Little John in particular knew that, if he were tortured a second time and were compelled to reveal the secrets of his clandestine profession, he would bring ruin not only upon himself, but also upon the entire recusant community.

Unfortunately one of the searchers turned back into the gallery and saw these unexpected strangers. Even now, Owen and Ashley attempted to bluff their way out by pretending to be mere recusants, rather than lay brothers. As for Sir Henry, in his report to Salisbury of the same day, he huffed and puffed about the impudence of the Catholics and their wicked lies, as though the host who hid the priests should have immediately revealed their whereabouts. He then expressed the proud hope that he had found Tesimond (Greenway) and Oldcorne (Hall).[12]

But of course Sir Henry had not found them. When this became apparent, the search was renewed. Bromley did attempt to evacuate the lady of the house, Mary Habington – sister to Monteagle, the hero of the hour – as her presence was obviously awkward for him. But Mary defiantly refused to leave 'without I should have carried her', and Bromley thought this would be conduct unbecoming towards one 'so well born'. On Friday, Saturday and Sunday, the searchers were as rampant as ever, calling to mind Anne Vaux's description of an earlier search at Baddesley Clinton in the 1590s: 'the poursuivants behaved just like a lot of boys playing Blind Man's Bluff, who, in their wild rush, bang into tables and chairs and walls and yet haven't the slightest suspicion that their playfellows are right on top of them and almost touching them'.[13]

It was on the Sunday, 26 January, that Humphrey Littleton, prisoner in nearby Worcester, decided to save his neck – as he hoped. The 'good service' which he offered to do was to betray the names and hiding-place of 'certain Jesuits and priests, which had been persuaders of him and others to these actions'. Hindlip was described as a haunt of priests in general and of Father Hall (Oldcorne) in particular. In addition, Littleton said he was quite sure that Hall was 'in Habington's house at this present', while Hall's own servant, currently in Worcester jail, 'can, he thinks, go directly to the secret places where Hall lies hid'. Littleton backed up these topographical details with a highly damaging account of a conversation he had had with Oldcorne.[14]

Littleton said that he had recently visited 'Father Hall' to consult him about the future of his nephew Stephen. Was it his, Humphrey's, duty to arrest him? According to Littleton, Oldcorne replied that on the contrary the Powder Treason itself had been 'commendable' and that it should not be in any way measured by its lack of success. This was just what the government wanted to hear – a Jesuit priest openly approving of the Plot. These promising confidences caused the Sheriff of Worcester to stay Littleton's execution, to see if he remembered anything else.

It transpired later that what Father Oldcorne had actually said was somewhat different. On the Plot's lack of success, he cited the instance of Louis XI of France, who had made a pilgrimage to the Holy Land, directed by St Bernard of Clairvaux. Plague had twice struck the King's camp, decimating his men the first time and killing the King himself the second, while his enemies went untouched. Nevertheless these disasters did not necessarily reflect upon the validity of the expedition. In short, an act was 'not to be condemned or justified' by the criterion of its success or failure but, rather, according to its objective and 'the means that is used for effecting the same'. Since Father Oldcorne knew nothing of Catesby's objectives, nor yet of his means, he declared himself as neither approving nor condemning the recent disastrous enterprise: he was content to leave it 'to God and their consciences'.[15] Given that Humphrey Littleton had been wondering whether to hand over his own nephew to the authorities, this was sensible and humane rather than bloodthirsty advice. But of course it could and would be twisted into a very different shape.

Ironically enough, Red Humphrey's treachery may not have been, strictly speaking, the key factor in the apprehension of Fathers Garnet and Oldcorne at Hindlip. On Monday 27 January, the two men emerged of their own accord, looking so like ghosts after an eight-day sojourn in a tiny cramped space that it was their pursuers who were the terrified ones and at first ran away from them. According to Garnet's own account, they had spent most of their time sitting as the hole was not high enough for them to stand up to their full height, nor long enough for them to stretch their legs completely. As a result, their legs, especially those of Father Garnet, were terribly swollen.[16]

The physical ordeal as the two priests listened to the searchers overhead had not been pleasant. It was true that they had been able to receive warm drinks through a quill or reed inserted into a narrow aperture which passed through one chimney – a typical Little John touch – into another chimney in 'the gentlewoman's chamber'. This chamber probably belonged to Anne Vaux, and she would have administered the liquids, including caudle, a sweet spicy kind of gruel especially designed for invalids, through the reed. Marmalade and sweetmeats, staples of this kind of siege, were found in their hole afterwards and must have been brought in with them by the priests themselves. But there was no drainage or earth closet (Little John sometimes managed to effect this – as at Sawston – but had not been able to do so in this particular hiding-place).

That was the trouble. Father Garnet said later that if only they had had half a day of freedom, they could have secured 'a close-stool' (commode). With the aid of that, they could have lasted for another three months. So it was what Sir Henry Bromley would call 'those customs of nature which must of necessity be done' that finally drove out the two priests. Even their captors blanched at the conditions which they found.[17]

Yet before we acquit Humphrey Littleton of all practical contribution to the arrest (morally his culpability remains the same) it must be remembered how long the search had already lasted without the result that the government really wanted. Bromley suspected that there were further priests to be discovered, but he was not absolutely sure – they could have escaped before 20 January. Without further information, Bromley might have given up just a moment before the priests themselves decided to surrender. Humphrey Littleton's Sunday revelations, however, clinched the matter. When the message came to Hindlip – only four miles from Worcester where Littleton was held – Bromley knew that sooner or later the prey would be his. On the Monday, Father Garnet and Father Oldcorne, emaciated and wretched, stepped out into his eager arms.

Garnet and Oldcorne were taken to Sir Henry Bromley's home at Holt Castle until further orders concerning their fate were received from London. They were neither shackled, nor held in collars, nor in any other way treated brutally. Although the whole basis of the official proclamation was that the Jesuits had been the prime persuaders in the recent devilish Plot, their treatment was in no sense that normally meted out to desperadoes. There was a paradox here. Sir Henry Bromley told Garnet that although the proclamation meant that he had to hold him 'strait' yet he honoured him as 'a learned man and a worthy priest'.[18]

In London, Parliament had reassembled on Tuesday 21

January; it had not met since that Saturday in November when the King had made his celebrated speech. In the Commons one of the first actions was to consider measures of safety, with reference to 'the Danger of Papistical Practices'. Two days later Sir Edward Montague, the Member for Northamptonshire, introduced a bill, drafted by himself, for a public thanksgiving to be said annually on 5 November. Sir Edward was often thought to be numbered among the Puritans, being 'a man of plain and downright English spirit'.[19] He was eager to be reinstated in the King's favour after delivering a petition against the suspension of non-conforming clergy which had annoyed James. The Papists' disgrace provided a perfect opening. Montague now introduced the concept of a plain and downright English festival which survived in one form or another for nearly four hundred years.

A more immediate festivity – of a sort – awaited the curious, many months before 5 November 1606. On Monday 27 January, the day of the capture of Father Garnet and Father Oldcorne, the trial of the eight surviving conspirators began in Westminster Hall. Seven of them were brought by barge from the Tower of London to Whitehall, early in the morning: these were Guy Fawkes, Thomas and Robert Wintour, John Grant, Ambrose Rookwood, Everard Digby and Robert Keyes. Thomas Bates' inferior status was marked by the fact that he was held in the less important Gatehouse prison. So 'these wretches', compared to whom villains of the Ancient World such as Nero and Caligula were said to be mere 'fly-killers', prepared to face judgement.[20]

The decision was never in doubt. The mere fact that these men were on trial for high treason meant that they would inevitably be found guilty, and equally inevitably sentenced to death. Refinements such as defending counsel were unknown. In the nineteenth century, Lord Macaulay would describe the process as 'merely a murder preceded by the uttering of certain gibberish and the performance of certain mummeries'. Yet one should be wary of too much anachronistic indignation. These were the rules of a treason trial at the time, proceedings which were quite literally intended as a show trial, one where the guilt of the prisoners would be demonstrated publicly. For this reason, the government encouraged popular attendance at such events. The real trial had already taken place in the form of interrogations before the Privy Council. It was here that guilt or otherwise was decided, since guilt was not a foregone conclusion at this point. Not every prisoner brought before the Privy Council as a suspect traitor was sent for trial.[21]

The prisoners were kept together in the Star Chamber for a short while before being brought into Westminster Hall. Here they were displayed on a scaffold which had been specially devised, and subjected to the fascinated scrutiny of the spectators. These included some secret watchers as well as many members of both Houses of Parliament. (There was a complaint the next day that MPs had been jostled and their reserved places 'pestered with others not of the House'; a committee was set up to investigate.) Among the secret watchers was the King himself, who occupied a room where he could see without being seen. He was said to have been present from eight in the morning until seven at night. Queen Anne and Prince Henry, not quite twelve years old – two potential victims of the Plot – were concealed in another secluded watch-post. Two private rooms were also erected so that foreign ambassadors and other notables could attend the trial discreetly.[22]

As for what they saw, a contemporary description conveys the sense of horrified wonder at the sight of the eight murderous 'wretches'. Some hung down their heads 'as if their hearts were full of doggedness', while others forced 'a stern look, as if they would frighten death with a frown'. None of them gave the impression of praying 'except it were by the dozen upon their beads'. (The Plotters were actually saying the rosary, a Catholic form of prayer much scorned by Protestants, beads being among the devotional objects which were unlawful.) One particular detail must have maddened King James. It was noticed throughout the trial that the conspirators were 'taking tobacco, as if hanging were no trouble to them'. Yet only in

1604 the King had energetically denounced smoking – 'a custom loathsome to the eye, hateful to the nose, harmful to the brain, dangerous to the lungs' – in his *Counterblaste to Tobacco*.²³ The conspirators' addiction was yet another proof of their moral obloquy.

The Lords Commissioners who sat in trial consisted of the Earls of Suffolk, Worcester, Northampton and Devonshire, as well as Salisbury, Sir John Popham as Lord Chief Justice, Sir Thomas Fleming as Lord Chief Baron of the Exchequer and two Justices of the Common Pleas, Sir Thomas Walmsley and Sir Peter Warburton. Of the peers, Worcester had been considered a Papist in the previous reign, and Northampton a Church Papist, but men of Catholic sympathies were of course specially keen to demonstrate their horror of the Powder Treason. Seven of the conspirators – Sir Everard Digby was the exception – were tried on the same indictment.*²⁴

This list of 'false traitors' to the King began, significantly, with the names and common aliases of the three Jesuits, Garnet, Tesimond and Gerard, who were described as 'not yet taken' since the morning's dramatic news had not reached London. The list then passed on to Thomas Wintour, followed by Guido Fawkes, 'otherwise called Guido Johnson', Robert Keyes and Thomas Bates, 'yeoman'. The names of the four slain conspirators came next: Catesby, Percy, the two Wrights, coupled with that of Francis Tresham, 'lately dead'. The names of the other three surviving conspirators, Robert Wintour, John Grant and Ambrose Rookwood, occurred in the course of the same indictment, an extremely long document which certainly did not underplay the drama of the occasion.

All seven of these conspirators pleaded 'Not Guilty', including Guy Fawkes. These pleas caused the authorities some surprise, as the previous confessions of the prisoners were 'notorious'. Guy Fawkes, in particular, had freely admitted his

---

* There was no mention of the statute under which they were being tried but it was presumably that of 1352 (25 Edw. st. 5 Cap. 2), which made it treason 'to compass or imagine the death of the king, his queen or the royal heir' (Bellamy, p. 9).

guilt from the first moment of his apprehension on 5 November. Digby had to be tried separately since, alone among his comrades, he pleaded 'Guilty'.

Sir Edward Phillips, Serjeant-at-Law, now sprang into action with what was termed the 'declaration'. His words were magisterial, eloquent and damning: 'The tongue of man never delivered, the ear of man never heard, the heart of man never conceived, or the malice of hellish or earthly devil ever practised...' such a treason. For if it was 'abominable to murder the least' of God's creatures, then how much more abominable to murder 'Such a King, Such a Queen, Such a Prince, Such a progeny, Such a State, Such a government...'.[25]

The Attorney-General Sir Edward Coke was the next to speak and he did not spare himself – or his audience. He made an extremely long speech, a fact he himself acknowledged when he used the word 'copious' of what was to follow: he did not intend to be 'so succinct as usual'.[26] One important aspect of this speech was however a negative one. Throughout, Coke implicitly denied that King James had made any promises of toleration to the Catholics before his accession. This was hardly surprising, given that Salisbury had written to Coke privately in advance in order to 'renew' his memory on the subject. Coke was to underline the fact that certain persons had gone to Spain to stir up an invasion 'as soon as the Queen's breath was out of her body'. This emphasis was the King's express wish and Salisbury explained his reason. The King was aware that there were some men who would suggest that only despair at the King's behaviour towards the Catholics, his severity, had produced 'such works of discontentment' as the recent treason.

The point was evidently important to James and one can guess why. Those vague Scottish promises of toleration were now a very long way away in the King's scope of things and such politically embarrassing intrigues of another time, another country, were best not recalled. It was far better to present the Catholics as a nest of malcontents from the word go, plotting

Garnet's straw: this 'miraculous' image, an object of reverence to Catholics was found on a straw spotted with Father Garnet's blood at his death; the straw, whose existence caused great annoyance to the English authorities, was smuggled abroad but vanished at the time of the French Revolution.

Father Henry Garnet SJ, by Jan Wiericx.

St Winifred's Well, Holywell, Clwyd; Father Garnet led an expedition to this ancient site of pilgrimage (still in existence today) in the late summer of 1605; his companions included Anne and Eliza Vaux, Father Gerard and Sir Everard and Lady Digby. Afterwards the government pretended the pilgrimage had been a cover for conspiracy.

The North View of S.ᵗWinefred's Well *and* Chapel, *in the County of* Flint

Father Garnet's last letter to his faithful protectress Anne Vaux, written from the Tower of London on 21 April 1606, twelve days before his execution; it ends 'yours *in eternum*, as I hope, H G'. He appended a rough drawing and the letters 'I H S' for the Sacred Heart of Jesus.

Sir Edward Coke, who, as Attorney-General, led the prosecution at the trials of the conspirators and Father Garnet.

The entry in the Commons' Journal for 5 November 1605 (which now hangs in the Noes voting lobby of the House of Commons); it records, in the margin: 'This last Night the Upper House of Parliament was searched by Sir Thomas Knevett; and one Johnson, Servant to Mr Thomas Percy was there apprehended; who had placed 36 Barrels of Gunpowder in the Vault under the House with a Purpose to blow the King, and the whole company, when they should there assemble. Afterwards divers other Gentle[men] were discovered to be of the Plot.'

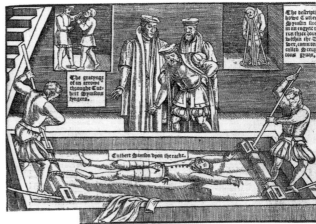

Letter of King James authorising the torture of Guy Fawkes which ends: 'the gentler Tortures are to be first used unto him et *sic per gradus ad ima tenditur* – and so by degrees proceeding to the worst – and so God speed your good work. James R.'

Instruments of torture at the time of the Gunpowder Plot: manacles and the rack.

A late eighteenth-century print of the execution of the conspirators.

Guido Fawkes' signatures before and after torture.

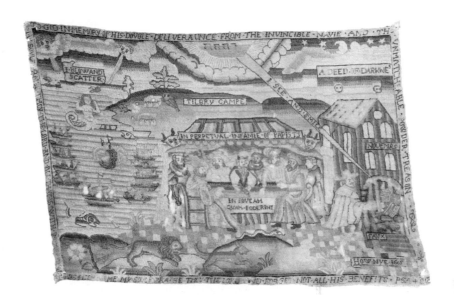

Embroidered cushion
depicting the defeat
of the Armada and the
Gunpowder Plot, *c.* 1621.

Engraving of Father Garnet
on the scaffold by C. Screta.

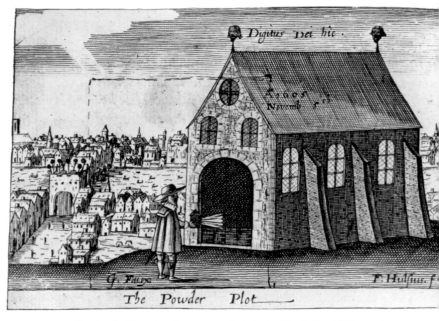

The Powder Plot, taken from an anti-Catholic booklet, 'A Thankful Remembrance of God's Mercie' by George Carleton, 1630.

Victorian impression of Guy Fawkes being taken to the scaffold.

Etching of Guy Fawkes laying his sinister trail, 1841; although Catesby was the leader of the band, Guy Fawkes has received the popular odium down the centuries.

The Papists' Powder Treason: an allegorical engraving done for 5 November 1612 'in aeternal memory of the divine bounty in England's preservation from the Hellish Powder Plot'.

A monument to the Plot's discovery erected in the council chamber in the house of the Lieutenant-Governor of the Tower of London, 1608 by Sir William Waad (still there today).

The search of the cellars of the House of Lords which still takes place on the eve of the Opening of Parliament by members of the Queen's Bodyguard of the Yeomen of the Guard; the traditional uniforms and lamps of the searchers contrast with the modern heating pipes above their heads.

Bonfire Night, 1994, in Lewes, Sussex, where celebrations, for better or for worse, continue to flourish.

to destroy the King 'before his Majesty's face was ever seen' – that is, in advance of his arrival in England. One may perhaps hear the delicate whisper of the King's guilty conscience in this firm rebuttal.

Salisbury's further instructions – all in his own handwriting – were interesting too. Monteagle was to be lauded for his part in the discovery of the Plot, but care was to be taken by Coke not to vary from the King's own account, already published. Coke, in short, was not to give credence to a story 'lewdly given out' that Monteagle had once been part of the Plot, and had betrayed it to Salisbury, still less that one of the conspirators had actually written the anonymous letter. (Monteagle's name was also obliterated in the published account of the Spanish Treason, as related by Francis Tresham.) Salisbury's last note was characteristic: 'You must remember to lay Owen as foul in this as you can.'[27]

Coke did not fail Salisbury and he did not fail King James. The Spanish Treason, including the two thousand horses promised by the English Catholics, featured strongly. So did the oaths taken by the conspirators and the alleged administration of the Sacrament – by Garnet, Tesimond and other Jesuits – to sanctify them. (Guy Fawkes' specific denial while being examined that Father Gerard knew anything of the Plot when he gave the Sacrament in May 1604 was not mentioned. To make quite sure this damaging statement was omitted, Coke underlined the passage in the examination in red and marked in the margin 'hucusque' – thus far and no further.)[28]

The Spanish King was however courteously handled. His Ambassador, listening intently in his private closet, must have been relieved to find that 'foreign princes' were (by the King's direct instructions) 'reverently and respectfully spoken of'. The priests, in contrast, were execrated. Their traitorous advice, their outright encouragement were underlined at every point, giving a picture of the Jesuits' behaviour which was so far at variance with the truth that it would have been laughable if it had not been so tragic – and so sinister.

With a flurry of classical and Biblical quotations, Coke

described the Powder Treason as having three roots, all planted and watered by the Jesuits. 'I never yet knew a treason without a Romish priest,' he declared, 'but in this, there are very many Jesuits.' In short the 'seducing Jesuits' were the principal offenders. All the old stories of the Jesuits seeking to remove crowns from rulers were trotted out, how the practices of 'this sect' principally consisted in 'two Ds, to wit, the deposing of kings, and disposing of kingdoms'. As for absolution, Catesby had received it in advance from the Jesuits and been encouraged to believe that his potential crime was 'both lawful and meritorious'. After that, 'he persuaded and settled' the rest of the Plotters when they raised some doubts, telling Rookwood, for example, that Father Garnet had given him absolution for the action, even if it involved 'the destruction of many innocents'.

The emotive subject of equivocation was also introduced by Coke. This was the art of lying as practised by Catholics – or so the government would have it. (The Catholics themselves, as we shall see in the next chapter, viewed it rather differently.) Coke spoke of how the 'perfidious and perjurious equivocating' of the conspirators, abetted and justified by the Jesuits, had allowed them not only to conceal the truth but also to swear to things which they themselves knew to be totally false. This was because 'certain heretical, treasonable and damnable books', including one which Coke entitled 'Of Equivocation', had been discovered among Francis Tresham's possessions. It was a subject to which Coke would return with eloquence in the future. In the meantime, the shade of Francis Tresham was beginning to haunt Father Garnet.

Coke's editorial concoction of what had actually taken place was accompanied by an even more colourful evocation of the horrors which might have taken place. Coke focused in turn on the probable fate of the Queen, Prince Henry 'the future hope', and, in a sense worst of all, the young Princess Elizabeth – 'God knoweth what would have become of her.' As he got into his stride, Coke even managed to feel sorry not only for the men and beasts who would have suffered from

the explosion but also for the very buildings of the neighbourhood: 'insensible creatures, churches and houses, and all places
near adjoining' – a remarkably modern concern.

When, however, Coke came to his delineation of the penalties traditionally meted out to traitors, he showed himself a
man of his own time. Each condemned prisoner would be
drawn along to his death, backwards at a horse's tail because
he 'hath been retrograde to nature': his head should be near
the ground, being not entitled to the common air. He was to
be put to death halfway between heaven and earth as unworthy
of both. His privy parts were to be cut off and burnt before
his face since he himself had been 'unworthily begotten' and
was in turn unfit 'to leave any generation after him'. The
bowels and heart which had conceived of these terrible things
were to be hacked out and the head 'which had imagined the
mischief' was to be cut off. Thereafter the various dismem-
bered portions of the traitor's body were to be publicly
exposed, that they might become 'prey for the fowls of the air'.

When Coke's speech was concluded, the various
'Examinations, Confessions and voluntary Declarations' of the
prisoners were read aloud.[29] These began with the testimonies
by Guy Fawkes and Francis Tresham about the Spanish
Treason, Tresham including the names of Father Garnet and
Father Tesimond as being 'acquainted with Wintour's employment in Spain'. After this followed the specific confessions to
do with the Powder Treason. Guy Fawkes' confession came
first, followed by the confession of the recently captured
Robert Wintour. This had been taken on 17 January in front of
the Lords Commissioners, and was accompanied by a long
statement signed by him four days later.

This statement had an important postscript: 'I confess that
on Thursday 7th of November, I did confess myself to Father
Hammond the priest, as other gentlemen did, and was
absolved, and received the Sacrament.' Hammond was in fact
the alias of the chaplain at Huddington, Father Hart. The
general confession of the conspirators at Huddington in the
small hours of the morning was probably more to do with

their expectation of death in the near future than with their guilt over the past. Nevertheless, the notion that the conspirators had been able to make a clean breast of their potential crimes and receive absolution from a priest – a Jesuit – two days after the discovery of the Plot was a damaging one.

More confessions were read, including that of Thomas Wintour as well as the examinations of Rookwood and Keyes. The last piece of evidence was not a confession, but it concerned a conversation which Robert Wintour was said to have had with Guido in the Tower after his capture. The two men found themselves in adjacent cells and took the opportunity to have what they believed to be an intimate conversation but was in fact overheard by a government spy. Wintour and Guido mentioned the taking of Nicholas Owen – 'the little man'. Then Robert Wintour said something to Fawkes to the effect that 'God will raise up seed to Abraham out of the very stones', meaning that God in the future would raise up others for the good of the Church, 'although they [the conspirators] were gone'.[30] These confidences were less important than the revelation of the government's methods of espionage among their prisoners. Sadly, Father Garnet never got to hear of this particular trick, otherwise his own conduct in the Tower might have been different.

After this evidence was heard, the seven were allowed at last to speak if they so wished, 'wherefore judgement of death should not be pronounced against them'. Only Ambrose Rookwood elected to make any real use of this privilege.[31]

Rookwood admitted that his offences were so dreadful that he could not expect mercy, and yet maybe there were some extenuating circumstances since he had been 'neither author nor actor', but had been drawn into the Plot by his feelings for Catesby, 'whom he loved above any worldly man'. In the end Rookwood craved for mercy, so as not to leave 'a blemish and blot unto all ages' upon his name and blood. Kings, he hoped, might imitate God who sometimes administered bodily punishments to mortals, but did not actually kill them.

The rest of the conspirators spoke shortly. Tom Wintour,

clearly suffering from remorse at having brought Robert into the Plot, asked to be hanged on behalf of his brother as well as himself. Guy Fawkes gave an explanation for his plea of 'Not Guilty' which had earlier baffled the court. He had done so, he said, in respect of certain conferences mentioned in the indictment 'which he knew not of'. The reaction of Robert Keyes was terse and stoic: death was as good now as at any other time, he said, and for this cause rather than for another. Thomas Bates and Robert Wintour merely asked for mercy.

John Grant kept up his reputation for taciturnity by remaining completely silent for a while. He then said that he was guilty of 'a conspiracy intended but never effected'. In a memorable phrase in the course of his speech, Coke had said that 'Truth is the daughter of Time [*Veritas temporis filia*]; especially in this case.' But John Grant's economical comment made before Time had had a chance to give birth to Truth was probably as just a verdict as any. It was indeed a conspiracy intended – but never carried out.

The trial of Sir Everard Digby followed. He pleaded 'Guilty' swiftly to the indictment, in order to have the privilege of making a speech. It was evidently not unmoving to some of those that heard it. Digby gave as his first motive his friendship and love for Catesby – how enduring was the influence and charisma of Robin! The cause of religion for which he had decided to neglect 'his estate, his life, his name, his memory, his posterity, and worldly and earthly felicity' took second place.[32]

He alluded to the broken promises of toleration – the King cannot have liked that – as well as mentioning the recusants' fear of harsher laws in the coming Parliament. This referred specifically to the subject of recusant wives, the fear that women as well as men would be liable for fines. Digby then argued passionately that since his offence was 'contained within himself' the guilt of it should not be passed on to his family, least of all to his little sons. His wife – the unfortunate, destitute Mary – should have her jointure, his sisters their marriage portions and his creditors their debts; his man of business should be admitted to him so that these arrangements could be made.

Coke, however, made short work of all this. The precious friendship with Catesby was 'mere folly and wicked conspiracy'; Digby's religion was 'error and heresy'. Over the question of the wives, Coke laid all the blame for their recusancy squarely on their husbands' shoulders in a fine seventeenth-century flourish. Either a man had married a woman knowing her to be a recusant, in which case he must expect to pay a fine, or she had become a recusant subsequent to her marriage, in which case the husband was equally at fault for not having kept her under better control. As for Digby's children! Coke sneered at Digby's pretended compassion for them when he had so easily accepted the prospect of the deaths of other people's children, including the 'tender princes'.[33]

Digby interrupted here – even now, he had enough spirit not to be cowed by Coke. He did not justify what he had done, Digby said, and he confessed that he deserved 'the vilest death'; he was merely a humble petitioner for mercy and 'some moderation of justice' for his family. By way of answer, Coke quoted back to Digby a singularly relentless passage from the Psalms: 'Let his wife be a widow, and his children vagabonds, let his posterity be destroyed, and in the next generation let his name be quite put out.'

Northampton was the next to make a speech, referring in elaborate terms to the favour which had been shown Digby by the late Queen Elizabeth and by King James. Northampton, too, was determined to put an end to the rumours that before he inherited the English crown King James had promised 'some further hope and comfort' for the Catholics. So he held forth on the subject of James' lifelong Protestantism: that faith which James 'had sucked from the breast of his nurse' (but not of course from the breast of his Catholic mother – for once, the name of Mary Queen of Scots was not dragged in). Lastly Salisbury himself thought it necessary to return to the theme of the King's alleged promises yet again. No promises had been broken. There were no promises. Never at any time had King James given 'the least hope, much less promise of toleration'.[34]

At the conclusion of Salisbury's speech, Serjeant-at-Law Phillips asked for the judgement of the court on the seven conspirators found guilty, and upon Sir Everard Digby, guilty on his own confession. After a few remarks from the Lord Chief Justice, the jury was directed to consider its verdict. It can have surprised no one present in Westminster Hall on that icy late January day that the verdict was equally chilling: Guilty, all of them.

The Lord Chief Justice then pronounced judgement of high treason upon all the prisoners. Seven of them listened to him in silence. Once more the exception was Sir Everard Digby. As the court rose, Digby cried out impulsively: 'If I may but hear any of your lordships say, you forgive me, I shall go more cheerfully to the gallows.' His speech had aroused a feeling of compassion if not of mercy – or perhaps it was his youth, the nobility of his bearing, the sense of utter waste. For the lords told him: 'God forgive you, and we do.'

PART FIVE
The Shadow of Death

He discovereth deep things out of darkness, and bringeth out to light the shadow of death.

JOB, 12:22
quoted in the Tower of London Memorial of the Powder Treason

CHAPTER FIFTEEN

The Heart of a Traitor

Behold the heart of a traitor!
Traditional cry of the executioner

The eight condemned men were put to death in two batches on consecutive days. On Thursday 30 January, Sir Everard Digby, Robert Wintour and John Grant were fetched from the Tower of London and Thomas Bates was brought from the Gatehouse. The time for executions was around eight o'clock in the morning, dark and bleak at this time of year. The site chosen on the first day was the western end of the churchyard of St Paul's 'over and against the Bishop of London's house'. Not everyone, however, approved of the decision. Sir Arthur Gorges, a poet and a friend of Ralegh, who had sailed with him against the Spaniards, protested to Salisbury against the quartering of 'these wicked and bloody conspirators' being carried out in a place of such 'happy memory', for it was here that Queen Elizabeth herself had thanked God for her nation's deliverance from the Armada.[1]

The custom of conveying certain miscreants to their place of death by dragging them at the horse's tail, to which the Attorney-General had alluded at the trial, tended to rob the executioner of the material upon which to do his appointed work. The damaging ordeal also robbed the public of the full ceremony, which it much enjoyed. This included speeches from the condemned men as well as those prolonged indignities to still-breathing bodies so graphically described by Sir Edward Coke. Therefore, in the case of important prisoners such as the Powder Plotters, it was government policy to convey them singly, each strapped to a wicker hurdle, used as a kind of sledge.[2]

This open passage through the crowd had, however, its own dangers. First, there was the possibility – however remote – of rescue. Secondly, in the case of known Catholics, tiresome recusant devotions might interrupt the desired spiritual process of last-minute repentance. Thirdly, there was the question of the wretches' wives and womenfolk, who had not seen their men for several months, since that dreadful day in early November when the reckless stand at Holbeach had been planned.* Recusants' wives, or the friends of condemned priests, often tried to say a last goodbye in this manner. Thus armed men were stationed at doorways along the route from seven in the morning: 'one able and sufficient person with a halberd in his hand' for every dwelling house in the open street.[3]

Even so, the women managed to get themselves into the crowds, and at the windows. There is a story of one little Digby boy calling out, 'Tata, Tata,' at the moment when his father was being drawn by on his hurdle, his face low down so that, in Coke's words, he should not pollute the common air. Thomas Bates' wife Martha was one of those who managed to find a place in the crowd; she was rewarded by finding that her husband was on the leading hurdle, presumably because he had joined the melancholy procession from the other direction, the Gatehouse being in Westminster. Eluding the halberdiers, Martha Bates managed to throw herself on her husband as he lay on his hurdle; she wailed aloud against the wretched fortune which had brought him to this 'untimely end'.

---

* There is a tradition that Robert Wintour's wife Gertrude had various secret meetings with her husband during the two months he was on the run; but, given the persistent official attention to Huddington as a known recusant centre, one wonders whether either of them would have run the risk – for the future of their children was at stake.

Bates, practical man to the last, took the opportunity to tell Martha where he had deposited a bag of money (originally entrusted to him by Jack Wright), and he begged his wife to hang on to it for her own relief and that of their children. Afterwards Martha got into trouble with the authorities over this bequest – perhaps they thought Bates' last instructions had been on some more conspiratorial level. But in the end she was allowed to keep the money.

At St Paul's, Sir Everard Digby was the first to mount the scaffold. He had spent his last days in the Tower writing letters to 'my dearest wife' Mary and then to Kenelm and John.[4] He urged the latter pair to support each other as brothers, and avoid the bad examples of Cain and Abel, and Philip of Macedon's sons (one of whom had murdered the other). Otherwise Everard Digby wrote poetry which expressed his own resignation to his fate – and explains perhaps further the affection in which contemporaries, even religious enemies, held him:

> Who's that which knocks? Oh, stay, my Lord, I come:
> I know that call, since first it made me know
> Myself, which makes me now with joy to run
> Lest he be gone that can my duty show.
> > Jesu, my Lord, I know thee by the Cross
> > Thou offer'st me, but not unto my loss.

In spite of Digby's resolution and his 'manly aspect', it was noted that his colour was pale and 'his eye heavy'. But he was determined to speak out strongly. He declared that he held what he had done to be no offence, according to his own conscience, informed by his own religion, but he acknowledged that he had broken the law. For this, he asked forgiveness of God, of the King and of the whole kingdom. Even at this moment, however, Digby took pains to deny that Father Gerard or the other Jesuits had known anything of the Plot. He then refused to pray with the attendant Protestant preachers and instead took refuge in 'vain and superstitious crossing', as one hostile observer noted, and 'mumbling to himself' in Latin.[5]

These private Catholic devotions performed, Digby reverted to the gallant courtier he had always been in public. He said goodbye to all the nobles who had been his friends – it was established procedure that dignitaries should witness state executions – with careful attention to their rank. He spoke to them all, as they said to each other afterwards, in such a cheerful and friendly manner, 'as he was wont to do when he went from Court or out of the City, to his own house in the country'.[6]

What followed however was not to be so casual or so pleasant. Digby was hung from the halter for a very short time before being cut down and he was therefore fully conscious when he was subjected to the prescribed penalties. Anthony à Wood had an extraordinary story to tell about what happened next.* 'When the executioner plucked out his heart and according to the manner held it up saying "Here is the heart of a traitor", Sir Everard made answer: "Thou liest".' Even if such a spirited riposte – any riposte – would have been anatomically possible under the circumstances, the fact that such a story was told is still further proof of the esteem in which Sir Everard Digby was held. As it was, the common people 'marvelled at his fortitude' and talked 'almost of nothing else'.[7]

Robert Wintour was the second to ascend the scaffold. He said little and was praying quietly to himself as he went to his death. John Grant, coming next, was the only one of the conspirators who actually justified what they had tried to do, and refused to confess to any offence, for it had been 'no sin against God'. A report by Salisbury to Edmondes in Brussels confirmed this obduracy. It was a defiance which was later embroidered by Protestant propaganda, with Grant claiming that the spiritual merits of the Plot would expiate all the sins he had committed in his life. 'Abominably blinded' by the fire

---

* He was writing long after the event but with information derived from Francis Bacon, who would have been present at the execution.

at Holbeach, he allowed himself to be led quietly up the ladder to the halter, resistance being impossible. After crossing himself, he went to his death.[8]

From the point of view of the onlookers, Thomas Bates was a more satisfactory criminal than these men with their crossings and their mumbled Latin prayers. If you could not be valiant – though misguided – like Sir Everard Digby, it was better to be abjectly penitent like Bates. He spoke of being inspired by affection for his master, Catesby, which had caused him to forget his duty 'to God, his King and Country'. This led Father Gerard to say afterwards that it was 'no marvel' that Bates had shown less courage than his companions, since he had acted for human rather than divine love; but Gerard concluded his verdict on a charitable note: 'It is to be hoped he found mercy at God's hands.' In general, Bates seemed deeply sorry for what he had done. He asked forgiveness of God and he also asked forgiveness of the King, and of the whole kingdom, praying humbly for 'the preservation of them all'.[9]

The four remaining executions took place in the Old Palace Yard at Westminster the next day, Friday 31 January. Possibly the patriotic reproaches of Sir Arthur Gorges had found echoes on other breasts, but more likely it was intended to put to death the major criminals – Tom Wintour and Guy Fawkes – in the very place which they had planned to demolish in order to hammer home the message of their wickedness. The route from the Tower was in consequence longer. In the course of it, Elizabeth Rookwood managed to watch her husband pass on his hurdle from the window of their lodgings in the Strand. As for Rookwood himself, he asked to be informed when he reached the appointed spot so that he could open his eyes and have one last glimpse of his beautiful wife (otherwise he kept his eyes shut in prayer). When he reached this point Ambrose Rookwood raised himself up as far as he could – he was tied with ropes – and called out: 'Pray for me, pray for me!'

'I will, and be of good courage,' his wife shouted back.

'Offer thyself wholly to God. I, for my part, do as freely restore thee to God as He gave thee unto me.'*[10]

Tom Wintour was the first of these men to mount the scaffold. He was 'a very pale and dead colour'. The spectators were anxious to hear a speech but Wintour, for all his pallor, riposted firmly that this was 'no time to discourse: he was come to die'. He too, like Digby, acquitted the Jesuits, including Father Tesimond, of all guilt, and asked for the prayers of all Catholics. Finally, crossing himself, he declared that he died a true Catholic. On the whole, professions of repentance were more likely to secure the hoped-for prolonged hanging which would result in unconsciousness. Although Tom Wintour had seemed 'after a sort, as it were, sorry for his offence', either his firm last-minute protestation of his Catholicism or his defence of the Jesuits denied him any relief. He was cut down after only 'a swing or two with a halter'.[11]

Ambrose Rookwood came next. He did choose to make a speech. This was a model of repentance, since he first freely confessed his sin in seeking to spill blood, and then asked God to bless the King, the Queen and all the 'royal progeny', that they might live long 'to reign in peace and happiness over this kingdom'. It was true that at the last Rookwood proceeded 'to spoil all the pottage with one filthy weed', in the words of an observer – evidently a Protestant – for Rookwood finally besought God to make the King a Catholic. But Rookwood's earlier sorrowful words seem to have been enough to secure him a long hanging, and he was more or less at his last gasp when he was cut down.[12]

Robert Keyes determined not to accept his fate passively. 'With small or no show of repentance', he went 'stoutly' up the ladder. Once at the top, and with his neck in the halter, he did not wait for the hangman's 'turn' but turned himself off, with a violent leap into space. His intention was presumably to die

---

* This is the version given by Father Gerard, who was not present; but it would have been pieced together carefully from the recollections of eye-witnesses: as was always done with the deaths of Catholics at the hands of the state, great trouble was taken to treasure the details of the final scenes.

quickly (although Father Gerard glossed this as meaning that Keyes wanted to die at a moment of his own choosing, with his mind set on his prayers, rather than be taken by surprise by the hangman). Unfortunately, the plan did not work. The halter broke, and he was taken, alive, to the quartering block.[13]

Guy Fawkes, 'the great devil of all', was the last to mount the scaffold. He did not make a long speech – he was probably not capable of it, since a contemporary reported his body as being visibly 'weak with torture and sickness'. He did ask forgiveness of the King and state, but at the same time kept up his 'crosses and idle ceremonies'. His last ordeal was to mount the ladder. He was scarcely able to do so, and had to be helped up by the hangman. Guido did, however, mount high enough for his neck to be broken with the fall.[14] Perhaps it was the physical punishment which he had endured in the months past which spared his consciousness at the end.

As Salisbury pointed out to Edmondes, all eight men had died Catholics. Nothing that had happened had caused them to abandon the religion for which they had sacrificed their liberty and finally their lives.

A few days after these executions, Father Garnet was sent for by the authorities to be brought to London. His treatment remained gracious, especially if one reflects on the recent ordeals of the men who were said to be his co-conspirators. While still at the house of Sir Henry Bromley, Father Garnet had been permitted to celebrate the lovely feast of Candlemas – the last feast of the Christian cycle before the beginning of Lent – together with Sir Henry and his family. A great white wax candle with 'Jesus' and 'Maria' on the sides, which had been confiscated at Hindlip, was produced. Father Garnet took it in his hands and passed it to Father Oldcorne, saying that he was glad to have carried 'a holy candle on Candlemas Day'. Then all present drank the King's health with their heads bared.[15] As an episode, it was a conspicuous illustration of the paradox of Catholic loyalty.

Nor was the Jesuit's dignity sacrificed in any way during the journey. Father Garnet was still very weak after his eight-day ordeal and his swollen legs were causing him pain. Salisbury ordered that he should be given the best horse, and his hospitality *en route* was paid for by the King (which meant that it was not stinted).

When a Puritan minister accompanying the cortège attempted to involve him in theological debate, Father Garnet immediately saw the dangers in this kind of exercise. Silence might be construed as inability to answer, while too impassioned a defence of the Catholic viewpoint could be held as evidence against him. Garnet consulted Sir Henry Bromley. The result was a discussion, in effect chaired by Sir Henry, in which the Puritan ranted at length without interruption, and Garnet then proceeded to speak 'briefly and clearly' as well as displaying remarkable erudition (the Puritans were wont to claim erudition as their special province). Sir Henry Bromley was much impressed and the egregious minister much disappointed.[16]

In London, Father Garnet was at first lodged in the Gatehouse prison in Westminster. His companion in hiding at Hindlip, Father Oldcorne, was also placed there, although housed in a separate cell. The arrival of the Superior of the Jesuits, with a fellow Jesuit, created a sensation in the Gatehouse prison. A flock of prisoners crowded at the entrance. Garnet cried out in a loud voice to know whether any of them were Catholics. When many replied that they were, Father Garnet responded: 'God help you all! And myself as well who come to keep you company here for the same cause.'[17] Father Garnet's nephew, Thomas Garnet, also a priest, who operated under an alias, was among the many Catholics currently held at the Gatehouse.

This interest in and response to Father Garnet draws attention to the ambivalent nature of Jacobean prisons as far as recusants were concerned. Prisons could serve as hotbeds of Catholicism, as well as centres for persecution. Paradoxically, it was often easier for recusants to attend a clandestine Mass in a prison containing priests than in the outside world. By modern standards, there was even a kind of informality prevalent in Jacobean prisons: inmates could send out to buy food, and, if necessary, could make purchases by stretching out money from prison windows. Obviously, more than mere food – information, letters – could be obtained by these means. In certain prisons, prostitutes and thieves would bribe their jailers to let them out under cover of darkness to go about their work, returning at dawn having earned the necessary money to make themselves comfortable.

Of the many prisons in the capital, one of them, the Clink, in Southwark near the present Blackfriars, was always full of Catholics: it has been described as a recusant 'propaganda cell for the whole capital'. Certainly Father Gerard had heard numerous confessions from his co-religionists when he was held there. Newgate, the chief criminal prison, also contained a 'great store of priests and other Catholics', to whom people of all sorts had 'continual access'.[18]

As for the Gatehouse, in January 1606 one of Salisbury's informants, Anne Lady Markham, complained about the sheer corruption of the place. Recusants were able to bribe their jailers to pass letters to their friends 'to tell what they have been examined of'; then they got back vital information which enabled them to guess 'shrewdly' how to answer.[19] Unfortunately the comparatively free conditions at the Gatehouse could also be used by the government for its own purposes. Unwittingly, Garnet's nephew, Father Thomas, was to be part of the entrapment which followed.

Another innocent agent was Anne Vaux, who with Thomas Habington's sister Dorothy (a convinced Protestant who had been converted into a fervent Catholic) had followed the Jesuits up to London, at a discreet distance. The two women lodged in Dorothy Habington's house in Fetter Lane, just off Fleet Street. They came into a London in which the main topic of discussion in official circles was religion and its consequences: this was emphasised by the House of Commons debate, a few days earlier, on the vexed subject of Protestant husbands having to pay the fines of their recusant wives. At the Plotters' trial, Sir Edward Coke had dealt with the matter tartly when Digby raised it, declaring that a recusant wife, one way or another, was always the husband's fault and he must pay up. But Sir Everard Digby's feelings were more in tune with the spirit of the times than those of the dismissive Coke. Members felt uneasy about the measure, and it was agreed that it should be 'further considered on'.[20]

The next day, 5 February, everyone felt much happier discussing the 'Armour and Munitions' to be seized from recusants, and their elimination from the army. Much virulent anti-Catholic talk followed. The Papists were divided into three, of which the first group, 'old, rooted, rotten', were unlikely to be reclaimed at this stage, but fortunately they were more superstitious than seditious. The second group, the converts (described as the 'Novelists'), were the greatest danger. As for the third, 'the future tense of the Papists' – its youth – this was a group which must be nipped in the bud, with great care taken that recusants should not get away with their own marriages and christenings, as opposed to those of the state. By the end of the month, the incoming Venetian Ambassador was struck by the universality of the discussion: 'here they attend to nothing else but great preparations for the annihilation of the Catholic religion'.[21]

This harsh talk from the male world did not mean that two recusant gentlewomen, both unmarried, could not manage to live at liberty in London. The social rule by which women were not persecuted to the hilt (as Martha Bates had been allowed her traitor husband's money for her relief) still obtained. So long as Anne Vaux remained quietly in Fetter Lane, living in the recusant world which was by definition discreet, she was unlikely to get into trouble. But of course for many years Anne Vaux had planned her life not so much to stay out of trouble as to help and protect Father Garnet. And that continued to be her motive in coming to London. She wanted news of him. She also wanted, if possible, to communicate with him directly.

Father Garnet's first examination in front of the Privy Council took place on 13 February.[22] His journey from the

Gatehouse prison to Whitehall did not pass unremarked. Father Garnet told Anne Vaux later that among other comments from the crowd he heard one man say derisively to another: 'There goes a young Pope.' The Council, however, treated him with outward respect. They addressed the Jesuit throughout as 'Mr Garnet' (they did not recognise his priesthood, but at the same time did not treat him with the contempt which would have been accorded a common criminal) and took off their hats when they spoke to him. These Councillors were the familiar band of Popham, Coke, Sir William Waad and Lords Worcester, Northampton and Nottingham, with Salisbury as their leader.

There was, however, one unpleasant indication of how the Council might promote derision in its own style. At some point in an early interview Salisbury leant forward and twitted the Jesuit about his relationship with 'Mistress Vaux' since Salisbury had intercepted a letter from her to the priest signed 'Your loving sister, A G'.

'What, are you married to Mrs Vaux! She calls herself Garnet. What, you old lecher [*senex fornicarius*]!' At the next interview, according to Garnet's account in a letter to Anne, Salisbury pretended to put the matter to rights. He put his arm around Garnet's shoulders and told him that he had spoken 'in jest'. The rest of the Councillors hastened to assure Garnet that they knew he led an exemplary life in that respect.[23]

If it was a jest, it was a strange one to make at that time and in that place to a middle-aged priest about his relationship with a Catholic spinster in her forties. But it was not a jest. On the contrary, it was part of a deliberate campaign to blacken the reputation of Father Garnet, so that the somewhat flimsy evidence which connected him to the Plot (of which he was supposed to be the leading conspirator) could be enhanced with hints of his personal depravity.

The charge was, inevitably, not an unfamiliar one in relation to celibate Catholic priests working clandestinely in England. Their very dependency on the women's domestic world, the false relationships to which they had to pretend for security's sake, meant that it was easy to spread such a smear. Father John Gerard had been charged with the same scandal concerning Lady Mary Percy, unmarried daughter of a previous Earl of Northumberland, who had founded the first English convent abroad since the Reformation. The accusation was made by Richard Topcliffe when Gerard was held in the Tower.

'It was you who stayed with the Earl of Northumberland's daughter,' said Topcliffe. 'No doubt you lay in bed together.' Even though Gerard knew Topcliffe was speaking 'without what even he considered the slightest evidence', the priest shook with anger at his indecency.[24]

Anne Vaux was not the only woman linked to Father Garnet (even though, according to the Councillors, his exemplary life was supposed to be well known). Dorothy Brooksby, from the prominent recusant family of Wiseman, was a young woman married to Anne Vaux's nephew William. Her two baby girls formed part of the extended household over which the Vaux sisters presided, and which included Father Garnet. At a later examination Coke taxed Garnet with attending a Catholic christening at White Webbs, and Sir William Waad went further, saying 'gibingly' that the priest was surely present at the baby's begetting also. Garnet protested against the unseemly insult as being not fit for 'this place of justice', at which Coke compounded it by suggesting that Mrs Brooksby's baby, being a priest's child, had 'a shaven crown'.[25]

This kind of crude badinage, however amusing for Coke and Waad, however distasteful to Father Garnet, was in a different class from the derogatory slant given to Garnet's twenty-year partnership – for that is the appropriate word to use – with Anne Vaux. For years, those who wished to denigrate the Jesuits had accused Garnet of effrontery – 'face' – in carrying a gentlewoman up and down the country with him.[26]

That partnership had indeed been at the very centre of recusant life. One of Digby's servants, examined about Father Garnet after his master's capture, unconsciously suggested a parallel between Anne and the Biblical Ruth: 'Mrs Anne Vaux doth usually go with him [Garnet] whithersoever he goeth.'[27]

Of course in one sense the relationship was paternal: Garnet was Anne Vaux's 'ghostly father', her spiritual director, and she was his penitent, his 'daughter in Christ'. Nevertheless it was a true partnership because without Anne Vaux's continuous, energetic, thoughtful loyalty Father Garnet could never have carried out his ministry in England for so many years without capture. But it was certainly not a partnership in any physical sense. Rather, it was a spiritual union, of the type experienced by saints in the Catholic Church such as St Francis and St Clare or the two founders of the Benedictine Order, St Benedict and another St Scholastica.

Unfortunately, as Father Gerard wrote later in this context: 'The sensual man perceiveth not these things which are of the spirit of God [*Animalis Homo non percepit ea quae Dei sunt*].' Garnet's enemies, in seizing on an apparent weakness, were measuring others by 'their own desires, not feeling any spark of that heat which moved so many Maries to follow Christ and his Apostles'. (Father Garnet himself, in bygone years, had sometimes in his thoughts likened Eleanor Brooksby and Anne Vaux, the widow and the virgin, to the two women 'who used to lodge our Lord'.)[28]

Of course no one who actually knew Anne Vaux credited the story. Her 'sober and modest behaviour' would impress even the government's interrogators. Anne Vaux was so manifestly that type of good woman, the backbone of many faiths, not only the Catholic one, who would 'willingly bestow her life' labouring to do God service.

She had never shown the slightest interest in getting married and her earliest struggles to obtain control of her fortune from Sir Thomas Tresham had been with the intention of using it to help the priesthood. Here was one who would surely have acted as a powerful abbess or reverend mother in pre-Reformation days. Many of Anne Vaux's similarly pious contemporaries had indeed fled the country to join the religious orders set up for expatriate Catholic women on the continent. Anne Vaux, encouraged by Father Garnet, discovered a different vocation: she was to be a practical and courageous Martha in England, rather than a contemplative Mary in a convent in Flanders.

Strangely enough, given the government's indictment of Garnet at the head of the list of conspirators, his early examinations contained very few allegations about the Plot itself. The smear concerning Anne Vaux might be unpleasant, but it was not proof of treason. In general, Garnet's admissions to the Council concerned those things of which he at least did not feel ashamed: that he had been at Coughton on 1 November, and that he had received Catesby's explanatory letter of 6 November. But he steadfastly denied any complicity in the Plot itself; nor did he reveal any names of conspirators.

What did take place at Garnet's interview while he was still in the Gatehouse was a prolonged questioning on matters of theology, including the doctrine of equivocation. Salisbury told Garnet this was 'the high point' on which he had to satisfy the King, in order to prove that he could be trusted as a loyal subject; in other words, that his was not the heart of a traitor. The discussion was given a special emphasis by the fact that the manuscript of a treatise on equivocation was lying displayed on the Council Table.[29]

At this moment the Jesuit, convinced that the examination was about details of the Powder Treason on which he could clear himself, was unaware how much weight was going to be attached to this subject. Nor indeed could he have foretold how the malevolent image of an equivocating Jesuit, fostered by Coke, would seize hold of the popular imagination.

The treatise had been among the 'heretical, treasonable and damnable books' belonging to Francis Tresham to which Coke had alluded at the trial of the Plotters. Coke had referred then to the 'equivocating' – swearing to things they knew to be false – by the conspirators: this, he said, had been encouraged and justified by the Jesuits.[30] But Father Garnet of course had no idea of the course of the trial: the only men who might have warned him – the defendants – were already dead by the time he reached London.

Since the book was to assume an enormous importance in the government's eyes, its discovery by Coke was either a lucky chance or a tribute to his sharp intelligence. It had happened like this: at the beginning of the previous December, Coke, who lodged in the Inner Temple, had the idea of searching a particular chamber there which Sir Thomas had obtained for the use of his two younger sons, Lewis and William, and where Sir Thomas himself sometimes stayed. Coke was rewarded. Two versions of the same book were found, one quarto and a folio copy of it in what turned out to be the handwriting of Francis' servant William Vavasour. What Coke did not realise, for some reason, was that Garnet had written the treatise himself. Coke imagined that he had merely made corrections. It was a strange oversight, given that the quarto was actually marked 'Newly overseen by the Authour and published for the defence of Innocency and for the Institution of Ignorants'.* But Garnet was asked only 'where and when he did peruse and correct' the treatise, and so was able – for what it was worth – to preserve his anonymity.[31]

The quarto version had originally been entitled *A Treatise of Equivocation*, but that title had in fact been crossed out, as Garnet pointed out to Salisbury. The title *A Treatise against Lying and Fraudulent Dissimulation* had been substituted (although the earlier title could still be made out). To Garnet, the alteration was an important one of clarification. Indeed, between the nature of Garnet's correction and the government's continued use of the original title lay the whole matter of the dispute between them. To Father Garnet, equivocation was a precise doctrine which had nothing to do with lying, a practice he roundly condemned. To the government, on the contrary, equivocation was not only lying but hypocrisy, since it wrapped a mantle of holiness round the lies.

What Coke had found, and now laid before the Councillors, had in fact been written by the Jesuit a few years earlier. The

---

* This quarto version is now in the Bodleian Library, with Garnet's corrections (and Coke's own marks) clearly visible (Bodleian, Laud MS., misc. 655). The folio copy in Vavasour's handwriting has disappeared.

inception of the treatise was due to a general disquiet on the subject of equivocation following the trial of Father Robert Southwell in 1595. This trial probably introduced knowledge of the doctrine into England, both among officials and among the public.

It is true that there were passages in the works of the Fathers of the Church which referred to the lawfulness of dissimulating under certain specific conditions. Furthermore, in late-sixteenth-century Europe numerous subjects, who differed from their rulers in religion, faced the problem of what has been described as 'secret adherence', which inevitably entailed a good deal of dissimulation along the way. It might well be impossible to profess one's true religion in public without vicious penalties or even massacre – this applied to crypto-Protestants in Catholic countries as much as to crypto-Catholics in Protestant countries. This kind of secret adherence was given the name Nicodemism by Calvin, after the Pharisee Nicodemus, a believer in Christ who out of fear visited Him only by night. It was a form of behaviour which received tacit acceptance.[32]

Equivocation as a particular method of procedure was, however, a novelty.* It was this procedure, rather than the mere fact of concealment, which seems to have caused general disquiet as a result of the Southwell trial. This disquiet, it must be emphasised, was shared by Catholics as well as by those Father Garnet called heretics; among the former, the 'strange' practice was 'much wondered at'.[33]

At Southwell's trial, Anne Bellamy, a Catholic woman who was the exception to the honourable record of her sex during this period, had testified that the priest had taught her to deny the truth in answer to the question 'Is there a priest in the house?' Francis Tresham's reaction was to have Vavasour make a copy of Garnet's treatise 'that we may see what they can say of this matter'. This was exactly the purpose for which Garnet had written the book.[34]

* The Oxford English Dictionary dates the use of the word in this doctrinal sense to 1599.

Equivocation was essentially a scrupulous way of behaving by Catholics who shrank from telling outright lies. 'He that sticketh not at lies, never needeth to equivocate': this observation by the Jesuit Robert Persons is at the heart of the doctrine of equivocation and central to its understanding. Father Garnet put it even more robustly: liars took 'a readier way to serve their turn, by plain untruths and evident perjuries'.[35] In times of danger, a flat lie to protect the truth (such as Thomas Habington's denial of the priests' presence at Hindlip) would be most people's instinct. In the same way, Catholic priests in front of the English authorities might have been expected to deny outright the truths which would have condemned them to death – notably the fact of their own priesthood. But they did not do so. Heroically, they attempted to balance the needs of their predicament with the prohibition of the Church on outright lying. Yet the lies they so painstakingly avoided, or believed they avoided, were of the nature that conspirators of all types – to say nothing of governments protecting national security – utter without a qualm.

The underlying principle of equivocation was that the speaker's words were capable of being taken in two ways, only one of which was true. A typical example, which caused a great deal of Protestant indignation, had occurred in February when a certain Father Ward swore to the Dean of Durham that he was 'no priest' – meaning, it transpired, that he was not 'Apollo's priest at Delphos'. Secondly, Father Ward swore that he had never been beyond the seas: 'it's true, sayeth he, for he was never beyond the Indian seas'. One can see the absurdity of this: at the same time one can admire the earnest conscience which found it necessary to justify such life-saving lies.

Obviously the authority of the questioner was an all-important point about equivocation, as well as the seriousness of the matter at issue. Father Robert Persons cited the case of a man who denied he was a priest to an unjust questioner, adding the mental reservation that he was not a priest 'so as I am bound to utter it to you'. As Father John Gerard wrote, the intention was not to deceive 'but simply to withhold the truth in cases where the questioned party was not bound to reveal it'.*[36] Furthermore, it could be argued that certain equivocating answers actually addressed themselves to the real question at issue. For example, the question ostensibly asked might be 'Are you a traitor?' A priest might therefore lawfully answer 'No' to his interrogator because, despite his priesthood, he knew himself not to be a traitor.

Father Garnet's treatise, because it was provoked by the trial of Southwell, took as its starting point the Bellamy question.[37] He justified the denial, saying that a Catholic could 'securely in conscience' answer 'No' when interrogated about the presence of a priest concealed in a house on the ground that he had a 'secret meaning reserved in his mind'. Similarly the question 'Did you hear Mass today?' could be answered negatively because the person interrogated 'did not hear it at St Paul's or such like'. Biblical precedents were meticulously cited in the cause of justifying equivocation, including the words of Jesus Christ himself. When Christ told his disciples that 'the girl is not dead but sleepeth', before raising Jaira's daughter from the dead, this was a form of equivocation. So was Christ's declaration that he did not know when the Day of Judgement was to be: since as God the Son he knew exactly when it was to be.†

Unfortunately there were severe disadvantages to the use of equivocation. A leading Catholic authority on the Gunpowder Plot has gone so far as to describe its use as 'the best weapon in Coke's armoury, and, admittedly, the Achilles heel of his opponents'. First of all, the practice gave an impression of insincerity, not to say deviousness, even to the recusants themselves. The Appellant priests, for example, enemies of the Jesuits, ridiculed the practice: 'in plain English', this was lying. This was something on which any government skilled in propaganda could easily build. Secondly, almost more damagingly,

---

* The real parallel was with a prisoner's plea of 'Not Guilty', as Father Gerard himself pointed out (Morris, *Gerard's Narrative*, p. ccxii).
† See Mark 13:32, where Christ observes: 'But of that day and that hour knoweth no man, no, not the angels which are in heaven, neither the Son, but the Father.' Matthew 24:36 is virtually identical.

the doctrine of equivocation could be presented as alien, somehow unEnglish, and thus used to underline the notion of the Jesuits as Roman spies with no allegiance to Britain. Anniversary sermons on 5 November would regularly denounce equivocation in strong language of unequivocal disgust.[38] At the trial, Coke, wondering aloud what the 'blessed' Protestant martyrs Cranmer and Ridley would have made of such 'shifts', argued that they would never have used them to save their lives.[39] Thirdly, the doctrine of equivocation could be belittled and mocked.

Father Garnet, in his treatise, was concerned to stress that the occasions when equivocation could be legitimately used were 'very limited'; anyone who swore upon his oath to a false-hood 'in cases wherein he was bound to deal plainly' committed a sin. But of course in the question as to which cases necessitated plain dealing by Catholic priests, and which did not, lay the crux of the dispute between Garnet and his captors. He might see himself as having a heart loyal to the King, but as a man imprisoned on a most serious charge he needed to convince the King's mighty Councillors. It was unlikely, however, that Salisbury, Coke and Popham wanted to be convinced.

On arrival in the Tower the next day, Father Garnet was housed comfortably enough. It took him time to get such items as bedding and coal for his fire, but he described his room as 'a very fine chamber'. He was allowed claret with his meals, as well as buying some sack out of his purse for himself and his neighbours.* Garnet even declared mildly that the dreaded Sir William Waad was a civil enough governor, except when Waad got on to the subject of religion, which caused him to indulge in 'violent and impotent [uncontrolled]' speeches.[40]

Father Garnet was lucky – for the time being at least. Others were not so lucky. On 19 February, the Privy Council

---

* No one ever drank water with their meals during this period – which would have been another kind of death sentence – so that it was a question of what kind of alcohol, beer being most common, was served. Private funds were also an essential component of even the most spartan regime in prison.

issued orders which allowed 'the inferior sort' of prisoners connected to the Powder Plot to be put to the torture.[41] The so-called inferiors included Little John and Ralph Ashley, as well as Father Strange, captured in the autumn, and the serving man from White Webbs, James Johnson. These orders, enlarged three days later, provided for those prisoners already in the Tower to be put to the manacles while other prisoners could be fetched thither for that purpose. The horrors were by no means over.

CHAPTER SIXTEEN

The Jesuits' Treason

I will name it the Jesuits' treason, as belonging to
them...

SIR EDWARD COKE

March 1606

In the Tower of London, the torturing of the 'inferior' prisoners was pursued without pity. James Johnson was
believed to have been racked for four or five days, and on
one occasion, according to the official record, for three hours
at a time. His crime was to have worked for Father Garnet
under the name of 'Mr Meaze', at White Webbs. As a result of
torture, he identified Garnet as Meaze when confronted with
him. Ralph Ashley, suspected of having assisted Little John in
his work, was among the other servants who were tortured.
Father Garnet asked Anne Vaux to try to get hold of some
money belonging to the Society of Jesus, in order to provide
beds for the sufferers (the alternative for these broken bodies
was the floor of a dungeon and straw).[1]

Nor were the priests, including Father Oldcorne, spared.
Father Strange, that 'gentleman-like priest' who loved tennis
and music, was a victim because of his friendship with Catesby,
even though Strange had never been involved in the treason.
Like Johnson, who was released in August, Father Strange
lived out the rest of his life disabled, and 'totally incapable of
any employment', as a result of his sojourn in the Tower.[2]

Most brutal of all was the treatment given to Nicholas

Owen, better known to the recusants as Little John. Since he had a hernia caused by the strain of his work, as well as a crippled leg, he should not have been physically tormented in the first place: as Gerard wrote in his *Narrative*, 'the civil law doth forbid to torture any man that is broken'. But Little John, unlike many of those interrogated, did have valuable information about the hiding-places he had constructed: if he had talked, all too many priests would have been snared 'as partridges in a net'. In this good cause, the government was prepared to ignore the dictates of the law and the demands of common humanity. A leading Councillor, on hearing his name, was said to have exclaimed: 'Is he taken that knows all the secret places? I am very glad of that. We will have a trick for him.'³

The trick was the prolonged use of the manacles, an exquisitely horrible torture for one in Owen's ruptured state. He was originally held in the milder prison of the Marshalsea, where it was hoped that other priests would try to contact him, but Little John was 'too wise to give any advantage' and spent his time safely and silently at prayer. In the Tower, he was brought to make two confessions on 26 February and 1 March. In the first one, he denied more or less everything – knowing Oldcorne (or Hall), knowing Garnet, under that name or any of his aliases, let alone serving him. He even remained vague about his own aliases: it was reported that 'he knoweth not whether he is called Little John'.⁴

By the time of the second confession, long and ghastly sessions in the manacles produced some results (his physical condition may be judged by the fact that his stomach had to be bound together with an iron plate, and even that was not effective for very long). Little John admitted to attending Father Garnet at White Webbs and elsewhere, that he had been at Coughton during that All Saints visit, and other details of his service and their itinerary. However, all this was known already. Little John never gave up one single detail of the hiding-places he had spent his adult life constructing for the safety of his co-religionists.

The lay brother died early in the morning of 2 March. He died directly as a result of his ordeal and in horrible, lingering circumstances. By popular standards of the day, this was a stage of cruelty too far. The government acknowledged the fact in its own way by putting out a story that Owen had ripped himself open with a knife given to him to eat his meat – while his keeper was conveniently looking elsewhere – rather than face renewed bouts of torture. Yet Owen's keeper had told a relative who wanted Owen to make a list of his needs that his prisoner's hands were so useless that he could not even feed himself, let alone write.[5]

The story of the suicide was so improbable that neither Owen's enemies nor his friends, 'so well acquainted' with his character over so many years, believed it. Suicide was a mortal sin in the Catholic Church, inviting damnation, and it was unthinkable that a convinced Catholic like Nicholas Owen should have imperilled his immortal soul in this manner. This 'false slander' concerning his death was contrasted by Catholics afterwards with Little John's calm and steadfast demeanour in the Marshalsea, when he certainly knew what lay ahead but showed no fear. Father Gerard called Nicholas Owen's end a glorious martyrdom.* His jailer's words were different but equally evocative: he said, 'the man is dead: he died in our hands'.[6]

The emollient handling of Little John's master, Garnet, did not however cease immediately. With the exception of Sir William Waad's angry ravings on the subject of Catholicism – which in any case the priest tried to bear patiently – Garnet considered himself well treated. Even his personal jailer (his 'keeper') appeared to be full of kindness towards him. One can imagine the Jesuit's pleasure when this fellow, Carey, confessed that Garnet's patient conduct had made such an impression upon him that 'he had even conceived a leaning for the Catholic religion'.[7]

As a kindness – which had to be kept, naturally, an absolute

---

* The Catholic Church has recognised Nicholas Owen as a martyr; he was canonised in 1970.

secret – Carey volunteered to convey letters from Father Garnet out of the prison. Garnet took the opportunity to write to his nephew Thomas, the priest held in the Gatehouse. Then, as the ultimate favour, Carey placed Father Garnet in a cell in the Tower which had a special hole in it through which he could talk to the prisoner in the next cell. This was Father Hall – in other words the Jesuit Edward Oldcorne.

Perhaps Father Garnet should have been suspicious about such a helpful arrangement. He did not of course know of the government's similar behaviour concerning Robert Wintour and Guy Fawkes. Unlike Gerard and Little John, both veteran prisoners, Garnet had never done time in captivity, thanks in large part to the inspired activities of Anne Vaux. Father Garnet, far from being the wily manipulator of government depiction, was, as Father Tesimond would sum him up, 'a charitable man... ready to believe all things, and to hope all things'.[8] He was not a worldly person, and as such did not fear the Greeks bearing gifts.

As a result, from 23 February, John Locherson and Edward Fawcett, two government observers, were able to overhear a series of conversations 'in a place which was made for this precise purpose'. (It was Locherson who had spied on Wintour and Fawkes.) The first conversation they reported introduced the name of Anne Vaux. Garnet had just heard that she was in London and was proposing to send her a note via Carey, who had offered to 'convey anything to her'. It was Anne Vaux, said Garnet, 'who will let us hear from all our friends'. There was an obvious risk for Anne in contacting her, but Anne – hopefully protected by the known 'weakness' of her sex – could play a vital role in passing on the recusant news. She could also supply Father Garnet with those necessaries which were essential to any kind of comfort in prison. Garnet proceeded to talk cheerfully to Oldcorne of his good relationship with Carey, how he had rewarded him financially already and proposed to go on doing so, quite apart from giving him 'a cup of sack' and another one for his wife. Garnet recommended Oldcorne to pursue the same course, including 'somewhat' for Mrs Carey.[9]

The task of the eavesdroppers was from time to time complicated by aspects of daily life in the Tower. For example, a
cock crowed and a hen cackled at exactly the same time
outside the window of the cell, drowning the priests' murmurs,
and since the names of various peers such as Northampton
and Rutland had been mentioned it was feared that vital confidences had been missed. Much of what the government's men
overheard was innocent and touching, rather than damaging,
although Father Garnet's admission to a human failing – that
he had drunk too much wine on one occasion – would be held
against him later. It emerged second or third hand in a letter
by John Chamberlain, who had heard that the Jesuit was drinking sack in his confinement 'so liberally as if he meant to
drown sorrow'. The two priests also took the opportunity to
confess to each other (as they had last done at Hindlip).[10]

But there were promising passages in the spies' report.
Garnet was concerned to inform Oldcorne about the content
of his examinations in front of the Council for the latter's sake
(what had and had not been admitted). He told his colleague
that he expected to be interrogated further about certain
prayers he had said at the time of the meeting of the last
Parliament 'for the good success of that business'. Garnet
added to Oldcorne: *'which is indeed true'*. The underlining of the
last phrase in the report was done by Coke, who obviously
intended to make out that Garnet had prayed for the success
of the Powder Treason. What Garnet had actually prayed for
was Catholic relief from persecution, but the phrase was all too
easily twisted.[11]

Not only were Garnet's intimate conversations being monitored, but his clandestine correspondence with his nephew
Thomas in the Gatehouse and with Anne Vaux was being similarly vetted. It was simple for Carey to take to the governor the
letters he had promised to 'convey'. Some of these were copied
and then taken onwards; some may have been altered; some
letters may even have been forged altogether. Even those places
where Father Garnet used orange juice to write the most secret
passages were not safe. Waad was able to heat up the letter and

read the contents, having either been forewarned by Carey, or else, as would be maintained later, made suspicious by the excessive size of the paper employed – a lot of it apparently blank – and the insignificant contents of the letters. However, words written in orange juice remain visible once they have been exposed to heat (as opposed to lemon juice, which becomes invisible once more when it is cold). These were some of the letters which were probably held back altogether.*[12]

Father Garnet's correspondence was shaped round a number of domestic articles essential for the daily round of a middle-aged prisoner. To Thomas Garnet, the Jesuit sent his spectacles wrapped in a long piece of paper which was apparently blank. He accompanied them with a note asking for the spectacles to be set in leather – 'and let the fold be fit for your nose' – and provided with a leather case. It was Anne Vaux who duly returned the spectacles to him. Her covering letter contained the optimistic phrase: 'If this come safe to you, I will write and so will more friends who would be glad to have direction.' She asked for spiritual guidance for herself – Garnet had been her protégé, but also her confessor for over twenty years and she needed a replacement (it is clear from their letters that neither the priest nor the woman was under any illusions about what the inevitable end of his imprisonment would be). She concluded, not with a signature – too dangerous – but with the simple words: 'O that I might see you.'[13]

That, decided the authorities who read the letter, was easily arranged. In the meantime, Father Garnet replied with a series of letters, between 26 February and 1 March, to 'his loving sister Alice'. In ink he acknowledged her presents of bedding and handkerchiefs, and asked for socks, a black nightcap and a Bible. In orange juice he warned her against the capture of more priests which might compromise the existing prisoners as well as themselves. 'Take heed no more of our friends come in to danger. It will breed new examinations.' He gave her practical

* Letters from Father Garnet to Anne Vaux which include passages originally written in orange juice are still in the Public Record Office; they can, therefore, never have reached their intended destination in this form (S.P. 14/216).

instructions for the reordering of the Jesuit organisation in England: Father Anthony Hoskins was to be the temporary Superior until a new one was chosen by the proper procedure.

As to Anne's obligation to him as her Father Confessor, he released her from it. Garnet implied that he would understand if she now decided to leave for Flanders and the placidly devout life of a convent there, a tranquillity which Anne Vaux had certainly earned. Yet if she could manage to stay in England, while somehow still getting to Mass and Communion, 'I think it absolutely the best.' In this case, Anne, her sister Eleanor Brooksby, her nephew William (and presumably the young mother Dorothy Brooksby) should lie low for a while.

At the end of February Father Garnet told Anne Vaux that the Council could find nothing against him 'but presumptions'. Such presumptions were not enough for a state trial since Parliament itself called for proper proof. Something better, something meatier would have to be established. The likelihood is that Father Garnet himself was put to the torture five days after the death of Little John on 7 March. As a result he made a 'Declaration' or confession the next day.[14]

It is true that torture can take many forms, and it is not absolutely clear which form was used on Father Garnet, only that, in the words of Father Tesimond, 'one suspects bad treatment somewhere'. Tesimond (who was by this time on the continent) believed that Garnet had been drugged, which would have been easy to achieve, given the draughts of sack he was imbibing, and which may explain the ease with which he was able to supply himself with wine. Then there was the question of sleep deprivation, an ageless technique of oppression which leaves no physical mark: Garnet was said to be confused, 'heavy with sleep, so that he could scarcely hold up his head or keep his eyes open' in front of the Commissioners. By early April, Garnet's 'partisans' in Brussels were spreading the news that he had confessed only after 'torments', including starvation and lack of sleep. This caused great annoyance to the English Ambassador there.[15]

It is possible the rack or manacles were merely shown to Father Garnet, and that imagination – the dread which had hung over him for so long – did the rest. The view does not however explain several references to a *second* proposed bout of torture which presuppose that a first one had already taken place. On 24 March Garnet himself protested that it was 'against common law' to torture someone over and over again for the same information, but the Councillors replied, 'No, not in cases of treason,' since that depended on the royal prerogative. In a letter to Anne Vaux of 11 April Garnet lamented the possibility of being tortured 'for the second time'. He resolved to tell the whole truth rather than face such an ordeal, accepting that he would die 'not as a victorious martyr' (as had Little John) but as a penitent thief. Another letter to Father Tesimond also talked of 'a second time'.[16]

No great attention need be paid to the fact that Father Garnet at his trial agreed with Salisbury that he had been well treated. The dialogue (for which of course we depend on the official record, not on any Catholic version) went as follows: Had not Garnet been well treated since his arrest? 'You have been as well attended for health or otherwise as a nurse-child' (infant at the breast). Garnet then replied: 'It is most true, my Lord, I confess it.'[17] Modern experience of show trials teaches us what to make of these public statements.

Torture of some sort did, however, make Father Garnet break at long last the seal of the confessional, which he had preserved with such agonies of conscience. His Declaration of 8 March was extremely dramatic.[18] By whatever method produced, it gave the government clear proof that, according to the law of England, Garnet had been guilty of misprision of treason – that is, of knowing about a treason in advance and not declaring it. And it was true, for in June 1605 Garnet had been told about Catesby's proposed conspiracy by Father Tesimond. Although Father Garnet had taken many steps to avert what he considered to be a catastrophe, he had not actually told the King or the English Council.

In order to clear himself of the graver charge of actual

treason – that he had personally directed the Powder Plot – Garnet decided to tell his interrogators 'the little that he knew'. Contrary to his previous denials, Garnet had known something of the plot beforehand, but he had heard it in such a way that, 'up to that moment, it could never have been lawful for him, without most grave offence to God, to breathe a word to a living soul'. This was because the seal of the confessional was 'inviolable'.[19] There was a direct conflict here between the common law of England – to which Mr Henry Garnet, born in Lancashire, was subject – and the doctrine of the Catholic Church – to which Father Henry Garnet, priest of the Society of Jesus, was bound. It was a conflict of loyalties which had been in theory possible ever since Father Tesimond came to him and made that walking confession.

When one of the Councillors asked the obvious question: why could he reveal the conversation now, in order to save his own life, and not do so earlier, 'in order to save the life of the King and peers of the realm', Father Garnet gave the orthodox Catholic reply. Breaking the seal depended on the will of the penitent (Catesby in this case), not that of the confessor.

Catesby had decreed that, in the event of the Plot's discovery, the matter of his confession was no longer to be regarded as sacred. If ever Garnet should be 'called in question for being accessory unto such a horrible action', either by the Pope, by his Superiors or by the English state, he would 'have liberty to utter all that passed in this conference'. But there was no doubt that the image of the equivocating – deceitful, malevolent and ultimately self-preserving – Jesuit was only deepened further by this revelation. As Salisbury observed on 9 March, it was 'a small matter' whether Garnet himself lived or died. The important thing was to demonstrate the treasonable practices of the Catholics and 'to prove to all the world' that it was for this reason, not for their religious beliefs, that they should be 'exterminated'.[20]

Some of the details of the Declaration may have been dictated or suggested by the government, notably the reference to Hugh Owen.[21] Garnet stated that Guy Fawkes told him he 'went over for Easter [to the continent] to acquaint Owen', adding, rather naively – or perhaps confusedly, given his state – 'which I never imagined before, nor thought any resolution to be in Fawkes'. But in general Garnet, while admitting to the fatal walking confession of Father Tesimond, stuck firmly to his thesis: his horror at the conspiracy, his sleepless nights after the confession, and his intense desire to get the Pope to forbid all such violent enterprises.

When the King was shown this confession in writing, he considered it 'too dry' and asked for something slightly more emotive. In particular, he wanted details of the nobles who were involved. But Garnet failed him on this subject yet again in his second Declaration.[22] Catesby, he said, had been close to the Earl of Rutland, yet did not try to spare him from the explosion. Even if Catesby had had some idea of disabling the (Catholic) Earl of Arundel to keep him from Parliament, he had avoided the company of Lady Derby and Lady Strange 'though he loved them above all others because it pitied him to think that they must also die'.

While Salisbury reported triumphantly in letters abroad that Garnet had declared the Powder Treason to be absolutely 'justifiable', this was at the very least a governmental equivocation. Garnet had justified his behaviour following the Catesby/ Tesimond confession: but he had never justified the conspiracy itself.

Some time before 11 March, Anne Vaux was taken into custody. She managed to disentangle herself from the trap laid by the government only to fall a victim to something she could not combat – sheer force. The keeper, Carey, using his mother as a go-between, had in his usual helpful fashion appointed a rendezvous at the Tower so that Anne might catch sight of Father Garnet, if not actually speak to him. But on her arrival Anne found the whole situation extremely suspicious. There were 'such signs and causes of distrust' that she cut short her visit, not even attempting to glimpse the Jesuit. Then, with that characteristic prudence which had enabled her to protect priests for so many years, she did not return to her own lodgings, realising full well she would be followed. She went instead to Newgate prison, ostensibly to visit the Catholic prisoners there 'unto which many of all sorts had continual access'.[23]

The stratagem infuriated the authorities, who had expected to be led towards a nest of recusants. Anne Vaux was arrested and 'with some rough usage' carried back to the Tower as a prisoner. This was highly unusual, as women were hardly ever committed to the Tower, and Anne Vaux, an unmarried gentlewoman, was not even suspected of being an active Plotter. In the Tower she was interrogated on two occasions, 11 and 24 March.[24] Since Father Garnet was also undergoing further interrogations at the same time – including interviews with the King, who was delighted to discuss such theological (and treasonable) matters as the seal of the confessional – the intention was obviously to play one prisoner off against the other.

From Anne Vaux the government learnt of the existence of a recusant safe house at Erith in Kent, unknown to them before. Here her first cousin, Francis Tresham, had come between Easter and Whitsuntide in 1605 and talked to Father Garnet. Anne also confirmed various movements of the conspirators, including a visit of Catesby, Tresham and Tom Wintour to White Webbs when Father Garnet was present. She talked of going to St Winifred's Well with Lady Digby and others she would not name: 'she will not say that Whalley [Garnet] was there'. She mentioned the gathering for the Feast of All Saints at Coughton, although she protested she knew nothing of Father Garnet's allegedly inflammatory prayer on the text: 'Take away the perfidious people from the territory of the Faithful.' She remembered the visit to Rushton shortly after the death of Sir Thomas when Lady Tresham had kept to her mourning chamber, although Francis Tresham had entertained them at dinner.

Unfortunately, all these movements described by Anne Vaux placed Father Garnet firmly in touch with Francis Tresham in recent years. This was nothing but the truth, but it suited Coke's plans. The government had been put out by Francis Tresham's inconvenient deathbed recantation on the subject of

Garnet and the Spanish Treason. Coke, with his agile and unscrupulous mind, intended to twist this truth into yet another denunciation of the evil doctrine of equivocation.

The government, however, had no intention of taking seriously Anne Vaux's positive evidence about Garnet's horror at the Powder Treason. They took what they wanted from her statements and ignored the rest. Yet Anne Vaux appended in her own hand a pathetic postscript to her first examination: she was sorry to hear 'that Father Garnet should be any least privy to this wicked action, as he himself ever called it', because he had made so many protestations to the contrary ever since. At her second examination, the Council was anxious that Anne should confirm that Garnet, while at White Webbs, had incited Francis Tresham to rebellion. Instead of this, Anne Vaux recalled the priest perpetually exhorting his friend to patience: 'She remembereth that he used these words, "Good gentlemen, be quiet. God will do all for the best."' As to toleration, Garnet had declared: 'we must get it by prayer at God's hands, in whose hands are the hearts of princes.'

Anne Vaux's dignity and decency impressed the Councillors, although this would not inhibit Coke from introducing her name gratuitously into his prosecution speech at Garnet's trial. In any case, by this time, the lewdly enjoyable story of their association had spread far outside the confines of the Council Chamber.

The trial of Mr Henry Garnet – as the government called him – took place on Friday 28 March at the Guildhall. It was, said Coke, the last act of that 'heavy and doleful tragedy' commonly called the Powder Treason. Before the tribulations of the Tower, Garnet had been much weakened by that ordeal at Hindlip and his physical condition was now very bad. It was unlikely that he could walk the distance to the Guildhall. This posed a problem which Sir William Waad solved by delivering the Jesuit in a closed coach. There were those who interpreted this unusual measure as fear of the Catholics among the crowds – it had not been granted, for example, to the conspirators, many of whom were 'of better birth and blood' than Garnet. But it seems clear from Waad's correspondence that it was Garnet's weakness which provoked the change: he was, in Waad's words, 'no good footman'.[25]

The trial started at about nine-thirty in the morning and lasted, as in January, all day.[26] The King was once again there 'privately', as were many courtiers, both male and female, including Lady Arbella Stuart and Catherine Countess of Suffolk. But there is no mention of Queen Anne (who had attended the Plotters' trial) being present. Either tact, given her known Catholic sympathies, kept her away or else the Queen's pregnancy – her eighth child was due in June – made the occasion unsuitable.

Father Garnet, throughout the trial, stood in something 'like unto a pulpit' which enabled the curious to feast their eyes on this creature of irredeemable evil who had planned to kill them all, but who appeared before them now in the guise of an unassuming middle-aged man with thinning hair who needed spectacles.

The indictment began by citing Garnet's various aliases: 'otherwise Whalley, otherwise Darcy, otherwise Roberts, otherwise Farmer, otherwise Philips'. This was a ploy which enabled Coke to make play with the fact that 'a true man' would never have had so many appellations. Garnet was described as 'Clerk, of the profession of Jesuits'. The date chosen for his treason was 9 June 1605, when he was said to have conspired with the late Robert Catesby not only to kill the King and his son, but also to 'alter and subvert the government of the kingdom and the true worship of God established in England'. After that, Garnet was accused of conspiring with Tesimond, and Thomas Wintour and other 'false traitors' including Catesby, to blow up and utterly destroy King, Prince Henry, Lords and Commons with gunpowder.

Garnet pleaded 'Not Guilty' and he was also allowed to object to a juror, John Burrell, a merchant like the other members of the jury. No reason had to be given for the challenge,* but presumably Burrell was a specially venomous anti-Catholic. After that, there was a brief – comparatively speaking – address from the Serjeant-at-Law. Then Sir Edward Coke got under way. From first to last, he was concerned to make it clear that the recent conspiracy had been dominated by the priests: 'I will name it the Jesuits' treason, as belonging to them...' He indulged in a long historic survey of conspiracies in the previous reign, as well as the present one, in all of which, said Coke, the Jesuits, with their doctrines of 'King-killing' and 'Queen-killing', had been central. As for Garnet, he had had 'his finger' in every treason since 1586.

Coke spoke eloquently in order to cover up one tricky area in the prosecution case: the fact that Garnet had not actually been personally involved in the actions which had brought the other Plotters to their doom in the midlands. By English law, he was undoubtedly guilty of misprision of treason, as has been noted, since he himself had admitted to foreknowledge of the conspiracy; but the greater charge of treason needed a little more manipulation if it was to stick. Coke's solution was to declare that Garnet as the 'author' of the Plot was immeasurably more sinful than the conspirators who were the 'actors' in it (*Plus peccat author quam actor*). Coke enlisted the Book of Genesis to his aid. Here the serpent received three punishments 'as the original plotter', Eve two 'being as the mediate procurer' and Adam only one, 'as the party seduced'. Garnet was the serpent.

Having laid down these principles, Coke proceeded to flesh them out by outlining at length the course of the Powder Treason. He was concerned to leave out no recent conspiracy which could conceivably be used to cast odium on what had happened. Thus the Main and Bye Plots of 1603 were said to be joined with the Gunpowder Plot, like foxes joined at the tails, 'however severed in their heads'.

At every stage, Garnet was said to be involved, whether in

* Sir Edward Coke in his *Third Part of the Institutes of the Laws of England, concerning High Treason* ... merely wrote that Garnet challenged Burrell 'peremptorily, and it was allowed unto him by the resolution of all the judges' (p. 27).

March 1603, cheering on Catesby with a 'warrant' for his enterprise, or in the summer of 1605 when he was accused of sending Sir Edmund Baynham to Rome to get the Pope's approval of the treason (the exact reversal of the truth). Then in late November at Coughton he had openly prayed 'for the success of the great action', and according to Coke prayer was much more than mere consent. Lastly, Coke denounced Garnet himself in terms which had become extended since his speech at the previous trial: where once he had referred to the 'two Ds' of the Jesuit sect, he now called Garnet 'a doctor of five Ds, namely, of dissimulation, of deposing of princes, of disposing of kingdoms, of daunting and deterring of subjects, and of destruction'.

Coke now concentrated at some length on 'dissimulation' as represented by that Treatise of Equivocation, 'seen and allowed [actually written] by Garnet'. Equivocation, said Coke, was an offence against chastity, since the tongue (speech) and heart (meaning) should rightly be joined together in marriage; equivocating statements were 'bastard children', conceived in adultery. This elaborate image gave Coke the opportunity to refer to Garnet's own vows of chastity, which he had broken: 'Witness Mrs Vaux for his chastity.'

Equivocation was certainly one of the two main prongs of the government's attack. It was, however, when Coke came to the subject of Francis Tresham and his dying letter that he was able to denounce equivocation in the most effective terms. He asked permission to read the fatal letter aloud. This was the document which Tresham had 'weakly and dyingly subscribed'. In the course of it Tresham exonerated Garnet from the Spanish Treason, mentioning, according to Coke, that he had not seen Garnet 'for fifteen or sixteen years before'. This gave Coke an open opportunity to elaborate on the contradictory testimony of Garnet personally, as well as that of Anne Vaux, who was 'otherwise a very obstinate woman'. Both had given evidence of ample meetings 'within two years space' and also many times before. According to Coke, Tresham had taken to heart the lessons of the 'book of equivocation', which had been found in his lodgings, and given vent to 'manifest falsehoods' even as he lay dying.

Garnet, never having seen Tresham's letter – despite the latter's instructions that he should do so – was in no position to contradict Coke's magisterial statements. But, for all Coke's indignation about a man who would equivocate on his deathbed, poor Tresham had not actually done so. His letter in fact referred to the long gap before 1602, not 1605.[27] All Garnet could do, however, was mutter lamely: 'It may be, my Lord, that he meant to equivocate.' It was just the kind of damaging admission that Coke wanted.

At various points in the trial, a great deal of time was spent in reading aloud statements. The first batch concerned plots encouraged by the Jesuits to assassinate Queen Elizabeth; then came extracts from the confessions of the conspirators – including Francis Tresham's original confession of 13 November in which he had implicated Garnet in the Spanish Treason and mentioned Monteagle. But times had changed: Monteagle was now an official hero for his association with the letter. Consequently, his name was omitted in court (the erasure can still be seen in the official document). Lastly, extracts from Garnet's own confessions were read aloud as well as those of Anne Vaux, and an account of his conversations with Oldcorne.

The Jesuit was however allowed to speak himself. He did as well as he could under the circumstances, although he could scarcely hope to extinguish the leaping flames of hatred – especially on the subject of equivocation – which Coke had ignited. His arguments in defence of the doctrine were those of his treatise. They included the words of Christ on the Last Judgement Day: 'in his godhead' Christ knew well when the day of judgement should be, but he did not know it 'so as to tell it to men'. Garnet explained that he had denied his conversation with Oldcorne because it had been a secret. In matters of Faith, however, Garnet stated firmly that equivocation could never be lawful.

The power of the Pope to excommunicate the sovereign of

a country, thus releasing his (or her) subjects from obedience, was the area of Garnet's weakness, as it had always been for Catholics because of the possible conflict of loyalties. Garnet argued valiantly enough, pointing to the fact that James had never been excommunicated. When he found the King 'fully settled' into his English kingdom, Garnet had burnt the briefs from the Pope calling for a Catholic successor to Elizabeth, and had constantly denied that these briefs legitimised any violent enterprise. Salisbury however pursued the point: if the King were to be excommunicated, were his Catholic subjects still bound to continue in their obedience? Garnet 'denied to answer', the most prudent thing he could do.

Coke now dismissed all Garnet's protests that he had tried hard to dissuade Catesby, and denounced equivocation yet again as 'open and broad lying and forswearing'. He also made little of the so-called seal of the confessional. The dismissal of this pretext – as the government considered it – was the other main theme of the trial. Under canon law, said Coke, Garnet could perfectly well have disclosed the matter communicated to him by Tesimond since it was 'a future thing to be done, not then already executed'. Others joined in the fray. The Earl of Northampton, who had a reputation as a public speaker, vented his talent to the full in a series of sonorous phrases. From Garnet's point of view, the most unfair of these was the Latin tag, *quod non prohibet cum potest, jubet*: what a man does not forbid when he can, he orders. Garnet asserted yet again that he *had* forbidden the treason.

But then this, like the earlier trial of the conspirators, was a showpiece. The odds had been weighted against Garnet from the beginning. Although treason as such – the charge on the indictment – was certainly never proved against him, misprision of treason was another matter. It was after all not likely that an English court would recognise the heavy burden that the seal of the confessional placed upon a Catholic priest (it was not part of common law).*

* Under English law today, Father Garnet would still be obliged to disclose the information he had received in the confessional from Father Tesimond, relevant

The matter was not dismissed without debate. Salisbury, by a characteristic sleight of hand, denied that there was such a thing as the seal of the confessional, and proceeded to demonstrate that Tesimond's observations had not been made under these privileged circumstances anyway. The ingenious mind of the great man, grappling with the net in which he intended to trap his adversary, can be traced in Salisbury's own handwritten comments on the subject in the state papers.[28] Examining Garnet, he pointed to the three necessary component parts of a Catholic confession. 'Satisfaction' had to follow contrition and confession, and without full repentance there could be no satisfaction. Since Catesby had not promised Tesimond to hold back from 'this evil act' he had not made a full repentance; the original confession was invalid, and Tesimond (and later Garnet) released from the seal.

Salisbury then made the quite different point that Garnet could have disclosed the conspiracy out of his 'general knowledge' of Catesby, following that conversation about the death of the innocents which was not privileged. Garnet's only answer to this was that he had not understood the significance of the conversation at the time. All along the King himself with his theological bent showed a keen interest in this topic. He had taken the opportunity to interview Garnet personally on the subject before the trial, and it was probably James who framed the questions subsequently put to him in court.[29] The key question was 'whether a priest is bound to reveal a treason dangerous to King and State if discovered unto him in confession, the party signifying his resolution to persist'. To this Garnet's answer was: 'The party cannot be absolved unless he come to submit himself; but the confessor is bound to find all lawful means to hinder and discover the treason.' This of course Garnet strongly

to Catesby's conspiracy. Under Section 18 of the Prevention of Terrorism (Temporary Provisions) Act 1989, it is an offence, punishable by up to five years' imprisonment, not to disclose information concerning an intended terrorist action. This applies to priests (as well as, for that matter, doctors and psychiatrists). Only lawyers can claim privilege in not revealing information received from their clients. (*Halsbury's Statutes of England and Wales*, 4th edn, 1994 reissue, 12, pp. 1339–40.)

maintained he had done. But the truth was that in the crucible of the Gunpowder Plot the responsibilities of a subject and of a priest were irreconcilable.

After all the sound and fury, the jury of wealthy London citizens took only fifteen minutes to deliver their verdict. Mr Henry Garnet, chief of the Jesuits, was found guilty of treason for conspiring to bring about the destruction of the King and government by the Powder Treason. The prisoner was asked, according to the law, whether there was any reason why judgement should not be passed. Garnet merely referred himself to the mercy of the King and God Almighty. The judgement, duly pronounced, was that he was to be hanged, drawn and quartered.

It had been a foul, wet spring while Father Garnet and his fellow prisoners languished in the Tower of London. The day after his trial, a westerly gale of hurricane intensity swept over England and on across the North Sea, destroying churches in the Low Countries. There had been nothing like it since 1570 – the year of the Pope's Bull excommunicating Queen Elizabeth, which had done so much to imperil the Jesuits in England.[30]

Dudley Carleton told John Chamberlain that Garnet had the air of being greatly surprised when finally told he was going to die: 'he shifts, falters and equivocates'. But, Carleton added gleefully, he will be 'hanged without equivocation'.[31] There is no other evidence of Garnet's faltering from what was surely an inevitable fate given the verdict of the trial. Carleton's comment merely symbolises the absolute obsession with the subject of equivocation in the minds of the public which followed upon the trial of Henry Garnet.

It did in fact take some weeks for Garnet to be hanged, with or without equivocation. Father Oldcorne, John Wintour, Humphrey Littleton and Ralph Ashley were put to death in the usual manner at Redhill, near Worcester, on 7 April, Father Oldcorne calling upon the name of St Winifred at the last. John Wintour, luckier than his two step-brothers, whose bodies were put up for public display, was allowed to be buried back at Huddington. There his body still lies in the Chancel 'under playne stones', along with that of his widowed sister-in-law Gertrude. Perhaps in the end the government heeded his plea that he had joined the conspirators at Dunchurch out of 'ignorance and not malice'. Humphrey Littleton met his death saying that it was deserved 'for his treason to God' in betraying the whereabouts of the two priests. Stephen Littleton and Henry Morgan were executed at Stafford.[32]

It was, however, the middle of Lent, Easter being very late in 1606 (Easter Sunday was not until 20 April, almost at the end of the possible cycle). This was not thought a suitable season for the great public festivity which the execution of the chief Jesuit would constitute in London. But the day eventually chosen – 1 May – seemed likely, on further consideration, to produce altogether too much festivity, not necessarily of the desired sort. Father Garnet reacted angrily to the unseemly news. 'What, will they make a May game of me?' he exclaimed. It was true that May Day was a celebratory date of great antiquity, reaching back to the pagan fire festival of Beltane, which marked the start of the summer. On this day, it was the custom for ordinary people to go into the country and gather green boughs in order to spend the day 'in triumph and pastime'.[33] Perhaps this did not strike quite the right note and a roistering crowd could never be absolutely trusted to do the right thing. So the Council chose 3 May, unaware that in the Catholic Church this was the Feast of the Invention (or Finding – from *invenire*, the Latin word for discovery) of the Holy Cross by the British Princess Helena. It was a feast to which Father Garnet had a particular devotion.

Despite Garnet's condemnation, the interrogations did not cease, nor did the concentration on the subject of equivocation. The day after the trial, Garnet made a new statement by which he hoped to clear up the Tresham affair. 'In cases of true and manifest treason a man is bound voluntarily to utter the very truth and in no way to equivocate', unless he knew about the treason by way of confession. In this case he was bound to seek all lawful ways to uncover the treason so long as the seal of the confessional was not broken. A few days later he wrote a letter to the King, protesting that he had been 'ever of the opinion' that it was unlawful to attempt any violence against the King's Majesty and the state, 'after he was once received by the realm'. When the government informed Garnet – a quite unequivocal lie – that they had captured Tesimond, Garnet took the opportunity to write his fellow priest a long letter apologising for the information he felt he must give away concerning Tesimond's walking confession.[34]

This letter, which was of course read – although Garnet was unaware of the fact – is the fullest account of what actually happened on that summer's day in the garden 'at the house in Essex' the previous year. Garnet maintained strongly to his fellow priest that everything had been told to him in confession, including as they walked 'because it was too tedious [painful] to hear all kneeling'. As for the Powder Treason, 'we both conspired to hinder it...I never approved it, nor, as I think, you'.

Although Waad in the Tower continued to insist that this so-called confession had in fact been nothing of the sort, the Jesuit never gave up. 'I took it as confession,' he said on one occasion, 'even if wrongly.' It would of course have suited the government's book to have eliminated this tiresome matter of Garnet's priestly oath of silence and to have concentrated on his treachery, pure and simple. This they never managed to do. The most Garnet ever conceded – somewhat dazed, and with the possibility at least of renewed torture – was this: 'If it [the news of the conspiracy] were not in confession, he conceived it to be delivered in confession.' There the irreconcilable matter rested.

Garnet's last letter to Anne Vaux was dated 21 April. He had already taken his leave of her and concerned himself with the various alternatives for her future in an earlier letter. This final missive was full of anguish, beginning: 'It pleaseth God daily to multiply my crosses.' Garnet hoped that God would grant him patience and perseverance to the end, as he related the various disasters which had occurred – first, his capture 'in a friend's house', then the confessions of the priests to each other and their secret conferences overheard at the Tower. After that, Tesimond had been captured (this was of course not true). Lastly, 'the slander of us both' – Garnet and Anne Vaux – had been spread abroad: this was all too true. Garnet concluded with a few lines in Latin which referred to the sufferings of Job. He signed himself: 'Yours *in eternum*, as I hope, H G.' Beneath the signature, he appended a rough drawing, a cross and the letters 'IHS' – the first three letters of the holy name of Jesus in Greek.[35]

CHAPTER SEVENTEEN

Farewells

Farewell, good friend Tom, this day I will save thee a
labour to provide my dinner.

FATHER HENRY GARNET
3 May 1606

Father Henry Garnet said his farewells in the Tower very
early on the morning of Saturday 3 May. King James was
no longer in London. The royal interest in the theological
arguments aroused by Henry Garnet's trial had waned in
favour of the other great kingly passion, the chase. James had
left for Newmarket in Suffolk on the Friday, hunting his way
happily northwards. Sir William Waad was left in charge of
delivering his prisoner, as he had been in charge of delivering
the conspirators in January.

The Jesuit, who had by now spent nearly three months as a
prisoner in the Tower, said a courteous goodbye to those who
had served him. To one of the cooks who called out, 'Farewell,
good sir,' he attempted a mild jest: 'Farewell, good friend Tom,
this day I will save thee a labour to provide my dinner.' Even
his captors were visibly moved. Lady Waad, well aware of what
lay ahead, told him that she would pray for him, adding: 'God
be with you and comfort you, good Mr Garnet...'[1]

At the last moment, as Garnet, wearing a black cloak over
his clothes and a hat, was being strapped to the hurdle which
would take him to his death, there was a commotion in the
courtyard. A woman rushed forward. It was Anne Vaux.

It was in fact an administrative mistake that she should have been let out of her prison for this harrowing moment. Waad had given instructions that Mistress Vaux should be permitted to watch the priest's departure at a window. But her keeper allowed Anne right out into the courtyard itself, where the wicker hurdle lay with its burden. Anne was however dragged away before she could exchange one last word with her mentor, or even utter a prayer over the man who for twenty years had been the centre of her world.[2]

Evidently the patriotic protests of Sir Arthur Gorges, who thought the site of St Paul's Churchyard holy to the memory of Queen Elizabeth, had been disregarded, for this was the place chosen for the execution. The hurdle was drawn by three horses all the way from the Tower. Father Garnet lay on it with his hands held together and his eyes closed; he had the air of 'a man in deep contemplation'.[3] An enormous crowd awaited him at St Paul's. A scaffold had been erected on the west side for the prisoner, and there were wooden stands set up for spectators. The surrounding windows were also packed with onlookers.

Not all of them, of course, were hostile. At least one priest was present in disguise, hoping to perform the last rites on Father Garnet's moribund body, as Garnet in the past had done for others. This priest spent twelve pence for a seat on the stand and, as a result, he was able to supply Father Gerard later with numerous details for his *Narrative*.[4]

A Protestant account described Father Garnet as looking guilty and fearful at the prospect of his final ordeal, but in fact his main problem, once he had left the hurdle, was to secure any kind of repose in which to prepare himself for death.[5] The Sheriff of London was present, as were Sir Henry Montague, the Recorder of London, the Dean of Winchester, Dr George Abbot, and the Dean of St Paul's, Dr John Overal. In their different ways, all these gentlemen were determined to secure the last-minute repentance and even the conversion of this notorious Jesuit. It might be thought that someone who had already endured so much for the sake of his Church was unlikely to desert it at the end: but even in the last weeks in the Tower Garnet had been subjected to various doctrinal debates – in all of which of course he remained firm in favour of the Catholic Faith.

The Jesuit dealt quite easily with the request, made by the Recorder in the name of the King, to reveal any further treasons of which he had secret knowledge. He had, said Garnet, nothing more to say on that subject. But when the divines set about arguing with him about the superior merits of Protestantism, the priest 'cut them off quickly', asking them not to trouble themselves – or him: 'he came prepared and was resolved'. Garnet then desired some place apart where he could pray.[6]

This was not to be. Montague stated his orders were that Garnet should acknowledge himself justly condemned, and then seek the King's forgiveness. Garnet replied that he had committed no treason or offence against the King. They could condemn him for nothing except for keeping the secrets of the confessional: this was the only way in which he had had 'knowledge of that Powder Treason'. However, Garnet added, if he had indeed offended the King or the state, he asked for forgiveness with all his heart.

These last words encouraged the Recorder to believe he had secured the vital admission he wanted. He called out to the crowd to pay attention: the Jesuit had just asked for the King's forgiveness for the Powder Treason. But Garnet refused to accept this and he repeated that he was not guilty. The same open disagreement then took place on the controversial subject of Catesby, and Tesimond's confession to Garnet. Once again the priest refused to be browbeaten into giving way.

'You do but equivocate,' exclaimed Sir Henry Montague, 'and if you deny it, after your death we will publish your own hand [writing], that the world may see your false dealing.'

'This is not the time to talk of equivocation,' answered Garnet. 'Neither do I equivocate. But in troth,' he went on and then reiterated it: '*in troth*, you shall not find my hand otherwise than I have said.' This solemn declaration, made twice over, impressed the spectators. The Recorder's own reputation was not enhanced when Garnet demanded to inspect the famous document in his own writing. Montague had to reply, somewhat foolishly, that he had left it at home.[7]

When Garnet was asked – according to custom – whether he had anything further to say, he apologised for his own weakness, including his failing voice. But he did call attention to the appropriate date on which he was to die: 'Upon this day is recorded the Invention [Finding] of the Cross of Christ, and upon this day I thank God I have found my cross...' Although Garnet continued to deny his own guilt, he did take the opportunity to express once more his horror at the fact that Catholics had planned such an enterprise. In the future, he directed all Catholics to remain 'quiet', possessing their souls in peace: 'And God will not be forgetful of them.'

At this point, someone standing in the crowd near by shouted out: 'But Mr Garnet, were you not married to Mrs Anne Vaux?' The accusation stung Garnet, in a way nothing else could.

The priest turned to the people, and answered: 'That honourable gentlewoman hath [suffered] great wrong by such false reports. For it is suspected and said that I should be married to her, and worse. But I protest the contrary... she is a virtuous good gentlewoman and, therefore, to impute any such thing into her cannot proceed but of malice.' Having delivered himself of this broadside, Garnet was at last allowed to pray – at the foot of the ladder he would shortly mount.[8]

He himself assisted in the stripping off of his clothes down to his shirt; this was very long and Garnet had had the sides sewn up almost to the bottom in the interests of modesty 'that the wind might not blow it up'. One more Protestant minister did come forward, but Garnet refused to listen to him, or even acknowledge his presence. On the ladder itself, he paused and made the sign of the Cross, desiring all good Catholics present to pray for him. However one member of the crowd had evidently been assured that there would be a dramatic last-minute conversion to Protestantism (a government-inspired rumour).

This disappointed person shouted out: 'Mr Garnet, it is expected you should recant.'

'God forbid,' he replied. 'I never had any such meaning, but ever meant to die a true and perfect Catholic.'

This aroused a protest from Dr Overal, the Dean of St Paul's: 'But Mr Garnet, we are all Catholics.' But this the Jesuit would not have, as for him there was only one Catholic Roman Church, and that was under the Pope.[9]

Henry Garnet was now ready. He prayed for the welfare of the King and the Royal Family. Then he made the sign of the Cross. His last prayers were in Latin, the language of the 'one' Church into which he had been born and in whose service he had spent his life. They included 'Into thy hands, O Lord, I commend my spirit', uttered several times, and 'Mary, Mother of grace, Mother of mercy, protect us from the enemy, and receive us at the hour of our death.' This was the last prayer he said before he was told that the hangman was ready. The priest crossed his arms over his breast – it had not been thought necessary to bind his arms – and 'so was cast off the ladder'.

Then an odd thing happened. Many of the spectators had deliberately made their way to St Paul's in order to see a spectacle which included drawing and quartering performed upon a living body. But the mood of the fickle crowd suddenly changed. A great number of those present – they cannot all have been Catholics – surged forward. With a loud cry of 'hold, hold', they stopped the hangman cutting down the body while Garnet was still alive. Others pulled on the priest's legs, something which was traditionally done by relatives in order to ensure a speedy death. This favour was not something the crowd had chosen to perform for the conspirators in January, even though these had been 'men of good sort', popular and much esteemed. As a result Father Garnet was 'perfectly dead' when he was finally cut down and taken to the block.[10]

Even the traditional words 'Behold the heart of a traitor' received no applause. Nor did anyone cry out, 'God save the King' as was customary. Instead, there was an uneasy murmuring among the spectators.

*

That same day, 3 May, Father John Gerard, who had himself been named in the January proclamation, managed at last to get away from England to the continent and safety. He believed he owed his preservation to the intercession of the martyred Father Garnet. Gerard planned to make the crucial Channel crossing among the attendants of two envoys, Baron Hoboken and the Marquis de Germain. Hoboken represented the Archdukes and had been summoned to hear complaints concerning Hugh Owen and Father Baldwin in Flanders. The Marquis had, ironically enough, come from Spain to congratulate King James on surviving the Gunpowder Plot. However, these 'high officials' took fright at having such an incriminating presence in their midst. But at the last moment, as Gerard believed, 'Father Garnet was received into heaven and did not forget me.' The officials changed their minds, and the Marquis de Germain came in person to help Gerard into the livery which would enable him to pass as one of his entourage. 'In my own mind,' Gerard wrote, 'I have no doubt that I owed this [reversal of decision] to Father Garnet's prayers.'[11]

Father John Gerard lived on for over thirty years after the death of his friend and colleague; he died in Rome in his early seventies. Like Father Tesimond, also named in the proclamation, who had escaped a few months earlier in that cargo of dead pigs, Father Gerard lived to write a full *Narrative* of the events of the Powder Treason, many of which he had experienced first hand, while meticulous researches among survivors filled in the gaps. In 1609 when he was at the Jesuit seminary in Louvain, he wrote an *Autobiography*, which gave an account of his missionary life in England. It has been suggested by his editor and translator (both books were written in Latin) Father Philip Caraman that Gerard in conversation with the novices must have frequently told 'anecdotes of hunted priests, of torture and everyday heroism of his friends among the English laity'. Someone then suggested to the General of the Jesuits that all this would make an inspiring if distressing record.[12]

Anne Vaux also lived for another thirty years, despite the ill-health and bad eyesight which had dogged her throughout her life. She was released from the Tower in August 1606, about the same time as her servant James Johnson was let go (although the intention with Johnson seems to have been to let him act as a decoy to lead the authorities to recusant safe houses). Shortly after her release, a priest mentioned that Anne Vaux was 'much discontented' that she had not been allowed to die with Garnet. He added discreetly on the subject of her work and health: 'I believe the customers [the priests] and she will live together, but I fear not long.' His forecast was however incorrect, for Anne Vaux proved to be one of those dedicated people in whom a strong vocation prevails over a weak physique.[13]

At first, with her sister Eleanor Brooksby, Anne remained in London, presumably to fulfil Father Garnet's last instructions to lie low until matters had quieted down (although Anne did suffer another spell in prison for recusancy in 1608). The sisters then moved to Leicestershire, where they continued to harbour and protect priests, their names appearing together on recusant rolls from time to time until Eleanor's death in 1626. Anne's toil over decades was acknowledged by at least two dedications in works by eminent Jesuits, translated into English, one of which, by Leonard Lessius, printed in St Omer in 1621, had the appropriate title of *The Treasure of Vowed Chastity in Secular Persons*...[14] She never gave up her work for the 'customers'. In 1635, the year of her death at the age of seventy-three, her name was reported to the Privy Council for harbouring a Jesuit school for the education of young English Catholic gentlemen at her mansion, Stanley Grange, near Derby.

It was Anne Vaux, in the early stages of her grief at the death of Father Garnet, who was responsible for nurturing the story of a miraculous straw-husk bearing his martyred image. She was, wrote one who knew her, 'sometimes too ardent in divine things' – although the priests she protected over so many years would not have agreed.[15]

The story of the straw-husk began with the usual desperate search for holy mementoes among those Catholics covertly present, after the death of Father Garnet. One of these was a young man called John Wilkinson who had been asked by a fellow recusant, Mrs Griffin, a tailor's wife, to procure her some kind of relic. Wilkinson was therefore standing right by the hangman as he deposited Garnet's severed head in the usual straw-lined basket. All of a sudden an empty husk of corn stained with the priest's blood 'did leap...in a strange manner' into his hand. Wilkinson gave the husk to Mrs Griffin, who put it in a crystal reliquary.[16]

There were two versions as to when the bloodstain revealed itself to bear 'the proportion, features and countenance of a pale, wan dead man's face' perfectly resembling Father Garnet, with his eyes closed, beard bespotted with blood and a bloody circle round his neck. Father Gerard heard that the image had been perceived by Mrs Griffin with a mixture of fear and joy, after three or four days. Another story linked the husk to the equally miraculous whiteness of Father Garnet's features, visible once his head was hoist on its pole by London Bridge. Although these heads were customarily parboiled (which made them black), Father Garnet's pallor was so remarkable as to cause general wonder. It also attracted a crowd of spectators, to the extent that after six weeks the government had to order the face to be turned upwards away from the inspection of the curious. According to this second (anonymous) account it was at this point that the likeness appeared in the corn-husk.

The husk in its reliquary was a natural focus of devotion among the faithful – including Anne Vaux who was shown it in the course of the autumn – and curiosity among the rest. As a counterpoint to the comfort the husk gave to the bereaved Catholics, it caused the English government and its representatives abroad considerable irritation. Sir Thomas Edmondes complained about a reproduction of the image being circulated in Brussels, and the Archduke Albert managed to have a book on the subject of the straw-husk suppressed. Sir Charles Cornwallis, however, had less success with Philip III in Spain. He did not manage to get pictures of 'Henry Garnet, an English man martyred in London' censored, even though they were specifically designed to show up the King of England as a tyrant.[17]

Zuñiga, the Spanish Ambassador in London, was in fact among those who inspected the straw-husk. He did so, as he told Philip III, 'from curiosity' after hearing about the husk from several sources, although he denied that he had paid for the privilege, being 'never such an enemy to my money as to give it for straws'.[18] In actual fact, the husk was probably concealed at the Spanish Embassy for a while, before being smuggled abroad. There it found a place among the relics in the possession of the Society of Jesus, before disappearing in the general turmoil of the French Revolution.

Like her sister-in-law Anne, Eliza Vaux of Harrowden maintained her fidelity to the recusant cause for the rest of her life. She was released from her house arrest in London in April 1606 after a series of protests at her condition, made with characteristic vigour. Free to live at Harrowden once more, she continued to harbour priests, Father Percy taking the place of Father Gerard as her chaplain. In 1611, however, she was arrested once again and Harrowden was ransacked, owing to a rumour (untrue) that Father Gerard had returned to England. The next year Eliza Vaux was indicted at the Old Bailey for refusing to take the Oath of Allegiance, and condemned to perpetual imprisonment in Newgate. In July 1613, she was released on grounds of ill-health; she died about twelve years later without ever deserting the Faith which she had proudly chosen, and admirably served.[19]

Eliza had done her best for the family of six children which had been her responsibility following the early death of her husband. The eldest, Mary, had married Sir George Symeon of Brightwell Baldwin in Oxfordshire in 1604; the youngest, Catherine, became the second wife of George Lord Abergavenny ten years later. The middle daughter, Joyce, became a nun in the recently founded Institute of the Blessed Virgin Mary and, dying in 1667, outlived all the family. After the suppression of the order by the Pope, 'Mother Joyce' spent her declining years at Eye in Suffolk, living with her brother

Henry.[20] Neither of Eliza's younger sons, Henry and William, married. It was the marital career of Eliza's eldest son Edward Lord Vaux which provided a strange, one might even say romantic, footnote, to the events of November 1605.

Edward's projected marriage to Lady Elizabeth Howard had been blighted by the discovery of the Powder Treason, and soon after Elizabeth had been married off to Lord Knollys, later the Earl of Banbury, forty years her senior. For a quarter of a century Edward himself did not marry. Then in 1632, he finally married his erstwhile sweetheart, Elizabeth Countess of Banbury, six weeks after the death of her aged husband.

Their love had evidently not been in abeyance all that length of time for Elizabeth, who bore no children to Lord Banbury for many years, gave birth to two sons in 1628 and 1630 respectively. These boys were widely supposed to be the offspring of Lord Vaux rather than Lord Banbury (who was by then over eighty). It was a view which Edward Vaux's testament only encouraged. Being theoretically without issue, he left Harrowden to his wife Elizabeth on his death, in remainder to her elder son, Nicholas, second Earl of Banbury. Unfortunately – if not altogether surprisingly – Nicholas' inheritance of the Banbury earldom was itself the subject of a long lawsuit, which, after Nicholas' death, his own son and heir Charles continued with zest.* The result was that Harrowden itself had to be sold in 1694, to meet the legal costs.[21]

So the house in which Edmund Campion and John Gerard had been hidden was replaced by the present structure by the new owner Thomas Watson-Wentworth in the early eighteenth century. It is surely legitimate to regard Edward Vaux and Elizabeth Howard as indirect victims of the Powder Treason, since, given their enduring passion for each other, they must surely have enjoyed a long and happy marriage had they been allowed to wed in November 1605.

The mothers, wives and children of the conspirators were not

---

* The present (10th) Lord Vaux of Harrowden descends in the female line from Mary Vaux, Lady Symeon, the eldest sister of Edward, 4th Lord Vaux.

coated with social ignominy, but they were, according to
custom where traitors' families were concerned, pursued with
financial vengeance. Guy Fawkes of course left no descendants
to suffer, no widow and no children. He died as he had lived
since the distant days of his Yorkshire childhood, a soldier of
fortune to outsiders, but to himself a latterday crusader, whose
strongest allegiance was to the Church in whose honour he
planned to wield his sword.

Robert Catesby's mother Anne – deprived of a farewell as
her son lurked in the fields by Ashby St Ledgers – was left
trying to rescue something from the wreckage. She concentrated on holding on to her own marriage settlement from Sir
William Catesby, for the benefit of her grandson, also named
Robert. Lady Catesby was successful, as the settlement was not
finally disturbed, despite the best efforts of the crown. But the
younger Robert left no descendants, and, for better or worse,
the direct Catesby line from the notorious conspirator died
out.*[22]

Lady Catesby's sister, Muriel Lady Tresham, who had similarly mothered a traitor in Francis Tresham – or at any rate one
whom the government treated as such – faced the same
problem of trying to salvage the Tresham estate. Unlike Lady
Catesby, Lady Tresham still had three unmarried daughters
needing portions (eight of her eleven children had survived
infancy, which was an astonishingly high proportion for the
late sixteenth century). Then there was the need to maintain
Francis' widow Anne and her small children. Although, as has
been noted, the entail upon male heirs saved the Tresham
estate from the worst effects of the attainder – Francis
Tresham had no son – all Lady Tresham's gallant efforts were
vitiated by the financial irresponsibility of Francis' brother Sir
Lewis Tresham (he acquired a baronetcy in 1611). In the
shadow of the 'Catholic Moses', as Sir Thomas Tresham had
been known, his sons had grown up reckless and selfish,

---

* The Catesby family, kin to Robert but not descended from him, is however
flourishing today. The famous eighteenth-century naturalist Mark Catesby, author
of *Natural History of Carolina, Florida and the Bahama Islands* (1731), was part of it.

inheriting their father's extravagance but not his moral strength, nor his grandeur. Already in difficulties before he inherited in 1605, Sir Lewis managed to complete the ruin of the family, and with the death of his son William in 1643 the Tresham baronetcy came to an end.[23]

Eliza Tresham, daughter of Francis, married Sir George Heneage of Lincolnshire. But her sister Lucy Tresham carried out her father's 'earnest desire', expressed on his deathbed, that one of his girls should become a nun. Taking the name of Mother Winifred – an allusion, no doubt, to St Winifred of Holywell, to whom recusants had so much devotion – Lucy Tresham lived her life out in St Monica's at Louvain, a new-founded convent in the Low Countries.[24] While in one sense she was far away from the tumults of English Catholicism, in another sense she was only one among many women in these convents who had connections to the Gunpowder Plot.

There were already twenty-two English nuns, Canonesses Regular of the Lateran, at St Ursula's, Louvain, in 1606, the year in which its offshoot St Monica's was founded. Father Garnet's sisters, Margaret and Helen, who had been professed at St Ursula's in the late 1590s, were among the first to move to St Monica's. Alongside them, Lucy Tresham found herself enjoying what Father Garnet had called 'that most secure and quiet haven of a religious life', in a letter to his sister Margaret.[25] Dorothea Rookwood, half-sister of Ambrose, was also there, and Mary Wintour, daughter of Robert and Gertrude, was professed in 1617.

One cannot help speculating about whether the subject of the Powder Treason was ever discussed in the convent refectory and, if so, in what terms. One can at least be sure that the most fervent prayers for the dead were offered on 3 May, the anniversary of Father Garnet's death. There were further connections and, one may assume, further prayers for the dead. Mary Ward, founder of the Institute of the Blessed Virgin Mary, was the niece of the Wright brothers, Jack and Christopher; Joyce Vaux and Susanna Rookwood, a further half-sister of Ambrose, were two of her earliest and closest associates.

The continued courageous and devout adherence to Catholicism was one thing that the families of the conspirators had in common after the event. Another daughter of Robert and Gertrude Wintour, Helena, was noted for her splendid gifts to the Jesuits,* while a son, Sir John Wintour, was 'a noted Papist' in the English Civil War. It is not absolutely clear whether Kenelm and John Digby, the sons of Sir Everard, were raised as Catholics after his death, since sources vary. But certainly the dazzling Sir Kenelm Digby – writer, diplomat, naval commander, lover and finally husband of Venetia Stanley – would describe himself in a memoir as a Catholic by the time he reached twenty, when he was living in Spain. It is likely that his devout mother had ensured a kind of covert Catholic instruction and influence all along, even if forbidden by law to bring up her sons in her own religion.[26]

Even the six children of Lord Monteagle, who had professed his new Anglican loyalties to King James, followed the religion of their pious Tresham mother, who remained a recusant. His eldest son Henry Lord Morley (the title which Monteagle inherited from his father in 1618) was a Catholic peer in the reign of Charles I. Monteagle was not at first disposed to grant the request of his eldest daughter Frances Parker, who was physically handicapped, to become a nun. But he finally surrendered, 'in respect that she was crooked, and therefore not fit for the world'. He gave her a handsome dowry of a thousand pounds.[27]

If the Catholic strain remained, the strain of dissidence and bravado appeared to vanish – with one exception. Ambrose Rookwood, great-grandson of the conspirator, was named for him – an ill-omened name, one might have thought, and so it proved. After the Restoration, Ambrose rose in the Stuart army to become a brigadier under James II. Unfortunately he preserved his Jacobite sympathies following the ejection of the

---

* Vestments, embroidered by her, including a set of white High Mass vestments of which the chasuble bears the words 'Ora pro me Helena Wintour', are still to be seen at the Jesuit-run Stonyhurst College, Clitheroe, in Lancashire (see plate section).

Catholic James from the throne in favour of his Protestant son-in-law and daughter, William and Mary.

In 1696 Brigadier Rookwood was involved in a plot to assassinate King William. When one of his co-conspirators turned King's evidence he was apprehended (in a well-known Jacobite ale-house) and taken to Newgate prison. After being tried for high treason, Ambrose Rookwood was put to death at Tyburn on 29 April 1696 – the second man of that name within the century to die for the ultimate offence. But Ambrose Rookwood the younger did not exhibit at the last quite the noble spirit of his ancestor; in a paper he delivered at the scaffold, he declared that he had only been obeying the orders of a superior officer.[28]

The Catholic peers who had been arrested at the time of the discovery of the Plot were subjected, like the conspirators' families, to a process of political forgiveness – provided they paid up. Lord Montague, who should somehow have known better than to employ a young Yorkshireman called Guy Fawkes as his footman fifteen years previously, was one who had always spoken up fearlessly for 'the ancient Faith'. At the moment of the Plot's discovery, he was questioned on the subject by his father-in-law, the powerful and venerable Lord High Treasurer, the Earl of Dorset. Montague expressed his absolute horror at such an undertaking and still further shock at the very idea that he, Montague, could be involved. 'I never knew what grief was until now,' he told Dorset. Montague also asked his father-in-law's advice on how he could get back into the King's good graces without violating the integrity of his religious principles. The short answer was, of course, money. Montague paid a fine and he also underwent a spell of imprisonment. Thanks to Dorset's influence, however, he escaped trial.[29]

His grandmother Magdalen Viscountess Montague, now in the evening of her life, certainly did not allow anything – including frequent searches of her establishments around the festivals of the Church such as Easter – to violate the integrity of her Faith: a Faith which she had held since her youth, when she had been Maid of Honour to Queen Mary Tudor. This representative of the grand old, unswervingly loyal Catholicism, whose prayers had been sought by Queen Elizabeth, died in 1608 at her house near Battle. There had been no less than five priests in the house to say Mass the day before, and William Byrd wrote an elegy to mark her death.[30]

Lords Mordaunt and Stourton were not so fortunate as Montague. Both Catholic peers – one connected to Robert Keyes, the other Francis Tresham's brother-in-law – faced trial in front of the Star Chamber, and were condemned to imprisonment in the Tower. In 1608 they were transferred to the Fleet prison. Lord Mordaunt was fined ten thousand pounds, although it is not clear whether the money was ever handed over, since his son was 'forgiven' the fine in 1620. Lord Stourton was fined six thousand pounds but was finally allowed to settle for paying a thousand.[31]

Meanwhile Monteagle, the other Tresham brother-in-law, enjoyed the pension granted to him for his heroic role in discovering the conspiracy, and he otherwise occupied himself with his interest in colonial enterprises. He donated to the second Virginia Company and was elected a member of its council in 1609, and he had shares in the East India and North-West Passage companies. However, it has to be said that his executors complained that his pension was in arrears to the tune of nearly two thousand pounds at his death in 1622.[32]

At least Monteagle used his influence to protect his brother-in-law Thomas Habington from the ultimate consequences of harbouring the forbidden priests at Hindlip, which could have been death. Although Habington was condemned, the pleas of his wife to her brother secured his reprieve. So he survived to pursue his antiquarian interests with vigour for the rest of his long life. Thomas Habington died in 1647 at the age of eighty-seven, his enthusiasm, as with Anne Vaux, leading to longevity. The baby William Habington, who had been born at Hindlip on the inauspicious day – from the Catholic point of view – of

5 November 1605, survived this traumatic birthdate to become a poet, author among other works of *Castara*. He estimated his own work as 'not so high as to be wondered at, nor so low as to be condemned'. Many recusants of the previous generation would have been happy to have been so judged.[33]

In political and personal terms, the clear loser from the affray of the Powder Treason was the Earl of Northumberland. Nothing was ever proved against him: none of the Plotters, tortured or self-preserving, confessed his name as the putative Protector; nor did the Jesuits incriminate him in the course of their overheard conversation. Salisbury was riding high at the time of Northumberland's trial in front of the Star Chamber in June 1606, having been made a Knight of the Garter in April.* Even he admitted that Northumberland would never have let those he loved perish in the explosion: a man of 'his birth, alliance and disposition'. It seems, therefore, to have been the personal distrust of the King which cast a fatal blight upon Northumberland.[34]

What caused this distrust? The indictment charged Northumberland with 'endeavouring to be the head of the English Papists, and to procure them Toleration'. The admission of Thomas Percy to the ranks of the King's bodyguards without causing him to take the Oath of Supremacy, knowing him to be a recusant, was cited as proof. This was a charge with which Coke was able to make merry, in his usual style, when he described the promotion of Percy to such an intimate position as putting 'an axe in his hand to carry it over the King's head'. There was also Northumberland's interest in the matter of the King's horoscope, and how long he would reign.[35] Northumberland's patronage of Thomas Percy was an ineluctable fact, and he admitted to the treasonable affair of the horoscope (although since the chart had – quite correctly – predicted a long reign for James I, it is difficult to see that much damage had been done).

---

* Although there were rumours that the lofty Kings of France and Denmark had protested at this, considering a Cecil too common for such an honour, Salisbury was installed a fortnight after Garnet's death.

But it was surely the question of toleration and, above all, those promises made (or not made) by the King while still in Scotland which were the key element in James' distrust of Northumberland. Coke himself summed it up when he said that the King himself had given his royal word (*in verbo regio*) that 'he never did promise or command' toleration.[36] Whatever the truth was of those distant dealings – whether Thomas Percy lied then or the King was lying now – it was wrapped in a convenient Scottish mist which obliterated all memories of such a very different era. It was Northumberland who in 1606 paid the penalty for being the front man of the Catholics, a position from which, in 1603, he had hoped to reap the reward.

At his trial, Northumberland, who was hampered by his deafness (he had of course no counsel), was fined thirty thousand pounds, and sentenced to imprisonment at the King's pleasure. He kept increasingly magnificent state during his incarceration. In the capacious Martin Tower he had a study, library, great chamber, withdrawing-room and two dining-rooms; while his personal cook (he was not reliant on Father Garnet's 'good friend Tom') lived in a rented house on Tower Hill. His accounts show not only considerable expenditure on clothing, but also that he was in the habit of wearing the blue ribbon signifying his membership of the Order of the Garter, since it frequently had to be renewed.[37] Nevertheless Northumberland remained in the Tower until 1621, when his son-in-law, the King's favourite Lord Hay, successfully pleaded for his release. He retired to his estate at Petworth, where he died in 1632.

The government had pinned down Northumberland for his part in the conspiracy, but those 'Plotters' abroad who were the bane of the English government's existence remained happily outside the long arm of its law. The Archdukes did not keep Hugh Owen long under house arrest and no charges were brought against him. When Owen moved on to Spain, Salisbury tried in vain to get him kidnapped and brought to England. However, Hugh Owen retired to Rome with a pension and lived to the age of eighty. That old soldier – and old intriguer – Sir William Stanley also lived on in freedom to the age of eighty. Only Father William Baldwin, the Cornish priest who had been named in the indictment of January 1606 as being part of the conspiracy, fell into the English net, although not for some years. The Archdukes had declined to extradite him then, but in the course of a journey to Rome in 1610 Baldwin was captured by the Protestant Elector Palatine, who despatched him to England. He remained in the Tower until 1618, even though no charge of treason was ever brought against him, presumably for lack of evidence. Father Baldwin's final release was due to the intervention of the Spanish Ambassador. He was then banished, and thereafter he spent eleven years as Rector of the English seminary at St Omer.[38]

Spared from destruction by gunpowder, the Royal Family, that domestic phenomenon still new to the English in 1603, was surely set to prosper. Where religion was concerned, Anne of Denmark maintained the discreet stance with which she had handled the difficult months following the discovery of the treason. The more or less public Catholicism on which the Pope and others had pinned so many hopes while she was still in Scotland (and which had deluded them about James' own Catholic sympathies) gave way to something more elegantly lethargic. In 1612 Pope Paul V would even go so far as to refer woundingly to the Queen's 'inconstancy'. In view of the many changes she had made in religious matters, he wondered if it was even true that she was a Catholic. Anne of Denmark *was* certainly a Catholic – she fitted up a chapel at her palace at Oatlands, and enjoyed having Catholic priests come to minister to her at Hampton Court.[39] But from 5 November 1605 onwards she lived her life as a royal version of a Church Papist. Like Church Papists in the reign of Elizabeth she wanted spiritual consolation in private, but no trouble in public.

There was however a fleeting quality to this perceived prosperity of the Royal Family, and May 1606, when Father Garnet on the scaffold prayed for its welfare, turned out to be the high point of its expansion. There were then four living children, two Princes and two Princesses, and the Queen was on the verge of giving birth yet again. But the expected baby, who was born on 22 June and named Sophia, died the next day.[40] Then Princess Mary, the special child because she had been born in England following her father's accession, died in September 1607 at the age of two and a half.*

No treasonable horoscope would have dared to predict that the glorious Prince of Wales would be the next to die. Prince Henry had been the hope of the nation ever since he won all hearts at the first royal procession of the reign. Alas for such expectations: he died of typhoid fever at the age of eighteen in November 1612. That left his brother Prince Charles, that timid, undersized child known to the conspirators as the Duke of York. He succeeded James in 1625 as King Charles I.

If the death of the healthy upstanding Prince Henry would have been an unlikely prediction for anyone in England in 1606, the execution of Charles I, by his own subjects in 1649, would have been an unthinkable one. The roundabout of history turned again. Nicholas Owen's cunningly devised hiding-places, designed to protect Catholic priests from the government of James I, enabled James' grandson Charles II to elude capture after his defeat by Cromwell at Worcester. Subsequently, the throne of England was lost to the male Stuarts. For all the seeming fecundity of the Stuart dynasty, the seventeenth century was destined to draw to a close exactly as the sixteenth century had done: with problems of succession and religion compounded by the reigns of two childless sisters – Mary II and Anne. On the death of Queen Anne in 1714, the Protestant succession passed as it had done in 1603 to a foreigner, the Elector George of Hanover.

King George I was the great-grandson of James I. His right to the throne was derived from his maternal grandmother. There is a delicate irony in the fact that this grandmother was

---

* She was buried, like the infant Princess Sophia, in Westminster Abbey. Poignant monuments to them both can be seen in the North Aisle of the Henry VII Chapel (see plate section).

none other than the Princess Elizabeth, that little girl whom the Gunpowder Plotters had intended to place upon the throne as their puppet monarch, and marry off to some suitably Catholic prince. A staunch Protestant all her life, even at the early age of nine, the Princess had once regarded with horror the prospect of receiving the crown in this unnatural manner. With the ripeness of time, however, the crown did come the way of her posterity. Indeed, it is the direct descendant of this same Princess Elizabeth, mooted in 1605 as sovereign in her own right, who sits upon the throne of Great Britain today as Queen Elizabeth II.

So the *dramatis personae* of the Powder Treason and of their descendants made their farewells, dead, fled or reintegrated in their different ways into English life. But the propaganda war was only just beginning.

CHAPTER EIGHTEEN

Satan's Policy?

The quintessence of Satan's policy, the furthest reach
and stain of human malice and cruelty, not to be paralleled ... as I am persuaded, among the more brutish
cannibals.

FRANCIS HERRING
Popish Pietie, 1610

Nearly four hundred years have passed since that dark
night in November when searchers found a 'desperate
fellow' with explosives in the vaulted room beneath
the House of Lords. In the time that has elapsed, the
Gunpowder Plot has meant many different things to many different people – including many different historians. The propaganda war has been long and vigorous and shows no signs of
abating, given that the most recent scholarly works on the
subject have taken diametrically opposite points of view.

Father Francis Edwards, S.J., in *Guy Fawkes: the real story of the
Gunpowder Plot?* (1969), maintains that the entire conspiracy was
devised by Robert Cecil, Earl of Salisbury, hereditary foe to the
moderate English Catholics, who used double-agents including
Robert Catesby himself (deliberately killed at Holbeach to stop
his mouth), Guy Fawkes and Thomas Percy. Mark Nicholls in
Investigating Gunpowder Plot (1992) believes that 'it is surely more
realistic to see the treason as one of the greatest challenges that
early modern state-security ever faced ...'*[1]

---

* The argument looks fair to continue, since Father Edwards has returned to the
attack in 'Still Investigating Gunpowder Plot', *Recusant History* (1993), a review of
Nicholls' book countering his arguments.

These two totally irreconcilable positions have in fact been present in the historiography of the Gunpowder Plot from the very beginning. Taking the government's official stance first, its invective on the subject (including the vituperative language of Sir Edward Coke) was based on the premise of an appalling danger narrowly averted. Succeeding writers and pamphleteers built energetically upon these foundations in what came to be a prolific body of literature. An extract from a work of 1610 entitled *Popish Pietie* by a physician named Francis Herring is a characteristic reflection of it, rather than an exaggerated version of the genre. For Herring, the Powder Treason – 'that monstrous birth of the Roman harlot' – was 'the quintessence of Satan's policy, the furthest reach and stain of human malice and cruelty, not to be paralleled among the savage Turks, the barbarous Indians, nor, as I am persuaded, among the more brutish cannibals'.[2]

In such estimates, there was an additional *frisson* in the status of the proposed victim. A King – God's chosen representative on earth – had been menaced. That meant that the conspiracy was not only wicked but actually sacrilegious. *Macbeth*, first performed in 1606 (possibly at Hampton Court in August to mark the state visit of Queen Anne's brother King Christian of Denmark),* is a work redolent with outrage at the monstrous upsetting of the natural order, which is brought about when subjects kill their lawful sovereign.

> O horror! horror! horror!
> Tongue nor heart cannot conceive, nor name thee!

Macduff's appalled cry when he discovered the bloodstained body of the murdered King Duncan would have certainly reminded his hearers in that summer of 1606 of the recent conspiracy against their own King. Macduff's words of

---

* Although this may have been a shortened version. Scholarly disputes on the dating of *Macbeth* agree at least on one thing: that the inspiration of the Porter's scene must have followed the trial and execution of Father Garnet. See *Macbeth* (Muir), pp. xv–xxv, for a discussion of the play's dating.

shocked expostulation even echoed the government indictment against the conspirators, which found the Gunpowder Plot to be a treason such as 'the tongue of man never delivered, the ear of man never heard, the heart of man never conceived ...'.[3]

Rumours concerning the King's safety – a monarch who was once threatened in such an appalling manner could always be threatened again – continued to rustle in the nervy months following the discovery of the Plot. At the end of March a story spread that James had been stabbed by a poisoned knife at Okingham, twenty miles from London, 'Which treason, some said, was performed by English Jesuits, some by Scots in women's apparel, and others by Spaniards or Frenchmen' (showing an even-handed list of contemporary prejudices).[4] The story was a complete fantasy, but it demonstrated the continued perturbation on the subject of the King's personal safety; he was 'the life o'th' building', as Macbeth described Duncan, whose presence guaranteed order.

The Papists' Powder Treason, an allegorical engraving done for 5 November 1612 'in aeternal memory of the divine bounty in England's preservation from the Hellish Powder Plot', was careful to glorify the King, as the central feature of what had been preserved. A series of royal portraits, including Prince Henry and Princess Elizabeth, loom over much smaller vignettes of Monteagle receiving the anonymous letter from a stranger and the conspirators taking their sacramental oath. It was unfortunate that the divine bounty failed the next day, when Prince Henry died of his fever on 6 November. The engraving had to be withdrawn (although it emerged in 1679, another period of virulent anti-Popery).*[5]

Such perturbation, personalised and focused on King James, was grist to the government's mill in its campaign against the treacherous Catholics. First, these traitors paid allegiance to the Pope rather than to their King; then, their perceived leaders,

---

* A painted version of this engraving hangs in New College, Oxford, today (see plate section); it was commissioned and donated by a physician named Richard Haydocke, who probably had a hand in the design, and maybe in the painting as well (Weller, *passim*).

the Jesuits, were actual 'King-killers'. A rhyming pamphlet of 1606 on the subject of the Powder Treason by the playwright Thomas Dekker contains 'The Picture of a Jesuit':

> A Harpy face, a Fox's head ...
> A Mandrake's voice, whose tunes are cries,
> So piercing that the hearer dies,
> Mouth'd like an Ape, his innate spite
> Being to mock those he cannot bite ... [6]

Like Francis Herring's disquisition on 'Satan's policy', this violent caricature was not atypical of the way Jesuits were portrayed henceforth. Not only were they 'King-killers', but they were also equivocators.

The doctrine of equivocation continued to be seen, like the Jesuits themselves, as at once alien and diabolical. In *Macbeth* Shakespeare began by amusing himself on the subject, when the drunken Porter of Macbeth's castle, awakened by knocking, imagined that he was at Hell's Gate, welcoming the new arrivals. His language recalled the popular gibes made on the subject of Garnet's death, including that jocular remark by Dudley Carleton to his correspondent John Chamberlain that Garnet would be hanged without 'equivocation' for all his shifting and faltering.* 'Faith, here's an equivocator,' exclaimed the Porter, 'that could swear in both the scales against either scale; who committed treason enough for God's sake, yet could not equivocate to heaven: O! come in, equivocator.' [7]

Towards the end of the play, a more serious use of the word occurred. Macbeth began to suspect that 'the equivocation of the fiend' was responsible for two comforting prophecies which had been made to him. One Apparition, summoned by the witches, had told him: 'Fear not, till Birnam Wood comes to Dunsinane'; the other Apparition had assured him that 'none of woman born shall harm Macbeth'. But Birnam Wood

---

* Another knocker at Hell's Gate – 'a farmer, that hang'd himself on th' expectation of plenty' – may also be a reference to Garnet, since Farmer was among his many aliases, those 'appellations' listed by Coke as evidence of deceit.

did advance on Dunsinane – in the shape of Macbeth's
enemies disguised as branches – and Macduff did have the
power to kill him, being 'from his mother's womb untimely
ripp'd'.[8] Both prophecies were classic examples of equivocation, since Macbeth had understood them in one sense, while
their hidden (sinister) meaning turned out to be very different.

This use of equivocation was seen as an essentially evil
process: 'a monster shapeless, two-headed, two-horned, and
also with a double mouth, and especially a double heart', as
William Gager described equivocation in *Pyramis*, a Latin poem
of 1608 dedicated to the King.[9] It was a shapeless mythical
monster that bore little relation to the actual Catholic doctrine
of equivocation – heroic if arguably ill-advised – which was
intended to avoid the sin of lying when in dangerous
conditions.

Such propaganda accompanied the political measures taken by
the government after the discovery of the Plot, and provided
the correct climate for persecution. Much of this was directed
at the blameless Catholic community, exactly as Father Garnet
and others had feared. The Catholics, like the Protestants,
trembled in the wake of the Plot, fearing a general massacre of
their number inspired by a spirit of 'vengeance and hatred'.[10]

In April 1606 Henri IV of France decided to give King
James a little lecture on the virtues of toleration – and who
better to do it than the man who had changed his religion to
secure a kingdom? 'His master had learned from experience',
said the French Ambassador in London, 'the strong hold
which religion has on the human breast' (if not perhaps on
Henry IV's own); it was a flame which tended to burn with
increasing fierceness in proportion to the violence employed to
extinguish it. Let King James, therefore, punish the guilty, but
let him equally spare the innocent.[11] These same admirable sentiments had in fact been expressed by James himself in his
speech to Parliament of 9 November 1605. Now he saw things
differently.

The King told the French Ambassador that the English

Catholics 'were so infected with the doctrine of the Jesuits, respecting the subordination of the royal to the papal authority', that he could do nothing. He would leave it to his Parliament. So another Oath of Allegiance was devised, with help from an Appellant Catholic priest, intended to increase the rift between those priests prepared to 'compromise' with the state, such as the Appellants, and those who could not, the Jesuits. It was an oath which resulted in a long propaganda war between King James and the defenders of the Pope's spiritual supremacy.[12] But from the point of view of the hapless recusants, such doctrinal wars were less important than the disabilities which came to burden their daily lives.

As these disabilities multiplied, Catholics could no longer practise law, nor serve in the Army or Navy as officers (on pain of a hundred pounds fine). No recusant could act as executor of a will or guardian to a minor, nor even possess a weapon except in cases of self-defence. Catholics could not receive a university degree, and could not vote in local elections (until 1797) nor in Parliamentary elections until Catholic Emancipation in 1829. All this was on top of the spiritual penalties by which Catholics were ordered to marry in the Anglican Church, take their children there for baptism, and finally rest in its burial ground.

In 1613 a bill was introduced into the House of Commons to compel Catholics to wear a red hat (as the Jews in Rome did) or parti-coloured stockings (like clowns did), not only so that they could be easily distinguished, but also so they could be 'hooted at' whenever they appeared. Wiser counsels prevailed and this unpleasant scapegoating was not carried through. Nevertheless a profound prejudice against Papists, with or without red hats and parti-coloured stockings, remained lurking in the popular consciousness after 1605, ready to emerge from its depths at any hint of leniency towards them. For many Protestants, a declaration of February 1606 on the subject of the Plot by Sir Thomas Smith summed the matter up: 'this bloody stain and mark will never be washed out of Popish religion'.[13]

It was a stain which could be passed on to unborn genera-
tions. It was the allegedly 'foreign' nature of Catholicism –
ruled by an alien Pope based in Rome – which made it peren-
nially vulnerable to attack. A political organisation could be
denounced where genuine religious convictions might evoke
sympathy. In 1651 Milton called Catholicism not so much a
religion as 'a [foreign] priestly despotism under the cloak of
religion arrayed in the spoils of temporal power'.[14] He was on
firm ground that would not be surrendered by every Protestant
until the late twentieth century (if then). Meanwhile, as the
contents of the anniversary sermons on 5 November reveal,
the notion of a conspiracy which was so frightful as to be
directed by Satan himself only deepened with the passing of
the years.

Was the Plot really 'Satan's policy' – that is, the work of
Satan carried out by the Catholics? Or was some other agency
responsible, rather closer to the King? The first rumours that
the mastermind was in fact Salisbury, not Satan, occurred in
November 1605. As early as 17 November, the Venetian
Ambassador, Niccolò Molin, reported: 'people say that this
plot must have its roots high up'. Another cynical account
described the fire which was to have 'burnt our King and
Council' as being but *'ignis fatuus* [will o' the wisp] or a flash of
some foolish fellow's brain'.[15]

Such stories suited the Catholic powers abroad, because they
shifted the embarrassing responsibility for the conspiracy away
from their own co-religionists (Philip III, for example, on first
hearing the news had hoped that Puritans would turn out to be
involved). On 25 November Sir Thomas Edmondes in
Brussels told Salisbury that he was ashamed to repeat the 'daily
new inventions at this court' which were intended to exonerate
the Catholics from scandal. An anonymous letter of December
held it as certain that 'there has been foul play', that some
members of the Council had spun the web which had
embroiled the Catholics.[16]

Not only were rumours of foul play convenient for the
Catholic powers, they also offered (and still offer) the most

convenient defence for those reluctant to face the fact that convinced, pious Catholics could also be terrorists. Bishop Godfrey Goodman's memoir *The Court of King James the First*, written about forty years after the event, provided material for this approach, albeit of a somewhat flimsy nature (the whole memoir has little scholarly quality). Goodman was the son of the Dean of Westminster and rose to become Bishop of Gloucester, despite being suspected of holding 'papistical views'. His special interest was in fact the reconciliation of the Anglican Church and Rome, which he described in his will as the 'mother church'.[17]

Goodman made Salisbury the clear villain of the piece. He began by drawing attention to the Catholics' acute feelings of grievance after the death of the 'old woman' (Queen Elizabeth) when they did not receive 'the mitigation' that they had expected. Salisbury's intelligence service had let him know all about this, whereupon he decided that in order to demonstrate his service to the state, 'he would first contrive and then discover a treason' – the more odious the treason, the greater the service. Thus Percy was an *agent provocateur* who was 'often seen' coming out of Salisbury's house at 2.00 a.m. Salisbury was meanwhile giving specific instructions for the convenient deaths of Catesby and Percy: 'Let me never see them alive.' But Goodman produces no proof for any of this, beyond second-hand gossip.

Nevertheless the sheer seductiveness of the story – from the Catholic point of view – prevented its dying away completely. In 1679, when the imaginary Popish Plot of Titus Oates created new waves of anti-Popery, Thomas Barlow, the fiercely anti-Catholic Bishop of Lincoln, saw fit to publish a fresh work on the Gunpowder Plot, which he called that 'villainy so black and horrid ... as has no parallel in any age or nation'. However, in the course of his narrative, Barlow also found it necessary to denounce the persistent 'wicked' rumours about Salisbury's role. The Plot, he reiterated fiercely, had been 'hatched in Hell' by the Jesuits.[18]

Of course Salisbury himself never tried to conceal the fact

that he had had knowledge of some impending 'stir'. He not only mentioned it in his official communication to the English ambassadors but told King James, who repeated it in his own account of the Plot. The reputation of Salisbury's intelligence service demanded no less and it would have ill become the King's chief minister to plead total ignorance of such a flagrant conspiracy under his very nose.

Salisbury's penetration of the Plot is one thing but the deliberate manufacture of the entire conspiracy with the aim of damning Catholicism for ever is quite another. There is far too much evidence of treasonable Catholic enterprises in late Elizabethan times for the Gunpowder Plot to be dismissed altogether as malevolent invention. It was, on the contrary, a terrorist conspiracy spurred on by resentment of the King's broken promises. The wrongs of the persecuted Catholics were thus to be righted by the classic terrorist method of violence, which encompassed the destruction of the innocent as well as the guilty.

The story told here has been of Salisbury's foreknowledge – at a comparatively late stage – thanks to the revelations of Francis Tresham repeated to Monteagle and his subsequent manipulation of the King by the stratagem of the anonymous letter. This limited foreknowledge makes sense of the extraordinary ten-day delay in searching the House of Lords for gunpowder – otherwise quite incomprehensible in a responsible and security-minded minister. In his Cold War against the forces of Catholicism, Salisbury scented the opportunity for a coup, particularly when it turned out that he could very likely entangle the hated Jesuits in the same net.

But foreknowledge is not fabrication, even if Salisbury, or perhaps Coke, did embellish the truth with certain vivid details afterwards, such as the celebrated – and infamous – mine which somehow vanished without trace. In the same way, the very different foreknowledge gained by Father Garnet, in the confessional, did not mean that he was, as Coke tried to suggest, the principal 'author' of the Plot. Neither Salisbury nor Father Garnet was the author of the Powder Treason, though both have been blamed for it. There is, however, a real difference between Salisbury and Garnet in that Salisbury gained by the Plot and Garnet suffered for it.

Could the Gunpowder Plot have succeeded? For it is certainly true that regimes have been triumphantly overthrown by violent means throughout history. If Salisbury's foreknowledge, albeit limited, is accepted, one must also accept that these conspirators never really had a chance once the Plot was in its last stages. Tresham's betrayal and Monteagle's eye to the King's preservation (and his own) saw to that, quite apart from Salisbury's industrious intelligence system.

But Salisbury's loyal activities, like the decisions of Tresham and Monteagle, were symptoms of a wider failure which was built into the scheme long before the last stages were reached. For the Gunpowder Plot to succeed, the conspirators needed to be sure of strong support at home and even stronger support abroad. King James understood the first point perfectly well, and expressed it eloquently when he said that the traitors had been 'dreaming to themselves that they had the virtues of a snow-ball' which would begin in a small way, but by 'tumbling down from a great hill' would grow to an enormous size, gathering snow all the way.[19]

In fact the snow-ball, far from increasing as it went, melted away in the light of the Plot's discovery. The Catholic community, whatever resistance it might have provided in the time of Elizabeth, had been cozened to believe that James, the son of the Catholic Mary Queen of Scots, would act as its deliverer once he ascended the throne. By the time the truth was discovered – James did not intend to keep the promises they thought he had made – it was too late. Two sorts of Catholic leaders, the peers and the priests, never gave encouragement to the violence of the Powder Treason.

Any support abroad had vanished as a genuine possibility even before the death of Elizabeth. It vanished when the King of Spain, for all his diplomatic dallying, refused to back a specific Catholic candidate for the English throne (such as his sister Isabella – herself in any case a reluctant nominee).

Thereafter the Anglo-Spanish Treaty confirmed the gloomy fact that there was to be no help from that quarter. Once again the Hapsburg – and Papal – belief in the impending Catholicism of King James was relevant. The King bamboozled two sets of Catholics into compliance by his slippery handling of his own religious convictions: English recusants and foreign potentates, including the Pope.

Quite apart from the continuing battle between Pro-Plotters and No-Plotters, the conspiracy has developed a rich historiographical life of its own. One feature of this has been the concentration on the figure of Guy Fawkes. It is Guy Fawkes who has had to accept the odium of being the arch-villain of the piece. William Hazlitt, in an essay of 1821 to commemorate 5 November, described him as 'this pale miner in the infernal regions, skulking in his retreat with his cloak and dark lanthorn, moving cautiously about among his barrels of gunpowder, loaded with death...'[20] It is Guy Fawkes who, in spite of having been generally known in his own time, including to the government, as Guido, has lent his forename to the stuffed, ragged figures on the pavement, whose placard solicits 'a penny for the guy', before being ritually burnt on 5 November. In all fairness, the reviled name should really be that of Robert Catesby, as leader of the conspiracy. But it may be some consolation to the shade of Guido, if it still wanders somewhere beneath the House of Lords, that Guy Fawkes is also the hero of some perennial subversive jokes as being 'the only man to get into Parliament with the right intentions'.

In memory of the failed endeavour of Guy Fawkes, the vaults of the House of Lords are still searched on the eve of the Opening of Parliament. The practice has become one of the many rituals which accompany and enhance British political procedures, connecting them to a vivid past. But the search has its origins in genuine panic about the Catholic menace. Nearly thirty-six years after the discovery of the Gunpowder Plot, the alleged massacres of Protestants by Irish Catholics aroused these fears. On 18 August 1641, Parliament, which was in a ferment over these supposed atrocities, believed that the threat might have moved closer to home. Orders were given to search 'Rosebie's House, the Tavern, and such other Houses and Vaults and Cellars as are near the Upper House of Parliament' for powder, arms or ammunition.[21]

A similar panic marked the period surrounding Titus Oates' revelations of a Popish Plot in 1678. In late October, the House of Lords was told by the Gentleman Usher of the Black Rod that coals and timber had been lodged in the cellars adjoining and that, even worse, 'a great knocking and digging' in the earth had been heard there. Seventy years after the Powder Treason, with Catholics still very much the prime suspects, this was enough to raise the alarm. The House of Lords set up a committee, which was to have the cellars cleared of firewood, so that sentinels, under the command of trusted officers, could patrol these dangerous areas day and night. A certain Mrs Dehaure, living in the Old Palace Yard, was ordered out of her home so that it could be filled with guards.[22]

Again in 1690, following the accession of William III, there were fears of Jacobite insurrection on behalf of the exiled Stuarts. The Marquess of Carmarthen reported to the House of Lords that there was strong cause to believe that there was 'a second Gunpowder Plot, or some such great Mischief', since notorious 'ill-wishers' were resorting to the house of one Hutchinson in the Old Palace, Westminster.[23] Nor were these fears totally imaginary. The assassination plot which led to the execution of Ambrose Rookwood the second occurred only six years later.

In the calmer weather of the eighteenth century, the search became progressively ritualised. In 1760 an agreeable new piece of ceremony was introduced, as is demonstrated by the accounts of a wine-merchant named Old Bellamy who was allowed to rent the vaults. The searchers ended their search by drinking the loyal toast in port which he supplied. By 1807 it had become the regular practice, supported by custom, for 'The Lord Chamberlain of England' to make a search for 'combustibles' under or near either House of Parliament before its Opening. After the fire which demolished much of the Palace of Westminster, Bellamy's wine-shop moved to nearby Parliament Street – but happily the custom of port-drinking continued.[24]

From the beginning of the twentieth century, a detachment of ten men of the Queen's Body Guard of the Yeomen of the Guard was accustomed to perform the search just before the Opening of Parliament by the sovereign and it still does. The Yeomen of the Guard, in their splendid scarlet uniforms and black Tudor hats, carrying lanterns, weave among the large modern pipes which heat the Palace of Westminster. Port is still drunk at the end of the search (after a lapse, the custom was revived, but without the loyal toast, in 1976).[25] So far as is known, however, the one successful search ever made – in the sense that perilous substances and a perilous person actually turned up – occurred on the night of 5 November 1605.

A second feature of the historiography of the Gunpowder Plot has been the attention paid to the date itself, variously known as Guy Fawkes Day and Bonfire Night.* Unlike many English celebrations, 5 November was not invented by the Victorians with their talent for conjuring up instant, rich, immemorial traditions. Nor for that matter are its origins lost in antiquity, linked over centuries to the Celtic fire festival at the beginning of winter (which later merged into the Catholic Feast of All Saints also on 1 November). As David Cressy has written in his study of the subject, there has been 'much speculative nonsense' floated along these lines: the English Bonfire Night comes directly from the date of the Opening of

---

* It is the day, not the year, which has proved '*utterly* and even maddeningly MEMORABLE' in the words of W. C. Sellar and R. C. Yeatman's *1066 and All That* (1930, pp. 62–3). It would be fair to say that there are many able to mutter:

> Please to remember the Fifth of November
> Gunpowder Treason and Plot
> We know no reason why Gunpowder Treason
> Should ever be forgot

(in one of its many variations) who, if challenged, would not be able to name the actual year in which these memorable events took place.

Parliament in 1605, and the proximity to 1 November is purely coincidental.*[26]

Nevertheless this emphasis on the day itself has, like the opposing arguments, been present since the beginning. The first bonfires were lit on 5 November 1605 itself, the first sermon preached soon after. An analysis of the Gunpowder sermons (those preached on the anniversary) shows a concentration on the day which is almost mystical in its fervour. In 1606 Bishop Lancelot Andrewes preached from the text 'This is the day which the Lord hath made; let us rejoice and be glad in it.' He went on, 'The day (we all know) was meant to be the day of all our deaths ... It is our Passe-over,' and made an even more solemn comparison to the Day of Resurrection. Altogether Andrewes, a fervent preacher of King James, would preach ten Gunpowder sermons. In 1618 he summed up the national feeling of patriotism mixed with religion: 'Here we have the making of a new Holy-day (over and above those of God's in the laws).'[27]

Predictably enough, celebrations waxed or waned according to the waves of anti-Catholicism which periodically shook England. Any apparent support given to that dangerous foreign-based religion, any renewed threat from its supporters, was enough to make the annual bonfires burn brighter. The marriage of Charles I to a French Catholic princess, the so-called Popish Plot of 1679, the Catholicism of James II – how convenient that his supplanter William III landed in England on 5 November! – all these events met with outbursts of conflagration.[28]

Yet there was one element present in the celebrations of the anniversary which would need diplomatic handling as the years passed. The original 5 November had been a date of royal deliverance: essentially it was a monarch who had been saved from destruction. Yet in 1647 – two years before the execution of Charles I – Parliament abolished all feasts *except* the 5 November celebration, on the ground that the day stood for

---

* It will be recalled that this date was changed twice: the last postponement was from 3 October. According to Cressy's argument, we might well have been chanting 'Please to remember the Third of October'.

the foiling of Papists, regardless of its other implications. Fifth of November continued to be celebrated under the Commonwealth, the only national feast to survive. This was despite a certain illogicality in commemorating the saving of a King from destruction by a people who had recently put their own King to death.[29]

Still stranger, in a sense, was the transmutation of Bonfire Night after it had crossed the Atlantic. Here were men and women who had come, very many of them, to throw off the chains of royalist absolutism: it might be questioned whether the annual memory of an English King's deliverance was really such an appropriate occasion for rejoicing. If celebrating a royal anniversary was too negative, the answer was to emphasise the positive: that is, to burn a Pope of Rome, still in charge, rather than Guy Fawkes, long vanished. Thus Pope Day, a rumbustious occasion of mob revelry and mob rivalries, came to be celebrated, mainly in New England, on 5 November. It was a special feature of Boston life among the 'lower elements', but spread as far south as Charleston.[30]

Increasingly, there was something anarchic about the occasion, with strong anti-governmental undertones, particularly so long as that government was British. During the struggles for American Independence, advantage was taken of the flexibility inherent in Pope Day (or Bonfire Night) when the effigy of any displeasing person could be burnt so long as that of the Pope went along too. Not everyone joined in the revelry: the custom was condemned by George Washington as 'ridiculous and childish'. Notwithstanding, Lord Bute, George III's Prime Minister, began to feature. In 1774, in Charleston, the Jacobite Pretender to the throne (Bonnie Prince Charlie), the Pope and the Devil all shared a bonfire with English tea. In another contemporary bonfire Lord North was burnt, wearing his Star and Garter, as well as Governor Hutchinson, once again accompanied by the Pope and the Devil. When an effigy was burnt in 1780 of Benedict Arnold, the turncoat American general who joined the British side, it was a symbolic protest which bore very little relation to the original 5 November celebration.[31]

So the bonfires of Pope Day died down, the celebration lingering on in the nineteenth century in places like Newburyport, Massachusetts, and Portsmouth and New Castle in New Hampshire mainly as an occasion for a boisterous outing for children, asking for money. Those in Newburyport who chanted, 'Here is the Pope that we have got / The whole promoter of the Plot,' had very little, if any, idea of the historical significance of what they were saying. In the United States, the coincidental proximity of 5 November to Hallowe'en on 31 October (to say nothing of the great national feast of Thanksgiving, roughly three weeks later) has meant that few folk memories of it survive, let alone celebrations, except among those of recent British descent, or with special British connections.*

In the Old World, as opposed to the New, Guy Fawkes Day was far from vanishing away. A study of popular prints on the subject of religion from 1600 up till 1832 shows anti-Catholicism and the political connotations of Popery as one theme that spans the whole period. The prayer of thanksgiving on 5 November remained in the Anglican Book of Prayer until 1859.† Protestant pastors annually remembered the hideous fate designed for King and Royal Family 'by Popish treachery appointed as sheep to the slaughter'. As they intoned, 'From this unnatural conspiracy not our merit but Thy mercy, not our foresight but Thy providence delivered us,' it was made clear that the unnatural conspiracy had been the work of *the* Catholics, not just a small group of them.[32]

This stubborn sense of Catholic menace did however mean

* Widespread enquiries by the author in 1993–4 failed to produce information concerning any indigenous celebration of 5 November in the United States – that is, festivals with continuity to the seventeenth century and Pope Day. All those who did mark Guy Fawkes Day in one form or another were careful to emphasise that their rituals were purely enjoyable and had absolutely no connotation of anti-Catholicism: as one correspondent wrote: 'much more Dionysian than anti-papal'.

† It was discontinued along with the official commemoration of two other days of monarchical significance, 30 January (execution of Charles I, 1649) and 29 May (restoration of Charles II, 1660).

that Guy Fawkes Day itself moved away, as in the United States, from the notion of royal deliverance. It moved in the direction of rowdy popular demonstrations on the one hand and anti-Popery on the other. Typical of the rowdy aspect was the running battle in Exeter, extending over forty years, between a popular force known as 'Young Exeter' and the authorities. In the course of it a High Churchman and right-wing Tory was burnt in effigy for his opposition to the Reform Bill in 1832.[33]

As for anti-Popery, the restoration of the Catholic hierarchy in 1850 was marked by the burning of the effigies of the new Catholic Archbishop of Westminster, Cardinal Wiseman, along with the Pope and certain Jesuits, on 5 November. For his part, Cardinal Wiseman protested against people being invited 'to feast their eyes upon the mock execution of individuals' (expressing the distaste that many have always felt for such practices).* At least Catholic priests in England could thank God 'that their effigies and not their persons' were in the hands of those who had made the effigies and lit the bonfires.[34]

This was not an exaggerated reaction, given the bursts of anti-Catholicism which continued to erupt publicly even in places where wiser counsels might have been expected. The publication of David Jardine's *A Narrative of the Gunpowder Plot* in 1857 merely stirred the controversy further. For Jardine placed a full measure of blame upon the Jesuits, with Garnet 'a willing, consenting and approving confederate'. He also made a thinly veiled accusation that certain documents condemning the Jesuits had been suppressed.[35]

In this way William Turnbull, a Scottish Catholic archivist working in the Public Record Office, became embroiled in the controversy as the supposed author of this suppression. Extreme Protestants – led by the rabidly anti-Catholic Tory

---

* One Catholic schoolmaster, Dom. Antony Sutch O.S.B. of Downside, used to celebrate 6 November as opposed to the 5th, as a protest against such practices: on this day he recalled to his pupils the sufferings of the Elizabethan and Jacobean Catholic martyrs (information supplied to the author).

MP for Warwickshire North, Charles Newdigate Newdegate –
howled for his resignation. In vain the Master of the Rolls,
Lord Romilly, issued a public statement which totally exculpated Turnbull. Newdegate, who also issued wild accusations
of treason against Cardinal Manning, had his way. Turnbull
resigned in 1861 and died, broken by the experience, not long
after. Certainly the Gunpowder Plot cast a long shadow.[36] One
of Newdegate's additional motives in his campaign of enmity
was to smear his Liberal political opponents in Warwickshire
who happened to be Catholics: the Throckmortons of
Coughton Court.

The immolation of current hate-figures – in effigy – was the
way Guy Fawkes Day was to go from the eighteenth century
onwards. It was, after all, a fertile field, and remains so. Joan
Courthope was the daughter of a late-nineteenth-century
Sussex squire. When she was thirteen, she recorded in her diary
angry British feeling concerning the Boer leader 'Oom Paul'
Kruger at the outset of the Boer War. On 5 November 1899,
at Ticehurst, a suitable effigy having been constructed, the
march 'The Downfall of Kruger' was played and a large
bonfire was lit. At the end, Joan noted laconically, 'Kruger
chucked in.'[37]

A hundred years later, the most famous Bonfire Night celebrations in England, those of Lewes in East Sussex, also con-
centrate, merrily enough, on burning the infamous – or just the
famous. In 1994 effigies included Mrs Thatcher, John Major on
a dinosaur taken from the film *Jurassic Park*, and the Home
Secretary Michael Howard in the week of the publication of
the unpopular Criminal Justice Bill, as well as Guy Fawkes
himself. The celebrations were attended by an estimated eighty
thousand people, with two thousand of them marching.[38]

The town festival has a long history – anti-Catholicism was
encouraged by the fact that seventeen Protestant martyrs were
burnt there under Queen Mary Tudor – and in 1785 the Riot
Act had to be read, owing to the conspicuous violence of the
crowd. Nowadays there are five rural Bonfire Societies, whose

members adopt various forms of historical fancy dress for their contests. Only one of them, however, the Cliffe, still burns an effigy of the Pope. (But the Cliffe is careful to make it clear that it is a seventeenth-century Pope which is being burnt, not the present incumbent.) An apt comparison can be made to the Palio in Siena with its similar loyalties and rivalries. In short, Lewes now provides 'a night of wildness and fun' rather than something more sinister, although there will always be those who will be made uneasy by the sight of the words 'No Popery' on a banner slung across an English street, let alone the burning of the Pope – any Pope – in effigy.* Perhaps those, including the present writer, who recoil from such sights, should take comfort from the sensible words in an American colonial almanac of 1746:

> Powder-plot is not forgot
> 'Twill be observed by many a sot.[39]

All these ebullient and on the whole light-hearted festivities have little connection to the serious men who plotted the downfall of the government in 1605. The courage of the Powder Plotters is undeniable and even those hottest in condemning their enterprise have paid tribute to it. A notable example of this is provided by the historian S. R. Gardiner, locked for many years in the late nineteenth century in a Pro-Plot versus No-Plot controversy. He even expressed a certain satisfaction that so many of the original conspirators cheated the scaffold by their doomed last stand at Holbeach. 'Atrocious as the whole undertaking was,' he wrote, 'great as must have been the moral obliquity of their minds before they could have conceived such a project, there was at least nothing mean or selfish about them. They had boldly risked their lives for what they honestly believed to be the cause of God and their country.'[40]

---

* The Catholic parish priest at St Pancras, Lewes, since the mid-1980s, whose church is passed by the bonfire processions, emphasises that he has not found Lewes to be an anti-Catholic town in any way.

In their own times this was understood, even by those – Catholics – who disapproved in principle of any such adventure based on the destruction of the innocent. Father John Gerard, in his *Narrative*, compared the conspirators (his intimate friends) to the Maccabees, the Jewish warriors who delivered their people from the Syrians in the second century. 'Seeing members of their brethren to suffer patiently the unjust oppression of their adversaries', the Maccabees decided that if everyone was similarly passive 'they will now quickly root us out of the earth'.* The comparison was an apt one as this was in essence the stance expressed by the conspirator Robert Keyes at his trial, when he spoke little but 'showed plenty of spirit'. Keyes thought it the lesser of two evils 'to die rather than live in the midst of so much tyranny'.[41]

It is not a position that the world can expect to see abandoned so long as the persecution of minorities – and for that matter of majorities – survives. Terrorism after all does not exist in a vacuum. 'I do not, however, deny that I planned sabotage. I did not plan it in a spirit of recklessness or because I have any love of violence. I planned it as a result of a calm and sober assessment of the political situation that had arisen after many years of tyranny, exploitation, and oppression of my people...' These are not the words of Robert Catesby, but *mutatis mutandis* they could in fact have been uttered by him had he lived to defend his actions to the world. This is in fact the speech, three hundred and fifty years later, of Nelson Mandela, in the dock for his leadership of the African National Congress, at the Rivonia Trial of 1964: he chose to quote it in his autobiography *The Long Walk to Freedom* as an explanation but not an excuse.[42]

Mandela was sentenced to life imprisonment (and served twenty-five years) before he was elected President of South Africa in 1991. In the end, President Mandela was not, therefore, to be one of the myriad 'defeated' human beings to whom 'History', in the lines of W. H. Auden on the Spanish

---

* The Maccabees decided (unlike their brethren) to fight on the Sabbath day: 'let us not all die as our brethren died in their hiding-places' (1 Maccabees 2:40–1).

Civil War, 'may say Alas but cannot help nor pardon ...' Yet this passage in his autobiography reminds us of one reason why terrorism, successful or otherwise, will probably always remain as the behaviour of last resort for some: 'The hard facts were that fifty years of non-violence had brought [my] people nothing but more repressive legislation, and fewer rights.'

The Gunpowder Plotters were terrorists and they were defeated. They were not good men – by no stretch of the imagination can they be described as that. The goodness in this tragic episode belongs to the priests and lay brothers such as Nicholas Owen (Little John) and the heroic women. But, under different circumstances, they might have been very differently regarded. One might go to the opposite extreme and represent the Plotters as brave, bad men: but perhaps brave, misguided men is a kinder verdict which may be allowed at this distance of time.[43]

The study of history can at least bring respect for those whose motives, if not their actions, were noble and idealistic. It was indeed a 'heavy and doleful tragedy' that men of such calibre were driven by continued religious persecution to Gunpowder, Treason and Plot.

Notes

〜

Details of books, documents etc., given here in abbreviated form, will be found in the list of Reference Books.

Prologue: Bountiful Beginnings

1 Weston, p. 222.
2 Hurstfield, 'Succession', p. 370; Caraman, *Garnet*, p. 299; Harrison, *Elizabethan*, p. 70; Byrne, p. 244.
3 Chamberlain, I, p. 188.
4 H.M.C. Salisbury, XIII, p. 668.
5 *Henry IV, Pt 2*, Induction.
6 *Carey*, pp. 57–8 and note.
7 *Carey*, p. 59.
8 *Carey*, p. 60; Williams, *Elizabeth*, p. 352. Somerset, *Elizabeth*, p. 568; C.S.P. Domestic, VIII, p. 1; Chamberlain, I, p. 188; Bruce, p. li; Neale, 'Sayings', p. 229 and note 1.
9 Handover, *Arbella*, pp. 158–60.
10 *Manningham*, p. 159; Birch, pp. 206–7; *Carey*, pp. 61ff.
11 Nichols, I, pp. 25ff.; Weston, p. 222.
12 Haigh, *Elizabeth*, p. 25; Clark, p. 212; Nichols, I, p. 30.
13 Caraman, *Garnet*, pp. 305–6 and note 1.
14 Anstruther, *Vaux*, pp. 258, 221.
15 Byrne, p. 190.

16 Nichols, I, p. 40; Smith, *James*, p. 4; Wormald, 'James', p. 188; Willson, p. 167.

17 Tierney, p. lxxii.

18 Edwards, *Tesimond*, p. 21.

19 Cuvelier, pp. 289–90.

20 Loomie, 'Toleration', p. 50.

21 Dekker, *Works*, I, p. 99.

22 Nichols, I, pp. 62ff.

23 Mathew, *James*, pp. 117, 122.

24 Nichols, I, p. 70.

25 Loomie, 'Toleration', pp. 14ff.; H.M.C. Salisbury, XV, p. 232.

26 H.M.C. Salisbury, XIV, p. 162.

27 Peck, *Mental World*, p. 4.

28 Chamberlain, I, p. 192; Nichols, I, p. 154.

29 Caraman, *Garnet*, p. 305.

30 Caraman, *Garnet*, p. 315; Weston, pp. 222–4.

Chapter One: Whose Head for the Crown?

1 Hale, pp. 124–5.

2 Lee, p. 420.

3 Mackie, pp. 267ff.

4 Wormald, 'James', p. 189.

5 It could be argued that the junior Suffolk line had a greater claim to legitimacy than the senior one, in that it descended from Lady Eleanor Brandon, who (unlike her elder sister Frances) had been born after the death of Suffolk's earlier wife.

6 Clancy, *Pamphleteers*, p. 79.

7 Clancy, 'Catholics', p. 115.

8 Published under the title *A Conference about the Next Succession to the Crowne of Ingland*, by R. Doleman; Hicks, 'Persons and *Succession*', p. 111.

9 Loomie, 'Philip', p. 509.

10 Klingenstein, pp. 8ff.

11 Klingenstein, pp. 85ff., 296; Chambers, I, p. 270; Harrison, *Elizabethan*, p. 530.

12 Parker, *Europe*, p. 137.

13 C.S.P. Venetian, X, p. 136; C.S.P. Domestic, VII, p. 725.

14 Parker, *Revolt*, p. 261; Dodd, p. 631 and note 5.

15 C.S.P. Spanish, IV, p. 726.

16 Doleman, p. 102; C.S.P. Spanish, IV, pp. 735, 660–2.

17 Holmes, *Resistance*, pp. 179–80.
18 Hurstfield, *Freedom*, p. 61.
19 Hicks, 'Cecil', pp. 99ff.; Clancy, 'Catholics', p. 132.
20 Bruce, p. xvi; MacCaffrey, p. 415.
21 Bruce, pp. xxxi–xxxiii.
22 Bruce, p. xxv.
23 Mackie, pp. 276, 280.
24 Bruce, p. 52.
25 Williams, *Anne*, p. 51; Willson, p. 94; Nichols, I, p. 190.
26 The identity of this 'great princess' is not known for certain; it may have been Anne's Catholic cousin Christina of Denmark, or Cecilia of Sweden; see Stevenson, pp. 256ff.; Stafford, p. 238.
27 Stevenson, p. 260.
28 Loomie, 'Catholic Consort', p. 305; Warner, pp. 124–7.
29 Hicks, 'Cecil', p. 164; Stafford, p. 233; Loomie, 'Philip', pp. 502ff.
30 Loomie, 'Philip', p. 512; Willson, pp. 143ff.
31 C.S.P. Domestic, VIII, p. 60; Loomie, 'Philip', p. 508.
32 Rodríguez-Villa, pp. 82–4; Stafford, p. 288.

Chapter Two: The Honest Papists

1 Weston, p. 31.
2 Vaux, pp. 48–9.
3 Rowse, *Cornwall*, p. 366.
4 Edwards, *Jesuits*, p. 30; Rose, p. 12.
5 Anstruther, *Vaux*, p. 321; Rowse, *Cornwall*, p. 360.
6 Willson, p. 122.
7 H.M.C. Salisbury, XIV, p. 178.
8 Trimble, p. 170.
9 Southern, pp. 39–43.
10 Southern, p. 63.
11 H.M.C. Salisbury, XII, p. 32.
12 Rowse, *Cornwall*, p. 353.
13 Holmes, *Resistance*, p. 202; Rose, p. 99.
14 Peck, *Northampton*, pp. 6ff.; Bossy, 'Character', pp. 241–2; Robinson, pp. 85–6.
15 Peck, *Northampton*, p. 70; Walsham, p. 83; *Manningham*, pp. 170–1.
16 Weston, p. 71; Bossy, *Bruno*, p. 121; Kerman, pp. 42ff., 189ff.
17 H.M.C. Salisbury, XVII, pp. 611–12.
18 Walsham, p. 1.
19 Hanlon, pp. 373ff.

20 Aveling, *Handle*, p. 66; Dickens, 'First Stages', p. 157.
21 Haigh, *Reformations*, p. 266.
22 *Lawes Resolutions*, p. 60.
23 Caraman, *Years*, p. 67; Walsham, p. 79; Hanlon, p. 394.
24 Rose, p. 113; Walsham, p. 79; Caraman, *Garnet*, p. 167.
25 Warnicke, p. 170; Neale, *Parliaments*, II, p. 294.
26 Rowlands, p. 157.
27 Clancy, *Pamphleteers*, p. 39; Holmes, *Resistance*, pp. 109ff.
28 Bruce, p. 37.
29 Rowlands, p. 158.
30 Anstruther, *Vaux*, pp. 205ff.
31 Gerard, *Autobiography*, p. 148.
32 Anstruther, *Vaux*, p. 224.
33 Gerard, *Autobiography*, p. 147; Anstruther, *Vaux*, p. 243.
34 Hamilton, II, pp. 151ff.
35 Caraman, *Garnet*, pp. 1ff.; Edwards, *Tesimond*, p. 174.
36 Anstruther, *Vaux*, p. 118; Caraman, *Garnet*, p. 132; Edwards, *Tesimond*, p. 185.
37 Anstruther, *Vaux*, pp. 191, 221ff.
38 Southwell, pp. 98–9.

Chapter Three: Diversity of Opinions

1 Bruce, pp. 31–2.
2 Bruce, pp. 33–4, 37.
3 Bruce, p. 36.
4 Nicholls, pp. 85ff.; Shirley, pp. 206–7.
5 Nicholls, pp. 102, 224.
6 Nicholls, p. 118; Bruce, p. 47.
7 Chamberlain, I, p. 212; Edwards, *Tesimond*, pp. 60–1; Edwards, *Fawkes*, p. 74.
8 Edwards, *Tesimond*, pp. 58ff.; Goodman, I, p. 102.
9 H.M.C. Salisbury, XVII, p. 550; Goodman, I, p. 102; although Nicholls, p. 109 note 47, thinks this bigamy is not proved he agrees that 'it *looks* as if both [wives] were alive in November 1605'.
10 Peters, p. 17; Aveling, *East Yorkshire*, p. 36.
11 Goodman, I, p. 102.
12 Nicholls, p. 98.
13 Nicholls, p. 98; Edwards, *Tesimond*, pp. 58–9.
14 Willson, pp. 148ff.; Nicholls, p. 98; Collinson, p. 447; Bruce, p. 56.

15 Bruce, pp. 53ff.
16 Aveling, *Handle*, p. 111; Hurstfield, 'Succession', pp. 382ff.; Bossy, 'English Catholic', pp. 92ff.; H.M.C. Salisbury, p. 44; Basset, pp. 85ff.
17 Basset, p. 61.
18 Bellamy, p. 108.
19 Pollen, *Archpriest*, p. 99; Caraman, *Garnet*, p. 289; Holmes, *Resistance*, pp. 187ff.; Basset, p. 87.
20 Basset, p. 87.
21 Bossy, 'Henri', p. 87.
22 Edwards, *Tesimond*, pp. 63–4, 83–4; Gerard, *Autobiography*, p. 59.
23 Peters, p. 34; Edwards, *Tesimond*, p. 63.
24 Edwards, *Tesimond*, pp. 55, 61, 69.
25 Caraman, *Garnet*, p. 283; Loomie, *Fawkes*, p. 2 note 3.
26 Gerard, *Plot and Plotters*, p. 21; Humphreys, 'Wyntours', pp. 55ff.
27 V.C.H. Worcestershire, III, pp. 123–7.
28 Nash, 'Littleton', p. 136; Edwards, *Tesimond*, pp. 55, 62.
29 Loomie, *Fawkes*, pp. 2ff.
30 S.T., I, pp. 169ff.
31 Loomie, *Fawkes*, pp. 43–4 note 4; Caraman, *Garnet*, p. 411 note 2.
32 Pollen, 'Accession', pp. 578ff.; Loomie, *Fawkes*, pp. 11–12.
33 Caraman, *Garnet*, p. 169; H.M.C. Salisbury, XV, p. 216.
34 Bruce, pp. 31–2.
35 Peck, *Northampton*, p. 23.
36 Kerman, p. 317.

Chapter Four: A King and his Cubs

1 Willson, p. 165.
2 Nichols, I, p. 22.
3 Barroll, pp. 191ff.; H.M.C. Salisbury, XV, pp. vii, 348.
4 Nichols, I, pp. 161, 124.
5 Rowse, *Forman*, p. 106.
6 Nichols, I, pp. 176ff.
7 Strong, p. 10; Nichols, I, p. 188; Harrison, *Jacobean*, p. 43.
8 S.T., II, p. 130.
9 Nichols, I, p. 128.
10 Edwards, *Tesimond*, pp. 28, 93; Morris, *Gerard's Narrative*, p. 11.
11 Gibbon, I, p. 167.
12 Barlow, p. 47.
13 Leatherbarrow, p. 150; H.M.C. Salisbury, XV, p. 119.

14 Loomie, *Fawkes*, p. 27; Stevenson, p. 265; Loomie, *Elizabethans*, p. 124.

15 C.S.P. Venetian, X, pp. 43, 40.

16 Stafford, p. 284; Nicholls, 'Treason's Reward', pp. 821–42.

17 Recent research has newly established Ralegh's involvement; see Nicholls, 'Ralegh's Treason'; Loomie, 'Toleration', pp. 15ff.; C.S.P. Venetian, X, p. 82.

18 Loomie, 'Toleration', p. 20 and note 63; Caraman, *Garnet*, p. 310; Dodd, p. 364.

19 H.M.C. Salisbury, XV, pp. 277–8; Morris, *Gerard's Narrative*, pp. 74–5.

20 Loomie, 'Toleration', p. 14.

21 Anstruther, *Vaux*, p. 278.

22 Willson, pp. 127–8.

23 Willson, pp. 28ff.

24 Loomie, 'Toleration', p. 23; *The Kings Majesties Speech*, 19 March 1603.

Chapter Five: Spanish Charity

1 Loomie, *Fawkes*, pp. 22ff.; Edwards, *Tesimond*, p. 69; H.M.C. Salisbury, XVII, pp. 479ff.

2 Longley, pp. 1–3; Spink, p. 30, Supplementum, I, p. 239; D.N.B. Fawkes; Aveling, 'Recusants', pp. 191ff.

3 Edwards, *Tesimond*, p. 69.

4 Goodman, II, pp. 121–2.

5 *Hyde Park Family History Centre*, The Church of Jesus Christ of Latter-Day Saints, Exhibition Road, London S.W.7; North Yorkshire County Council.

6 Loomie, 'Toleration', pp. 22ff.; Loomie, *Elizabethans*, pp. 178ff.

7 Loomie, *Elizabethans*, pp. 130ff.

8 Edwards, *Fawkes*, p. 89; Loomie, 'Toleration', p. 82.

9 In 1606 Christopher Wright would be lumbered with the charge of joining Guy Fawkes in Spain at this point (when he was no longer in a position to deny it) since Dutton had conveniently vanished from sight. See Loomie, *Fawkes, passim*.

10 Loomie, *Fawkes*, p. 21.

11 Loomie, *Fawkes*, App., pp. 61–2.

12 Loomie, *Fawkes*, p. 26.

13 Loomie, 'Toleration', p. 20.

14 Loomie, *Spain and Jacobean*, I, pp. 11ff.

15 Cuvelier, pp. 289–90; Loomie, 'Toleration', p. 10.
16 H.M.C. Salisbury, XV, pp. 245–6.
17 Loomie, *Spain and Jacobean*, p. 11; Loomie, 'Toleration', p. 170.
18 H.M.C. Salisbury, XV, pp. 245–6.
19 Loomie, *Spain and Jacobean*, pp. 14ff.
20 Loomie, 'Toleration', p. 25.
21 Loomie, 'Toleration', p. 27.
22 Loomie, *Fawkes*, p. 35.
23 Loomie, 'Toleration', p. 21.
24 Peck, *Court Patronage*, pp. 68–74; *Clifford*, p. 87 and note.
25 Loomie, *Spain and Jacobean*, pp. 71–2; Loomie, 'Toleration', p. 25; Croft, 'Reputation', p. 58.
26 Aveling, *Handle*, p. 131; Edwards, *Fawkes*, p. 75; Caraman, *Garnet*, pp. 308–9; Morris, *Gerard's Narrative*, pp. 23–4.
27 Caraman, *Years*, p. 82; Webb, p. 330; Bossy, 'English Catholic', pp. 98ff.; Magee, App. III, pp. 214–15.
28 Caraman, *Garnet*, p. 309.
29 H.M.C. Salisbury, XV, pp. 282–3, 278.

Chapter Six: Catesby as Phaeton

1 Ashton, p. 63; Akrigg, pp. 30–1; Salgãdo, p. 185.
2 Harrison, *Jacobean*, p. 110; Strong, p. 96.
3 Akrigg, p. 30; Strong, p. 10.
4 Edwards, *Tesimond*, p. 43; S.T., II, p. 77.
5 McIlwaine, pp. 269–80; Munden, p. 63.
6 C.J., pp. 176ff.
7 Peck, *Mental World*, p. 4; C.J., p. 177.
8 C.J., pp. 187–8.
9 Wormald, 'Gunpowder', pp. 158ff.; Peck, *Mental World*, p. 4.
10 *Eastward Ho!*, pp. xxiiiff., 61; De Luna, p. 115.
11 *Clifford*, p. 6; Cuddy, p. 163.
12 Haynes, *Cecil*, pp. 129ff.
13 C.S.P. Venetian, X, p. 230.
14 Edwards, *Tesimond*, p. 43.
15 Trans. Gavin Maxwell, *The Ten Pains of Death*, 1959.
16 Edwards, *Tesimond*, p. 43; Morris, *Gerard's Narrative*, p. 30.
17 H.M.C. Salisbury, XVI, pp. 44–5; Dickens, 'First Stages', pp. 24ff.; H.M.C. Salisbury, XVIII, p. 75.
18 Morris, *Gerard's Narrative*, p. 54.
19 S.T., II, p. 190; *Romeo and Juliet*, Act III, scene ii.

20 B.L., Cotton MSS, Titus B II, fol. 294.

21 Edwards, *Tesimond*, p. 61.

22 Wake, p. 39.

23 D.N.B. Robert Catesby.

24 Jones, pp. 1ff.; Chastleton, Oxon, Baptisms.

25 Williamson, p. 73.

26 Anstruther, *Vaux*, p. 305; B.L., MSS Royal, 12.E.X.

Chapter Seven: So Sharp a Remedy

1 Thomas Wintour's Confession, Gardiner, *Plot*, pp. 57–69, amended H.M.C. Salisbury, XVII, pp. 509–13.

2 Gardiner, *Plot*, p. 61.

3 Gardiner, *Plot*, p. 61.

4 Thomas Wintour was quite clear on the order of progression and, although there are some difficulties about his evidence, he had no reason to lie about Percy's slightly later involvement; Haynes, *Plot*, p. 45; Loomie, 'Toleration', p. 53.

5 Porter, p. 42; H.M.C. Salisbury, XVIII, p. 25; Hale, p. 456.

6 Andrewes, p. 94; C.S.P. Domestic, VIII, p. 279; Gardiner, *Plot*, p. 50; H.M.C. Salisbury, XVII, p. 479; Edwards, *Tesimond*, pp. 208–9 note.

7 Edwards, *Tesimond*, p. 153; Carswell, p. 40; S.P. 14/216/145; S.T., II, p. 230; H.M.C. Salisbury, XVII, p. 540; Morris, *Gerard's Narrative*, pp. ccxxxi–ccxxxii.

8 Morris, *Gerard's Narrative*, p. 140.

9 Edwards, *Tesimond*, pp. 87–8.

10 Caraman, *Garnet*, pp. 316–17.

11 Larkin and Hughes, I, p. 123 note 1.

12 Camm, p. 319.

13 Finch, App. VI, pp. 179–81.

14 Gearty, citing W. Laqueur, p. 10; Wilkinson, p. xii.

15 Wilkinson, pp. 5ff.; Clancy, 'Catholics', pp. 212ff.; Edwards, *Jesuits*, p. 22.

16 Scarisbrick, p. 18; Skinner, pp. 345ff.

17 Hale, p. 40.

18 Carswell, p. 159; Rose, p. 98.

19 Edwards, *Tesimond*, p. 80; Bossy, 'English Catholic', p. 95.

20 Edwards, *Tesimond*, p. 107; Edwards, *Fawkes*, p. 126.

21 Andrewes, p. 89.

22 Gardiner, 'Garnet's Declarations', p. 515; Magee, p. 39; Jordan, II, p. 64.

23 H.M.C. Salisbury, XI, pp. 156, 296; Gerard, *What Plot?*, App. H, pp. 256–7.

24 Dures, p. 42.

25 Edwards, *Tesimond*, p. 46 note.

26 Gardiner, *Plot*, p. 63 note 2.

27 Edwards, *Fawkes*, p. 124.

28 H.M.C. Salisbury, XVII, p. 528; XVI, pp. 208, 210, 220.

29 S.P. 14/216/145; Hales, p. 30; Edwards, *Tesimond*, p. 99 note.

30 S.T., II, pp. 175, 230.

31 Edwards, 'Still Investigating', p. 331; Williamson, p. 121; Gerard, *What Plot?*, pp. 122ff.; Edwards, *Fawkes*, p. 175; Edwards, *Tesimond*, p. 72.

32 Gerard, *What Plot?*, pp. 85–6; Williamson, p. 121.

33 S.T., II, p. 179; C.J., p. 260; Williamson, p. 72; Dekker, *Double P P*.

34 Seton, p. 373.

35 Nichols, I, pp. 472ff.

Chapter Eight: Pernicious Gunpowder

1 Edwards, *Tesimond*, p. 100–1; H.M.C. Salisbury, XVIII, p. 52.

2 H.M.C. Salisbury, XVII, pp. 500–1.

3 Peters, p. 57.

4 Paul, p. 226; Hales, pp. 26ff.; Milward, p. 21.

5 Hotson, pp. 188, 143ff.: Eleanor Bushell (Ned's sister) and Judith Shakespeare married two brothers called Quiney: they thus became 'sisters' according to contemporary usage.

6 Nichols, I, p. 429; Oman, p. 26.

7 C.S.P. Domestic, 1603–1610, pp. 246, 280.

8 C.S.P. Domestic, 1603–1610, p. 246; Gerard, *What Plot?*, p. 81; Wormald, 'Gunpowder', p. 162.

9 Morris, *Troubles*, 1st, p. 197.

10 Edwards, *Tesimond*, pp. 80–1; H.M.C. Salisbury, XVII, pp. 527–8; C.S.P. Domestic, VIII, p. 246.

11 Nicholls, p. 23.

12 C.S.P. Venetian, X, p. 301.

13 Nicholls, p. 23; but Nicholls, p. 205, points out that 'a strong circumstantial case' existed against Northumberland.

14 H.M.C. Salisbury, XVIII, p. 96; S.T., II, p. 230.

15 Chamberlain, I, p. 204; C.S.P. Venetian, X, p. 236.

16 Willson, p. 221; Wormald, 'Gunpowder', p. 157 note 43; Loomie, 'Toleration', p. 410.

17 Williamson, p. 118.
18 Vetusta Monumenta, V, pp. 3ff.; Smith, *Westminster*, pp. 39–41.
19 Edwards, *Fawkes*, pp. 111–12.
20 Williamson, p. 251; Gerard, *What Plot?*, p. 74; Carswell, p. 29 and note.
21 Dr Constam, Royal Armouries, to the author; H.M.C. Salisbury, XVI, p. 341; Bull, 'Furie of the Ordnance'; Cruickshank, p. 125.
22 Southern, p. 288; C.S.P. Domestic, 1603–1610, p. 256.
23 Constam; S.T., II, p. 183.
24 Hale, p. 136; Stow, p. 819.
25 Handover, *Cecil*, p. 265; Gerard, *What Plot?*, p. 99.
26 H.M.C. Salisbury, XVII, pp. 549–50.
27 Anstruther, *Vaux*, pp. 267ff.; Anstruther, 'Treason', pp. 452ff.
28 Anstruther, 'Treason', p. 454.
29 Anstruther, 'Treason', p. 456.
30 Anstruther, *Vaux*, p. 287.
31 H.M.C. Salisbury, XVII, p. 538; Gerard, *Autobiography*, p. 169.
32 H.M.C. Salisbury, XVII, pp. 538, 569–70; Anstruther, *Vaux*, p. 287.
33 Edwards, *Tesimond*, p. 90.
34 Duffy, p. 3; Caraman, *Garnet*, p. 320 and note 1.
35 Gardiner, 'Garnet's Declarations', pp. 510–11.
36 Edwards, *Tesimond*, p. 90.

Chapter Nine: There Is a Risk...

 1 S.T., II, p. 256.
 2 Edwards, *Tesimond*, p. 81.
 3 Caraman, *Garnet*, pp. 322ff.
 4 Caraman, *Garnet*, p. 322; S.T., II, pp. 107–11.
 5 H.M.C. Salisbury, XVIII, p. 97.
 6 Anstruther, *Vaux*, pp. 364ff.; S.T., II, p. 107; H.M.C. Salisbury, XVIII, pp. 96–7.
 7 S.T., II, p. 255.
 8 Caraman, *Garnet*, p. 91; Williamson, p. 143.
 9 H.M.C. Salisbury, XVIII, pp. 75–7; S.T., II, p. 231.
10 Loomie, *Fawkes*, pp. 52–3 and note 3.
11 C.J., pp. 256–7.
12 Wiener, p. 109.
13 Chamberlain, I, p. 201; S.T., II, p. 195.
14 Edwards, *Tesimond*, p. 45.

15 Nichols, I, pp. 530ff.; Chamberlain, I, pp. 208–9.
16 Paul, pp. 20ff.; *King Lear* (Muir), p. xxiii.
17 Anstruther, *Vaux*, p. 276; Caraman, *Garnet*, p. 325.
18 Caraman, *Garnet*, p. 412; S.T., II, p. 231.
19 Waugh, pp. 3ff.
20 Waugh, p. 23.
21 Waugh, p. 13.
22 Morris, *Gerard's Narrative*, pp. 182–3.
23 Mathew, *Catholicism*, p. 50; Squiers, p. 25; Edwards, *Tesimond*, p. 194.
24 Gerard, *Autobiography*, p. 46; App. C, pp. 265–6.
25 Charles-Edwards, pp. 1–24; Duffy, p. 44; Gerard, *Autobiography*, p. 46.
26 David, p. 70.
27 Anstruther, *Vaux*, p. 277
28 Finch, pp. 80ff.
29 Edwards, *Tesimond*, p. 108 and note; H.M.C. Salisbury, XVII, p. 513.
30 Anstruther, *Vaux*, p. 246.
31 Morris, *Gerard's Narrative*, pp. 164ff.; Sumner, p. 11.
32 Anstruther, *Vaux*, p. 278.
33 Williamson, p. 142.

Chapter Ten: Dark and Doubtful Letter

1 *King Lear*, Act I, scene ii; *King Lear* (Muir), pp. xviii–xix; S.T., II, p. 182.
2 Nicholls, p. 175.
3 Gerard, *Autobiography*, p. 33.
4 H.M.C. Salisbury, XVII, pp. 511–12.
5 Shakespeare Trust, ER 27/14; Hamilton, I, p. 214; Waugh, p. 80.
6 C.S.P. Domestic, VIII, p. 254.
7 Foley, I, p. 75; Anstruther, *Vaux*, p. 280.
8 Digby's examination, S.P. 14/216/94.
9 Lingard, VII, p. 57 and note 1.
10 Edwards, *Tesimond*, pp. 105–7.
11 S.P. 14/19/40; Astruther, *Vaux*, p. 279.
12 Goodman, I, pp. 120–2; C.S.P. Domestic, 1603–1610, p. 251.
13 Edwards, *Tesimond*, pp. 102–3.
14 De Luna, pp. 115ff.
15 S.P. 14/216/2.

16 Among the conspirators: Tresham (M. S. Giuseppi, ed., H.M.C. Salisbury, XVII, p. xvii; Hurstfield, *Freedom*, p. 329; Toyne, p. 21; Willson, p. 224); Percy (a possibility: Nicholls, p. 175); Christopher Wright (with Thomas Ward and Dr Oldcorne as 'aiders and abettors', Spink, p. 36); Thomas Wintour (Simons, p. 127). Others: Mary Habington (Nash, *Worcestershire*, I, p. 595; S.T., II, p. 197 note); Anne Vaux (Jardine, *Narrative*, pp. 83–6). Also: as a put-up job, Salisbury himself in a disguised hand (Edwards, *Fawkes*, p. 131); 'contrived' to scare Catesby into abandoning the plot, Rose, p. 105.

17 S.T., II, pp. 195–202.

18 Spink, p. 67.

19 Edwards, *Tesimond*, pp. 117ff.

20 See Elton, *Practice of History*, p. 77: 'there is a single question which the researcher must ask himself in assessing his evidence: how and why did this come into existence?'

21 Nash, *Worcestershire*, I, p. 585; Spink, pp. 112–19.

22 Nicholls, p. 175; H.M.C. Salisbury, XVII, p. 550.

23 Spink, p. 232. D.N.B. Monteagle (Parker).

24 Goodman, II, p. 106.

25 Wiener, p. 109.

26 Williamson, p. 69 and note 13, p. 260; but see Jardine, 'Remarks', p. 92, who questions the September 1605 dating.

27 Gerard, *What Plot?*, p. 117; Edwards, *Fawkes*, p. 131.

28 S.T., II, p. 209.

Chapter Eleven: Mr Fawkes Is Taken

1 S.T., II, pp. 197ff.

2 *Coughton Court and the Throckmortons, passim.*

3 Anstruther, *Vaux*, p. 281; S.T., II, pp. 232, 241; Tierney, IV, p. cii.

4 Morris, *Gerard's Narrative*, p. ccxxxvi.

5 *King's History*, S.T., II, p. 199.

6 Gardiner, *Plot*, p. 68.

7 C.S.P. Domestic, VIII, p. 246; Gardiner, *Plot*, p. 67.

8 Gerard, *What Plot?*, App. N, p. 276; Barlow, pp. 200ff.

9 Barlow, pp. 201–2; the Littletons are sometimes wrongly described as brothers; but see Nash, *Worcestershire*, I, p. 493; Edwards, *Tesimond*, pp. 132–3, note; Dures, pp. 42ff.

10 C.S.P. Domestic, VIII, p. 282; S.P. 14/216/178; Humphreys, 'Wyntours', p. 74.

11 Gardiner, *Plot*, p. 68; but see H.M.C. Salisbury, XVII, pp. 509–10 for lines omitted.

12 Nicholls, pp. 163ff.

13 Nicholls, p. 158 note 70.

14 Batho, *Northumberland*, pp. 5–6; Nicholls, p. 153; H.M.C. Salisbury, XVII, pp. 529–30.

15 S.T., II, p. 199; H.M.C. Salisbury, XVII, pp. 481–2; Gardiner, *Plot*, p. 131.

16 There was a No-Plot suggestion that Whynniard *died* on 5 November: possibly eliminated by the government as a cover for its own conspiracy. This has recently been shown to be incorrect since he signed his last will three weeks later; see Nicholls, p. 216.

17 Larkin, p. 123.

18 Gardiner, *Plot*, p. 68.

19 Anstruther, *Vaux*, p. 307.

20 Gardiner, *Plot*, p. 68.

21 S.P. 14/216/22.

22 Nicholls, p. 43; Williamson, pp. 174ff.; Digby's examination, C.S.P. Domestic, VIII, p. 260; S.P. 14/216/94.

23 Stow, p. 879; Nicholls, p. 13.

24 Stow, p. 881.

25 Nicholls, p. 10.

26 Bodleian, Ashmole MS., 363, fol. 241; Thomas, p. 312; Larkin, p. 123.

27 C.J., p. 257.

28 S.T., II, p. 201.

Chapter Twelve: The Gentler Tortures

1 Edwards, *Tesimond*, p. 33; Shakespeare Trust, ER 27/14.

2 Nicholls, p. 11.

3 S.P. 14/216/18.

4 Coke, *Third*, p. 35; Jardine, *Torture*, p. 35; Edwards, *Tesimond*, p. 49 note.

5 Bellamy, pp. 120ff.

6 Cooper, p. 119; Jardine, *Torture*, p. 23ff.

7 Bellamy, p. 119; Read, p. 37.

8 Cooper, pp. 105–19.

9 S.P. 14/216/37.

10 Bellamy, p. 113.

11 Bellamy, p. 112; Lingard, VII, pp. 261–2 note 135.

12 Goodman, II, p. 106; Morris, *Gerard's Narrative*, p. 105; S.T., II, p. 218; C.S.P. Domestic, VIII, p. 292; Edwards, *Tesimond*, p. 129.

13 H.M.C. Salisbury, XVII, p. 479; Goodman, II, p. 106.

14 H.M.C. Salisbury, XVII, p. 479.

15 H.M.C. Salisbury, XVII, p. 479.

16 Jardine, *Torture*, pp. 2–5.

17 Larkin, pp. 124–6; S.P. 14/216/22.

18 C.S.P. Domestic, p. 288; Edwards, *Tesimond*, p. 153.

19 Caraman, *Garnet*, p. 330.

20 Anstruther, *Vaux*, p. 310.

21 Anstruther, *Vaux*, pp. 300–1.

22 Caraman, *Garnet*, p. 330.

23 Hamilton, I, pp. 182–3; S.P. 14/216/178; C.S.P. Domestic, p. 282.

24 Tierney, IV, pp. cxi–cxii.

25 Gardiner, *Plot*, p. 69; S.P. 14/216/135; C.S.P. Domestic, VIII, p. 265.

26 Humphreys, 'Wyntours', pp. 65ff.

27 S.T., II, pp. 186–7.

28 Gardiner, *Plot*, p. 69.

29 Williamson, p. 182.

30 Gardiner, *Plot*, p. 69; H.M.C. Salisbury, XVII, p. 531.

31 H.M.C. Salisbury, XVII, p. 486; Bodleian, Ashmole MS. 363, fol. 241.

32 H.M.C. Salisbury, XVII, p. 486.

33 Edwards, *Tesimond*, pp. 134–5; H.M.C. Salisbury, XVII, p. 486.

34 Making a quantity of 1,800 lb since the Ordnance Board used a short hundredweight of 100 lbs; P.R.O., W.O. 49/31/101; Rodger, pp. 124–5. It used to be suggested by No-Plotters that the records had been removed for some reason, but this has been demonstrated to be untrue.

35 Anstruther, *Vaux*, pp. 290–1.

36 C.S.P. Venetian, X, p. 325; Magee, p. 38; De Luna, p. 138; H.M.C. Salisbury, XVII, p. 480; Goodman, I, pp. 120–2.

37 S.P. 14/216/49; S.T., II, pp. 202–3; Gerard, *What Plot?*, App. N, p. 268.

38 S.P. 14/216/54.

Chapter Thirteen: Fire and Brimstone

1 *King's Book*; McIlwain, pp. 281ff.

2 C.J., p. 257; *King's Book*; McIlwain, p. 289.

3 Larkin, p. 125.

4 Edwards, *Fawkes*, pp. 190–1.

5 Hurstfield, *Freedom*, p. 327; Edwards, *Fawkes*, p. 191.

6 See Nowak, *passim*; D.N.B. Barlow.

7 Nowak, p. 48.

8 Loomie, 'Catholic Consort', pp. 306ff.

9 Nichols, I, p. 592.

10 H.M.C. Salisbury, XVIII, p. 68; Nichols, I, p. 591.

11 Edwards, *Tesimond*, p. 136.

12 H.M.C. Salisbury, XVII, p. 490.

13 C.S.P. Domestic, VIII, p. 250; Anstruther, *Vaux*, pp. 283–5.

14 Gerard, *Autobiography*, pp. 197–8; H.M.C. Salisbury, XVII, pp. 490–1.

15 S.P. 14/216/156; S.P. 14/216/226; C.S.P. Domestic, VIII, p. 249; Anstruther, *Vaux*, pp. 295–6; G.E.C. Teynham.

16 Gerard, *Autobiography*, p. 208.

17 Anstruther, *Vaux*, p. 327.

18 Edwards, *Fawkes*, p. 181.

19 H.M.C. Salisbury, XVII, p. 534.

20 H.M.C. Salisbury, XVIII, pp. 38–40; H.M.C. Salisbury, XVII, p. 534.

21 S.T., II, p. 170; Nicholls, p. 38.

22 D.N.B. Waad; Caraman, *Garnet*, pp. 348–9.

23 The handy short title by which the official account came to be known. The full title was *His Majesties Speach in this Last Session of Parliament … Together with a discourse of the maner of the discouery of the late intended Treason, ioyned with an Examination of some of the prisoners.*

24 H.M.C. Salisbury, XVII, p. 541.

25 S.T., II, p. 22.

26 Anstruther, *Vaux*, p. 308.

27 C.S.P. Domestic, VIII, p. 254.

28 H.M.C. Salisbury, XVII, p. 534.

29 Hatfield MS 113/54; S.P. 14/216/114; 'apparently altered by Coke to 25', H.M.C. Salisbury, XVII, pp. xvi, 509–10, 512–13; Gardiner, *Plot*, pp. 57–69; Nicholls, p. 28 and notes 50–3; Williamson, App. I, pp. 247–500; Devlin, *Hamlet*, p. 148.

30 Williamson, App. I, p. 248 and Plates II and IV; H.M.C. Salisbury, XVII, pp. 512–13.

31 H.M.C. Salisbury, XVII, p. 502.

32 H.M.C. Salisbury, XVII, pp. 509–10.

33 Shirley, pp. 336–40; C.S.P. Domestic, VIII, 1603–1610, p. 257.

34 H.M.C. Salisbury, XVII, p. 535.
35 Batho, 'Wizard Earl', pp. 344ff.
36 S.P. 14/216/136; C.S.P. Domestic, VIII, p. 266.
37 Edwards, *Tesimond*, p. 137.
38 Barlow, p. 200.
39 S.P. 14/216/145; C.S.P. Domestic, VIII, p. 267.
40 S.P. 14/216/166; C.S.P. Domestic, VIII, p. 279.
41 The presence of Foster makes nonsense of the theory that the government poisoned Tresham for knowing too much about their machinations; Wake, pp. 31ff.
42 Wake, pp. 33–4; H.M.C. Salisbury, XVII, pp. 528, 553.
43 H.M.C. Salisbury, XVII, p. 558; Wake, p. 34.
44 S.P. 14/216/211; Wake, p. 40.
45 Wake, p. 34.
46 Wake, p. 40.
47 Finch, p. 92; Williamson, p. 196.

Chapter Fourteen: These Wretches

1 By 'J.M.', Harrison, *Jacobean*, p. 261.
2 C.S.P. Venetian, X, pp. 308–9.
3 Caraman, *Garnet*, p. 316.
4 Anstruther, *Vaux*, p. 200; Edwards, *Tesimond*, p. 163.
5 Larkin, p. 128; Humphreys, 'Wyntours', pp. 71ff.; H.M.C. Salisbury, XVIII, pp. 11–12.
6 H.M.C. Salisbury, XVIII, p. 34; Edwards, *Tesimond*, pp. 164–5.
7 Waugh, p. 18.
8 Anstruther, *Vaux*, pp. 333–5; Humphreys, 'Wyntours', p. 52.
9 Comment of an eye-witness, Anstruther, *Vaux*, p. 334.
10 Anstruther, *Vaux*, p. 334.
11 Morris, *Gerard's Narrative*, p. 153.
12 Anstruther, *Vaux*, p. 335.
13 Anstruther, *Vaux*, p. 190.
14 H.M.C. Salisbury, XVIII, pp. 35–6.
15 H.M.C. Salisbury, XVIII, pp. 34–5; S.P. 14/216/202; C.S.P. Domestic, VIII, p. 299.
16 Caraman, *Garnet*, pp. 339–40.
17 Caraman, *Garnet*, p. 339.
18 Edwards, *Tesimond*, p. 172; Anstruther, *Vaux*, p. 340.
19 C.J., pp. 257, 260; H.M.C. Montagu, pp. 47–9; D.N.B. Edward Montague.

20 Nichols, I, p. 590.
21 Anstruther, *Vaux*, pp. 132–3; Bellamy, pp. 9ff.; Carswell, p. 42.
22 Nichols, I, p. 35.
23 Somers, *Tracts*, XI, p. 113; Willson, p. 301.
24 S.T., II, pp. 159–64, 187.
25 S.T., II, pp. 164–6.
26 S.T., II, pp. 166–84.
27 Jardine, *Trials*, II, pp. 120–1 and note 2, 139 and note 2.
28 Jardine, *Trials*, II, p. 159 and note 1; Lingard, X, p. 44 and note 1.
29 S.T., II, pp. 185–7.
30 S.T., II, pp. 186–7.
31 S.T., II, p. 186.
32 S.T., II, pp. 187–8.
33 S.T., II, pp. 188–9.
34 S.T., II, pp. 189–94.

Chapter Fifteen: The Heart of a Traitor

1 H.M.C. Salisbury, XVIII, pp. 36–7.
2 Anstruther, *Vaux*, p. 339. It has been suggested that the government speeded up the executions in order to avoid confrontation with Father Garnet (still held captive in the midlands). But in fact executions at this period often did follow quickly upon convictions; see Bellamy, p. 182.
3 S.T., II, p. 182.
4 Barlow, pp. 197ff.
5 S.T., II, pp. 215–16.
6 Edwards, *Tesimond*, p. 226.
7 Wood, II, p. 241.
8 H.M.C. Salisbury, XVIII, p. 52; Edwards, *Tesimond*, p. 227.
9 Morris, *Gerard's Narrative*, p. 219; S.T., II, p. 182.
10 Morris, *Gerard's Narrative*, pp. 219–20.
11 S.T., II, p. 216.
12 S.T., II, p. 217.
13 S.T., II, p. 218; Morris, *Gerard's Narrative*, p. 221.
14 S.T., II, p. 218.
15 Humphreys, 'Habingtons', p. 57.
16 Morris, *Gerard's Narrative*, pp. 157–8.
17 Edwards, *Tesimond*, p. 175.
18 Hurstfield, 'Succession', p. 380; Gerard, *Autobiography*, p. 86; Anstruther, *Vaux*, p. 353.

19 Morris, *Gerard's Narrative*, p. clxxxix.

20 C.J., p. 264.

21 C.J., p. 265; C.S.P. Venetian, X, p. 321.

22 Caraman, *Garnet*, pp. 348ff.

23 Caraman, *Garnet*, pp. 350, 371, 422.

24 Gerard, *Autobiography*, p. 96.

25 Anstruther, *Vaux*, pp. 256, 347.

26 Anstruther, *Vaux*, p. 183.

27 C.S.P. Domestic, VIII, p. 263.

28 Morris, *Gerard's Narrative*, p. 172; Anstruther, *Vaux*, p. 186.

29 Caraman, *Garnet*, p. 351.

30 S.T., II, pp. 166–7.

31 Jardine, *Equivocation*, p. vii; Garnet, 'Equivocation', Bodleian, Laud MS., misc. 655, p. 1; Malloch, 'Garnet', p. 391; Allison, pp. 14–15.

32 Allison, p. 14; Malloch, 'Garnet', p. 387; Devlin, *Southwell*, App. C., pp. 333–5; Zagorin, pp. 12ff.; Holmes, *Resistance*, pp. 1ff.

33 Jardine, *Equivocation*, p. 3; Foley, VII, p. 1358.

34 Jardine, *Equivocation*, p. vii.

35 Basset, p. 135; Zagorin, p. 195.

36 Rose, pp. 80ff.; Zagorin, p. 210; Gerard, *Autobiography*, p. 125.

37 Jardine, *Equivocation*, p. 16.

38 Edwards, *Fawkes*, p. 215; Holmes, *Resistance*, p. 198; see Nowak, *passim*.

39 S.T., II, p. 180.

40 Caraman, *Garnet*, p. 354.

41 Anstruther, *Vaux*, p. 341.

Chapter Sixteen: The Jesuits' Treason

1 Anstruther, *Vaux*, p. 345; C.S.P. Domestic, VIII, p. 292.

2 Edwards, *Tesimond*, p. 159 note.

3 Morris, *Gerard's Narrative*, p. 186.

4 Morris, *Gerard's Narrative*, p. 186; Waugh, pp. 21–2.

5 Anstruther, *Vaux*, p. 345; H.M.C. Salisbury, XVIII, p. 98; Waugh, p. 23.

6 Morris, *Gerard's Narrative*, pp. 188–90.

7 Edwards, *Tesimond*, p. 184.

8 Edwards, *Tesimond*, p. 184.

9 Caraman, *Garnet*, pp. 360–2.

10 Chamberlain, I, p. 219.

11 Caraman, *Garnet*, pp. 362–3.

12 C.S.P. Domestic, VIII, p. 291 note.
13 S.P. 14/216/241; Anstruther, *Vaux*, p. 344.
14 Anstruther, *Vaux*, pp. 345ff.; Caraman, *Garnet*, p. 367; see Gardiner, 'Garnet's Declarations', pp. 510–19.
15 Edwards, *Tesimond*, p. 191; H.M.C. Salisbury, XVIII, p. 98.
16 Caraman, *Garnet*, p. 386; Anstruther, *Vaux*, pp. 341, 357; H.M.C. Salisbury, XVIII, p. 108.
17 S.T., II, p. 243.
18 Gardiner, 'Garnet's Declarations', pp. 510–17.
19 Edwards, *Tesimond*, pp. 191–2.
20 Gardiner, 'Garnet's Declarations', p. 515; Holmes, 'Casuistry', p. 37; Caraman, *Garnet*, p. 376.
21 Gardiner, 'Garnet's Declarations', p. 514; but Fr Caraman accepted that the handwriting was Fr Garnet's own, *Garnet*, p. 376 note 4.
22 Gardiner, 'Garnet's Declarations', pp. 517–19.
23 Morris, *Gerard's Narrative*, p. 171.
24 S.P. 14/216/200; 201, Anstruther, *Vaux*, pp. 353–6.
25 Morris, *Gerard's Narrative*, p. 225.
26 S.T., II, pp. 217–355; Morris, *Gerard's Narrative*, pp. 226–64.
27 Anstruther, *Vaux*, p. 360; Wake, p. 40.
28 Caraman, *Garnet*, p. 391.
29 Caraman, *Garnet*, pp. 390–1.
30 Paul, pp. 248–50.
31 *Macbeth* (Muir), p. xxi.
32 Habington, p. 119; Humphreys, 'Wyntours', p. 74; Morris, *Gerard's Narrative*, p. 269.
33 Morris, *Gerard's Narrative*, p. 288.
34 Caraman, *Garnet*, p. 424; H.M.C. Salisbury, XVIII, pp. 95–6.
35 Caraman, *Garnet*, p. 429.

Chapter Seventeen: Farewells

1 Morris, *Gerard's Narrative*, p. 289.
2 Anstruther, *Vaux*, p. 368.
3 Morris, *Gerard's Narrative*, p. 290.
4 Morris, *Gerard's Narrative*, p. 290.
5 S.T., II, p. 355.
6 S.T., II, pp. 355–6.
7 Morris, *Gerard's Narrative*, pp. 292–3.
8 S.T., II, p. 356; Morris, *Gerard's Narrative*, p. 293.

9   Morris, *Gerard's Narrative*, pp. 293–4.

10 Morris, *Gerard's Narrative*, p. 295; S.T., II, p. 358.

11 Loomie, 'Toleration', p. 48; Gerard, *Autobiography*, p. 209.

12 Gerard, *Autobiography*, p. xvii.

13 Warnicke, pp. 170 and note 20, 182.

14 Anstruther, *Vaux*, p. 183.

15 Anstruther, *Vaux*, p. 184.

16 Morris, *Gerard's Narrative*, pp. 300–1; Caraman, *Garnet*, App. D, pp. 442–3 and note 1.

17 Caraman, *Years*, p. 12.

18 Anstruther, *Vaux*, p. 385.

19 Anstruther, *Vaux*, pp. 396, 453.

20 Peters, p. 385; Anstruther, *Vaux*, p. 476.

21 Gotch, *Old Halls*, p. 62; G.E.C. Banbury.

22 Baker, I, p. 245.

23 Finch, pp. 92–9.

24 Wake, p. 39 note 6.

25 Foley, IV, p. 136.

26 D.N.B. Kenelm Digby.

27 G.E.C. Monteagle; Hamilton, II, p. 37.

28 D.N.B. Ambrose Rookwood, 1664–96.

29 Goodman, I, pp. 118–22.

30 Southern, pp. 46, 83 note 3; Kerman, p. 49.

31 Nicholls, p. 77.

32 G.E.C. Monteagle.

33 Morris, *Gerard's Narrative*, pp. 27–8, 271; D.N.B. William Habington.

34 G.E.C. Salisbury; Croft, 'Cecil and Court', p. 140; H.M.C. Salisbury, XVIII, p. 535.

35 Nicholls, pp. 185, 165–6; Shirley, pp. 353, 340.

36 Shirley, p. 354.

37 Batho, 'Wizard Earl', pp. 344–7.

38 Rowse, *Cornwall*, p. 371; Peters, p. 74.

39 Bliss, p. 110; Loomie, 'Catholic Consort', p. 308.

40 H.M.C. Salisbury, XVIII, p. 178.

Chapter Eighteen: Satan's Policy?

1   Nicholls, p. 218.

2   Cressy, 'November', p. 72.

3   Milward, p. 62; *Macbeth*, Act II, scene iii; S.T., II, p. 164.

4 Nichols, I, pp. 38–9.

5 Haynes, *Plot*, App. I, p. 138.

6 Dekker, *Double P P*, prelude.

7 *Macbeth*, Act II, scene iii; *Macbeth* (Muir), pp. xvff.

8 *Macbeth*, Act V, scene v.

9 *Gager's Pyramis*, pp. 250ff.

10 Edwards, *Tesimond*, p. 139.

11 Lingard, VII, pp. 86–7 and note 1.

12 Clancy, 'Deposing Power', pp. 209ff.

13 Caraman, *Years*, p. 14; Anstruther, *Vaux*, p. 373.

14 Milton, IV, pp. 320–1.

15 C.S.P. Venetian, X, pp. 291–2; Edwards, *Fawkes*, p. 138.

16 H.M.C. Salisbury, XVIII, p. 508; Gerard, *What Plot?*, p. 430.

17 Goodman, I, pp. ix, 102.

18 Barlow, Preface.

19 S.T., II, p. 211.

20 Hazlitt, XI, p. 319.

21 L.J., IV, p. 369a; reference supplied by Mr D. L. Jones, Librarian, House of Lords.

22 C.J., XXX, p. 530; L.J., XIII, pp. 305b–306a; Cressy, 'November', p. 87, who however dates the search only to the 1690s; but see note 21 supra.

23 L.J., XIV, pp. 570a, 571b–572a.

24 Smith, *Westminster*, p. 44.

25 Paget, pp. 73–4; information to the author.

26 Cressy, 'November', p. 69.

27 See Nowak, *passim*; Andrewes, pp. 889–90.

28 Cressy, 'November', pp. 73ff.; Cressy, *Bonfires*, pp. 162ff.

29 Hutton, p. 212.

30 Shaw, pp. 15–18; Whitehill, p. 29; *Folklore*, p. 386.

31 Shaw, pp. 15–18; Billington, pp. 18–19; *Folklore*, p. 386.

32 Miller, p. 15; Blunt, pp. 730–1; Cressy, 'November', pp. 71–2; Keeling, p. 398; Colley, p. 21.

33 Swift, 'Fawkes in Exeter', p. 61.

34 Norman, p. 61.

35 Jardine, *Narrative*, p. 155.

36 See Quinault, 'Warwickshire Landowners'.

37 'Diary of Joan Courthope', unpub.

38 Lewes Bonfire Night Special, *Sussex Express*, 11 November 1994.

39 *The Night of the Fires*, 11 November 1994; local information to the author; *Folklore*, p. 386.

40 Gardiner, *England*, I, pp. 263–4.
41 Morris, *Gerard's Narrative*, p. 10 and note 4; Edwards, *Tesimond*, p. 214.
42 Nelson Mandela, *Long Walk to Freedom*, 1994, pp. 350–1.
43 Recalling Clarendon's final judgement on Oliver Cromwell: 'a brave bad man'; Clarendon, Edward Earl of, *History of the Rebellion* ..., p. 97, Oxford, 1969.

Reference Books

〜

Details only of those books, documents, etc. cited in abbreviated form in the References; a full bibliography is impracticable for reasons of space. The place of publication is London unless otherwise stated.

Akrigg, G. P. V., *Jacobean Pageant*, 1962

Allen, Kenneth, *The Story of Gunpowder*, 1973

Allison, A. F., 'The Writings of Fr Henry Garnet, S.J. (1555–1606)', *Biographical Studies*, I, 1951

Andrewes, Lancelot, *XCVI Sermons*, 3rd edn, 1635

Anstruther, Godfrey, O.P., 'Powder Treason', *Blackfriars*, 33, 1952

Anstruther, Godfrey, O.P., *Vaux of Harrowden: a recusant family*, Newport, Mon., 1953

Ashton, Robert, ed., *James I by his Contemporaries*, 1969

Aveling, Dom. Hugh, O.S.B., 'The Catholic Recusants of the West Riding of Yorkshire, 1558–1790', *Proceedings of the Leeds Philosophical & Literary Society*, Leeds, X, 1963

Aveling, Dom. Hugh, O.S.B., 'The Marriages of Catholic Recusants', *Journal of Ecclesiastical History*, 14, 1963

Aveling, Dom. Hugh, O.S.B., *Post Reformation Catholicism in East Yorkshire 1558–1790*, York, 1960

Aveling, J. C. H., *The Handle and the Axe: the Catholic recusants in England from Reformation to Emancipation*, 1976

Baker, George, *History of Antiquities in the County of Northampton*, I, 1822

Barlow, Thomas, *The Gunpowder Treason...with Appendix of Several Papers written by Sir Everard Digby during his confinement*, 1679, reprinted 1850

Barroll, Leeds, 'The Court of the First Stuart Queen', in *The Mental World of the Jacobean Court*, ed. Linda L. Peck, Cambridge, 1991

Bassett, Bernard, S.J., *The English Jesuits from Campion to Martindale*, 1967

Batho, G. R., 'The Wizard Earl in the Tower 1605–1621', *History Today*, 6, 1956

Batho, G. R., *The Household Papers of Henry Percy, Ninth Earl of Northumberland (1564–1632)*, Camden Society, 3rd series, XCIII, 1962

Bellamy, John, *The Tudor Law of Treason: an introduction*, 1979

Billington, Ray Allen, *The Protestant Crusade, 1800–1860: a study of the origins of American nativism*, New York, 1938

Birch, Thomas, *An Historical View of Negotiations between the Courts of England, France and Brussels, 1592–1617*, 1749

(B.L.) British Library MSS

Bliss, W., 'Note on the Religious Belief of Anne of Denmark', *English Historical Review*, 4, 1889

Blunt, J. H., *The Annotated Book of Common Prayer*, new edn, 1888

Bodleian Library, Oxford

Bossy, John, 'Henri IV, the Appellants and the Jesuits', *Recusant History*, 8, 1965

Bossy, John, 'The Character of English Catholicism', in *Crisis in Europe 1560–1660*, ed. Trevor Aston, 1970

Bossy, John, 'The English Catholic Community. 1603–1605', in *The Reign of King James VI and I*, ed. A. G. R. Smith, 1973

Bossy, John, *Giordano Bruno and the Embassy Affair*, pbk, 1992

Boyle, Conall, *In the Footsteps of the Gunpowder Plotters: a journey through history in Middle England*, Meridian books, Oldbury, West Midlands, 1994

Bridges, John, *History of Northamptonshire*, 2 Vols, Oxford, 1791

Bruce, John, ed., *Correspondence of James VI with Sir Robert Cecil and others in England*, Camden Society, 1861

Bull, S., 'Furie of the Ordnance', unpublished thesis, University of Wales, 1988

Byrne, M. St Clare, *Elizabethan Life in Town and Country*, 8th revised edn, 1961

Camm, Dom. Bede, O.S.B., *Forgotten Shrines*, 1910

Caraman, Philip, ed., *The Other Face. Catholic life under Elizabeth I*, 1960

Caraman, Philip, *Henry Garnet 1555–1606 and the Gunpowder Plot*, 1964

Caraman, Philip, ed., *The Years of Siege: Catholic life from James I to Cromwell*, 1966

The Memoirs of Robert Carey, ed. F. H. Mares, Oxford, 1972

Carswell, Donald, ed., *Trial of Guy Fawkes and Others (The Gunpowder Plot)*, 1934

The Letters of John Chamberlain, ed. N. E. McClure, 2 Vols, Philadelphia, 1939

Chambers, M. C. E., *The Life of Mary Ward, 1585–1645*, 2 Vols, 1885

Charles-Edwards, T., *Saint Winefride and her Well: the historical background*, n.d.

(C.J.) *Journals of the House of Commons, 1547–1628*, 1803

Clancy, T., S.J., 'English Catholics and the Papal Disposing Power, 1570–1640', *Recusant History*, 6, 1961

Clancy, T. H., S.J., *Papist Pamphleteers*, Chicago, 1964

Clark, Sir George, 'Jacobean Northamptonshire, 1603–1625', *Northamptonshire Past and Present*, 2, 1958

The Diary of the Lady Anne Clifford, with an Introductory Note by V. Sackville-West, 1923

Coke, Edward, *The Third and Fourth Parts of the Institutes of the Laws of England…*, 1654

Colley, Linda, *Britons: Forging the nation, 1707–1837*, 1992

Collinson, Patrick, *The Elizabethan Puritan Movement*, 1967

Cooper, W. D., 'Further Particulars of Thomas Norton, and of State Proceedings in Matters of Religion in the Years 1581 and 1582', *Archaeologia*, 36, 1855

Coughton Court and the Throckmortons, National Trust, Norwich, 1993

'Diary of Joan Courthope 1886–1974', unpub., ed. Richard Rose

Cressy, David, *Bonfires and Bells: national memory and the Protestant calendar in Elizabethan and Stuart England*, 1989

Cressy, David, 'The Fifth of November Remembered', in *Myths of the English*, ed. Roy Porter, Oxford, 1992

Croft, Pauline, 'The Reputation of Robert Cecil: libels, political opinion and popular awareness in the early seventeenth century', *Transactions of the Royal Historical Society*, 6th Series, I, 1990

Croft, Pauline, 'Robert Cecil and the Early Jacobean Court', in *The Mental World of the Jacobean Court*, ed. Linda Levy Peck, Cambridge, 1991

Cruickshank, *Elizabeth's Army*, 2nd edn, Oxford, 1966

(C.S.P.) Calendar of State Papers, Domestic, in the reign of Elizabeth, 1601–1603, 1870

(C.S.P.) Calendar of State Papers, Domestic, 1603–1610, VIII, 1857

(C.S.P.) Calendar of State Papers, Spanish, IV, 1899

(C.S.P.) Calendar of State Papers, Venetian, X, 1900

Cuddy, Neil, 'The Revival of the Entourage: the bedchamber of James I, 1603–1625', in *The English Court: from the Wars of the Roses to the Civil War*, ed. David Starkey, 1987

Cuvelier, Joseph, 'Les Préliminaires du traité de Londres (29 âout 1604)', *Revue Belge de Philologie et d'Histoire*, 2, 1923, Bruxelles

David, Rev. Christopher, *St Winefride's Well: a history and guide. An illustrated description*, reprint, 1993

Dekker, Thomas, *The Double P P. A Papist in Armes. Bearing Ten severall Sheilds Encountred by the Protestant. At Ten severall Weapons. A Iesuite Marching before them*, 1606

Dekker, Thomas, *The Non-Dramatic Works*, ed. A. B. Crosart, 4 Vols, 1884

Devlin, Christopher, *Hamlet's Divinity*, 1963

Devlin, Christopher, *The Life of Robert Southwell: poet and martyr*, 1967

Dickens, A. G., 'The First Stages of Romanist Recusancy in Yorkshire, 1560–1590', *Yorkshire Archaeological Journal*, 35, 1943

Dickens, A. G., 'The Extent and Character of Recusancy in Yorkshire, 1604', *Yorkshire Archaeological Journal*, 37, 1945

(D.N.B.) Dictionary of National Biography

Dodd, A. H., 'The Spanish Treason, the Gunpowder Plot, and the Catholic Refugees', *English Historical Review*, 53, 1938

Doleman, R., *A Conference about the Next Succession to the Crowne of Ingland 1594*, ed. D. M. Rogers, Menston, Yorks., 1972

Duffy, Eamon, *The Stripping of the Altars: traditional religion in England c. 1400–c. 1580*, 1992

Dures, Alan, *English Catholicism 1558–1642: community and change*, 1983

Eastward Ho!, by Ben Jonson, George Chapman and John Marston, ed. C. G. Peter, 1973

Edwards, Francis, S.J., *Guy Fawkes: the real story of the Gunpowder Plot?*, 1969

Edwards, Francis, S.J., ed., *The Gunpowder Plot: the narrative of Oswald Tesimond alias Greenway*, trans. from the Italian of the Stonyhurst Manuscript, edited and annotated, 1973

Edwards, Francis, S.J., *The Jesuits in England: from 1580 to the present day*, 1985

Edwards, Francis, S.J., 'Still Investigating Gunpowder Plot', *Recusant History*, 21, 1993

Elliott, J. H., *Imperial Spain, 1469–1716*, 1969

Elton, G. R., *The Practice of History*, Sydney, 1967

Fea, Allan, *Secret Chambers and Hiding-Places*, 3rd & revised edn, 1908

Finch, Mary E., *The Wealth of Five Northamptonshire Families 1540–1640*, Oxford, 1956

Fisher, H. A. L., *Frederick William Maitland: a biographical sketch*, Cambridge, 1910

Foley, Henry, S.J., *Records of the English Province of the Society of Jesus*, 7 Vols, 1st Series, 1877–83

The Folklore of American Holidays, ed. Hennig Cohen and Tristram Potter Coffin, 2nd edn, Detroit, n.d.

Francis, Rev. P. H., *The Origins and Developments of Fire Arms and Gunpowder*, Bradford, 1961

William Gager's Pyramis, ed. C. F. Tucker Brooke, *Transactions of the Connecticut Academy of Arts and Sciences*, 32, 1936, New Haven, Conn.

Gardiner, S. R., *History of England, 1603–1607*, I, 1883

Gardiner, S. R., 'Two Declarations of Garnet relating to the Gunpowder Plot', *English Historical Review*, III, 1888

Gardiner, S. R., *What Gunpowder Plot Was*, 1897

[Garnet, Henry], 'Treatise of Equivocation', MS. Laud Misc. 655, Bodleian Library

Gearty, Conor, *Terror*, 1991

(G.E.C.) *The Complete Peerage ... Extant Extinct or Dormant*, by G. E. C., 6 Vols, reprint, Gloucester, 1982

Gerard, John, *The Autobiography of an Elizabethan*, trans. from the Latin by Philip Caraman, with an introduction by Graham Greene, 1951

Gerard, John, 'Traditional History and the Spanish Treason of 1601–1603', *The Month*, 87, 1896

Gerard, John, *The Gunpowder Plot and the Gunpowder Plotters, in reply to Professor Gardiner*, 1897

Gerard, John, S.J., *What was the Gunpowder Plot? The traditional story tested by original evidence*, 1897

Gibbon, Edward, *The History of the Decline and Fall of the Roman Empire*, ed. J. B. Bury, 7 Vols, 8th edn, 1923

Goodman, Dr Godfrey, *The Court of King James the First*, 2 Vols, 1839

Gotch, J. Alfred, *A complete account of the buildings erected in Northamptonshire by Sir Thomas Tresham*, 1883

Gotch, J. Alfred, *Old Halls and Manor Houses of Northamptonshire*, 1936

Grosvenor, Ian D., 'Catholics and Politics: the Worcester election of 1604', *Recusant History*, 14, 1977–80

Habington, Thomas, *A Survey of Worcestershire*, Worcestershire Historical Society, ed. John Amphlet of Cleat, Vol. II, Pt I, Oxford, 1896

Haigh, Christopher, ed., *The Reign of Elizabeth I*, 1984

Haigh, Christopher, *English Reformations*, Oxford, 1993

Hale, John, *The Civilization of Europe in the Renaissance*, 1993

Hales, J. W., 'Round about Stratford in 1605', *Notes and Essays*, 1884

Hamilton, Dom. Adam, O.S.B., ed., *The Chronicle of the English Augustinian Canonesses Regular of the Lateran, at St Monica's in Louvain*, 2 Vols, 1904–6

Handover, P. M., *Arbella Stuart: royal lady of Hardwick and cousin to King James*, 1957

Handover, P. M., *The Second Cecil: the rise to power 1563–1604 of Sir Robert Cecil, later first Earl of Salisbury*, 1959

Hanlon, Sr. Joseph Damian, 'These Be But Women', in *From the Renaissance to the Counter Reformation: essays in honour of Garrett Mattingly*, ed. C. H. Carter, 1966

Harrison, G. B., *A Last Elizabethan Journal: being a record of those things most talked of during the years 1599–1603*, 1933

Harrison, G. B., *A Jacobean Journal: being a record of those things most talked of during the years 1603–1606*, 1941

Hatfield MSS, Hatfield House, Herts

Haynes, Alan, *Robert Cecil, Earl of Salisbury, 1563–1612: servant of two sovereigns*, 1989

Haynes, Alan, *The Gunpowder Plot*, Stroud, Glos., 1994

The Collected Works of William Hazlitt, ed. A. R. Walter and A. Glover, 11, 1904

Hicks, L., S.J., 'Sir Robert Cecil, Father Persons and the Succession. 1600–1601', *Archivum Historicum Societatis Iesu*, 24, 1955

Hicks, L., S.J., 'Father Robert Persons S.J. and *The Book of Succession*', *Recusant History*, 4, 1957

Hicks, L., S.J., 'The Embassy of Sir Anthony Standen in 1603', *Recusant History*, 5, 1959

(H.M.C.) Historical Manuscripts Commission, Report on the Manuscripts of Lord Montagu of Beaulieu, 1900

(H.M.C.) Historical Manuscripts Commission, Calendar of the Manuscripts of the Most Honourable the Marquess of Salisbury, Vols XI–XVIII, 1906–40

Hogrefe, Pearl, *Tudor Women: commoners and queens*, Ames, Iowa, 1975

Holmes, P., 'Elizabethan Casuistry', *Catholic Record Society*, 67, 1981

Holmes, Peter, *Resistance and Compromise: the political thought of Elizabethan Catholics*, Cambridge, 1982

Gerard Manley Hopkins, ed. Catherine Phillips, Oxford, 1986

Hotson, Leslie, *I, William Shakespeare*, 1937

Humphreys, John, 'The Wyntours of Huddington and the Gunpowder Plot', *Transactions of the Birmingham and Midlands Institute*, 30, 1904

Humphreys, John, 'The Habingtons of Hindlip and the Gunpowder Plot', *Transactions of the Birmingham and Midlands Institute*, 31, 1905

Hurstfield, Joel, 'Robert Cecil Earl of Salisbury: minister of Elizabeth and James I', *History Today*, 7, 1957

Hurstfield, Joel, 'The Succession Struggle in late Elizabethan England', in *Elizabethan Government and Society: Essays presented to Sir John Neale*, ed. S. T. Bindoff, J. Hurstfield and C. H. Williams, 1961

Hurstfield, Joel, *Freedom, Corruption and Government in Elizabethan England*, 1973

Hutton, Ronald, *The Rise and Fall of Merry England 1400–1700*, Oxford, 1994

Jardine, David, ed., *Criminal Trials, II: The Gunpowder Plot*, 1835

Jardine, David, *A Reading on the Use of Torture in the Criminal Law of England previously to the Commonwealth*, 1837

Jardine, David, 'Observations on the historical evidence supporting the Implication of Lord Mounteagle as a Conspirator in the Gunpowder Treason', *Archaeologia*, XXIX, 1844

Jardine, David, 'Remarks upon Letters of Thomas Winter and Lord Mounteagle, lately discovered by John Bruce, Esq., F.S.A.', *Archaeologia*, XXIX, 1844

Jardine, David, ed., *A Treatise of Equivocation*, 1851

Jardine, David, *A Narrative of the Gunpowder Plot*, 1857

Johnson, Paul, *Elizabeth I: a study in power and intellect*, pbk, 1988

Jones, Mary Whitmore, *The Gunpowder Plot and Life of Robert Catesby also an account of Chastleton House*, 1909

Jordan, W. K., *The Development of Religious Toleration in England: from the accession of James I to the convention of the Long Parliament (1603–1640)*, II, 1936

Keeling, William D. D., *Liturgicae Britannicae*, 1842

Kerman, Joseph, *The Masses and Motets of William Byrd*, 1981

King James' History of the Gunpowder Plot, State Trials, II, 1809

King Lear, The Arden Shakespeare, ed. Kenneth Muir, reprinted with corrections, 1972

(*King's Book*) *His Majesties Speach in this Last Session of Parliament ... Together with a discourse of the maner of the discouery of the late intended Treason, ioyned with an Examination of some of the prisoners*, 1605

The Kings Majesties Speech ... to the Lords ... On Munday the 19 day of March 1603, 1604

Klingenstein, L., *The Great Infanta: Isabel, Sovereign of the Netherlands*, 1910

Laffleur De Kermaingant, P., *Mission de Christophe de Harlay Comte de Beaumont (1602–1605)*, Paris, 2 Vols, 1895

Larkin, James F., and Hughes, Paul L., eds, *Stuart Royal Proclamations*, 2 Vols, Oxford, 1973–80

The Lawes Resolutions of Woman's Rights, or the Lawes Provisions for Women, 1632

Leatherbarrow, J. S., *The Lancashire Elizabethan Recusants*, Chetham Society, New Series, 110, Manchester, 1947

Lee, Maurice, Jr, *James I and Henri VI: an essay in English foreign policy, 1603–1610*, Urbana, Ill., 1970

Lewalski, Barbara K., 'Lucy, Countess of Bedford: images of a Jacobean courtier and patroness', in *Politics of Discourse*, ed. Kevin Sharpe and Steven N. Zwicker, Berkeley, Calif., 1987

Lingard, John, *The History of England*, VII, 5th edn, 1849

(L.J.) *Journal of the House of Lords*, IV, XIV

Longley, Katharine M., 'Three Sites in the City of York', *Recusant History*, 12, 1973

Longueville, Thomas, *The Life of a Conspirator*, 1895

Loomie, Albert J., S.J., *The Spanish Elizabethans: exiles at the Court of Philip II*, 1963

Loomie, Albert J., S.J., 'Toleration and Diplomacy: the religious issue in Anglo-Spanish relations, 1603–1605', *Transactions of the American Philosophical Society*, Philadelphia, New series, 53, Pt 6, 1963

Loomie, Albert J., S.J., 'Philip III and the Stuart Succession in England, 1600–1603', *Revue Belge de Philologie et d'Histoire*, 43, 1965, Bruxelles

Loomie, Albert J., S.J., *Guy Fawkes in Spain: the 'Spanish Treason' in Spanish documents, Bulletin of the Institute of Historical Research*, Special Supplement no. 9, November 1971

Loomie, Albert J., S.J., 'King James I's Catholic Consort', *Huntington Library Quarterly*, 34, 1971

Loomie, Albert J., S.J., *Spain and the Jacobean Catholics*, I: *1603–1612*, Catholic Record Society, 1973

Luna, B. N. De, *Jonson's Romish Plot: a study of Catiline and its historical context*, Oxford, 1967

Macbeth, The Arden Shakespeare, ed. Kenneth Muir, reprinted with new introduction, 1992

MacCaffrey, Wallace, *Elizabeth I*, 1993

McIlwain, C. H., ed., *The Political Works of James I*, Cambridge, Mass., 1918

Mackie, J. D., 'The Secret Diplomacy of King James VI in Italy prior to his Accession to the English Throne', *Scottish Historical Review*, 21, 1923–4

Magee, Brian, *The English Recusants: a study of the post-Reformation Catholic survival and the operation of the recusancy laws*, with an introduction by Hilaire Belloc, 1938

Malloch, A. E., 'Father Henry Garnet's Treatise of Equivocation', *Recusant History*, 15, 1981

Diary of John Manningham, ed. John Bruce, Camden Society, 1868

Mathew, David, *Catholicism in England: the portrait of a minority: its culture and tradition*, 2nd revised edn, 1948

Mathew, David, *James I*, 1967

Miller, John, *Religion in the Popular Prints, 1600–1832*, Cambridge, 1986

Complete Prose Works of John Milton, IV, 1650–1655, Pt 1, New Haven, Conn., 1966

Milward, Peter, *Shakespeare's Religious Background*, 1973

Morris, John, S.J., *The Condition of Catholics under James I: Father Gerard's Narrative of the Gunpowder Plot*, 2nd edn, 1872

Morris, John, S.J., *The troubles of our Catholic forefathers*, First series, 1872

Munden, R. C., 'James I and "the Growth of Mutual Distrust": King, Commons and reform, 1603–1604', in *Faction and Parliament: essays in early Stuart History*, ed. Kevin Sharpe, Oxford, 1978

Nash, T. R., 'Copy of the original Death-Warrant of Humphrey Littleton', *Archaeologia*, 15, 1803

Nash, Thomas, *The History and Antiquities of Worcestershire*, 2 Vols, 1781

Neale, J. E., 'The Sayings of Queen Elizabeth', *History*, New Series, 10, 1925

Neale, J. E. *Elizabeth I and her Parliaments 1559–1581*, I, 1953

Neale, J. E. *Elizabeth I and her Parliaments 1584–1601*, II, 1957

(Nicholls) Nicholls, Mark, *Investigating Gunpowder Plot*, 1991

Nicholls, Mark, 'Sir Walter Ralegh's Treason: a prosecution document', *English Historical Review*, CX, 1995

Nicholls, Mark, 'Treason's Reward: the punishment of conspirators in the Bye Plot of 1603', *Historical Journal*, 38, 1995

Nichols, John, *The Progresses ... of King James the First*, 4 Vols, 1828

The Night of the Fires, compiled and produced by David Perry, Perryscope Productions, BBC Radio 3, 11 November 1994

Norman, E. R., *Anti-Catholicism in Victorian England*, 1968

Nowak, T. S., '"Remember, Remember the Fifth of November": Anglocentrism and anti-Catholicism in the English Gunpowder sermons, 1605–1651', Ph.D. thesis, State University of New York at Stony Brook, 1992

O'Halloran, Simon, *Bonfires in Lewes: a history of the celebrations on November the Fifth*, privately printed, 1967

Oman, Carola, *Elizabeth of Bohemia*, revised edn, 1964

Paget, Julian, *The Yeomen of the Guard: five hundred years of service. 1485–1985*, Poole, Dorset, 1984

Parker, Geoffrey, *The Dutch Revolt*, 1979

Parker, Geoffrey, *Europe in Crisis, 1598–1648*, Brighton, Sussex, 1980

Parnell, Geoffrey, *Book of the Tower of London*, English Heritage, 1993

Paul, H. N., *The Royal Play of Macbeth*, New York, 1950

Peck, Linda Levy, *Northampton: patronage and policy at the court of James I*, 1982

Peck, Linda Levy, *Court Patronage and Corruption in Early Stuart England*, Boston, Mass., 1990

Peck, Linda Levy, ed., *The Mental World of the Jacobean Court*, Cambridge, 1991

Peters, Henriette, *Mary Ward: a world in contemplation*, trans. Helen Butterworth, Leominster, Herefordshire, 1994

Pollen, J. H., S.J., 'The Accession of King James I', *The Month*, 101, 1903

Pollen, J. H., S.J., *The Institution of the Archpriest Blackwell*, 1916

Porter, Roy, *London. A social history*, 1994

(P.R.O.) Public Record Office, London

Quinault, Roland, 'Warwickshire Landowners and Parliamentary Politics 1841–1923', unpublished D.Phil. thesis, Oxford University, 1975

(R.C.H.) Royal Commission on Historical Monuments (England), London, V (East London), 1930

Read, Conyers, 'William Cecil and Elizabethan Public Relations', in *Elizabethan Government and Society: essays presented to Sir John Neale*, ed. S. T. Bindoff, J. Hurstfield and C. H. Williams, 1961

Ridley, Jasper, *Elizabeth I*, 1987

Robinson, John Martin, *The Dukes of Norfolk, A Quincentenniel History*, Oxford, 1982

Rodger, N. A. M., 'Ordnance Records and the Gunpowder Plot', *Bulletin of the Institute of Historical Research*, 53, 1980

Rodríguez-Villa, Antonio, ed., *Correspondencia de la Infanta Archiduquesa Doña Isabel Clara Eugenia de Austria con el Duque de Lerma y otros personajes*, Madrid, 1906

Rose, Elliot, *Cases of Conscience: alternatives open to recusants and Puritans under Elizabeth I and James I*, Cambridge, 1975

Rowlands, Marie B., 'Recusant Women 1560–1640', in *Women in English Society 1500–1800*, ed. Mary Prior, 1985

Rowse, A. L., *Tudor Cornwall: portrait of a society*, 1941

Rowse, A. L., *Raleigh and the Throckmortons*, 1962

Rowse, A. L., *Simon Forman: sex and society in Shakespeare's age*, 1974

Salgādo, Carmini, *The Elizabethan Underworld*, Stroud, Glos., 1992

Scarisbrick, J. J., *The Jesuits and the Catholic Reformation*, 1988

Seton, Walter W., 'The Early Years of Henry Frederick, Prince of Wales, and Charles, Duke of Albany (Charles I)', *Scottish Historical Review*, 13, 1915–16

Shakespeare Birthplace Trust, Shakespeare Centre, Stratford-upon-Avon

Shaw, Peter, *American Patriots and the Rituals of Revolution*, Cambridge, Mass., 1981

Shirley, John W., *Thomas Harriot: a biography*, Oxford, 1983

Simons, Eric N., *The Devil of the Vault*, 1963

Skinner, Quentin, *The Foundations of Modern Political Thought: The Age of Reformation*, Cambridge, 1978

Smith, Alan G. R., ed., *The Reign of James VI and I*, 1973

Smith, John Thomas, *Antiquities of Westminster; the Old Palace; St. Stephen's Chapel, (now the House of Commons) etc. etc.*, 1807

Somers, John, Baron, *A collection of scarce and valuable Tracts...*, 2nd revised edn, 13 Vols, 1809–15

Somerset, Anne, *Elizabeth I*, 1991

Southern A. C., ed., *The Elizabethan Recusant House, comprising The Life of the Lady Magdalen Viscountess Montague (1538–1608)*, 1954

The Poetical Works of the Rev. Robert Southwell, ed. William B. Turnbull, 1856

(S.P.) State Papers, Public Record Office, London

Spink, H. H., *The Gunpowder Plot and Lord Mounteagle's Letter*, 1902

Squiers, Granville, *Secret Hiding Places*, 1933

(S.T.) *State Trials, Cobbett's Complete Collection of...From the Earliest Period to the Present Time*, II, 1603–1627, 1809

Stafford, H. G., *James VI of Scotland and the Throne of England*, New York, 1940

Stevenson, Joseph, S.J., 'Anne of Denmark, Queen of Great Britain', *The Month*, 37, 1879

Stow, John, *Annales, or, A Generall Chronicle of England, Begun by John Stow. Continued by Edmund Howes*, 1631

Strong, Roy, *Henry, Prince of Wales and England's Lost Renaissance*, 1986

Sumner, Ann, ed., *Death, Passion and Politics*, Dulwich Picture Gallery, 1995.

Swift, Roger, 'Guy Fawkes Celebrations in Victorian Exeter', *History Today*, 31, 1981

Tierney, Rev. M. A., ed., *Dodd's Church History of England with Notes, Additions and a continuation*, 3 & 4, 1840–1

Torture and Punishment (Treasures of the Tower), H.M.S.O., 1973

Toyne, S. M., 'Guy Fawkes and the Powder Plot', *History Today*, I, 1951

Trimble, W. R., *The Catholic Laity in Elizabethan England*, Cambridge, Mass., 1964

Vaux, Laurence, *A Catechisme or Christian Doctrine*, with memoir by T. Law, Chetham Society, New Series, 4, 1885

(V.C.H.) Victoria County History, Worcestershire, III, 1913

Vetusta Monumenta, V, 1835

Wake, Joan, 'The Death of Francis Tresham', *Northamptonshire Past and Present*, 2, 1954

Walsham, Alexandra, *Church Papists: Catholicism, conformity and confessional polemic in early modern England*, Woodbridge, Suffolk, 1993

Ward, A. W., 'Review of W. Plenkers' "Was Frederick II's daughter Anne, Queen of Great Britain, a convert to Catholicism?"', *English Historical Review*, 2, 1888

Warner, G. F., 'James VI and Rome', *English Historical Review*, XX, 1905

Warnicke, Retha M., *Women of the English Renaissance and Reformation*, 1983

Waugh, Margaret, *Blessed Nicholas Owen: Jesuit Brother and maker of hiding holes*, 1959

Webb, William K. L., 'The Phantom Conspiracy', unpublished MS, Jesuit (Farm Street) Archives, London

Weller, Ralph B., 'Some Aspects of the Life of Richard Haydocke, Physician, Engraver, Painter and Translator (1569–?1642)', *The Hatcher Review*, 2, 1985

Weston, William, *Autobiography of an Elizabethan*, trans. from the Latin by Philip Caraman. With a foreword by Evelyn Waugh, 1955

Wharam, Alan, *Treason: famous English treason trials*, Stroud, Glos., 1995

Whitehill, W. M., *Boston: a topographical history*, Cambridge, Mass., 1959

Wiener, Carol Z., 'The Beleaguered Isle: a study of Elizabethan and early Jacobean anti-Catholicism', *Past and Present*, 51, 1971

The Journal of Sir Roger Wilbraham, ed. H. S. Scott, Camden Society, 10, 1902

Wilkinson, Paul, *Terrorism and the Liberal State*, New York, 1979

Williams, E. C., *Anne of Denmark*, 1970

Williams, Neville, *Elizabeth Queen of England*, 1967

Williamson, Hugh Ross, *The Gunpowder Plot*, 1951

Wills, Gary, *Witches and Jesuits: Shakespeare's Macbeth*, New York, 1995

Willson, D. H., *King James VI and I*, 1962 edn

Wood, Anthony à, *Athenae Oxonienses*, 1691

Wormald, Jenny, 'James VI and I: two Kings or one?' *History*, LXVIII, 1983

Wormald, Jenny, 'Gunpowder, Treason and Scots', *Journal of British Studies*, XXIV, Chicago, 1985

Zagorin, Perez, *Ways of Lying: dissimulation, persecution, and conformity in early modern Europe*, Cambridge, Mass., 1990

Index